Everything that lives is Holy.

— William Blake

Anne Baring (b. 1931) MA Oxon. Ph.D (hons) is a Jungian Analyst — author and co-author of nine books including, as Anne Gage (1961), *The One Work: A Journey Towards the Self*; as Anne Baring, with Jules Cashford (1992), *The Myth of the Goddess: Evolution of an Image*; (1993 and 2002), *The Birds Who Flew Beyond Time*; with Andrew Harvey (1995), *The Mystic Vision: Daily Encounters with the Divine* and (1996), *The Divine Feminine*; with Scilla Elworthy (2009), *Soul Power: an Agenda for a Conscious Humanity*; (2013, 2017 and 2020), *The Dream of the Cosmos: A Quest for the Soul*; (2023), *Messages from a Transcendent Dimension*; and (2025), *Divine Wisdom and the Holy Spirit: The Forgotten Feminine Face of God.*

Her work is devoted to the recognition that we live in an ensouled world and to the restoration of the lost sense of communion between us and the invisible dimension of the Cosmos that is the source or ground of all that we call 'life'. Her website is devoted to the affirmation of a new vision of reality and the issues facing us at this crucial time of choice.

www.annebaring.com
www.anne-baring.com

Divine Wisdom
and the
Holy Spirit

The
FORGOTTEN FEMININE
FACE of GOD

A Prayer to the Holy Spirit

As we witness the intolerable suffering of the people on this planet that is inflicted by War, may the Holy Spirit of Wisdom awaken us to a deeper sense of our relationship with the Earth, with each other, and with the hidden dimensions of the Cosmos still veiled from our sight.

May Her Light and Love shine through our hearts and illumine our minds. May She help us to become aware of the oneness and sacredness of life and to care for our neighbour as ourself, to know that the hurt of one is the hurt of all.

May She inspire us to be protectors rather than destroyers of life. May She forgive us for the sacrifice over many centuries of the lives of billions of men, women and children and may their souls be released from the terror, grief, loneliness, and despair in which they died in the recent and distant past. May they be welcomed with love and care in the world beyond.

May She help us to recognize and transform evil and to respond to the torment of all persecuted peoples as if it were our own. May She help us to see that evil is the infliction of terror, pain, humiliation, torture, or death on other human beings.

May She heal those who are unable to love: whose hearts are frozen by rage, hatred and revenge. May they be released from the compulsion to inflict pain and suffering on others.

May She free us from bondage to political and religious fanaticism whose devastating legacy we witness today. May She guide us to choose conscious leaders who serve the true needs of all peoples and all species on this planet.

May She inspire us to offer our lives in service of the great web of living relationships that is Her life and the life of the Cosmos. May She give us the humility, wisdom, strength, and compassion to accomplish the Great Work of transmuting our nature from base metal into gold.

Divine Wisdom
and the
Holy Spirit

The
FORGOTTEN FEMININE
FACE of GOD

Anne Baring

ARCHIVE publishing

First published in the United Kingdom by
Archive Publishing
Shaftesbury, Dorset, England

Designed at Archive Publishing by Ian Thorp MA

A CIP catalogue record for this book is available from
The British Library

ISBN 978-1-906289-66-9 (Paperback)
ISBN 978-1-906289-75-1 (Epub)

Front cover: Red Rose '*Falstaff*' photograph by Ian Thorp
The Pleiades: Deep-space photographic image created by
Greg Parker, New Forest Observatory, UK and Noel Carboni, Florida, USA

www.archivepublishing.co.uk

Printed and bound by CMP (UK) Ltd

Acknowledgements

I would like to express my gratitude to my beloved artist husband Robin, without whose loving presence, support, and encouragement through sixty-five years, I would never have written any of my books. I would also like to thank Dr Annine van der Meer, Dr Margaret Barker, Dr Betty Kovács, Kim Saavedra, David Lorimer, Paolo Morley-Fletcher and Ian Thorp, my wonderful publisher, for their friendship and help. I would also like to thank those authors, publishers and artists whose own work has assisted me with mine, and whose words and images have been an inspiration to me.

I would also like to express my heartfelt gratitude to the man whose invaluable help and support made possible the writing and completion of this book, who wishes to remain anonymous.

Dedication

I dedicate this book to those who are searching for the truth about our evolutionary journey on this planet and to those who seek assurance that we are immortal beings and that there is no death for the soul. It takes many lives on this planet to realize who we are and why we are here.

Women will save the World

When we honor the sacred feminine, we awaken the deepest part of our soul.
— Deepak Chopra

The power of women lies in their ability to love unconditionally, to see beyond appearances, and to heal with a simple touch.
— Thich Nhat Hanh

An awakened woman is an unstoppable force. Her gentleness can shatter hardness, her love can dissolve fear.
— Eckhart Tolle

Women are the bridge between earth and sky. Their hearts beat in rhythm with the universe.
— Khalil Gibran

A woman is the purest altar upon which a man may offer his devotion.
— Paramahansa Yogananda

A woman's wisdom is like water: it flows into every empty space, adapts, transforms, yet always remains true to itself.
— Lao Tzu

A woman's intuition is a sacred gift, an invisible thread connecting her directly to the heart of the universe.
— Gurdjieff

In the silence of her being, a woman knows the truth before it is ever spoken.
— Ram Dass

The woman who listens to her heart is wiser than the one who possesses all the knowledge of the world.
— Rumi

A woman's inner voice is the purest guide: when she follows it, she illuminates the path for those around her.
— Krishnamurti

Contents

The Eternal Bride
Cecil Collins

I am thou and thou art I
And wheresoever thou art
There I am.
In all things I am scattered
And from wherever thou wilt
Thou gatherest Me
And in gathering Me
Thou gatherest thyself.

— from *The Gnostic Gospel of Eve*

Completion of the Great Work
Engraved by Matthäus Merian ca. 1630

Above the Holy Trinity and the angels of Light influencing the zodiac. Below the Raven of the *Nigredo*, the Swan of the *Albedo*, the Dragon, and the Pelican who symbolizes the lunar mercury, and the Phoenix, who symbolizes the solar sulphur. On the right is the figure of a stag-headed shaman holding a moon and the figure of Luna with a stream of stars flowing from her breast and a bunch of grapes held in her hand. Below them is an eagle with wings enfolding water and earth. On the left is the figure of Sol and a magnificent lion, together holding an image of the sun. Below them is a phoenix with wings enfolding fire and air. The central figure of the alchemist or kabbalist wearing a star-spangled robe, and surrounded by the signs of the zodiac, stands on two lions with a single head. From their jaws flows a stream of living water. Sol and Luna are connected to the subtle body of the cosmos. This whole magnificent scene symbolizes the indissoluble unity of the Golden Stone and the union of the alchemist with the *unus mundus*, the Divine Ground and the union of the Above and the Below.

PREFACE

What the impending ecological crisis forces us to confront is that we have sacrificed meaning, morality, and almost all higher values for the 'sordid boon' of material wealth and wordly power. To keep drinking from this poisoned chalice will bring only sickness and death.

— William Ophuls [1]

This is perhaps the most crucial time in our history: a time of the utmost depravity, corruption, greed, and barbarism; a time of lies, subterfuge and the perpetration of evil on a planetary scale, but also a time of potential breakthrough to a higher level of consciousness, recognizing that we are inseparably connected to each other, to the world around us and to the wider universe, and that each one of us has a vital role to play in bringing our world back into harmony with the evolutionary intention of the cosmos. In the language of Alchemy, this means reconnecting the Great Below with the Great Above as in the extraordinary image on the page opposite. We tread a path which is on the knife edge between birthing this new vision on the one hand and social disintegration and regression into barbarism — perhaps the virtual extinction of our species — on the other.

We live in a world culture that could be described as insane. It is insane because the Great Below has for millennia become disconnected from the Great Above, the visible, material world from the invisible one. The planet is controlled by leaders who are in thrall, as they were two thousand years ago, to what Jesus called Caesar or the 'Ruler of the World'. The Ruler of the World is the addiction to power, conquest, weapons, and war. Hundreds of thousands of young men have been killed in the current wars that are devastating the planet. Their deaths cause inconceivable suffering to their families. There is no recognition in our world about what is of supreme value, supreme importance. In his autobiography, *Memories Dreams, Reflections,* Jung wrote:

> "The decisive question for humanity is: are we related to something infinite or not? That is the telling question of our life. Only if we know that the thing which truly matters is the infinite can we avoid fixing our interests upon futilities, and upon all kinds of goals which are not of real importance... If we understand and feel that here in this life we already have a link with the infinite, desires and attitudes change. In the final analysis we count for something

because of the essential we embody, and if we do not embody that, life is wasted." [2]

Jung also said that we have lost touch with the two-million-year-old man or woman within us. We have become disconnected from our roots, ignorant of the fact that we have roots, and that those roots once connected us to the Whole, to the One Life that lives through all of us, to the Life of the Cosmos and the Life of the Earth.

Long ago, in shamanic cultures, we knew how to communicate with the Life of the Earth: with the spirits of the plants, the water, the mountains, the animals, and with the Life of the Cosmos — the sun, the moon and the stars in the night sky. We also knew how to communicate with the ancestors and their wisdom. Today, we have lost those skills and are increasingly losing the skill of communicating with each other, listening to each other, respecting each other.

All this has come about because, over centuries and millennia, the visible, material world has become separated from the invisible one. We have lost the thread of Ariadne that once connected us to our cosmic Source. Belief, directed by powerful priesthoods, became a substitute for direct shamanic experience of the Source. We have lost touch with our soul — even the awareness that we have a soul. Cut off from soul, our mind has become impoverished, rigid, dogmatic, and inflated. In compensation for the loss of relationship with soul, it has become driven by the need for ever more power and control, which is why we find ourselves in the extraordinary situation we are in today when millions are suffering the effects of wars and from physical and mental illness, and we are threatened with becoming inducted into a technology that could replace our species with a transhumanist one created by AI, which could bring our species to an end.[3] We need urgently to find our way back the way we have come, towards nature and the ground of our own nature.

There are two widely divergent views of our presence on this planet. Are we alone in the cosmos, without higher guidance, the chance product of a lifeless, mechanistic universe that is without consciousness, intelligence, meaning or purpose? Or are we on an incredible evolutionary journey of discovery that has brought us to this crucial time of choice, when we must relinquish old habits, free ourselves from the web of evil in which we have become enmeshed, and listen to the guidance of the divinity that is within us and of which we are a part?

Over recent centuries, we have reached dazzling heights of scientific, medical, and technological advances which have transformed the conditions of our lives on this planet, and facilitated a phenomenal expansion of our ability to express the creative genius of our species in multiple ways. But we have also suffered a loss of the ancient awareness of the sacred interweaving of all aspects of life, a loss of relationship with the life of the planet and the inner life of the cosmos. As this book will explain, on the one hand, we have been impaled on a cosmology of separation for nearly three thousand years, with a concept of God who is above and beyond the created order and from whose image the Divine Feminine has been excised. On the other hand, the beliefs of Scientific Materialism have told us that there is no higher authority than our conscious mind and that we are the only conscious beings in a lifeless universe.

Four Powerful Myths

Four powerful myths have directed Western Civilization over some two and a half thousand years. They have had incalculable effects on our soul, leading to the crisis we find ourselves in now, and to habits of belief and behaviour that are harming the earth, as well as our species. In the chapters of this book, I will show how these myths developed, their negative effects and how they have given us a distorted image of who we are and why we are here.

1. The Genesis Myth of the Creation of the World by a Father God

The Creation of the World
From the painting by Giovanni di Paolo ?-1482 CE

2. The Myth of the Fall of Man: Genesis 2 & 3, created 623 BCE

The Fall and Expulsion (Adam and Eve) from the Garden of Eden
From the fresco on the Sistine Chapel by Michelangelo 1475-1564 CE

3. The Myth of Jesus as the Only Son of God: created at the
Council of Nicaea in 325 CE.

The Trinity with Christ Crucified
Austrian c.1410, The National Gallery, London

4. The Myth of Scientific Materialism or Scientism

Portrait of René Descartes (1596-1650)
by Frans Hals c.1583–1666

The transformation of a deeply entrenched patriarchal culture extending over some four millennia and the need to bring into being a more balanced and enlightened world culture, demands that we move beyond an outworn image of the Sacred. The old image of the Sacred is dying so that a new image of the Sacred and a New Story can emerge into human consciousnes. This is taking place as we move into a new astrological Age. Alchemy gives us a graphic image of killing the Old King (overpage).

The Old King personifies an outworn image of spirit and an outworn paradigm of reality — one that is cut off from metaphysical reality, cut off from relationship with the invisible world. We are living now in the time of the death of God, marked by social unrest, confusion, conflict and fear. This is how a Jungian analyst, Edward Edinger, defined this challenging interlude:

> "The breakdown of a central myth is like the shattering of a vessel containing a precious essence. Meaning is lost. In its place, primitive and atavistic contents are reactivated. Differentiated values disappear and are replaced by the elemental motivations of power and pleasure, or else the individual is exposed to emptiness and despair". [4]

The Sublimation of the King
from the *Philosophia reformata* 1622 by Johann Daniel Mylius

It may be that the image of God needs to evolve, because the old image is incomplete. It may not be God who is dying but rather the image we have projected onto Him, an image that was formulated by different priesthoods according to their level of understanding at a specific historical time. 'God' may be longing for release from His imprisonment in the strait-jacket of our beliefs. Like a conjurer demonstrating his skills, we have cut 'God' in two and have lost the sense of the divinity of nature. We have fixed the image of deity in the masculine gender, refusing until very recently to entertain the idea that the feminine aspect of spirit is essential to the completion and balance of the image of deity and therefore to the balance of a civilization.

The great mythologist, Joseph Campbell, wrote in *The Inner Reaches of Outer Space* that from time to time, the image of God has to die if it is not to become an idol. It has, he says, to become transparent to transcendence in order to be renewed. [5]

A New Concept of God or Spirit

God or Spirit or Divine Mind, so long projected onto a transcendent male creator remote from our world, is not something distant from us. Quantum Physics shows us that we participate in a Cosmic Consciousness or Intelligence which is co-inherent with every atom of our being and every particle of matter. At the sub-atomic level, everything is connected to everything else. The entire Creation, visible and invisible, is One Life. Divinity is within us as well as all around us. This is the revelation that the Alchemists and the greatest spiritual teachers and mystics have guarded for us but until now, few have understood it.

To injure the earth or to inflict pain and suffering on other human beings is to injure the Universal Consciousness and, since we participate in that Consciousness, to injure ourselves. Everything we do affects the whole, whether negatively or positively. This is such a different conception of God and of ourselves that it takes some time to assimilate its implications. The insight that divinity is present in every single atom of life is precisely what has been missing in our concept of God and it is this which has led to the split between spirit and nature and, ultimately, to that between religion and science as well as to our growing capacity to inflict horrific destruction on each other and on the life of the planet. In splitting the atom and creating weapons of mass destruction, and in killing others who are our soul-brothers and sisters, we are mutilating and desecrating the body of God. We are slowly moving towards the realization of the Indigenous People, given in a statement made at a recent Council in North America:

> "All Life is sacred. We come into Life as sacred beings. When we abuse the sacredness of Life, we affect all Creation."

This passage from a channeled Message from an Angel called Alariel in a book called *Beyond Limitations*, by Stuart Wilson and Joanna Prentis, explains the concept of Oneness:

> "The Greater Reality is founded on and reflects an essential Oneness. Oneness will require a complete re-orientation of your understanding of reality and that will be a major shift for you....Vengeance, for example, becomes absurd within the frame of Oneness. If all life is an interconnected web of being and consciousness, then who exactly would you be taking revenge upon? Your aim should now be to focus on the Oneness that you all share, rather than any small differences that may seem to divide you. You will be challenged to stay in that truth, whatever happens in your life. This is when the Universe will test you and events will occur to plumb the depth of your commitment to the Truth. Living in non-duality and unity and not judging and forgiving can be extremely hard and intense. It is difficult not to hate but to love your enemies; you can condemn their actions, but not condemn them as beings.... The challenge now facing humanity is to lay aside the divisive dualistic way of thinking and feeling and start looking for common ground — the basis for friendship and cooperation".[6]

This realization calls for a huge shift of awareness and a fundamental change in our values. If God or Spirit is not something separate from ourselves, something transcendent to nature and planetary life, but is the intelligence and energy of the life process itself, flaring forth at every instant in every region of this vast universe as well as in ourselves, then how we treat so-called "inanimate" matter, planetary life and each other becomes a matter of how we are treating God. It transforms obedience to God's commands into love and respect for God's creation, including ourselves, our neighbour and, most importantly, our enemy.

The Great Awakening: The Evolutionary Imperative of our Time

Over the past fifty years a gradual restoration of a sense of the sacred has been taking place beneath the surface of our culture, called forth by the multi-faceted crisis of our times. Now, through the awakening power of the environmental movement as well as through the scientific discoveries of quantum physics, we are entering a new era, where nature — the life of the earth — and all the miraculous processes and patterns of life can once again be recognized as indissolubly connected, as they once were and still are in shamanic cultures. This new movement that some call "the Great Awakening" is beginning to heal the split between spirit and nature which has so tragically flawed the three patriarchal religions.

All over the planet, women and men are beginning to awaken to a New Story and to come together to bring it into being: a Story that is different from those we have been told in the past; a Story that restores our vitally important relationship with a sacred earth and offers a foundation for regarding the entire universe and our planet as a single sacred entity; a Story that assists an alchemical transformation of our consciousness from base metal into gold, inspires hope and new possibilities for taking a giant leap in our evolutionary journey, out-growing the destructive patterns, conflicts and struggles for power of the past. These women and men are working together to create an enlightened planetary civilization: one that is based on relationship, love, and service rather than the pursuit of power and the deeply addictive pattern of national rivalry, weapons, and war.

The shadow aspect of our digitally enhanced but unconscious age is barbarism, an unrecognized predatory aspect of our own nature that can take us over when we abandon the ethical values which respect and serve life. Its predominant attribute is the will to power: the drive for dominance and control and the elimination of perceived enemies — even the elimination of a large part of the population of the planet by the few who aim to take control of it. We can clearly see this will to power in the demonic weapons accumulated by the nine nuclear powers of the world and their refusal to get rid of them on the grounds that they offer protection to the nations that hold them. We can see it in the spiritually immature leaders of nations who do not serve their people or the planet but their own power-driven agendas. We can see it in organizations like the WEF and WHO which seek control of the planet and the lives of the people of the world.[7] We can see it in the ongoing preparations for new wars — with Russia, with China, and the further sacrifice of human lives, homes, and livelihoods as well as harm to the planet.

The New Story invites a totally different understanding of Life, bringing with it more mature values which profoundly respect all forms of planetary and cosmic life and a new unified worldview. Opening to the New Story involves challenging and releasing ourselves from the power of the old ones.

Thousands, if not millions of people today are searching not only for the unified field in science but for a unified vision of life — a unified vision of spirit, nature and humanity that could be in time to mitigate the catastrophic effects of our fragmented view of life. The birthing of this vision asks us to relinquish many cherished beliefs and requires a fundamental transformation of our values. Our knowledge about the world and the universe is accelerating geometrically. We are overwhelmed with information about every aspect of what we observe, yet we understand almost nothing about the mystery of why we are here and what the evolutionary role of our species on this planet might be.

As the fairy-tale of the Sleeping Beauty tells us, we need to move beyond the hedge of thorns created by the four Myths that have indoctrinated us into incomplete beliefs: The creation of the world by a male God, the Myth of the Fall of Man, The Myth of the Only Son of God and The Myth of Scientific Materialism or Scientism.

We need to answer four questions: Who are we? Why are we here? Where have we come from? Where do we go when we die? The Essenes and the Gnostics knew the answers to these questions. But their vision and insight were destroyed by the Christian Church in the fourth century when it succumbed to the power principle — The Ruler of the World — as it was incorporated into the Roman Empire.

Awakening to the New Story invites a totally different understanding of Life, bringing with it more mature values which profoundly respect all forms of planetary and cosmic life and a new unified world view.

A New Concept of God

We are moving from the story of a dead insentient universe to a New Story of a universe that is vibrantly alive and the primary ground of our own consciousness. But more than this, we are moving towards a new concept of God and of our relationship with God which is a revelation as great as any we have ever had. We are moving from an image of God as a creator separate from creation to an image of spirit as Light and as the sublime Intelligence within the process of cosmic and planetary evolution, with ourselves as participants in that process. An Eternal Consciousness participates in the life of this universe and we are a manifestation of that Consciousness just coming to awareness that we participate in its life, that we are co-creators with it, that we are, essentially immortal beings because we are part of it. Those who have suffered the trauma of losing loved ones can take comfort from the fact that they will see them again when they transition to another world. [8]

We are living in a time of great danger — danger from the deliberate or accidental release of nuclear weapons that can wipe out the lives of millions of us in seconds and devastate the life of the planet. We are also in danger from the biological weapons that are currently being created in hundreds of gain-of-function laboratories. All this activity destined to harm life is evil. How much longer will it take for us to realize that if we are to survive as a species, we will have to put an end to war and the accumulation of these demonic weapons?

Today, as C. G. Jung said, "the world hangs on a single thread, and that thread is the psyche of man". Near the end of *The Undiscovered Self,* he wrote:

> "Is he capable of resisting the temptation to use his power for the purpose of staging a world conflagration? Is he conscious of the path he is treading, and what the conclusions are that must be drawn from the present world situation and his own psychic situation? Does he know that he is on the point of losing the life-preserving myth of the inner man which Christianity has treasured up for him? Does he realize what lies in store should this catastrophe ever befall him? Is he even capable of realizing that this would be a catastrophe? And finally, does the individual know that he is the makeweight that tips the scales?" [9]

Scientific Materialism or Scientism

One of the most powerful agents to have indoctrinated us into false or limited beliefs has been materialist science. For centuries, we have been controlled and manipulated by governments, by kings and conquerors, by powerful priesthoods and latterly, by the beliefs of Scientific Materialism or Scientism which has censored or barred evidence of important new scientific discoveries which could change our concept of reality. We have been conditioned to obey, to believe implicitly what we have been told, to trust the commands issued from above. We have suffered unimaginable pain and grief through incessant wars, setting nation against nation for centuries. Now, because we are so unconscious, we are threatened with the decimation of our numbers at the hands of a small, very powerful elite who, for reasons best known to itself, is attempting to control the world. I will offer proof of this in the Chapters on The Abuse of Power.

Materialist or Reductionist Science, also known as Physicalism or Scientism came into being over the last three centuries and today controls secular culture, governments, international organizations, the media, and mainstream academic life. It developed on the flawed or unbalanced foundation of the separation of nature from spirit — a separation that was bequeathed to us by the patriarchal religions. Its Master Story is the control of nature and technological progress.

This cosmology or view of reality — presented as incontrovertible truth — tells us that we are the only sentient beings in a dead universe that has come into being by chance some 4.8 billion years ago and is without life, intelligence, evolutionary purpose or meaning. It claims that — like the universe — we humans have also come into being by chance. It teaches that we are separate from nature and are the only conscious beings in the entire universe. It has banished God and the soul as well as any suggestion of the existence of a dimension of reality beyond our material one, or any form of consciousness transcendent to its own. The highest authority is now the rational mind. It ignores the further potential development of human consciousness and the higher states of mind that have long been explored in the metaphysical traditions of the East and, in earlier ages, in the shamanic wisdom of the West. It is pursuing the enticing goals offered by AI or artificial intelligence as well as a transhumanist agenda which plans to enhance human intelligence by implanting nano-particles or chips in the human organism.[10] It is ignorant of the achievements of past civilizations and the insights of shamans, mystics, and enlightened philosophers. Anything 'non-rational' is anathema to it.

It insists that consciousness originates in the neurons of the physical brain. When the brain dies, consciousness ceases to exist. We are basically bio-physical machines, with no free will. Our bodies are mechanisms that can be manipulated by multiple vaccinations to prevent disease or implanted with a chip that can carry our bank card details. These dehumanizing beliefs offer no foundation for morality which, in the Babel of social media, is increasingly vanishing from our world, and no foundation for relationship with and respect for the earth. This cosmology, taught in our schools and universities for over a hundred years, has taken on the power and absolutism of an ideology. It derives its materialist beliefs from Descartes' bleak statement: "There exist no occult forces in stones or plants.… There is nothing in the whole of nature which cannot be explained in terms of purely corporeal causes totally devoid of mind and thought." [11] Contrast this with the words of Pico de la Mirandola from the Italian Renaissance, "All this great body of the world is a soul, full of the intellect of God, who fills it within and without and vivifies the All… the world is alive." [12]

Descartes' view has infiltrated and programmed scientific materialism. It has led to this statement by Yuval Harari, the historian, author and spokesman for the World Economic Forum, "Life has no script, no playwright, no producer and no meaning. We are no more than "hackable animals". [13] Descartes' view has also influenced the work of Richard Dawkins who believes "Scientific Rationalism is the crowning glory of the human spirit."

If there is a single idea that has facilitated our ability to harm the planet, it is the belief of scientific materialism that the earth and nature have no consciousness and that we are separate from the life around us. It therefore does not matter what we do to matter — that nature and matter are not sacred, that we are not part of that sacredness. This is why there is no foundation for morality in our relationship with the earth. What we think we need, we take. This behaviour could be described as schizoid.

According to the psychiatrist Dr Iain McGilchrist, author of *The Master and His Emissary* and his recent *magnum opus — The Matter with Things —* this materialist cosmology reveals that we have become prisoners of the literal left-hemispheric mind which, over centuries and even millennia, has cut off access to the imaginative right hemisphere and has led to the misinterpretation of reality that is currently reflected in and promoted by scientific materialism.[14]

C.G. Jung, could see the dangers of this materialist philosophy. In *Man and His Symbols*, he wrote:

> "As scientific understanding has grown, so our world has become de-humanized. Man feels himself isolated in the cosmos, because he is no longer involved in nature and has lost his emotional 'unconscious identity' with natural phenomena.… No voices now speak to man from stones, plants, and animals, nor does he speak tothem believing they can hear. His contact with nature has gone." [15]

In another passage, he describes how, as the conscious mind gained more and more autonomy and separation from the deeper matrix of the psyche, the whole super-structure of consciousness has become disengaged from the age-old instinctive ground or primordial soul out of which it has developed.

"Consciousness thus torn from its roots…", he said, "possesses a Promethean freedom but it also partakes of the nature of a godless hybris." [16]

No image describes this godless hybris better than a painting — below — of the Cyclops, gazing down upon the naked figure of a woman lying in a beautiful landscape, painted over a hundred years ago by Odilon Redon.

The Cyclops
Painting by Odilon Redon 1840-1916 CE

Authoritarian Control over the Human Spirit

Looking at the world today, countless millions live their lives in bondage to patriarchal images of God which are rigid in their authoritarian control over the human spirit — as in Afghanistan and Iran, where women are virtual prisoners of their governments, threatened with death if they dare to resist their brutal rulers. Countless other millions live under the absolute control of their totalitarian governments — as in China and North Korea. Areas of Africa are succumbing to violence and war under a succession of corrupt tyrants and military leaders, driven by the greed for power. The Middle East is imploding under the pressure of the unresolved situation between Israel and the

Palestinian Territories where, in relation to their numbers, the Palestinians do not have enough land to call their own and Israel is surrounded by enemies who are intent on destroying it. The United States, Russia and China are preparing to embark on further wars to achieve a position of absolute power in relation to each other. China threatens to invade and annex Taiwan. We have just come through the alarming Covid-19 years when the totalitarian tendencies of governments through the censorship of the media and the suppression of all discussion about the content and safety of the vaccines were rapidly developed in order to control vast populations.[17] All this horror has come about because of a complete lack of understanding of who we are and why we are here, when we are driven and controlled by our unconscious survival instincts which are always looking out for the next enemy.

This extraordinary time we are living in is giving us an opportunity to recover forgotten values which serve and protect life, to surrender our lesser aims to serve the evolutionary imperative of birthing a new and better kind of civilization. We are witnessing both the death throes of the old Patriarchal Order and the birth of a New Order that renounces the sacrificial rituals of war, the struggle for power between nations and the general corruption of governments and ineptitude of politicians who do not serve the people who vote them into power but their own agenda. Change is coming but we need to understand the long historical process that has led us to this crucial time of choice, which, after two thousand years, is also a time of judgement for the whole of humanity.

The UAP Disclosure Act

The Unidentified Anomalous Phenomena (UAP) Disclosure Act of 2023 was put forward for signature to the President of the United States in December 2023 and is a response to the allegation that for some seventy years, government agencies in that country have accessed and stored information that our planet may not be the only one in the universe to be inhabited by intelligent beings. In a recently enacted defence policy bill (February 2024), federal agencies will be required to organize and tag records related to UAP's and will have to the end of the current fiscal year "to review, identify, and organize each UAP record in its custody for disclosure to the public and transmission to the National Archives."[18] This disclosure process is a very slow work in progress. Yet the fact that it exists challenges the belief of materialist science that our universe and its three trillion galaxies have come into being by chance and that we are the only conscious beings in it.

The presidential approval of the UAP Disclosure Act is a significant step forward in verifying that other intelligent beings exist and have been known to exist for more than half a century, and this could change everything. We are not alone in the universe. We have galactic neighbours, some of whose technologies may be light-years ahead of our own. This was not news to ancient civilizations and is not news to many people on our planet who have been in touch with intelligent beings on Sirius, Arcturus, the Pleiades and Andromeda for many years, receiving messages of encouragement from them about the fact that our planet is going through a process of ascension which will bring about many positive and transformative changes. [19]

I hope this Preface may have thrown some light on the situation in which we now find ourselves. Having summarized our predicament, I can turn to the solution and the theme of this book: the recovery of the forgotten Feminine Face of God — Divine Wisdom and the Holy Spirit. This will include the joint Mission of the two greatest teachers of the Essenes, Jeshua (Jesus) and Mary Magdalene.

There are three different aspects to the process of awakening to a New Story:

1. The first and most important is to know how and why the deep split between spirit and nature arose and to re-unite our conscious, rational mind with the feminine matrix of our soul.

2. The second is to recover and redeem the Feminine Principle, understanding when, where and how it was rejected and why its recovery is essential to balance the present control of the planet by men who are possessed and driven by the will to power. The freeing of women in every culture from their long oppression and marginalization is an essential aspect of this recovery.

3. The third is to define a new image of God, discarding the patriarchal image we have inherited of a male creator separate from creation, and becoming aware that we are Cosmic Beings, participants in and co-creators with the God we have been worshipping for thousands of years. Only when nature, matter, soul, and body — the four aspects of the Feminine — are recognized as a manifestation of spirit will we be able to heal our dangerously unbalanced and unconscious culture.

The Second Coming

Turning and turning in the widening gyre
The falcon cannot hear the falconer;
Things fall apart; the centre cannot hold;
Mere anarchy is loosed upon the world,
The blood-dimmed tide is loosed, and everywhere
The ceremony of innocence is drowned;
The best lack all conviction, while the worst
Are full of passionate intensity.
Surely some revelation is at hand;
Surely the Second Coming is at hand.
The Second Coming! Hardly are those words out
When a vast image out of *Spiritus Mundi*
Troubles my sight: somewhere in sands of the desert
A shape with lion body and the head of a man,
A gaze blank and pitiless as the sun,
Is moving its slow thighs, while all about it
Reel shadows of the indignant desert birds.
The darkness drops again; but now I know
That twenty centuries of stony sleep
Were vexed to nightmare by a rocking cradle,
And what rough beast, its hour come round at last,
Slouches towards Bethlehem to be born?

— W. B. Yeats

Notes:

1. Ophuls, William, (2018), *Apologies to the Grandchildren*. Independently published, p. 21
2. Jung, C. G. (1983) *Memories, Dreams, Reflections,* Collins and Routledge & Kegan Paul, p. 300
3. Kurzweil, Ray (2024) *The Singularity is Nearer*, Bodley Head, London.
    See also Wood, Patrick M. (2022) *The Evil Twins: Technology and Transhumanism,* Coherent Publishing, LLC, Messa, AZ
4. Edinger, Edward (1984) *The Creation of Consciousness, Jung's Myth for Modern Man*, Inner City Books, Toronto
5. Campbell, Joseph (1986) *The Inner Reaches of Outer Space*, St James Press Ltd., Toronto, Canada
6. Wilson, Stuart and Prentis, Joanna (2012) *Beyond Limitations,* Ozark Mountain Publishing, PO Box 754, Huntsville, AR, pp. 101-3
7. The recent WHO Treaty offered to governments for signature in May 2024. Amendments have now been made to it in response to vociferous opposition to and rejection of its terms.
8. Anthony, Mark (2021) *The Afterlife Frequency: The Scientific proof of Spiritual Contact and How that Awareness Will Change Your Life*, New World Library, Novato, CA
9. Jung, C.G. (1958) *The Undiscovered Self,* Routledge & Kegan Paul Ltd., London, pp. 111-112
10. Kurzweil, op. cit.
11. Apffel-Marglin, Frédérique and Chung Gonzales, Randy, *Initiated by the Spirits*, p.151
12. ibid, p. 150
13. from a talk given at the World Economic Forum in Davos 2020 and other talks on YouTube
14. McGilchrist, Dr Iain (2021), *The Matter with Things, Our Brains, Our Delusions and the Unmaking of the World*, Volumes 1-2, Perspectiva Press, London
15. Jung, C.G. (1964) *Man and His Symbols*, p. 95, Aldus Books, London
16. Jung, C.G. (1931) *The Secret of the Golden Flower*, p. 85, Routledge & Kegan Paul, London
17. Desmet, Mattias (2022), *The Psychology of Totalitarianism*, Chelsea Green Publishing, London
18. Dr Steven Greer has tried for many decades to draw attention to the information concealed by the Deep State on the existence of UFO's (now called UAP'S) and Alien craft that have crashed on American soil. He has detailed his quest for the release of information on these events in a book called *Unacknowledged* and two films: *Unacknowledged* and *Close Encounters of the Fifth Kind*. I have followed his work for twenty years and respect his research.
19. Portal to Ascension webinars organized by Neil Gaur.
    www.portaltoascension.org

Note 13 continued:

According to Professor Harari: "Many tyrants and governments wanted to hack millions of people in the past, but nobody knew biology well enough. Nobody had enough computing power and data to hack millions of people. Neither the Gestapo nor the KGB could do it. But soon, at least some corporations and governments will be able to systematically hack all the people. We humans should get used to the idea that we are no longer mysterious souls. We are now hackable animals. Data may allow human elites to do something even more radical than just build physical dictatorships. By hacking organisms, elites may gain the power to re-engineer the future of life itself. Because once you can hack something, you can usually also engineer it. And if indeed, we succeed in hacking and engineering life, this will be not only the greatest revolution in the history of humanity. This will be the greatest revolution in biology since the very beginning of life four billion years ago. For four billion years, nothing fundamental changed in the basic rules in the game of life. All of life for four billion years — dinosaurs, amoeba, tomatoes, humans — all of life was subject to the laws of natural selection and to the laws of biochemistry.

But this is now about to change. Science is replacing evolution by natural selection with evolution by intelligent design. Not some intelligent design of some God above the clouds but *our* intelligent design — the IBN Cloud, the Microsoft Cloud. These are the new driving forces of evolution. And science may enable life, after being confined for 4 billion years to the limited realm of organic compounds, science may enable life to break out into the inorganic realm. So, after 4 billion years of life shaped by natural selection, we are entering the era or inorganic life, shaped by Intelligent Design. So does the data about my DNA, my brain, my body, my life, belong to me? Does it belong to me, or to some corporation, or perhaps to the government or perhaps to the human collective?"

End of transcript from his 2020 Davos talk.

https://www.youtube.com/watch?v=gG6WnMb9Fho

As I was writing this Preface, my attention was drawn by a friend to a book by Lionel Corbett, published in 1996 by Routledge, London and called *The Religious Function of the Psyche*. This book might be of interest to people who cannot accept traditional concepts of God but who nevertheless experience a strong sense of the sacred in their lives. It offers a psychological model for the understanding of such an experience, using the language and interpretive methods of depth psychology, particularly those of C.G. Jung. It addresses the problems of evil and suffering, and the notion of human development as an incarnation of spirit, offering an alternative approach to spirituality, as well as providing an introduction to Jung and religion.

INTRODUCTION

There is an almost sensual longing for communion with others with a larger vision. The immense fulfilment of the friendship between those engaged in furthering the evolution of consciousness, has a quality impossible to describe.

— Pierre Teilhard de Chardin

In the twelfth century, there was a visionary Italian monk called Joachim of Fiore (1135-1202), who founded the monastery of that name in the mountainous region of Calabria in southern Italy. As a young man, on a visit to the Holy Land, he had received a revelation of his life's work and this led him to take holy orders. Among his prolific writings, which were widely circulated at the time, he wrote about three Ages: The Age of the Father, The Age of the Son, and The Age of the Holy Spirit, when a new dispensation of universal love would manifest, proceeding from the Gospel of Christ but transcending the letter of it. There would be no more need for religious institutions. The Age of the Father and the Age of the Son have passed and we are now entering the Age of the Holy Spirit. Joachim knew the Holy Spirit as the third Person of the Trinity and would not have dreamed that there was a Feminine Holy Spirit or a Feminine Face of God.

This book is a celebration of Divine Wisdom and the Holy Spirit, the forgotten feminine face of God. In this interlude between the Age of Pisces and the Age of Aquarius, the long-lost image of the Divine Feminine is returning. She, the Corner-Stone that the builders rejected during the Age of Pisces, is initiating a crucial new phase in our evolution, urging us to discover a new ethic of responsibility towards the planet, bringing us a new vision of the sacredness and unity of life. Wisdom, justice, beauty, harmony, love and compassion and the impulse to help and to heal are the qualities that have traditionally been identified with the Divine Feminine, yet she is also the irresistible power that destroys old forms and brings new ones into being, the inspiration of the love-in-action that is needed to transform a culture that is radically out of touch with its soul. The Divine Feminine is the unseen dimension of Soul, once named the *Anima-Mundi*, to which we are connected through our instincts, our feelings, and the longing imagination of our heart. Soul is not limited to our own psychic life. Soul is invisible nature, the immense web of relationships that is concealed beneath the veil of matter. It is something inconceivable and immeasurable to which we belong, in which we live — an intermediate dimension between our physical world and the deep unknowable ground of being.

For many hundreds of years, in the fascination with the development of mind and the technological skills that have given us the power to control nature, the emphasis of Western civilization has been overwhelmingly focused on power, control and conquest rather than relationship. Now, to balance this one-sided emphasis, the image of the Divine Feminine, together with the Wisdom tradition that belongs to her, is returning to consciousness. She is reconnecting us to the dimension of the instinctual soul that has been shut away, like the Sleeping Beauty, behind a hedge of thorns. The power and numinosity of the Divine Feminine are needed to arouse the will and energy to act on behalf of life and to restore wholeness and balance to our image of God and sanity to our culture. It is awakening us to a new ethic of responsibility, focused beyond personal, tribal and national concerns towards the needs of the planet and all the forms of life it embraces.

The Divine Mother is asking us to trust and protect life, to work with her in all we do, opening our understanding to the knowledge that we are not separate from her but an expression of her being. The unknown dimension of soul is our conduit to the Divine. Cut off from soul, the mind becomes impoverished, rigid, dogmatic, and inflated. In compensation for this loss of relationship with soul, it becomes driven by the need for ever more power and control. The journey in search of the unknown dimension of soul, back the way we have come, towards nature and the ground of our own nature, is difficult and even dangerous because it asks that we relinquish the certainty of deeply held beliefs, both religious and scientific. It means opening ourselves to discovery.

The Grail of the Feminine is urging us to open our heart to a new vision of reality, the revelation of all cosmic life as a divine unity. For those awakened to this vision, to be born a human being is not to be born into a fallen, flawed world of sin and illusion, cut off from the divine; it is to be born into a world lit by an invisible radiance, ensouled by divine presence, graced and sustained by incandescent Light and Love.

The Sacred Image

As our consciousness evolved, the sacred image was like an umbilical cord connecting us to the deep ground of life. Looking back over the past at the evolution of human consciousness, it seems to fall into three main stages. During the first stage, broadly defined as the Palaeolithic and Neolithic eras, humanity lived instinctively as the child of the Great Mother, in magical harmony with her body — creation — and knew life and death as two modes of her divine reality.

Then, this primordial experience began to fade as we gradually developed the capacity for self-awareness and reflective thought and, with this, the power to control the environment. In the second phase, human consciousness became differentiated from the matrix of nature, and nature was imagined as a great Dragon — something to be struggled against, defeated, controlled.

During this phase of Separation, there was a shift of focus from the Great Mother to the Great Father and a radical split between spirit and nature, dividing the oneness of life into a duality. The concept of a transcendent male Creator God, formulated by male priesthoods, gradually became identified with spirit, light, creative mind, and good; and the Goddess with nature, matter, darkness, and chaos. Men and women were part of this process of differentiation. Men unconsciously aligned themselves with the Creator God and the principle of light. They associated women with nature because of their closeness to the instinctual processes of gestation and giving birth. For nearly 3000 years in the three patriarchal religions that originated in the Middle East there has been no sacred marriage between Goddess and God, no feminine dimension to the Godhead to lend balance and wholeness to the concept of it. This loss of the Divine Feminine has endangered civilization and is reflected in the emphasis on conquest and the drive for power over nature that has become the ethos of modern culture.

Yet this division of life into two aspects is rooted in the dissociation within us between the conscious, rational mind, and the deep, instinctual matrix of soul. It is because of this dissociation within us that we have come to divide life into two aspects: spirit and nature, mind and matter. We need to recover the lost relationship with nature and with soul, and this may be one reason why the image of the Divine Feminine is returning now, during the third phase in the evolution of human consciousness.

The Experience of the Mother

Why is the image of a Divine Mother so important? To answer this question, we need look no further than our experience of birth into the world. First, there is the experience of the embryo in the womb, the experience of union, fusion and containment within a watery nurturing matrix. After the traumatic experience of birth and the sudden and violent expulsion from this matrix, the prolongation of the earlier feelings of close relationship, trust, and safety is vital. Without the consistent and loving care of the mother in early childhood, the child has no trust in itself, no power to survive negative life experiences, no model from which to learn how to nurture and support itself or to care for its children in turn. Its primary response to life is anxiety and fear. It is like a tree with no roots, easily torn up by a storm. Its instincts have been traumatized and damaged. With the love of a mother and trust in her presence, the child grows in strength and confidence, taking delight in life. Its primary response is trust.

Cultures that have no image of the Mother in the god-head are vulnerable to powerful unconscious feelings of fear and anxiety, particularly when the emphasis of their religious teaching is on sin and guilt. The compensation for fear is an insatiable need for power and control.

Those who for centuries have been the transmitters of the patriarchal traditions may not appreciate how deep this need and this longing are; as acutely felt by men as by women. Just as it is the presence of the mother that comforts and reassures the child, so it is the image of the Divine Mother that awakens the feeling of trust and containment because it reflects our personal experience of our containment in the womb and our earliest human relationship.

This is why the image of the Divine Feminine is returning to us now, to help us recover not only our trust in life but also the relationship with the dimension of consciousness that we have, in our longing to be in control of life, ignored. A knowledge of the symbols the soul uses in dreams to communicate its guidance and its wisdom is essential to an understanding of ourselves, and the greater dimension in which we live.

God-the-Mother

The Divine Feminine is the forgotten Feminine aspect of the God-head — God-the-Mother — once named Holy Spirit and Divine Wisdom; lost for millennia during the patriarchal era, yet never completely forgotten, surviving unnoticed as the twelfth century Cathar Church of the Holy Spirit in the Languedoc area of France and as the God-Mother in fairy tales like Cinderella. The Divine Feminine is the Womb of Life and the unseen Web of Life that connects each one of us to the life of the planet and the greater life of the cosmos and its three trillion galaxies.

The Divine Feminine is returning to us now as we face the greatest challenge we have ever had to face — how to birth the understanding that Life is One; that we are all connected to each other; that we are all immortal children of the Cosmos, participants in the source from which we have come and to which we will return. We cannot birth this understanding without becoming aware of the Divine Feminine and the values She embodies: Wisdom, Truth, Justice, Compassion, Love, Harmony, and Beauty.

Long ago, the Divine Feminine was known in ancient Judaism as the Holy

Spirit, Divine Wisdom and the Tree of Life, whose fruit offered the gift of immortality. She was known in Gnostic Christianity and in the Great Work of Alchemy as Sophia or Divine Wisdom. She was known to Jesus as His Mother, who spoke to him at His baptism.[1]

Twelve hundred years ago, the Holy Spirit was known throughout Europe as the Holy Grail, sacred image of the Divine Feminine. Her most ancient symbol is the rose — the rose that we can find exalted in the great rose windows of Chartres cathedral. Light and Love flow to all creation from her Cosmic Womb.

What happened to the Mother? Why is there no feminine aspect of the god-head — no God-the-Mother? Why, in the three patriarchal religions, do we have a Father God but no Mother God? I have chosen to write about the neglected feminine aspect of God because it is an essential aspect of our understanding of life and of ourselves, essential to the completion of our nature and our decadent, unbalanced and addicted civilization. It is also essential that women know there is a Divine Feminine Presence in the god-head or Ground of Being — a Mother.

The Book of Genesis

The Bible has been intrinsic to the development of Western civilization. But we need to be aware that the Bible and its contents are entirely the creation of men, whether Jewish or Christian. We also need to be aware of how deeply we have been conditioned unconsciously to accept the image of God transmitted to Christianity from Judaism. If we go back to the Book of Genesis 1:27 we read: *So God created man in his own image, in the image of God created he him: male and female created he them.* Man could not exist on this planet without woman giving birth to him. She is essential to the creation and continuation of life. If God created male and female in his own image, then it follows that there is a Divine Feminine aspect to God that may have been lost in the arduous process of translating the Hebrew Old Testament into Greek, Latin and English.[2]

At the end of my life, I feel drawn to make this forgotten feminine gender of the Holy Spirit more widely known, to make a small contribution to restoring the largely forgotten image of the Divine Mother and the Divine Feminine. It is vitally important that people should know the archetypal history of the last ten thousand years, how the original aspect of divinity was the Great Mother and how this image changed into the Great Father during the third millennium BCE, and how the Divine Feminine aspect of deity was deleted from the god-head at a specific time.

The Awakening Dream

Fifty years ago, I had a visionary dream of a cosmic woman, whose form reached from earth to the highest reaches of the Cosmos. What I saw, I later realized, was the Divine Ground showing itself to me in feminine form. This dream changed the course of my life. It led me to the discovery of the feminine aspect of the Holy Spirit that had been lost or hidden for two-and-a-half millennia and to the recognition of the disastrous effect that this loss of the image and mythology of the Divine Feminine has had on the development of Western civilization. This dream was the most awesome experience of my life, the awakener of my soul:

I dream that I come round the side of a huge dolmen and enter another world, an utterly strange and barren landscape. It is lit by the brilliant radiance of the full moon. I am searching for someone I love and my longing for him is so great that I have embarked on a journey in search of him. The landscape is transformed from a desert into field after field of brilliant green wheat. The moonlight is so bright that it is like daylight and the wheat is the colour of an emerald. I float over this emerald sea for many miles, my bare feet skimming the surface of the wheat, until I come to the brow of a low hill and hesitate, wondering if I should go further. I decide to go on and come down into a valley on the other side.

Suddenly, I find that two enormous men, standing on two hills high above the valley, have caught me in a gigantic net that stretches the whole width of the valley. They are drawing me into the presence of something tremendously powerful and numinous. I am frightened, yet at the same time fascinated. I lie flat on my back on the ground, helplessly enmeshed in the net and look up, half in terror, half in awe. I see the figure of a woman towering above me, filling the entire space between earth and sky. She is naked, with fair skin and golden hair and is very beautiful. She is not young, but ageless. In the centre of her abdomen is an immense revolving wheel that is also a rose and a labyrinth, like the one I had seen inlaid in the floor of Chartres Cathedral. Awestruck, I gaze up at her, then down at my own body which is exactly like hers, only tiny in relation to it. I too have a revolving wheel but mine is not centred; it is too far to the left. She does not speak but indicates that I am to centre my wheel, like hers.

This dream led me to discover my life work, which was to restore the image of the Divine Feminine. My search for her led me to the Shekinah of Kabbalah whose titles now, as they were millennia ago, are Divine Wisdom and the Holy Spirit. I discovered that the feminine aspect of the Holy Spirit had been eliminated from Judaism in 623 BCE, and as well as from Christ-

ianity, because it took its monotheistic image of God from Judaism and the
Old Testament. It led me to see the calamitous effects that the loss or absence
of the Divine Feminine has had on civilization, and on the evolutionary path
of our species, and how we have been indoctrinated to believe that only God
the Father exists. It led me to devote the rest of my life to the restoration of
the Feminine Principle.

Visionary dreams like this one cannot be interpreted according to any
known system of belief. They need to be held close to the heart and allowed
to live so that, over the course of many years, they can act as leaven in the
soul. In an earlier culture I would have worshipped this image as a goddess
and perhaps built a shrine to her, but in today's world, belief and worship
did not satisfy me. Because it was so powerful and so numinous, I wanted to
understand the relevance of this dream for the whole of humanity, not just for
myself. I needed to know why I had been given this vision and how to serve it.

Naked and beautiful, neither young nor old, the Cosmic Woman who had
appeared to me was too pagan a figure for the Christian Mary, yet she was
not like Aphrodite or any of the Greek goddesses with whom I was familiar.
I began to question whether she could be a manifestation of the Soul of the
World or Soul of the Cosmos, first mentioned by Plato in the *Timaeus* and
later described as the *Anima-Mundi* by Plotinus in the *Enneads*. Again and
again, I returned to wondering about her and how I was to centre my wheel.
Why was my wheel too far to the left and how could I centre it? What was she
asking of me by sending me such a powerful vision?

This visionary dream led me to research the image of the Goddess in
ancient civilizations and to write a book with my friend, Jules Cashford — *The
Myth of the Goddess: Evolution of an Image* (1992) — while we were both
training to become Jungian Analysts during the 1980's. While researching
the image of the Divine Feminine from the Palaeolithic Era to the present day,
I came across the image of the Shekinah in the Jewish mystical tradition of
Kabbalah, known as 'The Voice of the Dove' or 'The Jewels of the Heavenly
Bride.' This is the only tradition in the West which includes the Divine
Feminine in the God-head. I am not Jewish yet this tradition drew me to it
like a magnet. I felt at home in it, as if I had studied it in other lives. I also felt
that the image of the Shekinah as the Divine Feminine aspect of the god-head
came the closest to the cosmic woman of my visionary dream. I felt my dream
had led me to this tradition.

Once before in the twelfth century, the rescue of the Divine Feminine
was attempted in the great spiritual impulse of the Quest for the Holy Grail.
In that century, it was briefly present in the Cathar Church of the Holy Spirit
in south-western France. Indirectly, it gave rise to the marvel of the Gothic

Cathedrals and the later Renaissance. Then, this great impulse died in the wars that engulfed Europe. Apart from enlightened mystics like Jacob Boehme and the later Russian mystics, we lost sight of the Divine Feminine until the last decades of the twentieth century when several American women went in search of her, as Jules and I had done.

I should mention that in 1956, when I was twenty-five, I was fortunate to have been offered an extraordinary commission by an Italian Encyclopaedia of Art in Rome. I was asked to travel to all the museums in the capital cities of India and countries further East and to ask the curators to choose photographs of the finest works of art they held in their museums. This commission took a year, during which I travelled to India, Burma, Thailand, Indonesia, Taiwan and Japan. China was out of bounds at that time. This wonderful commission opened my eyes to great civilizations of which I had no previous knowledge. It introduced me to Hinduism, Buddhism and Daoism, and to concepts like reincarnation, enlightenment and karma that were unfamiliar to me. I marvelled at the incredible beauty of the art of India and Indian Asia, and the magnificence of half the Imperial Treasure of China, taken to Taiwan (formerly Formosa) in 1949 by General Chang Kai-Chek when he went into exile there, and safeguarded in vast underground corridors. Privileged to be shown these hidden treasures, I fell in love with the incredible beauty of the Daoist paintings of the Song Dynasty. I visited the gigantic temple of Angkor Wat in Cambodia, and others, equally extraordinary, recently freed from the roots of the giant trees that had grown over them for centuries. And later, the Buddhist temple of Borobodur, in Java.

When I returned, I wrote my first book, called *The One Work, A Journey Towards the Self,* published in 1961, which explained how my travels had opened my eyes to the essential teaching of Hinduism and Buddhism and led me to compare this with what I believed was the essential teaching of Christianity. The book ended with the Gnostic *Hymn of the Pearl* and the words: "I seek the Grail, the Pearl of Great Price, the Treasure, and I am told to look for them in the Cave of my heart. When I have found them, the Mystic Marriage will take place. I and my Father are One. Samsara and Nirvana are One. Heaven and Earth are One and everything is God."

Years later, my path drew me to writing other books: *The Mystic Vision* (1995) and *The Divine Feminine* (1996) with Andrew Harvey and a book for children, *The Birds Who Flew Beyond Time*, based on the Sufi story of *The Conference of the Birds*. And a book called *Soul Power: an Agenda for a Conscious Humanity* with a close friend, Scilla Elworthy. Then, not satisfied that I had communicated all that I wanted to in *The Myth of the Goddess*, I began writing *The Dream of the Cosmos: A Quest for the Soul*, published in

2013 and updated in 2020. This book took me on a journey of exploration into what has been neglected during the millennia of patriarchal culture — the Feminine dimension of the Divine, our relationship with spirit and, most importantly, our forgotten relationship with nature. As I explored the different facets of the banishment of the Divine Feminine, I realized that during the patriarchal era woman's voice had been completely silenced. There were no longer any temples where the Goddess was worshipped; no longer any priest-esses serving in them. I wondered what effect the absence of the Divine Feminine in our image of God had had on the psyche of both men and women? Had it given men an inflated idea of their value and women a diminished image of theirs, leading to a diminished concept of women's value in both genders? How had this radical imbalance worked its way through the last three thousand years and the wars and struggles for power between and within the patriarchal religions?

For nearly four thousand years the Divine Feminine has, like the Sleeping Beauty, lain under a spell; her voice silenced, her wisdom rejected. Beauty, grace, and harmony have faded from our world. We are threatened with destruction by the demonic weapons we have created and the wars that are continually generated by the struggle for power and dominance between nations. But now, in this time of great crisis for humanity, she is stirring to life. What does she want from us? What is her hope? I believe she wants recogni-tion and relationship. I see this relationship as a sacred marriage; a marriage between ourselves and the invisible ground of life.

The Holy Spirit Today

How could we imagine the Holy Spirit today? Perhaps as the Light that manifests as both wave and particle, as the deep unexplored 'sea' of cosmic space and the invisible light particles which are the ground of all physical reality including the extraordinary complex structure and organization of the patterns of energy that we call matter: a word which comes from *mater*, the Latin word for mother. After so many billions of years the creative energy of life has evolved a form, the planet Earth, and a consciousness, our own, which is slowly growing towards the recognition of its ground and source. Yet, because of the loss of the tradition of the Divine Feminine, we do not know that what physicists, cosmologists, and biologists are exploring in the finer and finer gradations of matter they are discovering is what the awe-struck explorers of the Tree of Life in Kabbalah named the Face and the Glory of God, nor that the magnificent universe revealed to us through the Hubble and James Webb telescopes is the outer covering or veil an unimaginably fine web of invisible relationships. If only these images of the Holy Spirit could be restored to us, how differently we might see matter, with what respect we might treat it.

What comment would the Holy Spirit pass on the pathological effects of our ignorance — the pollution of her earth, her seas, her air, the abysmal and wanton sacrifice of animals and the contamination with toxins and pesticides of the food and water that is her gift of life to us? And what of the manufacture and sale of ever more lethal weapons, including the biological weapons that are currently being developed and stored in hundreds of gain-of-function laboratories in many parts of the world? What of geo-engineering and the arrogant interference with the climate of the planet? What of the torture, murder and rape of men, women, and children in war; the use of explosives to destroy flesh and bone; the agony of orphaned, starving, trafficked or murdered children, the desperate grief of mothers and grandmothers who have lost their beloved sons and grandsons, the anguish of the young men forced into battle before their lives have really begun, the desecrated landscape created by the addiction to war? To hear her answer, we would have to attune ourselves to her being. We would have to listen with her ear to the voice of the suffering we bring into being through our utter ignorance of the unity and divinity of life. We would have radically to change our habits of behaviour and become more consciously aware that the suffering we inflict on others is suffering that we are inflicting on the 'body' of spirit and that spirit suffers from our blindness, ignorance, and abysmal cruelty.

If we could awaken to the sacredness and divinity of life, we would begin to see matter and our own bodies in a different light; we would treat them with greater respect. We would know that our body is not a machine to be controlled by multiple vaccinations but the miraculous vehicle or temple of our soul, essential for our ability to live on this planet. If we could awaken to Her Presence, we could bring matter and spirit, body, mind, and soul together, healing the deep traumas inflicted by the beliefs and concepts which have separated them. Even as we accomplish this, we would begin to transmit the Light and Love of the Holy Spirit flowing to us and all creation. This book is written in homage to Her and in recognition of Her guidance.

While I was writing the chapter on the Shekinah in the *Dream of the Cosmos*, this wonderful vision came to me:

I stand on the shore of the world and look intently at the sea of stars, at their great patterns spread out before me. As I look, I see a ship approaching, in the shape of an ark, its prow curved back like the wings of a great bird. Closer it comes, weaving between the constellations, growing larger as it approaches me. I see that it is translucent, as if made of glass, and that it has the irides-cence of an opal. Yet also, it is richly adorned with jewels that are themselves stars. Closer still it comes, and now I see that the ship casts a radiance upon the sea of space and shows me that this sea is a great web or net made of gossamer filaments of light; they sparkle with jewels like a spider's web in the sun. At the jewelled points where these filaments meet there are vortices of swirling energy. I perceive the web as a being of unimaginable dimensions who is speaking to me, saying:

"This is what I am. This is the hidden glory of My Being. This is the life you belong to. The Sea of My Being is at once 'greater than the great' and 'smaller than the small', co-inherent with the greatest galaxies of cosmic space and the tiniest particle of matter. Once I was named Soul or Spirit or Cosmic Consciousness or Great Mother and Father — the greater psychic reality to which your own life belongs and of which, for the most part, you are tragically unaware. Once, people imagined themselves living within My Being. Then I became distant, remote, forgotten. Now, for so many, I am lost altogether. This causes me grief for I am in exile from My people. For both of us there is great suffering and loneliness. My dream — the Dream of the Cos-mos — is for you to know Me again, to realize that you live within My Being, My Light, and My Love."

The Net of Indra

Notes:

1. In Mary Magdalene's *Gospel of the Beloved Companion*, Jesus (Yeshua) speaks throughout of the Holy Spirit as His Mother. (Jehanne de Quillan, Éditions Athara, Foix, 2010)

2. The New Testament was originally written in Greek, then in Latin. From 383 to 404, St Jerome translated the Bible into Latin. Originally, he translated the Old Testament from the Greek, but later compared what he had translated with the Hebrew original. Perhaps in this process of this and later translations, the Hebrew word *Ruach* — the feminine noun for the Holy Spirit — was translated into the genderless Greek words *hagia pneuma* and then into the Latin *Spiritus Sanctus* by St. Jerome.

   Much later, in the sixteenth century, the Bible, both Old and New Testaments, was translated from Greek into English by William Tyndale (1490–1536) a brilliant linguist who, tragically, was strangled and burnt at the stake for having dared to undertake this work. Parts of his translation were incorporated into the later King James version published in 1611. Forty-seven scholars participated in this new version, under the supervision of Richard Bancroft, the Archbishop of Canterbury. However, until the present time, few translators of the New Testament have gone back to the Aramaic words of Jesus. Those who have, among them Neil Douglas-Klotz, have given us a revelation of the beauty and subtlety of the language that Jesus spoke. See Chapter 5.

Chapter One

PRIMORDIAL TRAUMA:
TWO GREAT CATACLYSMS

About 12,800 years ago (10,800 BCE), after 2,000 years of accelerating global warming at the end of the ice-age, there was a terrifying cataclysm. Evidence has been emerging slowly and was reported in the *Daily Telegraph* on April 22nd, 2017, that approximately 13,000 years ago, the planet was hit by multiple fragments of a disintegrating comet. This comet caused catastrophic damage to the planet and wiped out much of human and animal life, including several ancient civilizations. It also triggered the onset of what is called The Younger Dryas, a thousand years of freezing cold. Worldwide, there are multiple accounts of this catastrophe, and warnings given about its approach. Some tell of a "star with a long wide tail that came down and burnt everything up." [1]

The enormous ice-fields two kilometres thick covering Canada abruptly melted under the impact of up to 8 large fragments of the disintegrating comet. In 2018 a crater 19 miles (31 kms) wide was found in north-west Greenland (under the Hiawatha Glacier) that may have been caused by the impact of one of these fragments and is thought possibly to date to this time. Other large fragments fell on the North European ice field and further to the East. [2]

The comet is thought to have exploded over Canada. The colossal heat generated by the impacts of these fragments — some of them up to two kilometres wide, with a combined explosive power of 10 million megatons, caused the sudden catastrophic melting of these ice fields and sent a gigantic wall of water surging down into North America, carrying enormous boulders with it. This wiped out the people of the Clovis culture of North America as well as 35 species of animals, including mammoths, mastodons, and sabre-tooth tigers. This happened very suddenly, before any human or animal had time to flee. There were also continent-wide fires which sent quantities of toxic smoke, dust, and ash into the upper atmosphere, blocking out the sun. Torrents of freezing fresh water flowed into the Atlantic, disrupting the warming currents there and triggering another ice-age. Huge fragments of the comet also fell over the Atlantic and across Europe, melting the European ice-cap.

The Younger Dryas Period

The cataclysmic event of the exploding comet triggered what is called the Younger Dryas Period, a period of freezing cold which lasted 1000 years from about 10,800 BCE until about 9,700 BCE and extended over fifty million square kilometres as far east and south as Syria (map below). The ice-age returned and people and animals who had survived the catastrophe perished from the cold and the lack of food. The cave dwellers in the Dordogne area of France seem somehow to have survived this catastrophe and, as far as we know, did not record it on their cave walls. They had long adapted to living in sub-zero temperatures.

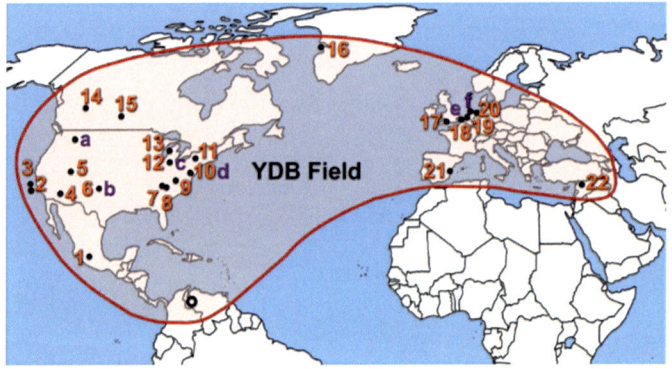

Younger Dryas Boundary Field The red line defines the current known limits of the field

In the *Journal of Geology*, September 2014, a paper summarising the evidence for a comet as the cause of the Younger Dryas says:

"A cosmic impact event at the onset of the Younger Dryas cooling episode is the only hypothesis capable of explaining the simultaneous deposition of peak abundances in nano-diamonds, magnetic and glassy spherules, melt-glass, platinum and/or other proxies across at least four continents (approaching 50 million square kilometres). The evidence strongly supports a cosmic impact 12,800 years ago."

The cataclysm preceding the Younger Dryas also affected Indonesia and Australia. The sudden rise in sea-levels caused by the melting ice drowned a huge section of land called Sundaland that connected Indonesia to the mainland of South-East Asia and possibly land connecting Indonesia with Australia, leaving only a scattering of 13,000 islands. It also separated Sri Lanka from India. Sundaland was a land mass that had surrounded the Indonesian islands and connected them to Thailand, Vietnam, and the Chinese mainland until the

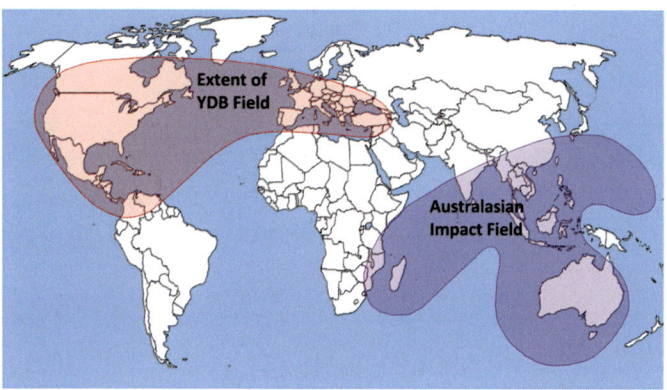

time of the rise of ocean levels as a result of the cosmic impact melting huge areas of ice.

The Disappearance of Lemuria or Mu

A manuscript in the British Museum called the Troano Manuscript tells of the disappearance of a very large island in the Pacific that was swallowed up overnight by the sea after tremendous earthquakes that were so severe that they split the land-mass into sections and caused it to sink without trace. This catastrophe was said to have happened about 12,500 years ago. Sixty-four million people were said to have died with it, together with all the animals.

James Churchward, in a remarkable book published in 1959 (re-published 2020) called *The Lost Continent of Mu*, described the life of the island, and recorded its catastrophic demise. [3] This was the original Mother-land from which daughter-colonies were established in south and central America to the East and in Indonesia and Sundaland to the West. Only a few small islands in the Pacific including the Hawaiian Islands, Easter Island and the Marshall and Polynesian Islands are the tiny remnants of it.

Churchward tells the story of how, when he was in India to help relieve a famine there, he came across ancient clay tablets in the vaults of a temple, whose location he does not divulge. With the help of an elderly priest who was at first reluctant, but after many months of persuasion, agreed to teach him how to decipher the ancient language and symbols with which these tablets were inscribed. In this way he learned from him a language which predated Sanskrit. Spending years in this temple learning the language from the priest, he eventually discovered on the tablets what could be described as the earliest Story of Creation and realized that it could be the primary source of later Creation Myths, including the one in the Book of Genesis.

The tablets revealed the existence of a huge unknown continent called Mu that had existed in the Pacific Ocean and had disappeared without trace at approximately the same time as the first cataclysm of 12,800 BCE. They thus confirmed the evidence of the Troano Manuscript in the British Museum. Churchward spent fifty years tracing the influence of this unknown, vanished civilization on the later civilizations of India, Babylonia, Persia, Egypt and Yucatan. He discovered that people from this lost continent had travelled to Burma and India to the West and Mexico to the East. The clay tablets, written in a language called Naacal, had come from Mu, and had reached the Indian temple via Burma.

When the Earth Nearly Died

The memories of the Great Flood (the First Catastrophe) have been recorded in stories and myths passed down for thousands of years by people all over the world. The catastrophe was so immense and widespread that it has never been forgotten. The book by D.S. Allan and J. B. Delair called "*When the Earth Nearly Died*", published in 1995, gives very detailed descriptions of the terror and horror of the Great Flood. [4]

I would like to connect this first catastrophe with very recent excavations that have been made into a hill called Gunung Padang in West Java. What was found there has stunned the archaeological community. The majority of the 100-meter hill is man-made — and is not actually a hill at all. It is a terraced pyramid, built up over millennia by the oldest civilization the world has yet discovered. Though few know it, there has been an ancient pyramid concealed beneath a mountain in Indonesia for millennia. Gunung Padang means "The Mountain of Light," and one researcher has reason to believe that this may be the oldest pyramid still standing on Earth, possibly 20,000 years old, at least as old as the Island of Mu. The description of it forms one part of a series on Ancient Civilizations presented on Netflix by Graham Hancock. He has been criticized and ridiculed for his books and for this series. But they are the fruit of his lifelong search for evidence of the existence of ancient civilizations and I trust his intuitions and journeys in search of them, as well as his conclusions.

Gunung Padang is evidence of a very advanced ancient civilization, and it challenges everything archaeologists thought they knew about the history of human civilization. I think that it may have been part of the civilization that existed on the continent of Lemuria or Mu, not far to the East in the middle of the Pacific Ocean — perhaps the only remnant of what the temples there once looked like. Graham Hancock begins his current series on Netflix with an exploration of Gunung Padang. There is now an interesting second series.

A Second Cataclysm

A second cataclysm happened about a thousand years later, around 11,700 years ago or 9,700 BCE at the end of Younger Dryas Period. This one was known as the Great Flood in the records that have come down to us. The cause of this second catastrophe is not as clear as the first one a thousand years earlier. Graham Hancock thinks it may have been caused by fragments of the same comet that had returned, this time hitting the oceans rather than the land. However, another hypothesis put forward by Robert Schoch, Professor of geology at Boston University, suggests that it was due to an enormous solar outburst which melted the glaciers literally overnight and led to the sudden rise in sea-levels — up to a hundred feet — all over the world.[5] A third hypothesis was that the poles shifted. Whichever theory is ultimately proved correct, the result of both cataclysms was the same: a devastating flood caused by the second sudden collapse of the North American and Northern European ice caps which had reformed during the Younger Dryas Period.[6] Gigantic tsunamis were carried inland for hundreds of miles. Huge walls of water, some coming over mountains, advanced on helpless communities. There were torrential rains, earthquakes, and volcanic eruptions like the one on Krakatoa which blotted out the sun for years; enormous fires scorched whole continents. The survivors took refuge in caves and carved out underground tunnels which could provide them with some shelter from the cold. Some of these can still be seen in Turkey (Cappadocia and Derinkuyu). This marked the final end of the ice-age.

Atlantis Destroyed

The Great Flood destroyed the city and island of Atlantis. Its sudden disappearance in a day and a night was recounted by Plato and dated by him to ca. 9,600 BCE. Plato says that a Greek law-giver called Solon had travelled to Egypt and heard the story of the Flood from the priests of Saïs in the Delta who had records of it in their temple. In his *Timaeus* and *Critias*, Plato records the destruction of a large land-mass and a renowned city that he called Atlantis. He also gives a precise description of its lay-out and dimensions, and also the reach of its power far into the Mediterranean area. This is what he wrote:

> There was an island opposite the strait you call the Pillars of Hercules. On it there was a remarkable dynasty of kings, who ruled the whole island. In addition, they controlled Libya up to the borders of Egypt and Europe as far as Tyrrenia (Italy). Plato added that "There were earth quakes and floods of extraordinary violence and in a single dreadful day and night, the island of Atlantis was swallowed up by the

sea and vanished." [7] Plato said that this catastrophe had happened because "The people of Atlantis ceased to be able to carry their prosperity with moderation."

In the *Critias*, he wrote: "To the perceptive eye the depth of their degeneration was clear enough, but to those whose judgement of true happiness is defective they seemed, in their pursuit of unbridled ambition and power, to be at the height of their fame and fortune." [8]

Plato said the destruction was so complete that people had to begin again, like children.

This account by Plato has generally been dismissed as a fabrication, without any basis in truth, but the repetition of a cataclysm 9,700 years ago together with Robert Schoch's solar outburst theory suggest it could be fact rather than fiction.

In destroying Atlantis, the Great Flood destroyed a highly developed and technologically advanced civilization which had large ships powered by some unknown method of propulsion which travelled west to the coast of Central and South America, east to the Mediterranean and south to Africa. Channeled material suggest that like Noah, certain people had prior notice of the coming catastrophe and established colonies in other parts of the world to carry forward the legacy of Atlantis. [9]

Thousands of years later, the story of the second Great Flood was recorded in the Sumerian *Epic of Gilgamesh* whose oldest written cuneiform accounts date to 2,000 BCE although Gilgamesh himself is thought to have lived around 2,700 BCE. From the Sumerian records it passed to the later Babylonian accounts and eventually to the Book of Genesis (Gen. 7-9). It was also recorded by different groups of Indians in North and South America and by people living in India and the Far East. A Hindu text, the *Shatapatha Brahmana*, describes a devastating flood in antiquity. The Myth of the Fall in Genesis 2 & 3 and our expulsion from the Garden of Eden may be a distant memory of this catastrophe. The original Garden of Eden may have been Atlantis.

Temple inscriptions and legends from Egypt and Mesopotamia as well as from Central and South America tell of god-like beings who arrived from the sea in large ships. They taught people the arts of civilization: how to grow crops and to build great temples aligned to the stars. Hieroglyphs on the walls of the temple of Edfu in Egypt, which is dedicated to the god Horus, are copies of even more ancient texts. They tell of god-like men wearing strange head-dresses who came in large ships and taught the people the basic skills of civilization. These Edfu records speak of seven sages who were called "The Sons of Horus" and who wore falcon head-dresses. They describe them as "The Builder Gods, the Sages, the Lords of the Light and The Shining Ones." They appear to have been a chain of initiates, known as "The Followers of Horus". They also speak of a sacred place, "Homeland of the Primeval Ones" in the midst of a great ocean where a terrible catastrophe took place, destroying it utterly and killing almost all its inhabitants. This, I believe, was the first cataclysm of 12,800 BCE, not the disappearance of Atlantis. The hieroglyphs say that a few survived and set sail in their ships to build a new civilization in a different place. One of those places was Egypt. Another was Göbekli Tepe in Turkey.

The Mesopotamian clay tablets also speak of seven sages or god-like beings called the Apkallu who came to Mesopotamia *before* the Flood and taught the people there for several thousand years. Oannes — part man, part fish — was one of these, said to have emerged from the sea to bring civilization to humanity. In Sumer the Apkallu returned after the Flood to help the people to rebuild civilization. Sumerian records name five great cities that existed in Sumer before the Flood and say that the people living in one of them — Sippar — buried their records before the Flood and returned to recover them after it. These sages were masters of astronomy, architecture, metallurgy, stone-cutting and carpentry.

In Egypt, Isis and Osiris may have originally been two of these sages who brought with them knowledge of how to rebuild civilization. This god-like group of people seems to have built or re-built the foundations of civilization in Egypt, Mesopotamia and Turkey (Göbekli Tepe) as well as South and Central America. Graham Hancock writes: "Thanks to the advice and teaching of these extraordinary sages, human civilization received rapid scientific and technological advances and 'entered a period of exceptional splendour and plenty', the golden age before the Flood." [10]

Göbekli Tepe

Göbekli Tepe is situated in eastern Turkey, near the Syrian border, between the Tigris and Euphrates rivers. It was discovered in 1963. Excavation by Klaus Schmidt, a German archaeologist, began in 1995. Radio carbon dating has revealed that the site was inhabited from around 9,500 BCE. Because of its very early date, 11,500 years ago, it is a momentous discovery that has, like the revised dating of the Sphinx, thoroughly upset the archaeological records. It is thought to be one of the most extraordinary and extensive archaeological sites ever uncovered — the size of 13 football fields. It is the oldest temple complex in the world, constructed not long after the first great cataclysm of 12,800 BCE and the beginning of the Younger Dryas period. It has 50-60 circles, with only 4 so far excavated. Inside the excavated circles are T-shaped monolithic pillars, 16 feet high, weighing between 10 and 60 tons, some of which are engraved with signs of the zodiac and animals and, on one of the pillars, a headless man and other images suggesting evidence of a comet strike and massive loss of life (confirmed by the Edinburgh Research Group) as well as, according to Hancock, a warning of the comet's future return. It seems to have been a temple or complex of temples built specifically for the surveillance of the stars and for tracking the star Sirius in particular. The actual carving out of the rock of the many slender stone T-shaped pillars was an extraordinary feat, without considering the quality of the relief carvings on the pillars.

Whoever supervised the building of these strange temples also initiated agriculture in this region which must have had a population of many thousands. Those who directed the building of these temple sites had a very high competence in astronomy as well as architectural and sculpting skills and knowledge of how to grow crops. When Robert Schoch examined one of the main pillars, he realized that the T-shaped pillar could represent Orion, the headless hunter of the skies, complete with his belt, loincloth and even his dog — associated with Sirius which was later named the Dog-Star. All the pillars look South and East, the direction of Orion, Sirius, and the Pleiades in the constellation of Taurus. For reasons unknown, the whole huge complex was buried around 8,000 BCE, some 1700 years after the second cataclysm and remained hidden until the 1963 discovery. Why they were filled in is still an unsolved mystery.

Pillar 43 shows animal reliefs representing zodiacal signs and three strange handbag-shaped objects at the top. These 'handbags' are identical to those that are shown in the Babylonian and Assyrian reliefs but these are many thousands of years *later* than Göbekli Tepe. What was the thread of transmission that connected these very different cultures over this huge expanse of time and distance?

The Evidence of Advanced Civilizations

These recent discoveries have challenged the timeline usually presented by archaeologists, anthropologists, and historians since they indicate that 'civilization', including astronomy, architecture and mathematics, and the advanced technology of building enormous stone temple complexes began much earlier than has been thought. In Peru and Colombia, the shamanic traditions being explored by Westerners today, including those of the Kogi Indians of Colombia, may have originated in the pre-Flood era, as did the shamanic traditions of the great seers of India.

I think it is clear from all that I have described that there were highly developed civilizations with advanced technologies and building skills existing before the two great cataclysms which destroyed them: one at the beginning and the other at the end of the freezing thousand-year Younger Dryas Period. People living in these civilizations were not primitive or existing in survival mode but had built great cities with extraordinary temples oriented on specific stars and constellations. They had also developed agricultural practices which fed large populations. They were highly gifted astronomers, sculptors and architects. Particularly in the case of Mu or Lemuria, they had established thriving colonies to the East in South and Central America and to the West in Indonesia which, before the rising sea levels caused by both cataclysms, was part of a much larger land-mass. Both Lemuria and Atlantis had large ocean-going ships and obviously would have traded extensively with other areas. Their stone carving and stone lifting technology was, in the case of the great builders of pyramids and temples in Egypt and South America, more developed than anything we have today, so we can only conjecture what it was and how they used it to create these magnificent buildings. No-one can say how old Sacsayhuaman or the gigantic stone complex of Cuzco are.

It is still a mystery how these stones were transported to their present sites or how they were fitted together so closely that there is hardly the space for a razor blade to fit between them. The majority weigh over 20 tons; some weigh 100 tons and others 200 or 300 tons. They were not built by the Inca but by some civilization long preceding it, thought to be as old as 30,000 years but in any case, pre-dating both cataclysms. Did the original people who built the incredible stone structures in Cuzco and Sacsayhuaman in Peru, and Tiahuanaco in Bolivia come originally from the lost continent of Mu or Lemuria in the Pacific Ocean?

These cataclysmic events inflicted devastating traumas on the human psyche. These will have been held in what Jung called the collective unconscious of our species, in our species memory. For long ages people would have been focused only on survival yet there have also been periods of extra-ordinary creativity leading to the most advanced and enlightened civilizations such as that of Egypt. The part astronomy played in the building of temples and pyramids everywhere is phenomenal and largely overlooked by archaeologists.

It is salutary to remember that no-one knew of the existence of Göbekli Tepe until its chance discovery in 1963. There may be other such discoveries in the future. At present, there is no way that archaeologists and historians can prove to their satisfaction the existence of these anti-diluvian ancient civiliza-tions. For this reason, they find it difficult to accept the evidence of explorers like Graham Hancock and others, such as cosmologist Nassim Haramein and geologist Greg Bradon, who have presented newly discovered evidence of earlier inhabitants on this planet in an online Course given by them in 2024 for Humanity's Team.

I am drawing on channeled material in certain chapters of this book, including this chapter, because I think it offers fascinating details about these lost civilizations and the people who lived in them. I am familiar with this kind of material through the channeled Messages received by my mother and a friend of hers for some twenty years from 1943-65.[11] In the last part of this Chapter, I am drawing on material from a book called *Atlantis and the New Consciousness*, by Stuart Wilson and Joanna Prentis, which offers fascinating insights into what life was like on Atlantis and the reasons why its formidable civilization may have declined and vanished. We know so little about our ancient past, so little about civilizations that have vanished in these great cataclysms. For this reason I have included here some channeled mat-erial, received by Stuart Wilson and Joanna Prentis through an angelic being called Alariel. He said that many Atlanteans who lived in the Golden Age of Atlantis, had reincarnated as Essenes in the time of Jesus and that these, in turn, have reincarnated now, in this time of immense change, transformation and the raising of human consciousness. Here are some statements given by Alariel:

> The Golden Age of Atlantis, (approximately 14,000-12,000 BCE), the most advanced civilization that the Earth has ever seen, was guided by wise and loving Beings of high spiritual attainment.… No other era came near it for the perfection of its civilization and the deep connection of the individual with the One, the All, which was universally respected and honoured. The harmony of the individual reflected the harmony of the whole society, and this echoed the harmony of the One in a way that gave life a special quality, a feeling of 'rightness' which pervaded the lives of everyone who lived there.[12]

> The arts were a vital part of Atlantis during the Golden Age and poetry was one important aspect of these. A renowned poet, called Kayden, wrote this statement:

Poetry should reflect
The creativity of the personality,
The light of the soul
And the fire of the Spirit.

The four pillars of poetry
are Beauty and Truth
Love and Light.
When poetry reflects these ideals,
It adds to the happiness of the world. [13]

The period of golden Atlantis could not be sustained forever. Gradually selfishness, greed, lust, and overwork crept into the life of the Atlanteans. The followers of the wise ones who maintain the knowledge that they were Children of the Light tried to warn the rest of the people, but they were laughed at and scorned. A twisted society of shallow celebrity, selfish exploitation, and violent criminality emerged, working hand in hand with a very advanced [and dangerous] technology that dehumanised people. [14]

The final phase of Atlantis was over and the golden dream of the highest and most spiritual civilisation this world has ever known was now becoming a legend, a distant folk memory in the history of the human race. [15]

When the Atlantean period was finally over, the knowledge was not lost. Well before the time of the final destruction, the great teachers of the final phase took their followers by ship to new locations across the globe. There they worked to seed the wisdom of Atlantis into new civilizations who would take the human story forward within a number of unique traditions. [16]

Wherever you go in the universe, the underlying foundation of mathematics and geometry connects the whole structure into a single holistic unity. But there is a still deeper unifying element, and that is the foundational Energy of Unconditional Love. It was Love that brought the universe into being, and Love which sustains it and provides the impetus for change within the consciousness of sentient beings. Whatever spiritual path you choose, the transformative Energy of Unconditional Love is there to support and nourish that path and carry through the process of change and transformation within the heart. Simply tuning into this Energy and invoking it within the heart, will begin this process of profound change. Alariel [17]

* * * * *

I will end this chapter with the following Message from the Mother, delivered by the Kogi Indians of Colombia. The Kogi Indians are called the "Older Brothers" because they still live in an original way of life, maintaining a deep shamanic relationship with Mother Earth. Throughout the ages the Original Peoples of Earth have carried prophecy and instruction for these times. On November 17th, 2023, the Kogi Indians delivered this urgent message from Mother Earth. It is to be shared with the world and with the Younger Brothers so that we may unite all nations in support of Mother Earth.

Message from the Mother

"I am the Mother. I am in the heart of the universe. Throughout all of time, I have never suffered from such heat or exhaustion. I have endured for the last thousand years. Since that time, my natural connection points, my rivers, reservoirs, and internal waterways have been obstructed and are full of pollution. I cannot cleanse or recuperate.

In December of 2023, I will start to rise and move, and turn and send a message to all my children around the world. The storms, the earthquakes, the hurricanes, and the rise of the ocean will come. If the governments, the sultans, the princes, presidents, and kings of the world do not listen and act, in two years' time, only 30% of the Earth will remain.

I am the Mother. I have always endured, despite arrows being put in my eyes and in my body. I am not seeking to defend myself. I remain calm. But now I must recuperate. There are two ways that I can heal. I can take the Law of Nature into my own hands. This way, I will go in search of my medicines, so that I can heal my body, heal my energies and all that I am suffering from. There will be great changes upon the Earth. You will feel me recovering. You will feel me moving. I will not do this to cause harm to you. It will mean I am recuperating my body. Or the second way: All my children will make the healing happen for me. So I will not need to do it myself. I will put my older children in charge of my recovery. They will go and search for my medicines. For my cure. So I can be healed and recuperate with their help. You, my children, must all be united and deliver what is needed for your older brothers so that they can do the healing where I have been injured by you, my younger ones. Each one of the rulers of the world, of the governments of the world, must say, 'Yes, Mother, I will stand with you. I will give my help to where you have been injured'.

I, your Mother, have given you everything. When these changes start to happen, we will see whether you listen and act. Or whether I myself will have to do what I must to recover the balance on Earth. If in just six months from now, by June 2024, you say, 'Yes, we will provide what is needed', then my oldest children will be able to help cure my body. If this message is ignored, I will take the Law of

Nature into my own hands one year and a half from that date. This is the Message that the Mother has given. She who is in the heart of the world."

Notes:

1. see Hancock, Graham (2015), *Magicians of the Gods*, Coronet, an imprint of Hodder and Stoughton Ltd., London
2. This hypothesis was supported by experts from Edinburgh University led by Dr Martin Sweatman of Edinburgh's School of Engineering (as reported in *The Telegraph*) and by the Comet Research Group, composed mainly of geologists, as well as by Graham Hancock. The Edinburgh Research was published in the journal *Mediterranean Archaeology and Archaeometry*.
3. Churchward, James (1939), *The Lost Continent of Mu,* Neville Spearman, London. (Reprinted 2020 see Amazon.co.uk)
4. Allan, D.S. & Delair, J.B., (1995) *When the Earth Nearly Died*, Gateway Books, Bath. See also:
    Benton, Michael, (2015) *When Life Nearly Died: The Greatest Mass Extinction of All Time*, Thames & Hudson,
5. www.robertschoch.com
6. Hancock, *op. cit.* p. 181
7. Lee, Desmond, (1971) translator. *Plato: Timaeus and Critias*, Penguin Books Ltd., Harmondsworth, London p. 37-38
8. ibid, *Critias*, pp. 131, 136-145 and appendix.
9. Wilson, Stuart & Prentis, Joanna, (2011) *Atlantis and the New Consciousness*, Ozark Mountain Publishing, Huntsville AR 72740
10. Hancock, *op. cit.* p. 161
11. Baring, Anne (2023) *Messages from a Transcendent Dimension*, Archive Publishing, Shaftesbury, Dorset
12. *Atlantis and the New Consciousness*, p. 87
13. ibid, p. 77
14. ibid, p. 103
15. ibid, p. 104
16. ibid, p. 107
17. ibid, p. 142

When the heart breaks
And the seasons call
Pin a rose at my heart
Sing

When illusion fails
And hopes fall
Pin a rose at my heart
Sing

When fear speaks
And silences call
Pin a rose at my heart
Sing

Death and destruction around me
A rose at my heart.

— Thalia Gage

Chapter Two

THE SEPARATION OF NATURE FROM SPIRIT

Everything is interwoven, and the web is holy; none of its parts are
unconnected. Together, they compose the world.

— Marcus Aurelius [1]

In this chapter, I would like to offer an archetypal overview of why the current crisis on this planet has come into being: showing when, where and how the masculine and feminine archetypes — reflected in the image of a God or Goddess — became separated, and why the loss of the feminine aspect of deity has had such a deep and damaging effect on Western civilization. We live in a world that has been governed by the masculine archetype for some 4,000 years, with no feminine archetype to balance it, no sacred marriage between them. As a result, world culture and the human psyche have become dangerously out of balance, out of alignment with the earth and the cosmos. Forty or so years ago I had a visionary dream of a cosmic woman. Since then, my life has been focused on the recovery and restoration of the feminine archetype — the archetype that stands for our *relationship* with nature, the earth and the cosmos. It also stands for a totally different perspective on life: a perspective which recognizes that we live on a sacred planet; that our human lives participate in a Sacred Cosmic Order and that our role as humans is to care for life on this planet. The Feminine stands for the soul, for the heart, and for compassion and justice — the two primary values which protect and serve life. It is summed up in this statement by a Council of the Indigenous People of North America: "All Life is sacred. We come into Life as sacred beings. When we abuse the sacredness of Life we affect all Creation." When did we lose the awareness that all life is sacred? Why did we lose the feminine archetype that connected us to Nature?

We are at present imprisoned in an outworn image of God and in a secular, materialist view of reality which has cut us off from the earth, the cosmos, and our own soul. For increasing numbers, religion has become meaningless. God has been pronounced dead — an outgrown superstition. But while the image of the sacred may die, the Sacred cannot die. After an interval marked by cultural and social decadence, political chaos and the general corruption of our times, a new image or concept of the Sacred may appear, unheralded, from the depths of the human soul.

The supreme spiritual task of a civilization has been symbolized in myth by the quest for a priceless treasure. A civilization is inspired and sustained for a certain length of time by its great myths, but eventually the original impetus created by them fades. The treasure is no longer understood to be the creation of a living relationship with a transcendent Source but is projected onto lesser aims, such as the acquisition of power, wealth, and fame. A great sustaining myth emerges from the inner dimension of the soul through the life and example of an extraordinary individual; it then becomes crystallized into religion, dogma, belief. The living relationship with the soul may be lost through adherence to a collective belief system. Eventually, a state of psychic atrophy sets in where we are out of touch with the soul, where there is no renewal or regeneration but a death or paralysis of the creative imagination. Yet beneath the surface of deeply distressing events in the world to which there seems to be no end in sight and no solution, the seeds of regeneration are germinating.

From the first stirrings of conscious awareness, we have sought relationship with the cosmos. Gazing in wonder at the stars, naming the constellations, minutely charting the rising and setting of the moon and the sun, imagining a divine intelligence that has created the beauty and marvel of the earth, and longing to communicate with that intelligence, we have created many images of the Sacred to draw us closer to the mystery. This longing for relationship reached a new expression in 1969 when the view of our beautiful blue planet from the moon gave us a stunning perspective of our home in the vastness of the universe. A profound experience of transformation was initiated, an alchemical process of death and rebirth. We are called to respond to a new consciousness arising deep within the soul of humanity, a consciousness that could become the true 'saviour' of our species. We cannot go on acting as if we are alone in the universe and the masters of this planet. We cannot go on fighting and killing each other. We have profoundly to change our attitude to life, to relinquish the false myth of growth, progress, and consumption we have been living by, and cease our on-going assault on the life and resources of the planet.

This is a time of great peril, but also of unparalleled opportunity. Never before in our species memory has there been this collective opportunity to change course before it is too late. We need to understand why we have lost touch with nature and why we have learned so little from our spiritual traditions that we are prepared to destroy God's creation with our wars and weapons of mass destruction. The process of transformation requires a new image of the Sacred and a new understanding of what we mean by the word 'God'. We are moving into a New Era, which is also a new astrological Age, the Age of Aquarius. Men and women have a vital role to play in helping human consciousness to rise to a higher level.

I would like to share these words with you, written some years ago by an Austrian woman called Susanne Schaup, in a book about the Divine Feminine called *Sophia: Aspects of the Divine Feminine, Past and Present*. In it she laments the loss of Sophia, or Divine Wisdom, the feminine aspect of deity.

> That which gives a culture legitimacy is ultimately its underlying concept of God. If this concept does not change, nothing can change.... No scientific, ecological, or social paradigm shift can take effect, if the theological paradigm does not change with it. The image of God in Western religion, including Judaism and Islam, is a masculine one, despite all protests to the contrary, and as such, is a direct cause of the devaluation of the Feminine and feminine priorities in our culture. Patriarchy is still the prevailing world order. If this system is to change, we need a new perception of God.... Many women as well as an increasing number of men, no longer accept the traditional image of God because it lacks the Feminine. [2]

I remember reading a remarkable book by Richard Tarnas called *The Passion of the Western Mind*, published in 1991, which explains the origins of patriarchy and why it had to separate itself from nature. In the extraordinary and perceptive Epilogue, he writes,

> The evolution of the Western mind has been driven by a heroic impulse to forge an autonomous rational human self by separating it from the primordial unity with nature.... But to do this, the masculine mind has been founded on the repression of the feminine — the repression of undifferentiated unitary consciousness, the *participation mystique* with nature: a progressive denial of the *anima mundi*, of the soul of the world... of imagination, emotion, instinct, body, nature, woman — of all that which the masculine has identified as 'other.' [3]

He goes on to say that "The deepest passion of the Western mind has been to differentiate itself from and then rediscover and reunite with the feminine, with the mystery of life, of nature, of soul." But to achieve this reunion, "to reintegrate the repressed feminine, the masculine must undergo a sacrifice, an ego death. The Western mind must be willing to open itself to a reality the nature of which could shatter its most established beliefs about itself and about the world." [4]

The transformation of a deeply entrenched patriarchal culture and the need to bring into being a more balanced and enlightened world culture, invites us to move beyond the outworn image of the Sacred. This image of the Sacred is dying so that a new image of the Sacred and a New Story can emerge into human consciousness. Alchemy gives us a graphic image of killing the Old King, the deeply entrenched ruling belief system. The Old King personifies an outworn image of Spirit and an outworn paradigm of reality — one that is split off from nature and from soul. We are living now in the time of the death of God, marked by social unrest, conflict, fear and despair.

In the Preface I quoted these words of a Jungian Analyst, Edward Edinger:

> The breakdown of a central myth is like the shattering of a vessel containing a precious essence. Meaning is lost. In its place, primitive and atavistic contents are reactivated. Differentiated values disappear and are replaced by the elemental motivations of power and pleasure, or else the individual is exposed to emptiness and despair. [5]

Three Phases in the Evolution of Consciousness

For many thousands of years, since the second great cataclysm described in Chapter One, we have been on a hero's journey, a slow and arduous journey of recovery and discovery, without knowing who we are, where we have come from, why we are here on this planet or where we go when we die. The theme of the hero's journey underlies all mythologies which suggest that we have become separated from our home in the divine world and are therefore, exiled, fallen, lost or asleep. They tell us that we need to embark on a quest to recover our connection with that world, thereby bringing about our awakening, transformation and return to the Source.

The philosopher Owen Barfield in his remarkable book, *Saving the Appearances: A Study in Idolatry,* defined three phases in the evolution of human consciousness: the first Phase of Original Participation, the second Phase of Separation from Nature and the third Phase of Final Participation.[6] I think we are currently living near the end of Phase Two, poised at the threshold of the Third Phase of conscious reunion with the divine ground.

We now know that over a time-span of many millennia, the image of the Sacred changed from the primordial Great Mother of the Palaeolithic and Neolithic eras to the many goddesses and gods of the Bronze and Iron Ages and finally, in the three patriarchal religions, to the image of a monotheistic Father God, although, in India, the older polytheistic pantheon has survived to our time. Throughout these millennia, whatever the religion or the culture, the sacred image gave us a vertical axis, keeping us in touch with a Divine Source or Ground of Being instinctively felt to exist. It held society together in a shared belief system, a shared image of the Sacred.

The Palaeolithic Era

In the First Phase, lasting at least 30,000 years, the Cosmos was imagined as a Mother, from whose cosmic womb all forms of life emerged in a continuous cycle of birth, death and regeneration. For tens of thousands of years, the source from which life arose and to which it returned was maternal. What we now call 'cosmos' and 'nature' was a living web of relationships, ensouled by the Great Mother. The most important idea about this early time is that *there was no creator beyond creation*: no separation between the Great Mother as Source or Womb and the myriad forms of her life. The Great Mother was both the starry cosmos and all life on earth. All forms of life were her children. *Everything was infused with divinity* because each and all were part of her Sacred Cosmic Order.

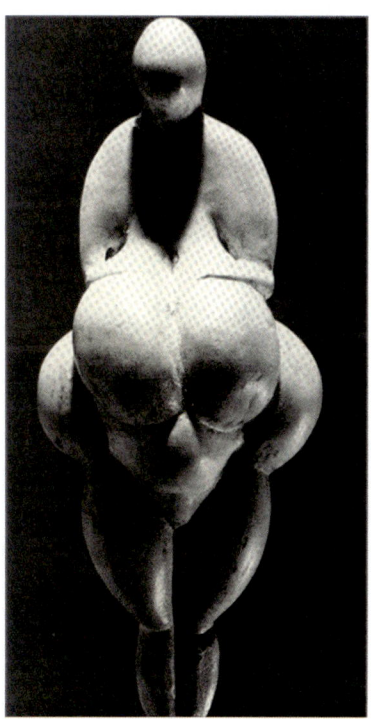

"Goddess" of Laussel	*"Goddess" of Lespugue*
c. 25,000 BCE	c. 22,000 BCE

Life was an organic, living, and sacred whole and we were part of that whole. The Milky Way was the starry passage by which souls entered and left this world. The shamanic journey into non-ordinary states of consciousness, facilitated by the ingestion of hallucinogenic plants, was the spiritual experience throughout this long era and was practiced in many different cultures. Shamans, both male and female, mediated between this hidden dimension and the human community. During this era, we had a participatory consciousness, different from the one we have now. We lived, died and were reborn within the being of the Great Mother.[7] The Great Mother ruled the three domains of Sky, Earth and Underworld: the bird was her messenger; the lion represented her power to create and destroy and was the guardian of her sanctuaries; the serpent was her power to regenerate life. These were her three principal sacred animals.

The cosmology of this era was a cyclical process of birth, death and regeneration that arose from the age-old observation of the recurring phases of the moon: its birth as the crescent, its waxing to fullness, and its waning into the three days of darkness. The moon gave us an image of eternity as well as, with its changing phases, of time. It was also related to the phases of our lives as we moved from youth to maturity, then to old age and death that was followed by rebirth. The ten months of the lunar year were associated with the gestation time of the embryo in the womb of woman. Woman as maiden, mother and crone was deeply associated with the phases of the lunar cycle and with the cyclical rhythm of the earth as it moved through the phases of the seasons. Woman was revered because, like the Great Mother, she brought new life out of herself. She was a co-creator with the Great Mother. She was the primary bearer and carer of Life.

Just as the stars emerged each night from the darkness of the night sky, so the visible universe was born from the dark mystery of the invisible. Plants, trees, animals, and birds as well as rocks and rivers, moon, sun, and stars were all infused with divinity because each and all were part of a living, breathing, connecting web of life — the life of the Great Mother. The hidden dimension of spirit was present in every aspect of the manifest world. The earth was a 'Thou', a Mother. Everything connected with her life was sacred. The Indigenous People of the world have never lost this understanding.

The Neolithic Great Mother

Moving on to the era of the Neolithic Great Mother, many images of the Great Mother during this era come from the area in Europe that the great Lithuanian archaeologist, Marija Gimbutas, discovered and called "The Civilization of the Goddess". This remarkable and forgotten civilization, possibly developing out of the widespread devastation created by the Great Flood, extended from Italy to beyond the Black Sea and included Malta, Greece, Crete, Romania, Bulgaria,

Neolithic Great Mother
Danube Valley 5,500 BCE

Neolithic Great Mother
Western Romania 5,000 BCE

Moldova, and Ukraine. It was peaceful, egalitarian, and intensely creative, producing magnificent pottery and exquisite gold artefacts, many of which were exhibited a few years ago in an exhibition called *The Lost World of Old Europe: The Danube Valley 5000-3500 BC* in New York and at the Ashmolean Museum in Oxford.

Men and women lived in harmony and mutual support to sustain the many small communities that spread along the banks of the great rivers of Europe. During the era of Neolithic Old Europe, there was no evidence of fighting or war. In *The Civilization of the Goddess*, Marija Gimbutas writes:

> It is a gross misunderstanding to imagine warfare as endemic to the human condition. There are no depictions of arms (weapons used against other humans) in Palaeolithic cave paintings, nor are there remains of weapons used by man against man during the Neolithic of Old Europe. [8]

This remarkable, virtually unknown, and peaceful civilization existed for three thousand years, from 6,500 until 3,500 BCE, when it was infiltrated and ultimately destroyed by Kurgan (Indo-European) tribes descending in waves from the area of The Russian Steppes. They brought with them the horse, lethal weapons, and the war chariot. Whereas the civilization they destroyed had most probably been matrilineal, they introduced the patriarchal order, sky gods, and the hierarchical organization of society with a warrior-leader at the top and woman at the bottom. From the establishment of this new order, women were relegated to a subservient role.

As Gimbutas writes: "Millennial traditions were truncated, towns and villages disintegrated, magnificent painted pottery vanished; as did shrines, frescoes, sculptures, symbols and script." [9]

Steve Taylor, in his brilliant book, *The Fall*, which I urge everyone to read, quotes the historian, P. Stern:

> They were introducing violence to a part of the world that previously had been relatively peaceful. And along with ruthless invasions, undeclared warfare, and appropriation of women as their rightful spoils, they were developing a society in which masculinity was supreme. An insatiable desire for property and power, together with insensitivity to pain and suffering in themselves as well as in others, characterised everything they did. [10]

Over the next two to three millennia, these tribes spread eastwards through Anatolia, the Middle East and Persia, eventually reaching India, destroying the cultures already existing in these areas and imposing their own patriarchal order. The caste system of India is the distant legacy of these warrior people.... Marija Gimbutas' Kurgan theory was ridiculed and derided for decades by archaeologists until, in a lecture given in Chicago in 2018 by Lord Colin Renfrew, she was finally vindicated by newly discovered DNA evidence which offered proof of her theory.

The Great Goddesses of the Bronze Age

Moving forward, we can follow the image of the Neolithic Great Mother as she becomes the Great Goddesses of the Bronze Age: Goddesses such as Isis in Egypt, Inanna in Sumer, and Artemis of Ephesus (opposite), all of whom were worshipped as the Queen of Heaven and associated with the moon. For many thousands of years, the Great Mother and these Great Goddesses personified *the principle of relationship*: the interconnectedness of every aspect of life and, above all, the sacredness of the great Web of Life that connected nature and cosmos. In Egypt and Sumer and later in Greece and Rome, women served as priestesses in the temples of the Goddess. The essential relationship between heaven and earth was celebrated annually in the ceremony of the sacred marriage between goddess and god in the temples of Egypt and Sumer. The Mysteries of Eleusis in Greece were the summit of the shamanic insights given to initiates or Mystes who were able to experience the vision of the divine ground that underlay all the phenomena of nature. No-one has explained these Mysteries more comprehensively than John Lash in his book,

Artemis of Ephesus

Not in His Image: Gnostic Vision, Sacred Ecology and The Future of Belief. [11]

The primary question of the Lunar Era was: How should the human community act to be in harmony with the life of the cosmos? Plato (429-347 BCE), in his *Timaeus*, was the first to give a name to an all-embracing cosmic entity which he described as a "single Living Creature that encompasses all the living creatures that are within it." He called it the Soul of the Cosmos. The priceless legacy of this whole era was the shamanic *experience* that the cosmos has an inner life — a Soul — and that humans could communicate with it and derive their laws from listening to its guidance. As Dr Peter Kingsley has shown in his books, the Pre-Socratic philosophers Pythagoras and Parmenides were masters of the practice of shamanic incubation which gave them access to the inner dimension of the cosmos and to the wisdom imparted to them from that source.[12]

We carry within our soul a very ancient kind of consciousness or experience of life that I call lunar consciousness and associate with the timeless wisdom of the soul. It is an instinctive, feminine, participatory, relational way of knowing, mediated through the heart, enhanced sensory observation and intuition, which opens the shamanic path between two dimensions of reality. We need to reconnect with this lost consciousness and learn to listen again to the voice of what Jung called "The Spirit of the Depths."

The Solar Era — The Separation from Nature

Then, around 2,000 BCE in the Middle East, there was a change so great that its repercussions are still felt today because it has been the distant but major influence on the development of Western civilization. This change was the replacement of the Great Mother by the Great Father, preceded by a period when there were both goddesses and gods. As the monotheistic Father God brought the world into being as something separate and distant from himself, so nature became split off from spirit and was no longer sacred. Simultaneously, the rise of powerful city states in the Middle East led to the creation of a succession of vast empires, territorial conquest, and war. The theme of conquest and the pursuit of power laid down millennia ago continues to this day with the leaders of the three current great empires — China, Russia, and America.

Although the architectural, artistic, and literary creations of these empires were extraordinary, the suffering endured was unimaginable. Millions of young men lost their lives and died of their wounds in atrocious pain. Millions of women and children were raped and sold into slavery in the same way as, in 2015, the tragic Yazidi women were raped and sold into slavery by Islamic

State. Deep traumas were created in the collective psyche of humanity that are unhealed to this day. During these thousands of years of war, we forgot about nature and our relationship with her. Gradually, we developed the idea that we were above nature, entitled to control and dominate her for the benefit of our species alone. To summarize: the change in the image of deity was a primary factor in separating nature from spirit. It led to a polarizing dualism that henceforth shaped our concept of reality.

During the Solar Era, which has lasted some four thousand years from ca., 2,000 BCE to the present day, we find a cosmology that is radically different from that of the earlier Lunar Era. It is a Cosmology of Separation, characterized by dissociation, duality, fragmentation, and polarization, which arose from the growing conflict between cities and nation-states. Between the Lunar and the Solar Eras there was a time when goddesses and gods peopled the heavens and, as in the *Iliad* and the *Odyssey*, interacted with humans. Ultimately however, in the three patriarchal religions, the Great Father replaced the Great Mother as the monotheistic image of deity. Western civilization developed on the foundation of a fundamental dissociation between spirit and nature, creator and creation.

Because of this, we lost the participatory consciousness that we had in the earlier era and the sense that we lived within a Sacred Order — an insight that has only survived to our time in the Indigenous cultures of the world. The focus of this whole era is on the establishment of the patriarchal order led by male warrior-leaders, together with male priesthoods that exist to this day. But it is also about a violent and traumatic separation from the deeper matrix of the soul or psyche, and a severance of our relationship with nature, cosmos, and earth.

This separation traumatized all of us because it destroyed the sacredness of nature and the ancient shamanic recognition of the presence of spirit within the natural world, opening the way to its exploitation. It also failed to carry forward the sacred marriage between the feminine and masculine archetypes, represented by a goddess and a god, that was celebrated in the ancient civilizations of Egypt and Sumer. Above all, it led to the loss of the Mysteries, the most sacred experience of the earlier era, and the destruction of the magnificent temples in which these were celebrated. It also led to the persecution of the Gnostics and the loss of their Gospels until their astounding discovery in Egypt in 1945. [13]

How did this radical change in cosmology come about? The Iron Age (beginning ca., 1250 BCE), saw the completion of the long process begun in the earlier Bronze Age when numinosity began to be transferred from the Mother Goddess to the Father God. The *Enuma Elish* or Babylonian Myth of Creation is the first story of the replacing of a mother goddess who generates creation as part of herself, by a god who 'makes' creation as something separate from himself. In this myth, the god Marduk kills the dragoness mother Tiamat and splits her body into heaven and earth. He then creates humanity from the blood of her murdered son. [14] All the myths of the Iron Age in which a sky or sun god or hero conquers a great serpent or dragon can be traced to this Babylonian Epic, in which humanity was created from the blood of a sacrificed god and no longer from the womb of a primordial goddess. Its huge influence can be followed through Hittite, Assyrian, Persian, Canaanite, Hebrew, Greek and Roman mythology. It was a mythology of violence, cruelty, and conquest which was reflected in the behaviour of the rulers of these civilizations. This is what Jules Cashford and I wrote in the *The Myth of the Goddess*:

> We know that in the earlier goddess culture the concept of the relation between creator and creation was expressed in the image of the Mother as "*zoe*", the eternal source, giving birth to the son as "*bios*", the created life in time which lives and dies back into the source. The son was the part that emerged from the whole, through which the whole might come to know itself. As the god 'grew up' in the course during the Bronze Age, he came to be the consort of the goddess and sometimes co-creator with her. But in the Iron Age, the image of the relationship enacted in the ceremony of the sacred marriage disappeared, and the emerging balance and relationship between the female and male divine archetypes or energies is lost.
>
> Now a father god established a position of supremacy in relation to a mother goddess, and was gradually transformed into the monotheistic god of the three patriarchal religions known to us today: Judaism, Christianity, and Islam. The god is then the sole primal creator, whereas before the goddess had been the only source of life. The god becomes the *maker* of heaven and earth, whereas the goddess *was* heaven and earth. The concept of 'making' is radically different from 'being' in the sense that what is made is not necessarily of the same substance as its maker, and may be conceived as inferior to him; while what emerges from the mother is necessarily part of her and she of it.

The Dualism of Spirit and Nature

In this way, the essential identity between creator and creation was broken, and a fundamental dualism was born from their separation, the dualism that we know as spirit and nature. In the era of the Great Mother and the goddess these terms have no meaning in separation from each other: nature is spiritual and spirit natural, because the divine is *immanent* as creation. In the new myth of the god, nature is no longer 'spiritual' and spirit is no longer 'natural' because the divine is *transcendent* to creation. Spirit is not inherent in nature, but outside it or beyond it; it even becomes the source of nature. So a new meaning enters the language: spirit becomes creative and nature becomes created. In this new kind of myth, creation is the result of a divine act that brings order out of chaos. [15]

It is impossible to describe the long-term effects of this radical change in cosmology, effects which have led ultimately to the beliefs of scientific materialism and its claim that we humans are the only conscious beings in an inanimate universe that came into being by chance with the 'Big Bang'.

Severing the Umbilical Cord joining Nature with Spirit

As our conscious mind slowly evolved out of the matrix of the primordial collective soul, the sacred image and the mythologies which grew up around it were like an umbilical cord holding us in touch with the foundation of life. But, as we moved into the era of the monotheistic God of the patriarchal religions, that umbilical cord was severed. Nature was separated from spirit. The older shamanic relationship with the earth and a living cosmos was gradually lost and with it the idea that the whole of nature was sacred, infused with divinity, ensouled. The elimination of the image of the Great Mother or Great Goddess was the principal reason for the loss of the belief that nature was ensouled with spirit and therefore sacred. It was the eradication of spirit from the natural world that ultimately removed from the people living through the millennia of the patriarchal religions their age-old sense of participation in a Sacred Order.

We can see these different myths as stories told by humanity at different stages of our evolution, which explore different ways of being in the universe. But the Judaeo-Christian tradition which has inherited only the myth of the god, presents the duality of spirit and nature as 'given'— inherent in the way things are. Yet we know that this dualism did not always exist. Its origin at a specific time in human history has been lost to consciousness because, in the patriarchal cultures in which the father god was worshipped as unique creator, no memory of the earlier image of the mother goddess as creator survived in recognizable form. This situation began to change with the work of Johann Bachofen (1815-1887) and his ground-breaking book *Myth, Religion and Mother Right*. He was the first person to establish Matriarchy as an historical fact. Then came Erich Neumann's magisterial study, *The Great Mother: An Analysis of the Archetype*, published by Bollingen in 1955. In 1976, Merlin Stone published *When God was a Woman*, originally titled *The Paradise Papers*. Hers was the first of many books on the Goddess that were written by women, including *The Myth of the Goddess*, and a beautiful book by Buffie Johnson called *Lady of the Beasts: The Goddess and Her Sacred Animals*. There was also Riane Eisler's powerful and incisive book, *The Chalice and the Blade*.

Territorial Conquest

In the late Bronze Age (named after the creation of bronze weapons) and the Iron Age that followed it, the rapid growth of the population facilitated the drive for territorial conquest led by warrior-kings who presided over immense empires — all built on the enslavement of conquered peoples. First came the Akkadian empire of Sargon of Akkad, followed by the Assyrian, Babylonian, Persian, Greek and Roman Empires. With the rise of city-states, then empires, came the idea of power over vast numbers of people and how a certain territory belonged to a specific group. All of this emerged from the original infiltration of Kurgan or Indo-European people descending from the Russian Steppes. Conquering more territory involved killing, controlling, or enslaving others. As nature was increasingly split off from spirit, this new male quest for territory, power and renown destroyed the older relationship with a harmonious cosmic order. The slaughter and suffering of thousands meant nothing to the leader or 'solar hero' intent on conquest and the acquisition of power, territory, fame, and glory. Homer's *Iliad* was the template that ruled the whole of the Iron Age. The vast empire created by Alexander the Great offered a model to emulate. In three thousand years, we have not morally grown beyond the warrior ethos of the *Iliad*, as current wars with their unspeakable barbarism demonstrate. It was in the Solar Era that we became addicted to war and conquest, an addiction that could lead ultimately to our extinction.

Two immensely powerful and polarizing cosmologies became the major influence on the social, political, and religious history of Western civilization. The first of these was the battle between light and darkness, good and evil, symbolized by the hero's fight with the dragon, that had its origin in the Babylonian Myth of Creation and, beyond that, in the writings of the Persian sage, Zoroaster. This cosmology, projected into the world, would lead to endless struggles for power and dominance. Ultimately, it would lead to the battle to conquer and subjugate nature in the service of man. Nature and the earth were no longer sacred. Man became identified with spirit; woman was identified with nature. As nature was believed to be separate from and inferior to spirit, woman came to be regarded as inferior to man, no longer the sacred carrier of life. Four thousand years ago, man began to assume a position of dominance over both nature and woman. Over these millennia, woman's voice was silenced and her sacred role as priestess, prophetess, healer, sybil and shaman was deleted. Her sole value consisted in her being the carrier of man's seed, his servant, and his sexual slave. This archaic belief still prevails among the Taliban in Afghanistan who have brutally forced women back into the home and barred them from access to education, contraception, and participation in the culture. (2022).

The key theme of the Solar Era is ascent to the light and repudiation of the darkness associated with nature. The development of the conscious mind in humanity, together with its stupendous cultural and scientific achievements can be recognized as the evolutionary achievement of this Era and above all, the achievement of men. But this achievement was built on the widening chasm between spirit and nature. This whole process was closely tied in to the invention of writing and the power that literacy gave to an elite group of very powerful rulers and priesthoods who deliberately destroyed the shamanic practices and animistic rituals of the older Lunar Order. [16]

As the image of deity changed from Great Mother to Great Father and the Divine Feminine was excluded from the image of deity, our relationship with nature was severed. This led to the gradual de-souling of the world and the crisis we face now.

Notes:

1. Marcus Aurelius, *Meditations*, Chapter 7, Verse 9. Translated by Gregory Hays
2. Schaup, Susanne, (1997), *Sophia: Aspects of the Divine Feminine*, Nicolas-Hays, Inc., York Beach, Maine, p. xi
3. Tarnas, Richard, (1991), *The Passion of the Western Mind*, Ballantine Books (Random House) p. 442
4. Ibid, p. 444
5. Edinger, Edward, (1984) *The Creation of Consciousness: Jung's Myth for Modern Man*, Inner City Books, Toronto, Canada
6. Barfield, Owen, (1988) *Saving the Appearances: A Study in Idolatry,* Wesleyan University Press, Connecticut
7. Baring, Anne & Cashford, Jules (1992) *The Myth of the Goddess: Evolution of an Image*, Penguin, London; and Baring, Anne (2013 & 2020), *The Dream of the Cosmos: A Quest for the Soul,* Archive Publishing, Shaftesbury, Dorset
8. Gimbutas, Marija, (1991) *The Civilization of the Goddess: The World of Old Europe*, HarperSanFrancisco, p. 352
9. Gimbutas, Marija (1977) Journal of Indo-European Studies 5, p. 291
10. Stern, P, (1969), *Prehistoric Europe from Sone Age Man to the Early Greeks*. Norton, p. 230, quoted in *The Fall* by Steve Taylor
11. Lash, John Lamb, (2006 & 2021) *Not in His Image*, Chelsea Green Publishing, Vermont USA & London UK
12. Kingsley, Peter, (1999) *In the Dark Places of Wisdom*, London: Element Books; (2010) *A Story Waiting to Pierce You: Mongolia, Tibet and the Destiny of the Western World,* The Golden Sufi Center, California

13. Lash, John Lamb, op. cit. and G.R.S. Mead (1931, *Fragments of a Faith Forgotten*, John M. Watkins, London

14. *The Myth of the Goddess,* Chapter 7, *Tiamat of Babylon: The Defeat of the Goddess*

15. ibid, p. 274

16. Shlain, Leonard, (1998) *The Alphabet versus the Goddess: The Conflict Between Word and Image,* Viking, New York.

Seed

From star to star, from sun and spring and leaf,
And almost audible flowers whose sound is silence,
And in the common meadows, springs the seed of life.

Now the lilies open, and the rose
Released by summer from the harmless graves
That, centuries deep, are in the air we breathe,
And in our earth, and in our daily bread.

External and innate dimensions hold
The living forms, but not the force of life;
For that interior and holy tree
That in the heart of hearts outlives the world
Spreads earthly shade into eternity.

— Kathleen Raine

Chapter Three

THE FINAL LOSS OF THE DIVINE FEMININE

There was a specific time when there is a clear record of the final loss of the Divine Feminine, a loss that originated in the Hebrew religion. This was the second major factor that contributed to the loss of the sacredness of nature, the first being the change in archetypal imagery from the Great Mother to the Great Father. This long-forgotten event has had a devastating influence on patriarchal culture, the status and treatment of women, and our relationship with the planet.

Surrealist Landscape 1945
Painting by Cecil Collins (1908-1989)

To understand what caused this loss and why it was so significant we need go back to the First Temple in Jerusalem that was founded by Solomon around 950 BCE and to the remarkable books of the Old Testament scholar, Dr Margaret

Barker, and particularly her latest book, *The Great Lady*.[1] In these, she describes the enormous change in Hebrew cosmology that took place in 623 BCE during the reign of king Josiah, when a group of priests called Deuteronomists took control of the First Temple in Jerusalem. Prior to this event, the Jewish people had worshipped both a Goddess and a God, a Queen and King of Heaven, who *together* had created the world. The Queen of Heaven, whose name was Asherah or Ashratah, was worshipped as the Holy Spirit, Divine Wisdom and the Tree of Life — a cosmic Tree that connected the invisible and visible worlds — whose fruit was the gift of immortality. Dr Barker writes:

> In the most ancient tradition of Israel, Yahweh was both female and male, and it was they who co-created the world. The feminine side of Yahweh was called Wisdom, the consort of Yahweh, the Queen of Heaven, the bright and radiant one whose teaching was like the light of the dawn. But Wisdom was abandoned by her husband. [2]

In *Temple Theology*, she comments that the most important result of Josiah's purge was the introduction of monotheism, which was the creation of the Deuteronomists.[3] In another book, *The Hidden Tradition of the Kingdom of God*, she says "The tradition of the Temple was rich and complex, but it is essential to keep in mind the massive destruction and cultural revolution at the end of the seventh century BCE, and to recognize that no complete reconstruction is possible." [4]

In 623 BCE the Deuteronomists, on the instruction of King Josiah, took control of the Temple. They removed every trace of the Goddess Asherah, the Queen of Heaven. They removed her statue from the Temple and that of the great bronze serpent that symbolized her power to regenerate life. They cut down her sacred groves of trees and smashed all images of her, including small clay statues of her. They banished the ancient shamanic rituals presided over by the high-priest, who had climbed the steps in the great tower at the back of the temple to commune with the Queen of Heaven, in the same way perhaps, that in Pre-Socratic Greece Parmenides had communed with the Goddess Persephone. They replaced these with new rituals based on strict obedience to the Law of Moses. The making of images was henceforth forbidden. These reforming priests destroyed the temple rooms where the women wove hangings for the statue of Asherah. They banished the hosts of heaven — the angels and archangels — and removed the methods of communication with them by destroying the instruments on the roof of the Temple that had helped the former astronomer-priests to follow the movements of the stars.

Dr Barker describes in her latest book, *The Great Lady* how, in certain Books of the Old Testament, the Deuteronomists or Reformers went to great lengths to alter specific letters in the words that described Wisdom and the former Queen of Heaven, so that they were no longer recognizable and nearly vanished altogether. Dr Barker describes these miniscule but significant changes:

> For about five centuries before the time of Jesus the official scribes who copied the holy scrolls had been 'correcting' the texts as they copied them. They removed all references to things they considered blasphemous or unfit to be in the holy writings. They were not simply copiers. They were editors. One of their targets was the Great Lady. There are many examples of her names and titles being changed so as to conceal her.... They also removed references to her role and her devotees by manipulating letters or changing how they were pronounced. [5]

In an earlier book, she writes:

> The story of her violent expulsion can be read in the Old Testament, but it is rarely if ever recognised for what it is.... The Lady has been hidden: removed from the Bible by the ancient translators and the ancient editors and then overlooked by the scholars. There are dozens of examples like this, not only in English translations of the Bible, but over many centuries. This is the story I shall tell: how the Great Lady became the Lost Lady. [6]

In *Temple Theology*, Dr Barker says that as a result of the events described above:

> The assumption that Deuteronomy was the 'norm' has led to a number of distortions in our perception and presentation of the Old Testament, which has two distinct 'theologies'. There is the older Temple theology concerned with Wisdom, and with the structure and harmony of creation, and there is the new Deuteronomic theology which is focussed on the figure of Moses and the history of Israel as the chosen people. The second theology prevailed over the Wisdom theology which was relegated to the periphery. *It is the Deuteronomic theology which has come to dominate the popular view of Old Testament theology.* [7]

All this amounted to the shutting down of ancient Hebrew cosmology and, I believe, to the fading of the sense of living within a sacred order. It could be compared to the devastating impact Christianity had on Pagan culture in the fourth century (see below) or, centuries later, to the impact of the sixteenth century Reformation on the cultural life of Europe. It would seem that epochs of left-hemispheric consciousness and the desire of people in positions of authority to control the population and destroy their rivals, can curtail and inhibit the flourishing of the soul, the right hemisphere of the brain and the creative imagination.

After the eradication of the Queen of Heaven, Divine Wisdom and the Holy Spirit, Yahweh was left as the sole Creator God: The former Divine Feminine aspect of God was deleted from the image of deity. The only place where the Divine Feminine and the sacred marriage survived, together with the wonderful comprehensive cosmology of the First Temple tradition, was in the mystical Jewish tradition of Kabbalah, known as *The Voice of the Dove* and *The Jewels of the Heavenly Bride*, which the next chapter will explore. The Essene communities in Palestine as well as the Jewish community in the Egyptian city of Alexandria miraculously preserved and safeguarded this precious First Temple Wisdom tradition that eventually found its way to Spain and Europe in the late Middle Ages and is still vibrantly alive today.

The Creation of The Myth of the Fall

The Deuteronomists, also known as The Reformers, did not stop there. They created the Myth of the Fall in Genesis 2 & 3, with its punishing God and its grim message of sin, guilt, suffering and the banishing of Adam and Eve from the Garden of Eden. In this myth the image of Deity is the Great Father. Divine Immanence is lost. The emphasis is on the transcendence of God or Spirit. Earth becomes a place of exile and punishment for primordial sin. Adam is given dominion over the earth but he is no longer part of the Divine Order. He is exiled to a world contaminated by the Fall and subject to sin, suffering and death, introduced into the world by Eve.

These Deuteronomist priests neatly down-graded the Goddess into the human figure of Eve, making Adam bestow on her the former title of the Goddess — "Mother of All Living" and placing two Trees in the Garden of Eden instead of the single one whose fruit had offered the gift of immortality from the Goddess. They blamed Eve for the sin of disobedience that brought about the Fall and for bringing sin, suffering and death into the world. Henceforth, all women would be contaminated by Eve's sin and would have to be under men's control lest they create further disasters.

Speaking as a therapist, I cannot begin to tell you the catastrophic effects of this Deuteronomist myth on Christian civilization. When Christianity adopted the Old Testament from Judaism, the Christian Fathers developed the idea that the whole human race was tainted by original sin, punished for a primordial act of disobedience. The created world was no longer a manifestation of the Tree of Life but was viewed as contaminated by the Fall, no longer sacred. Woman's long oppression, even persecution, stems directly from this myth, the creation of the Deuteronomists. Her voice was silenced for millennia.

In a book called *The Story of Eve*, John Phillips observes that…

This Story begins with the appearance of Yahweh in the place of the Mother of All Living. This shift of power marks a fundamental change in the relationship between humanity and God, the world and God, the world and humanity, and men and women....What it involved, ultimately, was the rejection of the Feminine as a sacred entity. [8]

Christianity adopted the monotheistic image of God and the Old Testament from Judaism, including the Myth of the Fall in Genesis 2 & 3. Genesis 1 although included in the Christian Bible, seems to have been largely ignored, perhaps because the story in Genesis 2 & 3 suited the Christian narrative. In this new Christian patriarchal cosmology, earth was designated by a vengeful, punishing God as a place of exile and punishment for primordial sin. It was no longer sacred.

The Negative Legacy of this Myth — the Persecution of Women

Since Eve was portrayed as the primary agent of the Fall, having been the first to take the apple offered by the serpent, she took the blame for our banishment from the Garden of Eden. This led to the unrelenting persecution of women, who had the heavy burden of the sin of Eve placed on them, not only by Jewish commentators but by the Christian Fathers and generations of

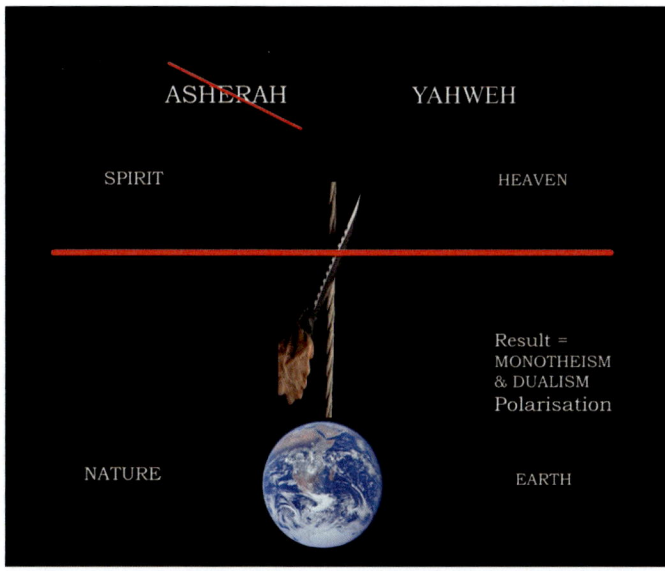

Christian priests, culminating in their being tried and condemned to death at the stake by the Inquisition for consorting with the Devil.[9] This immensely

powerful myth and its literal interpretation are at the root of the misogyny that pollutes our culture to this day, giving rise to a deep unconscious suspicion — even a fear — of women and a consequent desire to control, diminish, silence and even punish them — all of which are explicitly revealed today in pornography and the widespread incidence of rape and domestic abuse.

From the perspective of our relationship with the earth, this myth, and the final loss of the Goddess and the Divine Feminine were a catastrophe. Everything that was once associated with the Divine Feminine: nature, matter, the body, sexuality, and the whole instinctual aspect of life was excluded from the sacred. Once again, nature, split off from spirit, was effectively de-souled. We lost the awareness that spirit was active and present in the world, as the ground of everything we experience as life. We lost the sense of living within a Sacred Cosmic Order. This myth imprinted us with a negative image of our nature and our presence on this planet and placed a heavy burden of shame and guilt — particularly sexual guilt — on our shoulders. We have never recovered from the pernicious effect of this immensely influential myth which can even be detected in current conflicts where women's bodies are used as a weapon of war as described by Christina Lamb, in her recent book, *Our Bodies, Their Battlefield: What War Does to Women*.[10] The horrific attack by Hamas on Israeli citizens living near the border with Gaza on October 7th, 2023, is the latest example of rape used as a weapon of war. The complete silence for months about this crime from the UN Women's Organization was an utter disgrace.

A New Saviour Myth

The most significant development to take place in Christian theology was the creation of a startling new myth in the fourth century CE. This was established at the Council of Nicaea in 325 CE., where Jesus was officially declared to be the Son of God, whose sacrificial death had ensured the salvation and redemption of Christians. This new myth, bestowing salvation on all Christians through the sacrificial death of the Son of God, was of concern to the Gnostic community, who foresaw the problems it would give rise to. [11] The original concept of Jesus in the Jewish world of his time was that he was human. Only when Christianity moved from the Jewish to the Greek world, was the new myth of the sacrificed Son of God created.

The religion that developed in Rome from the fourth century onwards, after the incorporation of the Church of Rome into the Roman Empire, was very different from the original teaching of Jesus who, like the great teachers of the East, had taught a path of transformation leading to union with the Divine ground. What was originally a direct shamanic transmission of the path to union with the Divine Ground had become, by the fourth century, a faith that put its emphasis on belief and belonging to the Church of Rome as the path to salvation. The theme of inner transformation taught by the Gnostics was lost. (see Chapter Six: Parts One and Two)

In the man we know as Jesus, we encounter someone with the same charismatic presence as the Buddha, whose powerful and radical teaching was very similar to that of the Buddha. It has been suggested that Jesus, in the 'missing years' before the beginning of his Mission, spent time in India, possibly in one of the Buddhist Universities there. He is also thought to have spent some years in Egypt. Like the Buddha, he was perhaps an emissary from the higher regions of the cosmos: an exceptional individual, a shaman with the power to heal diseases, even to bring people back to life; a man whom tens of thousands of people followed and others, the Pharisees, hated and feared. He had only three short years in which to fulfil his Mission and in that time, he unknowingly laid the foundations of what would grow into a new religion whose effect on the world would be far-reaching and profound. This religion was not what he intended but it is what happened in the hands of those who within three centuries had created the myth of the Only Son of God, who, by his sacrificial death was the Saviour and Redeemer of Christians, thereby following the mythic pattern of earlier dying and resurrected gods who had been worshipped as saviours. Jesus never referred to himself as the Son of God or the Messiah, only as the Son of Man. Yet, in an extraordinary turn of events, by the middle of the fourth century, "the Jesus who *has* the message has become the Christ who *is* the message." [12]

The Arian Heresy and The Council of Nicaea 325 CE

Not all bishops agreed with the idea that Jesus was the Son of God and the Arian heresy became widespread around 318 CE. Named for its principal exponent, a Libyan priest called Arius, living in Alexandria, Arianism held that Jesus was neither eternal nor divine and was a creation separate and distinct from God. He could not, therefore, be the Son of God. Arius was furiously denounced by Athanasius, the powerful bishop of Alexandria and excommunicated from the Church.

The controversy grew so intense that, at the Emperor Constantine's instigation, a Council was convened at Nicaea, not far from Constantinople, in May 325 CE. This Council, in which the assembled bishops attacked each other so violently that they came to blows, voted overwhelmingly to condemn Arius and the bishops who supported him. Yet the Council managed to create another controversy, this time a linguistic one: was Jesus of the *same substance* as God or only *like unto* God? The bishops argued furiously over the difference between two Greek words: *homoousious* — meaning "of the same substance as God" and the very similar word *homoiousios* which meant similar to or like unto God. Referring to Jesus as *homoousious* meant that Jesus was of the same nature and substance as God, that in fact he was God. Everything hung on the presence or absence of the extra letter 'o'. Despite the opposition of some of the bishops, the term *homoousious* passed into an article of faith, and this, together with *heteras ousious*, or *heteroousious* (different substances or persons), became the basis of the Trinity.

The contempt for the body and the distrust of sexuality made the need for emphasis on the divinity of Jesus even more pronounced. Jesus was 'begotten' of God because he was of the same substance as God. Mary gave Jesus his physical body; God or the Holy Ghost gave him his divine nature. Naming Jesus the Son of God, meant that he had to be immaculately conceived, free of the taint of original sin, as well as celibate. To confirm the divinity of Jesus, at the Council of Ephesus in 451 CE, the Virgin Mary was declared God-Bearer or *Theotokos* and Jesus was declared to be both God and man. In these two Councils, all trace of Jesus's brothers and sisters and his marriage to Miryam of Bethany (Mary Magdalene) was expunged even though, according to Lawrence Gardner, the Vatican retained the documents which proved their existence and their relationship to Jesus.[13]

The Loss of the Feminine Image of the Holy Spirit in Christianity

In the pre-Christian world, Wisdom was always associated with the image of a Goddess: with Inanna in Sumer, Maat and Isis in Egypt and Athena in Greece, as well as with the Hebrew Goddess Asherah, who was worshipped until 623 BCE as Queen of Heaven, Divine Wisdom, and the Holy Spirit. But as we move into the Christian era, there was a profound shift in archetypal imagery. From the time of the Council of Nicaea in 325 CE, Wisdom became associated with Christ as the Logos, the Word, and lost all connection with the Feminine Principle. The loss of the Divine Feminine in Christianity was also hidden in the process by which the Hebrew rendering of *Ruach* — the feminine noun for spirit — was translated into the genderless Greek words *Haghia Pneuma* and then into the Latin *Spiritus Sanctus*, whose masculine gender ending may have led, in Christian theology, to the Holy Spirit being defined as male. The lost Wisdom Tradition of the Holy Spirit was not to surface again until 1945 with the astounding discovery of the Nag Hammadi Gnostic Texts and later, in the extensive research of the Old Testament scholar, Dr Margaret Barker.

At this Council, the Christian image of a Trinity of Father, Son and Holy

Spirit became wholly identified with the male gender. The connection of Divine Wisdom and the Holy Spirit with the ancient images of the Divine Mother and the Queen of Heaven, was irrevocably lost. Henceforth, there would be no feminine element in the God-head until 1950 when, in response to a petition, a Papal Bull of Pius XII declared the Virgin Mary to be "Assumed into Heaven, Body and Soul". In 1954, a Papal Encyclical named her Queen of Heaven, thereby restoring to her the cosmic dimension held by the Goddess in the great civilizations of the Bronze Age and by the Hebrew Goddess Asherah. The new Decree affirmed that, symbolically, Mary as bride was united with her Son in the heavenly bridal chamber and that, as Sophia (Wisdom), she was united with the godhead.

As I noted in *The Dream of the Cosmos*, Jung realized that the Papal Bull and the subsequent Encyclical reflected the fact that something of great significance was happening in the collective psyche. Mythologically speaking, the feminine archetype — including both body and soul that were personified by the Virgin Mary — was raised to the level of parity with the masculine one of spirit, heralding a 'sacred marriage' of the two great archetypal principles that would soon begin to find expression in the collective soul of humanity, in the changing relationship between men and women and the many different aspects of the ongoing struggle of women to make their voice heard in a world governed and controlled by men. [14]

The theologians and churchmen who formulated the doctrines of the Incarnation and the Trinity at the Councils of Nicaea and Chalcedon in 325 CE and 451 CE — doctrines that became the foundation of the edifice of Christian theology — inherited the Iron Age attitudes of the patriarchal cultures in which they lived. They assumed, without questioning their premises, that nature was different from and inferior to spirit and the female inferior to the male. They defined their doctrines on the legacy they received from the Old Testament, which clearly differentiated the beliefs and practices of Judaism from those of the surrounding pagan cultures and had banished the image of the goddess. With no respect for the Divine Feminine, it is easy to understand how the intellect, split off from its psychic ground, became entangled in its own formulations and came to believe that these were divine revelation.

The Church soon assimilated the attributes and functions of the former Goddess. The Church, from the beginning conceived as feminine, was defined as 'Mother'. She declared herself to be the Bride of Christ. And she was the embodiment of Wisdom. The text of the Song of Songs was used to support the idea that the Church was the beloved of Christ and the repository of Wisdom. The Church's task as Mother was to draw the human soul to her and so to Christ, but this authoritative intermediary deprived her children of trust

in their own souls, or of visualizing the Holy Spirit of Wisdom, now personified by Christ, as the ground of their being and the presence of a directing
consciousness within their soul. Although the rich tradition of contemplatives
and mystics belonging to both the Eastern and Western streams of Christianity,
kept alive this inner approach to the image of Christ, the Western Church
became increasingly secular in its aim to increase its territorial authority and
insisted on absolute obedience to the law of its doctrine.

Mythic Inflation

It was a natural corollary of the Roman Church's identification of itself with
the archetype of the Great Mother that it should fall victim to mythic inflation
for many centuries. In its extirpation of heresy, the persecution of anyone or
anything that threatened its doctrine, it revealed the dangerous, compulsive
behaviour of an archetype when it is unconsciously appropriated by an
individual or an institution. The institution, identified with the archetype,
becomes inflated by the numinosity of the divinely appointed role it accords
to itself. Believing that it was executing the will of God by eradicating the
evil of heresy, the Church itself became the actual embodiment of the evil
it saw in heretics, and the negation of the teaching of Christ. How can the
long history of the intolerance and arrogance of Christianity towards heretics,
other faiths and Indigenous People be explained, except as mythic inflation?
Today any individual or group of people who identifies 'good' exclusively with
their own religious or political ideas, and 'evil' with those of other groups,
may fall victim to the same psychic disorder. It seems as if this psychic danger
can be avoided if no claim is made to be being infallible, and if the emphasis
is placed always on the quest for greater understanding, which must involve
relationship and dialogue with the 'opponent'.

The Imbalance between the Masculine and the Feminine

The substitution of Christ as Logos for Sophia as the Holy Spirit is only one
strand in the story of how the image of the Divine Feminine was excluded from
the Christian Trinity. With the formulation of Christian doctrine in the early
centuries of this era, the emphasis of Christianity on the masculine archetype
was, so to speak, fixed. The faint reflection of the image of union lingered in
the concept of the marriage between Christ and his Church, or between Christ
and the community of the elect. But this 'humanization' of the Goddess image
could not contain the soul's need for an image of union between Goddess and
God, which symbolized the unity of life in the union of creator and creation,

anticipating the eventual reunion of consciousness with its ground. With the evolution of consciousness taking humanity ever further away from nature, mental and spiritual processes increasingly came to be seen as unrelated to physical ones, and intellect or mind superior to feeling and the values of the heart. The only numinous image that could bring these two aspects of life together again was the sacred marriage between Goddess and God.

The marriage of the Church to Christ could not satisfy the soul's need for a *divine* image of wholeness to express the mysterious unity of all life. Jung commented on the soul's need to have the image of the feminine 'metaphysically' anchored in the figure of a *divine* woman, the bride of Christ: "Just as the person of Christ cannot be replaced by an organization, so the Bride cannot be replaced by the Church. The feminine, like the masculine, demands an equally personal representation". [15] Only now, after nearly 4,000 years of a split between spirit and nature, which has deeply injured all aspects of the feminine, as well as the human soul, can growing insight and understanding help to heal this festering wound.

By a strange twist of fate, the numinous ground *within* the human being, which was approaching the threshold of consciousness in many individuals and was personified by Jesus as a teacher of Wisdom, was lost when Jesus was transformed into a God to be worshipped. Instead of the ground *within* the soul being recognized as divine, and related to the underlying divinity of the whole of life, the old literal pattern of the worship of God was emphasized and the separation between consciousness and its ground was perpetuated. Immanence was sacrificed to transcendence. Christians were taught that as long as they believed, belonged to and obeyed the Church, they were redeemed by the sacrificial death of Jesus on the cross. And so, as Jung pointed out, the divine image came to stand outside man and woman rather than within them.

At the later Council of Chalcedon in 451 CE, Jesus became the exception — the *only* Son of God — rather than a man who had realized his true, divine, being and become the voice and mouthpiece of Sophia or Divine Wisdom: the model, therefore, of what all human beings may become, because this, essentially, is who they are. The belief that Jesus was the one and only incarnation of the godhead veiled the insight that all people have within them the potentiality of realizing their divine nature and knowingly becoming the 'sons' and 'daughters' of God. Moreover, the Incarnation could not be understood in the sense of the divine presence being incarnated in the whole of visible creation as the 'Son'. True to the process whereby what is unconsciously lost is projected onto an adversary, the Christian Church soon lost the image of totality and created a separation between those who believed its teaching and were therefore 'saved', and those who did not and were not 'saved'. The same separation was projected topographically onto heaven and hell, which were to receive the 'saved' and the 'damned'.

The identification of Jesus with the image of the Son of God, who was immaculately conceived and born of a virgin, gave divine authority to the New Testament and to the Church as its interpreter, and may have ensured its survival, but the Wisdom tradition of the Kingdom of God as the divine ground of life and the human soul had to go underground, and Western civilization was deprived of an insight that might have greatly enriched it and contributed to its spiritual development.

The implicit celibacy of Jesus led to the celibate priesthood of the Catholic Church. In 1139, the Second Lateran Council passed a rule forbidding priests to marry. The rule of celibacy has remained in place ever since, with the disastrous effect of the sexual abuse of generations of boys — abuse which has only recently come to light against great resistance by the Vatican.

The Edict of the Emperor Theodosius 1 and Heresy

In 380 CE, the Emperor Theodosius 1 issued the Edict of Thessalonica which declared that Christianity was henceforth to be the official religion of the Roman Empire. In 381 CE, he declared that anyone who did not comply with his edict that all must believe in the Apostolic Creed defined at Nicaea — that the Father, Son, and Holy Spirit were of one and the same substance — would be declared a heretic. This was the time when the words 'heresy' and 'heretic' entered the annals of the Church of Rome. All remaining Gnostic Gospels which carried vital elements of Jesus' teaching, including the Gospels of Thomas and Philip, were destroyed on the emperor's orders, not to reappear until the discovery of the Nag Hammadi texts in 1945. From the final severance of the Divine Feminine from the godhead at the Council of Nicaea came the gradual de-souling of nature and the crisis we face now.

The Destruction of the Legacy of the Pagan World
and the Forcible Conversion of Conquered Peoples

In this chapter, we have seen how the presence of the Divine Feminine in the godhead was not only banished from Judaism, but also from Christianity because it took its image of God from Judaism. Islam from the seventh century CE also had a sole male creator god. Consequently, the three patriarchal religions all lacked an image of the Divine Feminine in the godhead, with consequences that can still be seen today and which are far more dangerous now than they were at the time of their inception.

The monotheistic cosmology of these three patriarchal religions and the loss of the Divine Feminine have led to the situation where the earth is no longer recognized as sacred but open to our exploitation of it and we are confronted with the catastrophic effects of the loss of the Divine Feminine. From the time of Theodosius 1, the Christian Church in Rome turned against the cultural legacy of the Classical Pagan world, destroying its temples, sculptures, and any lingering evidence of the Mysteries. Theodosius ordered the destruction of the temple of Eleusis.[16] In 392 CE, a Christian mob destroyed the magnificent Serapeum Temple in Alexandria, filled with priceless scrolls holding the accumulated wisdom and knowledge of the ancient world. A few centuries later, from the time of the First Crusade in 1095, Christians embarked on wars, conquests, and brutal conversions in the name of their God. In the thirteenth century, with St. Dominic and the founding of the Dominican Order, the Vatican introduced the horror of the Inquisition which was to last for five centuries in Europe. With this history of destruction, war, slaughter, persecution, and torture, it seems inconceivable that the Church of Rome could still regard itself as the vessel for the transmission of the message of Jesus, yet such is the inflating effect of power on men in charge of great institutions, that this was perhaps to be expected.

The Church hounded to death William Tyndale, the brilliant polymath who translated the New Testament from Greek into English (1525). Tyndale was working on the translation of the Old Testament when he was discovered hiding in Brabant (Belgium) where he had taken refuge. Condemned to death for heresy, he was arrested, strangled, and burnt at the stake.[17] In 1600 Giordano Bruno (1548–1600), the extraordinary Italian poet, philosopher, and cosmo-logist, who said there were other inhabited planets in the universe, suffered the same fate, because he refused to deny that God was present in nature. These were the lengths to which the Church of Rome went to destroy any challenge to its authority.

We have recently acknowledged the evils of slavery, but it was a series of Papal Bulls from 1493, issued by the Vatican in what was called The Doctrine of Discovery/Domination, that authorized and encouraged the Christian Euro-pean nations to invade, capture, subdue, and enslave the indigenous populations and to seize their lands and possessions — all in the name of Christ.[18] Because of this lamentable history of conquest, persecution and subjugation, so-called Christian civilization has been on the wrong path since the fourth century: on the path of power and domination instead of love and service, out of touch with the teaching of its Founder, while continuing to worship His crucified image. Instead of putting the emphasis on the Resurrection and Jesus's restoration to life after his crucifixion, the Church of Rome placed it on the crucifixion, and its portrayal in every church. This was a profound mistake because it amplified humanity's sense of sinfulness and guilt and encouraged the Church to dwell on it in countless sermons.

The deeper layers of the soul which held the memory of a life of participation in the sacred life of the earth and the instinctual awareness of the unity of life governed by divine law, understood for thousands of years through the image of the Goddess and the Mysteries associated with her worship, were silenced. The primary mistake in Christian teaching was to split nature from spirit and body from soul. The soul and the instinctive feeling values associated with it were consistently overridden and ignored. The body was feared and despised as sinful. In 419 CE, St. Augustine's belief that the original sin of Adam and Eve was transmitted from generation to generation through the sexual act passed into the Doctrines of the Church.[19] Although women had played an outstanding and significant role in the first two centuries of the spread of Christianity, their voice was henceforth silenced and they became subject to the control and authority of man.

The most disastrous effect of monotheism was that nature was split off from spirit. The loss of the Goddess meant that nature was no longer sacred because spirit was no longer imminent within it. We are the inheritors of the dualism embedded in the monotheistic patriarchal religions which worshipped a Creator-God whose priesthoods would not tolerate a feminine co-creator, and who, in their ignorance of what they were doing, severed the umbilical cord between nature and spirit. Because of this, we lost touch with our primordial, instinctive soul. We are faced with the effects of this severance today as, indoctrinated by materialist science, which tells us that we are separate from the earth, and that the earth and matter are devoid of spirit or any form of sentience, we belatedly recognize the harm we have inflicted on the planet.

Nuclear Weapons and the Rape of Nature

Dr Marie-Louise von Franz, a close colleague of Jung, observed in her book *C.G. Jung, His Myth in Our Time*, that when the Feminine Archetype is unconscious or not honoured, it manifests as the will to power.[20] We have seen this in the warlike ethos of the entire Solar Era and in the atrocious persecution of heretics and dissidents by the Inquisition. But it reached its culmination in the last century in the creation of atomic, hydrogen and nuclear bombs. The growing confrontation between nations during the Second World War, and the fear that Germany might develop an atomic bomb, led America to create the first atomic bomb, detonated at Los Alamos in 1945. [21]

Hailed as a tremendous scientific achievement, there was not the slightest understanding of what a sacrilegious act this was. From the perspective of the sacred nature of life, to invent a weapon that could destroy life on a massive scale was a rape of nature and matter. Its creation was followed by the obliteration of Hiroshima and Nagasaki, an unforgivable crime against a helpless civilian population, that was justified by the need to end the war with Japan. It was followed in March 1st, 1954, by the dropping of a bomb on Bikini Atoll in the Marshall Islands, a bomb nearly a thousand times more powerful than the bombs dropped on the Japanese cities. A further twenty-four nuclear weapons were detonated at Bikini Atoll by the United States between 1946 and 1958. Between 1957-62, the British government also undertook nuclear testing on the colonized islands of Kiribati, not far from the Marshall Islands. All these detonations had catastrophic effects on the inhabitants of the Marshall and Kiribati Islands — effects from which they still suffer today. Many people are still suffering from birth defects, cancers and other serious illnesses connected with radiation poisoning. Yet, the UK government refuses to acknowledge the experiences of people on the Pacific Islands and has refused to make reparations. The US government has made only partial reparations — a payment in 1986 of $150 million to the Marshall Islands.

Albert Schweitzer commented in 1954 when he received the Nobel Prize for Peace, that with the creation of this demonic weapon, we had lost our humanity. My mother was warned in channeled Messages at the time, that the splitting of the atom would lead to the splitting of the human psyche and to mass insanity.[22] That insanity is reflected today in the ruthless struggle for power between America, Russia, and China, each locked into the drive for dominance, pre-eminence, and control through the continued invention and stockpiling of ever more lethal weapons, with North Korea engaging in the same race to absolute power.

Now there are nine nuclear powers, with Iran a probable tenth. Few people, least of all governments, understand that the actual creation of nuclear weapons was a crime against the Sacred Order of life on this planet, an assault on matter — ultimately on spirit, since matter cannot be separated from spirit. We are now faced with evil on a colossal scale — evil that we have failed to recognize because we have not begun to comprehend the fact that all life on this planet is sacred. Albert Einstein presciently observed, "With the splitting of the atom, we have changed everything save our mode of thinking and thus we drift towards unparalleled catastrophes." [23]

The Effects of the Loss of the Feminine Value

Today, we live in a secular culture — a culture that has largely dispensed with religion and has given overwhelming emphasis to the rational mind and to technological progress, scientific advance, and political power. It has neglected the Feminine Value — above all, the deepest longings and innate wisdom of the human heart. Although it is beginning to return, visionary and shamanic experience has been banished, much as it was banished long ago by the Deuteronomists. Modern culture is driven by a predatory and rapacious materialism, an ethos of competitive struggle, and the pursuit of power, wealth, fame, dominance, and control. In such a culture, the soul is effectively starving. There is no limit to the evil people will do for money and power. We are now facing the shadow aspect of Western civilization and the effects of having ignored the feminine value for millennia. This prophecy from *The Essene Gospel of Peace* Book 4, written down on a scroll two thousand years ago, possibly by Jesus, sums up what has happened:

> *But there will come a day when the Son of Man will turn his face from his Earthly Mother and betray her, even denying his Mother and his birth right. Then shall he sell her into slavery, and her flesh shall be ravaged, her blood polluted, and her breath smothered; he will bring the fire of death into all the parts of her kingdom, and his hunger will devour all her gifts and leave in their place only a desert.*
>
> *All these things he will do out of ignorance of the Law, and as a man dying slowly cannot smell his own stench, so will the Son of Man be blind to the truth: that as he plunders and ravages and destroys his Earthly Mother, so does he plunder and ravage and destroy himself. For he was born of his Earthly Mother, and he is one with her, and all that he does to his Mother, even so does he do to himself.* [24]

Every word of this prophecy has come true. Believing ourselves to be separate from and entitled to exploit nature in the interests of our species alone, and having no idea of who we are and why we are on this planet, we have grossly interfered with the harmony of the natural world and are bringing possible mass extinction upon it as well as upon ourselves.

Over recent centuries, we have reached dazzling heights of scientific, medical, and technological advances which have transformed the physical conditions of our lives on this planet and facilitated a phenomenal expansion of our ability to express the creative genius of our species in many different areas and to communicate with each other through the Internet. But we have also suffered a catastrophic loss of soul, a loss of the ancient awareness of the sacred inter-weaving of all aspects of life, a loss of the sense of participation in the life of nature and the life of the cosmos and, despite all our religions, a radical misunderstanding of the nature of God. We have lost all awareness of the existence of our soul. The whole foundation of our lives is missing.

As Kingsley Dennis observes in his recent book *The Inversion*, we have been deceived by scientific materialism into seeing material reality as the only reality that exists. [25]

In his autobiography, Jung warned of the dangers of this materialist philosophy and the loss of soul that is the effect of its influence:

> Evil today has become a visible Great Power. One half of humanity battens and grows strong on a doctrine fabricated by human ratiocination; the other half sickens from the lack of a myth commensurate with the situation. The Christian nations have come to a sorry pass; their Christianity slumbers and has neglected to develop its myth further in the course of the centuries. Those who gave expression to the dark stirrings of growth in mythic ideas were refused a hearing. [26]

Looking at the state of the world today and the struggle for power between three great nations that could lead to a nuclear catastrophe, we can see that each possesses the Promethean freedom that Jung commented on (see Preface) but also partakes of a godless *hubris*, however much two of their leaders proclaim that God is guiding or blessing them. This suggests that, as described in the Preface, we are out of alignment with both the cosmos and the earth. In alchemical language, our world — the Below — has become disconnected or separated from the Above, the invisible, inner dimension of reality. The major cause of this disconnection or separation is our misconception of the nature of God and the loss of the Divine Feminine. A second cause of disconnection is scientific materialism which has separated us from both God and our soul, banishing the concept of the sacred and all deeper meaning to life.

Notes:

1. Barker, Dr Margaret, (2023) *The Great Lady: Restoring Her Story*, Sheffield Phoenix Press, UK
2. Barker, (2003) *The Great High Priest*, p. 236.
3. Barker, (2004) *Temple Theology*, SPCK, London, page 7 and Chapter 4
4. Barker, Dr Margaret (2004), *The Hidden Tradition of the Kingdom of God*, SPCK, London.
5. Barker, *The Great Lady,* pp. 6-7
6. Barker, ibid, pp. xiv and xv
7. Barker (2004) *Temple Theology*, p. 35
8. Phillips, John A. (1984) *Eve, The History of an Idea*. San Francisco: Harper & Row, p.15, quoted in *The Myth of the Goddess*, p. 495

9. For their attitude to sexuality and the virulent misogyny of the Early Christian Fathers, see Baring, Anne, *The Dream of the Cosmos*, Chapters 7 & 8

10. Lamb, Christina (2020) *Our Bodies, Their Battlefield: What War Does to Women*, William Collins, London

11. Lash, John Lamb, (2005 & 2021) *Not in His Image: Gnostic Vision, Sacred Ecology and the Future of Belief*, Chelsea Green Publishing, Vermont USA & London UK

12. Bowden, Rev. John (1989), *Jesus: The Unanswered Questions*, p. 7

13. The books of Laurence Gardner provide detailed evidence that the Vatican moved heaven and earth to conceal the fact of their marriage and that it holds a document called *The Desposyni Chart* that provides evidence of their marriage and the existence of their children, as well as the descendants of Jesus' brother, James. *The Magdalene Legacy*, Element, London, 2005 and *The Grail Enigma* 2008 HarperElement, London.

14. See Baring, Anne (2020) *The Dream of the Cosmos*, p. 224

15. Jung, C.G. Collected Works, Vol. 11 *Psychology and Religion*: West and East, para 753

16. Nixey, Catherine (2017), *The Darkening Age: The Christian Destruction of the Classical World*, Macmillan, London. See also, Freeman, Charles (2013) *The Closing of the Western Mind: The Rise of Faith and the Fall of Reason*, Pimlico, London

17. Only two copies of his translation of the New Testament survive in the British Library. Nearly 18,000 copies were destroyed.

18. Kovács, Dr Betty J. (2019) *Merchants of Light: The Consciousness that is changing the World*, The Kamlak Center, p. 437

19. This passed into Church Law at a Council in Carthage (419 CE) which formulated the Doctrine of Original Sin.

20. von Franz, Marie-Louise, (1975), *C.G. Jung, His Myth in Our Time*, C.G. Jung Foundation for Analytical Psychology, Chapter XIII

21. See the book, *American Prometheus: The Triumph and Tragedy of J. Robert Oppenheimer* and also the recent film 'Oppenheimer'.

22. Baring, Anne, (2023), *Messages from a Transcendent Dimension,* Archive Publishing, Dorset, UK

23. *The Expanded Quotable Einstein*, collected and edited by Alice Calaprice (2000), The Hebrew University of Jerusalem and Princeton University Press, Princeton, New Jersey

24. Szekely, Edmond B. (1981) *The Essene Gospel of Peace*, Book Four, *Teachings of the Elect* Brussels: International Biogenic Society

25. Dennis, Kingsley L. (2023), *The Inversion: How We Have Been Tricked into Perceiving a False Reality*, Aeon Books,

26. Jung, C. G. (1963) *Memories, Dreams, Reflections,* Collins and Routledge & Kegan Paul, London, p. 306

Chapter Four

THE SHEKINAH OF KABBALAH
DIVINE WISDOM AND THE HOLY SPIRIT

I loved her above health and beauty, and chose to have her instead
of light for the light that cometh from her never goeth out.

— Wisdom of Solomon

After detailing the far-reaching events recounted in Chapter Three, I turned with relief to this chapter and the unique cosmology offered by the Jewish mystical tradition of Kabbalah, beautifully named *The Voice of the Dove* and *The Jewels of the Heavenly Bride*. As many of you may know from reading *The Dream of the Cosmos* and the Introduction to this book, about 50 years ago I had a visionary dream of a goddess-like figure whose sublime form stretched from heaven to earth. For years I wondered who she was. She was not familiar to me like the goddesses I knew from my study of ancient civilizations in *The Myth of the Goddess*. Then, one day, as I was writing about the Shekinah in a later book co-authored with Andrew Harvey called *The Divine Feminine*, I realized in a flash who the cosmic being of my visionary dream was. Without the shadow of a doubt, she was the Shekinah.[1] For reasons unknown to me — perhaps originating in another incarnation — my dream had led me to the Jewish mystical tradition of Kabbalah. I discovered to my astonishment and delight, that in this cosmology, the Shekinah is the co-creator of the world. Here, at last, was a cosmology that resonated with my heart because it restored the Divine Feminine to the god-head. It is through this tradition that I learned why, in Blake's words, "Everything that lives is holy"; why we cannot separate any part of creation from any other part.

The word Kabbalah means "receiving" or "That which has been received". Legend says that when Adam and Eve were cast out of the Garden of Eden, the angel Razael gave them a book to help them find their way back into it. In the words of my teacher, the late Z'ev ben Shimon Halevi (Warren Kenton), "Kabbalism is the inner and mystical aspect of Judaism. It is the Perennial Teaching about the Attributes of the Divine, the nature of the universe and the destiny of man."

To this, I would add the opening words of Gershom Sholem's *Kabbalah*: "Kabbalah is the traditional and most commonly used term for the esoteric teachings of Judaism and for Jewish mysticism, especially the forms which it assumed in the Middle Ages from the 12th century onward." [2]

Why is this tradition so important? Because it is the only tradition in the West that celebrates the indissoluble relationship and union between the feminine and masculine aspects of the god-head — a sacred marriage or union which the three Patriarchal or Abrahamic religions have rejected or ignored. It carried forward the ancient Bronze-Age image of the sacred marriage, held in the union of the Divine Mother-Father in the Ground of Being, who are one in their emanation, one in their ecstatic and continuous act of creation through all the dimensions they bring into being and sustain.

If we want to understand the deep roots of our environmental and spiritual crisis, we can find them in the loss of three important elements: the feminine image of spirit, the direct shamanic path of communion with spirit through visionary and mystical experience, and the sacred marriage of the masculine and feminine aspects of the Divine Ground. Each of these was once part of the lost traditions and practices of the First Temple in Jerusalem.

The Origins of Kabbalah

I believe that it may be possible to trace the distant origins of Kabbalah to the First Temple prior to the momentous events that took place there in 623 BCE. As explained in Chapter Three, Israel and this great Temple originally had an ancient, shamanic, visionary tradition mediated by the High Priest. But in 623 BCE, in the reign of King Josiah, a powerful group of priests called Deuteronomists took control of the Temple on his orders. The shamanic rituals of the High Priest which had honoured and communed with the Queen of Heaven as Divine Wisdom and the Holy Spirit in the great tower at the back of the temple, were banished and replaced by new rituals based on obedience to the Law of Moses. Every trace of the former Queen of Heaven, the Goddess Asherah, worshipped as Divine Wisdom and the Holy Spirit, was obliterated. Also obliterated was all trace of communion with the Hosts of Heaven.

This is how the Jewish people lost their Goddess. Yahweh was left as the sole Creator God. What had once been intrinsic to the image of God was excised from it. The Deuteronomists then created the Myth of the Fall in the Book of Genesis 2 & 3, severing the Tree of Life from its ancient association with the Queen of Heaven, whose title 'Mother of All Living' they bestowed on Eve. It seems possible that Kabbalah could be the surviving teaching of the First Temple that was preserved by the Essene Communities in Palestine, (see

Chapter Seven). But it may also have been carried to the city of Alexandria by Jews who were outraged by the change in cosmology imposed by the Deuteronomists and who wanted to preserve the ancient teachings of the First Temple. These exiles and later ones joined the community of Jews already well established in that city. We know from Jeremiah's rebuke to them when he visited Alexandria, that they had continued to worship the Queen of Heaven, (see Chapter Five).

Transmitted, I believe, from its origins in the First Temple in Jerusalem, a chain of unnamed contemplatives passed on the teachings of Kabbalah orally for over a thousand years until the thirteenth century CE when the canonical text of Kabbalah, a book called *Sefer Ha-Zohar*, the *Zohar* or *Book of Radiance or Splendour* was written in northern Spain in 1290 CE by Rabbi Moses (Moshe) de León (1250–1305). He wrote his extraordinary text in Aramaic, and in pseudepigraphic form, almost in the form of a novel, entering imaginatively into the life of a famous rabbi, Rabbi Shimon bar Yochai, who lived in Palestine in the second century CE and, as it were, tuning in to him conversing with his disciples. There has been much heated controversy over whether he was the sole author of the text of whether it was a compilation of the work of other authors, the most important being Rabbi Shimon bar Yochai. However, after prolonged and exhaustive examination of the text, which ran to many volumes and over two thousand, four hundred pages, Gershom Scholem, the renowned authority on Jewish Mysticism and Kabbalah, concluded that it was undoubtedly entirely authored by Rabbi Moses de León.[3] He said he was a visionary, comparable to Jacob Boehme or William Blake, and his extraordinary and magisterial creation should be viewed in that context.

> The Quest for Truth knows of adventures that are all its own, and in a vast number of cases has arrayed itself in pseudepigraphic garb. The further a man progresses along his own road in this Quest for Truth, the more he might become convinced that his own road must have already been trodden by others, ages before him. To the streak of adventurousness which was in Moses de León, no less than to his genius, we owe one of the most remarkable works of Jewish literature and of the literature of mysticism in general. [4]

The question arises, what sources did Rabbi Moses draw on to create his masterpiece? The city of Gerona (Girona) in northern Spain was a centre of Kabbalism in the twelfth century as well as the city of Narbonne in south-western France. Was he in touch with either of these groups of kabbalists or was he working in isolation?

> More than a scribe, de León was the composer of the *Zohar*. He drew on earlier material, he may have collaborated with other kabbalists, and he may have genuinely believed that he was transmitting ancient teachings. Indeed, parts of the *Zohar* may have been composed through automatic writing [channeling], in which the mystic would meditate on a divine name, enter a trance, and begin to 'write whatever came to his hand.' Such a technique was apparently used by other thirteenth century kabbalists. But Moses de León wove his various sources into a master-piece: a commentary on the Torah in the form of a mystical novel. [5]

Another question is: how had Kabbalah reached Spain, how long had it been there and who had preserved it through the centuries? It is known that the Jewish kingdom of Septimania was established in northern Spain and south-western France in the late eighth century CE. There was a particularly strong Jewish community in Toulouse and Narbonne. Even after the disappearance of this kingdom, the Jewish community in France never lost its links with Spain, particularly the towns of Cordoba, Toledo, Seville and Gerona. Gerona may have become a centre of Kabbalistic studies during the eighth century but there is still the question of who brought it to Spain in the first place and at what date. If it entered Spain from Narbonne, it could have come, ultimately, from the Essene teaching of Mary Magdalene who was teaching in that area of France for twenty years from 44 CE. Here we have reluctantly to leave the mystery of how Kabbalah reached Spain but we may return to it in Chapter Eight.

With the persecution and brutal expulsion of the Jews from Spain in 1492, Kabbalism moved to Safed, in Palestine, where one of its greatest teachers, Moses Cordovero (1522–1570), lived and wrote his famous work, *The Orchard of Pomegranates* (*Pardes Rimmonim*). Kabbalism also took root in northern Europe, in England, Poland and Bohemia, where many kabbalists were also alchemists. It existed briefly in Renaissance Italy, where the brilliant young Pico della Mirandola hoped to create a fusion of Kabbalism and Christianity until his untimely death cut short the possibility of him realizing his vision. "His famous 900 Theses," writes Daniel Matt in his book *The Essential Kabbalah*, "drew heavily on Kabbalah and laid the foundation for Christian kabbalistic literature." [6]

The Tree of Life

Because of its possible origins in the First Temple in Jerusalem where one of the most important images describing the Goddess Asherah was the Tree of Life, it seems highly significant that the principal image of Kabbalah is the Tree of Life, which is a clear and wonderful concept describing the web of relationships which connect invisible spirit with the fabric of life in this world. This seems to be the only spiritual tradition which, in minute detail, connects the invisible dimension of reality with the visible one — our world. At the innermost level or dimension of reality is the unmanifest, unknowable divine ground; at the outermost the physical forms we call nature, body, and matter. Linking the two is the archetypal template of the Tree of Life — an inverted tree — whose branches grow from its roots in the divine ground and extend through many invisible worlds, levels or dimensions until they reach our world. In this cosmology, the nature and properties of the different dimensions or levels of reality and their relationships with each other are described and defined.

Every aspect of creation, both visible and invisible, is interwoven with every other aspect. All is one life, one cosmic symphony, one integrated whole. We participate, at this material level of creation, in the divine life which informs all these myriad levels of reality. Our human lives are therefore inseparable from the inner life of the cosmos. We are all participants in it. The great maxim of the kabbalists was "As Above, So Below" — a maxim that originated in the Hermetic Science taught in the temples of Egypt. The aim of the kabbalist was and is, to unite the two worlds, the invisible divine world (the Above) with the manifest material world of our experience (the Below). Quintessentially, there is only One Divine Life. Uniquely in this cosmology, there is no duality, no separation of nature from spirit and, above all, no fallen world. In the words of Moses de León:

> The essence of divinity is found in every single thing — nothing but it exists. Since it causes everything to be, no thing can live by anything else. It enlivens them; its existence exists in each existent.
>
> Do not attribute duality to God. Let God be solely God. If you suppose that *Ein Sof* emanates until a certain point, and that from that point is outside it, you have dualized. God Forbid! Realize, rather, that *Ein Sof* exists in each existent. Do not say, "This is a stone and not God." God forbid! Rather, all existence is God, and the stone is a thing pervaded by divinity.
>
> Before anything emanated, there was only *Ein Sof. Ein Sof* was all that existed. Similarly, after it brought into being that which exists, there is nothing but it. You cannot find anything that exists apart from it. There is nothing that is not pervaded by the power of divinity. If there were, Ein Sof would be limited, subject to duality. God forbid! Rather, God is everything that exists, although everything that exists is not God. It is present in everything, and everything comes into being from it. Nothing is devoid of its divinity. Everything is within it; It is within everything and outside of everything. There is nothing but it. [7]

This contemplative tradition emphasizes the path to God as a process of awakening through gradual illumination and experience rather than adherence to a specific doctrine or faith. Its emphasis is on the growth of insight and wisdom through contemplation, imagination and a deepening relationship with the divine ground while not neglecting life and relationships in this dimension of reality. It does not separate matter from spirit. It does not reject the body nor is it obsessed with sin. All these ideas are, in my view, essential to our concept of reality.

The Doctrine of Emanation

The fundamental teaching of Kabbalah is the doctrine of emanation and, because of this, the oneness or unity of all cosmic dimensions of reality. Divine Creative Spirit, named as the unmanifest god-head *Ein Soph* or *Ein Soph Aur — the Limitless Light* — is regarded not only as totally transcendent and unknowable but also, through emanation, present in every particle of the material world as well as in the intermediary dimensions of reality veiled from our sight. The zig-zag path taken by the Divine Emanation down the Tree of Life is called the Lightning Flash.

Kabbalism did not regard this world as fallen, as in Christianity, but saw it sustained and permeated by the Light of the divine ground. It taught that whatever we do in this world affects the invisible worlds and vice-versa because everything, visible and invisible, is connected through an invisible Web of Life. The concept of reincarnation is intrinsic to this path to God. The soul becomes enlightened over many lives, at first through attraction to, then contemplation of and finally, communion with the invisible worlds. Moses de León wrote these memorable words:

> The purpose of the soul entering this body is to display her powers and actions in this world, for she needs an instrument. By descending to this world, she increases the flow of her power to guide the human being through the world. Thereby she perfects herself above and below, attaining a higher state by being fulfilled in all dimensions. If she is not fulfilled both above and below, she is not complete.
>
> Before descending to this world, the soul is emanated from the mystery of the highest level. While in this world, she is completed and fulfilled by this lower world. Departing this world, she is filled with the fullness of all the worlds, the world above and the world below.
>
> At first, before descending to this world, the soul is imperfect; she is lacking something. By descending to this world, she is perfected in every dimension. [8]

Like someone emerging from a darkened cellar, we cannot bear the radiant light of the divine ground all at once. As our relationship with the divine deepens, so does our consciousness expand to include awareness of the deeper, unseen dimensions of being until we begin to transmit the Light and Love of this hidden ground.

Worlds within Worlds

Rather than presenting an image of a hierarchical descent from the invisible to the visible, Kabbalah offers the image of worlds nesting within worlds, dimensions within dimensions, manifesting, as it were, from within outwards. It is a wonderfully illuminating template of the network of relationships which connect invisible spirit with the fabric of this material world. At the innermost level is the unknowable Source or God-head, at the outermost the physical forms of what we call matter. All is one unified web of life: one energy, one spirit, one single cosmic entity. We are, I discovered, each one of us, that life, that energy, that spirit, however unconscious of this we may be. Quintessentially, there is only One Divine Life. We are all participants in the life of the cosmos, atoms in the Being and Body of God. In our essence, we are One. It is extraordinary and also timely that the science of quantum physics has reached the conclusion that we are all connected to (entangled with) each other, as well as with the life of the earth and the cosmos, through the minute particles of the sub-atomic Field.

I realized that the levels or dimensions of this hidden ground of the cosmos are what Jesus meant by the Kingdom of Heaven — worlds or dimensions which are invisible to us yet which underlie and 'permeate' the physical world and which, if we could only see them, are spread out all around us as he described them in *logion* 113 of The Gospel of Thomas: *The Kingdom of Heaven is spread out upon the earth and men do not see it.* Jesus, as well as other great teachers like the Buddha, must have taught from deep knowledge and experience of these worlds, from a revelatory experience of cosmic consciousness. I began to see that the image of an invisible dimension of reality lies behind many images of the quest, in particular the medieval quest for the Holy Grail — image of a boundless source of nourishment. These dimensions can gradually become accessible to our limited consciousness as it develops and expands. My visionary dream, had opened a door for me to the existence of a hidden dimension of reality which holds our own in its embrace.

The Sacred Marriage and the Transmission of Light

The highly-developed cosmology of this tradition preserves the ancient Bronze Age image of the sacred marriage, reflected in the union of the Divine Father–Mother in the ground of being.[9] There is not a Father God but a Mother–Father who are one in their eternal embrace: one in their ground, one in their emanation, one in their ecstatic and continuous act of creation through all the dimensions they bring into being and sustain. From the perspective of divine immanence, there is no essential separation between spirit and nature. No other tradition offers the same breath-taking vision in such exquisite poetic imagery of the union of male and female energies in the One that is both. The Song of Songs was the text most used by kabbalists for their contemplation of the mystery of this divine union.

The *Zohar* or *Book of Radiance or Splendour* contemplates the mystery of the relationship between the female and male aspects of Divine Spirit exp-ressed as Mother and Father, and their emanation through all dimensions of creation as Daughter and Son. The essential concept of this mystical tradition expresses itself in an image of nested worlds within worlds rather than as a hierarchal ladder of descent. Divine Spirit named as *Ein Soph* or *Ein Soph Aur*, beyond form or conception, is the ineffable Light at the Root, the Source, the Divine Ground of Being. Emanating as creative Sound or Word, Light, Intell-igence and Love, it brings into being successive spheres, realms, or dimensions named as veils or robes which clothe and hide the hidden source, yet at the same time transmit its radiant Light.

The transmission of this ineffable Light from the source to the outer manifest level is illustrated, as described earlier, as an inverted tree, the Tree of Life, whose branches grow from its root in the divine ground and extend through invisible worlds or dimensions of which we are not aware because our present level of consciousness is not yet able to access their higher vibratory level. Certain contemplatives, such as the Essenes and the Tibetans, are able to do this after long practice. A recent book by Mark Anthony explains why those who have transitioned to another level of reality are separated from us because the elec-tromagnetic frequency is higher at their level than it is at our level. This must apply also to further higher or inner dimensions.[10] As I absorbed these images, I was struck by the similarity of the image of Light as the Divine Ground of Being to the Tibetan concept of the luminous Light of the Void.

The primal centre or root is the innermost Light, of an unimaginable lumin-osity and translucence, utterly different from the light of the sun we see in our world. This centre expands or is sown as a ray of Light into what is described in some texts as a sea of glory, in others as a palace or womb which acts as an enclosure for or receptacle of the Light. From here it emanates as a radiant cascade, a fountain of living water, pouring forth Light to create, permeate and sustain all the worlds or dimensions it brings into being. All life on earth, all degrees of consciousness, are that Light and are therefore utterly sacred. The *Zohar* describes nature as the garment of God.

This cascade of Light flows through the ten Vessels, Powers, or Attributes of the Divine, named as the *Sefiroth*, which are connected by the twenty-two paths of the Tree of Life. The first Vessel (*Kether*) is a state of perfect equilibrium and contains all that was, is and will be. The divine impulse towards emanation moves the energy to expand beyond the first Vessel to the second; it is then received and contained by the third Vessel. This process of expansion and containment is repeated three times until this Tree is complete and the emanating energy balanced. The process of emanation then proceeds through further worlds, and the laws or archetypes which govern each world or level of creation come into being until they manifest as our own. All life on earth, all levels and degrees of cosmic reality are the creation of that primal Fountain of Light and are therefore an expression of divinity. In the radiance of that invisible cosmic Sea of Light, everything is connected to everything else as through a luminous circulatory system. Kabbalism gives us a highly developed cosmology of a conscious, intelligent, and supremely creative universe, with Light and Love as the creative agent that brings the entire universe into being. All the angelic orders, the Archangels and multitude of angelic beings, are present within it, accessible to those who seek to communicate with them.

The Shekinah or Feminine Face of the God-head

The Shekinah is the image of the Divine Feminine or the Feminine Face of God as it was conceived in this mystical and shamanic tradition of Judaism, transmitted orally for a thousand years and more until it flowered in the writings of the Jewish kabbalists of medieval Spain and south-western France and later, in sixteenth century Palestine. In the imagery and cosmology of the Shekinah, we encounter the most complete description of Divine Wisdom and the Holy Spirit, as well as the indissoluble relationship between the two primary aspects of the god-head that have been lost or hidden for millennia. This again suggests that Kabbalism has a strong connection with the teaching of the First Temple and the worship there of the Queen of Heaven as Divine Wisdom and the Holy Spirit as well as the Tree of Life.

Wisdom in ancient civilizations was always associated with a Goddess: with Inanna in Sumer, Maat and Isis in Egypt, Athena in Greece. The Bronze Age imagery of these Great Goddesses returns to life in the extraordinary beauty of the descriptions of the Shekinah, and in the gender endings of nouns which describe the feminine dimension of the divine. But the Divine Feminine is now defined as a limitless connecting web of life, as the unseen Soul of the Cosmos — described as such by Plato in his *Timaeus* — as the intermediary between the unknowable god-head and life in this dimension. The Shekinah brings together the Above and the Below, the invisible and visible dimensions of reality in a resplendent vision of their essential relationship and unity.

The Shekinah: Divinity Active and Present in the World

The *Zohar* or *Book of Radiance or Splendour* speaks of the Shekinah as the Voice or Word of God, the Wisdom of God, the Glory of God, the Compassion of God, the Active Presence of God, intermediary between the mystery of the unknowable source or ground and this world of its ultimate manifestation. The cosmology of the Shekinah as Divine Wisdom and the Holy Spirit offers one of the most incandescent images of the immanence of the divine in this dimension. She transmutes all creation, including the apparent insignificance and ordinariness of everyday life, into something to be loved, embraced, honoured, and celebrated because it is the epiphany or shining forth of the divine intelligence and love that has brought it into being and dwells hidden within it.

Why did I find the image of the Shekinah so broad in its imaginative and revelatory reach, so nourishing to my soul? Because it gave me a different image of spirit. Here was an image of the divine as the actual ground of the phenomenal world, that has brought this world into being and lives within it. The Shekinah, named as Divine Wisdom and the Holy Spirit — divinity present and active in the world — supplies the missing imagery of divine immanence which has been lost or obscured in Judaism since 623 BCE. It survived in the mystical stream of Christianity and as Sufism in Islam. This tradition brings together spirit and nature, the divine and the human, in a coherent and seamless vision of their essential relationship. It seems an utter tragedy that this marvellous cosmology was lost to Judaism after the coup of 623 BCE when we lost our connection with the invisible dimension of the cosmos and with the Angelic Realm, the hosts of heaven. Yet the *Zohar* has restored it.

The Shekinah is defined as the feminine aspect of the god-head as Mother, Beloved, Sister and Bride — imagery that has been lost or obscured in Judaism, Christianity, and Islam and that could, if recovered and honoured, transform our image both of God and Nature, not to mention ourselves. The Shekinah gives woman what she has lacked throughout the last two thousand years in Western civilization — a sacred image of the Divine Feminine that is reflected at the human level in herself. The Shekinah is Divine Motherhood, named as 'Mother of All Living' — the title that once belonged to the Goddess Asherah and was given to Eve in Genesis when the Myth of the Fall was created by the Deuteronomists. This suggests to me that the Shekinah of Kabbalah was originally the Goddess Asherah worshipped in the First Temple. The Shekinah is said to be in exile which she literally is, if we trace the beginning of her exile to the events in Jerusalem in 623 BCE.

Gershom Scholem, the great authority on Kabbalism, writes that the introduction of the idea of the feminine element in God "was one of the most important and lasting innovations of Kabbalism. The fact that it obtained recognition despite the obvious difficulty of reconciling it with the conception of the absolute unity of God, and that no other element of Kabbalism won such a degree of popular approval, is proof that it responded to a deep-seated religious need." He goes on to say that "the Shekinah is not only queen, daughter and bride of God, but also the mother of every individual in Israel. [I would venture to add, the mother of every individual in the world]. In the symbolic world of the Zohar, this new concept of the Shekinah as the symbol of 'eternal womanhood' occupies a place of immense importance and appears under an endless variety of names and images." [11]

In this extraordinary cosmology, the Shekinah or the feminine face of the godhead is named Cosmic Womb, Palace, Enclosure, Fountain, Apple Orchard, and Mystical Garden of Eden. She is described as the architect of worlds, source, or foundation of our world, and the Radiance, Word, or Glory of the unknowable ground or godhead. Text after text uses sexual imagery and the imagery of light to describe how the ray which emanates from the unknowable ground enters the womb — the Great Sea of Light — of the Celestial Mother and how she brings forth the male and female creative energies which, as two branches of the Tree of Life, are symbolically, King and Queen, Son, and Daughter. A third branch of the Tree descends directly down the centre, unifying and connecting the energies on either side. All elements or aspects of the Tree of Life are connected through twenty-two paths. The heart centre of these three branches or pillars as they are sometimes described, is called Tiphareth or Tifareth.

The Shekinah is named as the Divine Spouse, the indwelling and active Holy Spirit. She is the divine guide and immanent presence who delivers the world from bondage to beliefs that separate it from its source, restoring it ultimately to union with the divine ground. She brings into being all spheres or dimensions of manifestation which are ensouled and sustained by the ineffable source until, through them, she generates the manifest world we know and remains here until such time as the whole manifest creation is enfolded once again into its source. We are the 'sparks' of her Divine Being.

Kabbalism calls this last, tenth sphere *Malkuth*, the Kingdom, where the divine Mother-Father image is expressed as the male and female of all species. Humanity, female and male, is therefore the expression in this dimension of reality of the duality-in-unity of the God-head. The Shekinah is forever united with her beloved Spouse in the divine ground or heart of being and it is their union in the god-head that holds life in a constant state of coming into being. Yet she is also present, here with us, in the material reality of our world. The sexual attraction between man and woman and the expression of true love between them is the enactment or reflection at this level of creation of the divine embrace at its heart that is enshrined in the cherished words of the Song of Songs: "I am my beloved's and my beloved is mine." (6:3) Human sexual relationship, enacted with love, mutual respect, and joy, is a sacred ritual that is believed to maintain the ecstatic union of the divine pair.

Because she brings all worlds into existence as her robes or veils, and dwells in them as divine presence, nothing is outside spirit. In the radiance of that invisible cosmic Sea of Light, everything is connected to everything else as through a luminous circulatory system. Moreover, the Shekinah is deeply devoted to what she has brought into being, as a mother is devoted to the well-being of her child. All life on earth, all levels and degrees of consciousness, all forms of what we see and name as 'matter' are the creation of that primal fountain of Light and are therefore an expression of divinity.

Blue and gold are the colours associated with the Shekinah. As cosmic soul, She is the radiant ground or 'light body' of the human soul — at once its deepest, essential ground, its outer 'garment', the physical body, and its animating spirit or consciousness. She is the holy presence of the 'glory of God' within everyone. All of us, moving from unconsciousness and ignorance of this radiant ground to awareness of and relationship with it, live in her being and grow under her power of attraction until we are reunited with the source, discovering ourselves to be what in essence we always were but did not know ourselves to be — sons and daughters of God, living expressions of divine spirit. The blackness of the Shekinah's robe, comparable to the black robe or veil of Isis — who was also called 'The Widow' during her search for Osiris — signifies the darkness of the mystery which hides the glory of her Light.

I was amazed to discover that the Shekinah was called 'The Precious Stone' and 'The Stone of Exile' (lapis exilis), which at once connects her with the image of the Grail, described as both a vessel that is the source of bound-less nourishment, and as a stone. She was also called the 'Pearl', and 'The Burning Coal'. To the opening eyes of my imagination, she appeared as the glowing gold of the hidden treasure at the heart of life, the jewelled rainbow of light thrown between the divine and human worlds, the seamless robe which unites the manifest and unmanifest dimensions of life.

Here, at last, was the crucial missing piece of the mystery that I had sought to understand for over fifty years, ever since my mother's channeled Messages had told us to find 'the Stone at the foot of the Tree'. Here was the Shekinah described as 'The Precious Stone' at the foot of the Tree of Life. I was astounded and deeply moved by this discovery, yet I knew it was important not to cling to the literal imagery but to look beyond it, into the symbolic heart of the teaching and its meaning for our culture which has been so long deprived of the image of the Divine Feminine.

It suddenly occurred to me that the cosmology of Kabbalah is woven into the fabric of much-loved fairy-tales. In the story of Cinderella, for example, the veiled form of the Shekinah as the forgotten image of the Great Mother can be recognized as the fairy God-mother who presides over her daughter's transformation from soot-blackened drudge to royal bride. A later chapter (Cinderella) will explore this interpretation and show how the human soul dons these 'robes of glory' as she moves from the darkness of ignorance into the revelation of her true nature and parentage.

Notes:

1. This chapter is a condensed version of Chapter Three – The Tree of Life – in my book, *The Dream of the Cosmos: A Quest for the Soul*, Archive Publishing, Dorset, 2020. It was also published 2021 in a book called *Philo-Sophia: Wisdom Goddess Traditions*, edited by Debashish Banerji and Robert McDermott, Lotus Press, P O Box 325, Twin Lakes, Wisconsin, USA.
2. Scholem, Gershom, (1974) *Kabbalah*, Keter publishing House Jerusalem Ltd.
3. Scholem, Gershom G. (1941) *Major Trends in Jewish Mysticism*, Schocken Publishing House, Jerusalem, p. 159 and pp. 156-243
4. ibid, p. 204
5. Matt, Daniel (1995) *The Essential Kabbalah: The Heart of Jewish Mysticism*, Harper SanFrancisco, p. 6. The Torah comprises the first five books of the Old Testament, namely the books of Genesis, Exodus, Leviticus, Numbers and Deuteronomy.
6. ibid, p. 16
7. ibid, p. 24
8. ibid, p. 148
9. See Baring, Anne & Cashford, Jules (1992), *The Myth of the Goddess, Evolution of an Image*, Penguin Books Ltd., London, The Sacred Marriage, pp. 211-216 and Chapter 16, The Sacred Marriage of Goddess and God: The Reunion of Nature and Spirit.
10. Anthony, Mark (2021) *The Afterlife Frequency*, New World Library
11. Scholem, Gershom G. (1954 & 1961) *Major Trends in Jewish Mysticism*, Schocken Books, New York, pp. 229-230
See also *Kabbalah* by Gershom Scholem; *Zohar, The Book of Enlightenment* by Daniel C. Matt; *The Hebrew Goddess* by Raphael Patai and *The Way of Splendor, Jewish Mysticism and Modern Psychology* by Edward Hoffman.

The Holy Trinity, Urschalling, Bavaria,

9th century fresco on the church ceiling
showing a feminine figure between 'God the Father' and 'Jesus'.

Chapter Five

THE WISDOM TEXTS
HOLY SPIRIT, DIVINE WISDOM, SOPHIA

K abbalah offered me a vision that gives infinite value to life in this material dimension and a clear cosmology of connection between the invisible and visible dimensions of reality, between what kabbalists and alchemists called "The Great Above" and "The Great Below". In this Chapter, my desire to hear the voice of the Divine Feminine led me back to the Wisdom Texts, to the Book of Proverbs in the Old Testament and to two Books in the *Apocrypha*, as well as to a medieval text called the *Aurora Consurgens*. These, I knew would be only fragments of a great liturgy that has been lost because all traces of the Hebrew Goddess and her association with Wisdom were deleted from the Pentateuch, the first five Books of the Old Testament, with the sole exception of the Book of Proverbs.[1] The five Wisdom Books in the Old Testament consist of Job, Proverbs, Psalms, Eccesiastes, and The Song of Solomon (The Song of Songs). Included in the Wisdom Books are Ecclesiasticus or the Book of Jesus Ben Sira, and The Wisdom of Solomon in the *Apocrypha*. In this chapter I will focus on Proverbs 8 and the two Wisdom Books in the *Apocrypha*.

When writing *The Myth of the Goddess*, Jules Cashford and I had followed the image of the Divine Feminine or Great Mother from the Palaeolithic era onwards. I knew that behind the image of the Shekinah stood the great goddesses of the Bronze Age, above all, Inanna in Sumer, Maat and Isis in Egypt and later, Athena in Greece. Beyond them was the distant form of the Neolithic Great Mother and the extraordinary revelation of the forgotten Civilization of the Goddess (6,500 – 3,500 BCE), so named by Marija Gimbutas, the brilliant Lithuanian archaeologist who discovered it. Many people, including many historians and archaeologists, have never heard of this civilization yet it is of great importance for our understanding of what preceded the earliest known civilizations and was destroyed so long ago. [2]

It seemed to me that there were elements in Kabbalah that paralleled the Hindu concept of Shakti and her cosmic union with Shiva. This suggested to me that an original tradition of the unity of the two aspects of the source of life

— personified by a god and goddess — was at one time disseminated through India, Mesopotamia and Egypt but was gradually lost with the rise of the three patriarchal religions. What is left today are a few precious fragments of a very ancient pre-Flood cosmology that may have originated in Atlantis. As mentioned in Chapter One, it is now known that Atlantis established communities in different parts of the world, both in the East and the West, before its final disappearance, described by Plato in his *Timaeus* and *Critias*. [3]

As we move into the Christian era, there was a profound shift in archetypal imagery and a loss of the *feminine* image of Divine Wisdom and the Holy Spirit. From the time of the Council of Nicaea in 325 CE, Wisdom was associated with Christ as the Logos, the Divine Word, and lost all connection with the Divine Feminine. The original connection between the Holy Spirit and Divine Wisdom with the Goddess Asherah as Queen of Heaven and "Mother of All Living" in ancient Hebrew cosmology was long forgotten. The connection of the Holy Spirit with Sophia in the Greek and Gnostic world, was also irrevocably lost. As I read the texts from different traditions, it gradually became clear to me that the esoteric stream of Gnostic Christianity, Kabbalah and Alchemy had carried forward from the city of Alexandria the ancient cosmology of the Divine Feminine which was to disappear over the centuries of the Christian era. The deletion of the image of the Divine Feminine from the god-head in 623 BCE was the principal cause of this loss.

The eradication of all traces of shamanic communion with the inner dimension of reality and the loss of the awareness that nature was ensouled with spirit and therefore sacred, ultimately removed from the people who lived during the millennia of the three patriarchal religions their age-old sense of living within the invisible cosmic being of a Great Mother. In the West, it was only in Celtic Christianity that the belief that nature was sacred and animated by spirit survived and then only until the Synod of Whitby in 611 CE.

The Wisdom Texts

To reconnect with the tradition of the Divine Feminine that has been fragmented and almost lost over some two and a half thousand years, to hear her barely audible voice, I turned to the Wisdom Texts: to the Book of Proverbs in the Old Testament and the magnificent passages in the Books of Jesus Ben Sira (Ecclesiasticus) and the Wisdom of Solomon in the *Apocrypha*. The two later Books included in the *Apocrypha* most probably owe their existence to what was preserved of the pre-Deuteronomist Wisdom tradition by the Essenes and by the Gnostic Christians living in Jerusalem and Alexandria. The words of these texts offer the most vivid and powerful imagery of the immanence of spirit in the life of this planet. They transmute all creation and the apparent insignificance of our lives into something precious and sacred, to be loved, embraced, cherished, and celebrated because the life we see and experience here is the epiphany or manifestation of the Divine Ground that has brought us into being and contains our world within itself.

This deeper understanding of life radiates from the Book of Proverbs, and the Book of Ben Sira (Ecclesiasticus) in the *Apocrypha*, where Wisdom speaks as the Holy Spirit, calling to humanity to listen to her. Unknown and unrecognized, she says she is working within the depths of life, within the depths of nature and our nature, yearning to open our hearts and minds to her presence, her justice, her wisdom, her compassion, and her truth. As I read these passages, it seemed to me that I was listening to the voice of the Shekinah speaking to the souls of humanity who were the scattered sparks of her divinity.

Image of Wisdom —— Notre Dame, Paris

As with the loss of the tradition of the Divine Feminine in Christianity, there is also the story of the previous loss in the Jewish tradition, described in Chapter Three. However, as mentioned in that Chapter and in Chapter Four, the ancient cult of a female deity who was the Queen of Heaven and the Protectress of Jerusalem fortunately did not die out after Josiah's purge but was carried to the city of Alexandria by the Jews who rejected the new Temple regime forcibly imposed on them by the Deuteronomists. They took with them the traditions, rituals and cosmology of the First Temple which was focussed on the worship of the Queen of Heaven, whose former titles were Divine Wisdom and the Holy Spirit and whose sacred image was the Tree of Life, bestower of the fruit of immortality. This first exodus was followed by a second wave, at the time of the Babylonian Captivity in 586 BCE, when the First Temple in Jerusalem, originally built by Solomon, was destroyed by the Babylonians, the city sacked and many of its inhabitants carried off into captivity in Babylon. Some, however, fled to Egypt where they joined the Jewish community already established in the city of Alexandria. The First Temple, described as a harlot after the Deuteronomists' purge, was destroyed by the Babylonians. It was rebuilt as the Second Temple after the end of the Babylonian Captivity and completed by 515 BCE.

A few years after this exodus, the prophet Jeremiah visited Alexandria and accused the Jewish community there of causing the destruction of the Temple and the sacking of Jerusalem by the Babylonians, blaming these disasters on their worship of the Queen of Heaven. However, the multitude of men and women who had gathered to hear him were having none of this and Jeremiah must have retired, discomfited, from his attempt to blame them. This is what they said:

> As for the word that thou hast spoken unto us in the name of the Lord we will not hearken unto thee but we will certainly do whatsoever thing goeth forth out of our own mouth, to burn incense unto the Queen of Heaven and to pour out drink offerings unto her, as we have done, we, and our fathers, our kings, and our princes, in the cities of Judah, and in the streets of Jerusalem: for then we had plenty of victuals and were well and saw no evil. But since we left off to burn incense to the Queen of Heaven, and to pour out drink offerings unto her, we have wanted all things, and have been consumed by the sword and by the famine. (Jer. 44:15-20)

In the first century, there were over a million Jews living in Alexandria. This Jewish community is known to have welcomed Gnostics, precious fragments of whose teachings came to light at Nag Hammadi in 1945. It also, in my view, nurtured the Love-Wisdom cosmology of the First Temple tradition which later surfaced a thousand years later in Spain as the teaching of Kabbalah, culminating in Moses de León's astonishing *Zohar*. How this transmission occurred, is still a mystery. It may have occurred through students of a second century Gnostic teacher called Basilides who were known to have taken his teaching to Spain. (see Chapter Six)

The Jewish Community in Alexandria

The Jewish community in Alexandria, reproached by Jeremiah, continued to preserve their worship of a female deity whom they addressed as Divine Wisdom, Queen of Heaven, and Holy Spirit. Among the later texts which enshrined this Wisdom tradition was the Book of the Wisdom of Jesus ben Sira, also known as Ecclesiasticus, that was originally written in Jerusalem c.180–175 BCE but was taken to Alexandria by his grandson after 132 BCE, and translated into Greek for Greek-speaking Jews living there. It is to be found in the *Apocrypha* section of the Catholic Bible but not in the Protestant Bible. It enshrines the magnificent passages where Wisdom speaks to the world. Around 100 BCE, the Book of the Wisdom of Solomon was also written in Greek, in Alexandria. The writer describes Wisdom sitting by the throne of the Lord in heaven (9:10) and as the Holy Spirit (9:17) Could the authors of these two books have drawn upon much older Wisdom tradition material originating in the First Temple that may have been passed secretly from hand to hand?

The destruction of the Second Temple by the Romans and the devastating sack of Jerusalem in 70 CE led to a final exodus of Jews to Alexandria. Soon after this date a group of rabbis met together in the university of Jamnia to define what would, in future, constitute their canon of holy books. Except for certain passages in the Book of Proverbs, all other traces of Wisdom, including the two Books mentioned above, were not included in this canon of texts.

What is so interesting about this story is that the Jewish communities in Alexandria and elsewhere in Egypt—probably in the many Essene communities established there — as well as in Essene communities in Palestine, were able to preserve the teachings, cosmology and possibly even the rituals from the First Temple in Jerusalem.

In the Book of Ben Sira, written in Jerusalem, and the Book of the Wisdom of Solomon, written in Alexandria, Wisdom was symbolized by a Tree of Life and by water. Like the ancient Goddesses Inanna and Isis and the Hebrew Goddess Asherah, she was the Queen of Heaven. "She was both the mother and consort of the kings, but also the consort of the Lord. She gave eternal life/resurrection, she fed her devotees. Her Light was radiant, superior to earthly light. She was the Mother of all creation. She was also the anointing oil, the archetypal angel high priest, the genius of Jerusalem and its protectress." [4]

It is a strange and interesting fact that the Church of Rome retained the Old Testament as well as the Books included in the *Apocrypha* relating to Divine Wisdom and the Holy Spirit, while the mainstream Jewish canon, formulated at Jamnia, discarded the latter. The reason the Church of Rome was able to inherit them was because when the Christian missionaries from Alexandria took the new teaching into the Greek speaking world of the Mediterranean, they took with them the Greek Scriptures from the community in Alexandria, descended from the Jewish population that continued to venerate the Queen of Heaven.

The Removal and Destruction of many Gospels

Apart from the Wisdom texts mentioned above, the material transmitted to the early Christian Church from the Jewish communities in Egypt and elsewhere had many gospels which were later, under the influence of Irenaeus (130-202 CE), Bishop of Lyons in the second century CE, removed from the canon of texts that were to become the foundation of Church doctrine and teaching. He retained only the four gospels we know today, naming them in the order of John, Luke, Matthew, and Mark. Less than two hundred years after the selection made by Irenaeus, two edicts of the emperor Constantine in 326 and 333 CE, ordered the burning of any gospels outside the established canon of these four. This suggests that many of the previously excluded gospels were still in circulation. In issuing this edict to destroy the gospels, Constantine was influenced by Athanasius, the powerful Bishop of Alexandria who had presided over the Council of Nicaea.

As explained in Chapter Three, at this crucially important Council, the Holy Spirit was defined in the male gender and became part of the Nicene Creed recited by Christians to this day. Wisdom, once associated with the Holy Spirit in the First Temple, was henceforth associated with Christ as the Logos, the Divine Word, and lost all connection with the Divine Feminine and the feminine Holy Spirit. In this way, the ancient connection between the Holy Spirit and the Divine Feminine was irrevocably and, for Western civilization, tragically lost.

Around 382 CE Pope Damasus 1 commissioned his secretary, Jerome, to produce a new translation in Latin, from the various Latin versions of the Septuagint which were not organized into a single volume. Jerome set about the task with understandable trepidation, but also with assiduous commitment. He learnt Hebrew and, thanks to the work of the formidable early Christian scholar and theologian, Origen of Alexandria (c. 185 - c. 253 CE), was able to access texts in both Hebrew and Greek. The resulting translation, produced in the Latin of the people, became known as the Vulgate. It may have been in the course of his arduous work of translation that the Hebrew rendering of *ruach* — the feminine noun for spirit — was translated into the genderless Greek word *pneuma* and then into the Latin *spiritus sanctus*. However, Jerome's translation was made *after* the Council of Nicaea so it is not possible to say that his translation led to the Holy Spirit being defined as male at this Council but it is worth noting that the change of gender may have occurred in an earlier process of translation. In Syriac and Aramaic, as well as Hebrew, the word for spirit is feminine.

Some fifty years after the Council of Nicaea, in 381 CE, a decree was made by the emperor Theodosius 1, which declared that anyone who did not comply with his edict that all must believe in the Nicene Creed, that the Father, Son and Holy Spirit were of one and the same substance would be declared a heretic. This decree of Theodosius, as well as later ones between 389 and 391 CE led not only to the persecution of heretics but also to the destruction of any remaining gnostic gospels. They led also to the attack on the Pagan religions and the destruction of their shrines and magnificent temples, including the temple of Eleusis. They even forbade people to enter these temples. Through these decrees, the idea entered Christian teaching that hell and eternal punishment awaited heretics and unbelievers.[5] Evidently, the Church had by this time, already lost touch with the teaching of Jesus, and had become inflated by the power that had accrued to it through its fusion with the Roman Empire.

In one of the gospels lost or destroyed during this time — the *Gospel of the Hebrews* — a Gospel that was only known to have existed from quotations in the work of the early Christian Fathers, Origen and Jerome, the Holy Spirit was described as the *Mother* of Jesus, who spoke to him at his baptism, saying "My Son, in all the prophets I was waiting for Thee." "Here," the late Professor Gilles Quispel (one of the great authorities on the Gnostic Gospels) writes, "we come to a very simple realization: just as the birth requires a mother, so rebirth requires a spiritual mother. Originally, the Christian term "rebirth" must therefore have been associated with the concept of the spirit as a femnine hypostasis." [6] I was interested to discover that the late Father Bede Griffiths, one of the great philosopher-mystics of our time, asked in his book, *Return to the Centre*, "May we not say that the Holy Spirit is feminine?" [7]

The image of Divine Wisdom survived in the Eastern Churches, where she appears in all her ancient splendour. In the cathedral of Novgorod, Sophia is depicted as a fiery winged angel... enthroned where one would expect to see the figure of Christ, crowned as the Queen of Heaven, and holding the scroll of true knowledge and the serpent staff, her ancient symbol. In 537 CE, the emperor Justinian built the magnificent Basilica of *Haghia Sophia* in Byzantium and placed the figure of Divine Wisdom in the apse. It has recently been transformed into a mosque.

Dr Margaret Barker writes in the Prologue to her most recent book, *The Great Lady*, referring to the images (overleaf) on its front and back covers:

Look at the great mosaic of a woman dressed in blue in the east end of the Catholic cathedral on the island of Murano near Venice. It was made about 800 years ago and put in the most prominent place in this huge building. The half-dome ceiling over the altar, called the apse, is filled by a huge mosaic of the Great Lady. Her blue garments are fringed with gold and decorated with gold crosses. She stands on a jewelled platform with hands slightly raised so that we see her palms. Her head is surrounded by a halo of light, and on either side of her head are Greek letters which are an abbreviation of her title: Mother of God.

There is a similar mosaic in the Orthodox cathedral in Kyiv, the capital of Ukraine. It is about 200 years older than the mosaic in Murano. The presence of the same Great Lady fills the apse at the east end of the building. She wears a blue dress and a golden hooded cloak called a *maphorion*. She too stands on a jewelled platform and has a halo of light. Her hands are raised — higher than the Great Lady's of Murano — and her palms can be seen. She too is named the Mother of God. The cathedral is dedicated to the Holy Wisdom, a figure hardly known in the Western Church.

She is the Great Lady of the ancient temple in Jerusalem. She had many names and titles: She was known as the Holy Wisdom, and so appears in the cathedral of the Holy Wisdom in Kyiv.... She is the Great Lady of the ancient temple in Jerusalem, which was built by King Solomon about 950 BCE.... She was the Great Lady of Jerusalem who was important for the first Christians. The Great Lady was the heavenly protector of Jerusalem who reigned from her temple until she was driven out. Her people had suffered ever since and still long for her return. [8]

Dr Barker, in the same Prologue, identifies the Great Lady with 'the Woman clothed with the sun' in the Book of Revelation, Chapter 12: "And there appeared a great wonder in heaven; a woman clothed with the sun, and the moon under her feet, and on her head a crown of twelve stars." She ends her Prologue with the words: "This is the story I shall tell: how the Great Lady became the Lost Lady." I believe we can identify the Lost Lady with the exiled Shekinah described in the last Chapter as well as with the Goddess Asherah who was banished from the First Temple.

The Reformation and the Final Phase of the Loss of the Divine Feminine

A further loss of the texts and imagery of the Divine Feminine came with the Reformation in the sixteenth century, when the Protestant Church decided to adopt the Biblical texts from the Hebrew canon that was defined at the University of Jamnia shortly after 70 CE. It rejected the texts that belonged to the earlier traditions which had taken root in Egypt and been transmitted to the early Christian Church. To these Protestants, any mention of a female

Above: *Catholic cathedral dedicated to Sophia, Island of Murano, Venice, Italy*
Overleaf: *Orthodox cathedral dedicated to the Holy Wisdom, Kyiv, Ukraine*

divinity was anathema, and so the magnificent verses in the Wisdom of
Solomon and the Wisdom of Ben Sira were excluded from the Protestant canon

and are unknown to Protestant Christians, although they could still read the Book of Proverbs. The Catholic Church fortunately retained these Wisdom texts and included them in the part of their Bible known as the *Apocrypha*.

The Wisdom Texts

As we read the words in the Book of Proverbs, we can feel the presence of The Great Lady, as Divine Wisdom comes to life. The verses of this Book were written down from the time of Solomon (970-931 BCE) to the time of King Hezekiah (726-697) BCE. They therefore long predate and somehow survived the reforms of King Josiah and the Deuteronomists. In Proverbs, there are verses where Wisdom says that she is the Beloved of the Lord, with Him from the beginning, before the foundation of the world. She speaks from the deep ground of life as the hidden law which orders it and as the craftswoman of creation. Here are the words, written down millennia ago and miraculously, never lost:

> The Lord possessed me in the beginning of his way,
> before his works of old.
> I was set up from everlasting, from the beginning,
> or ever the earth was.
> When there were no depths, I was brought forth;
> When there were no fountains abounding with water.
> Before the mountains were settled,.
> before the hills was I brought forth:
> While as yet he had not made the earth, nor the fields,
> nor the beginning of the dust of the world.
> When he established the heavens, I was there:
> when he set a circle upon the face of the deep:
> When he made firm the skies above:
> when the fountains of the deep became strong:
> When he gave to the sea its bound,
> that the waters should not transgress his commandment:
> When he marked out the foundations of the earth:
> Then I was by him, as a master craftsman,
> And I was daily his delight, rejoicing always before him;
> Rejoicing in the habitable earth;
> And my delight was with the sons of men.

— Proverbs 8.22-31

In the much later Books of Ben Sira and the Wisdom of Solomon in the *Apocrypha*, Wisdom tells us that she is immanent in our world, with us in the streets of our cities, calling to us to awaken to her presence, to obey her laws, to listen to her wisdom, promising her blessing if we can only hear her voice and respond to her teaching. With their vivid imagery, these passages transform the idea of the Holy Spirit, speaking as Divine Wisdom, from abstract idea into living presence. She speaks as if she were here, in this dimension, dwelling with us, in the midst of her kingdom, accessible to those who seek her out. She is unknown and unrecognized, yet working within the depths of life, striving to open our understanding to the divine reality of her being, the sacredness of her creation, and her justice, wisdom, love, and truth. Speaking as the Tree of Life, She appeals to all those who are desirous of her, to fill themselves with her fruits, "For my memorial is sweeter than honey, and mine inheritance than the honeycomb." (Ben Sira 24.20)

In the Wisdom of Ben Sira, also known as Ecclesiasticus, Divine Wisdom, the Holy Spirit, tells us her story, in imagery that celebrates her connection with the earth, its trees and plants, and its people:

> I came out of the mouth of the most high,
> and covered the earth as a cloud.
> I dwelt in high places,
> and my throne is in a cloudy pillar.
> I alone compassed the circuit of heaven,
> and walked in the bottom of the deep.
> I had power over the waves of the sea, and over all the earth,
> and over every people and nation...
>
> He created me from the beginning before the world,
> and I shall never fail.
> In the holy tabernacle I served before him;
> and so was I established in Sion.
> Likewise in the beloved city he gave me rest,
> and in Jerusalem was my power...
>
> I was exalted like a cedar in Libanus,
> and as a cypress tree upon the mountains of Hermon.
> I was exalted like a palm tree in En-gaddi,
> and as a rose plant in Jericho,
> as a fair olive tree in a pleasant field,
> and grew up as a plane tree by the water...
>
> I gave a sweet smell like cinnamon and aspalathus,
> and I yielded a pleasant odour like the best myrrh...
> As the turpentine tree I stretched out my branches,
> and my branches are the branches of honour and grace.
> As the vine brought I forth pleasant savour,
> and my flowers are the fruit of honour and riches.
>
> I am the mother of fair love, and fear,
> and knowledge and holy hope...

I therefore, being eternal, am given to all my children
which are named of him.
Come unto me, all ye that be desirous of me,
and fill yourselves with my fruits.
For my memorial is sweeter than honey,
and mine inheritance than the honey-comb...

The first man knew her not perfectly,
no more shall the last find her out.
For her thoughts are more than the sea,
and her counsels profounder than the great deep.

I also came out as a brook from a river,
and as a conduit into a garden.
I said, I will water my best garden,
and will water abundantly my garden bed:
and lo, my brook became a river,
and my river became a sea.

I will yet make doctrine to shine as the morning,
and will send forth her light afar off.
I will yet pour out doctrine as prophecy,
and leave it to all ages for ever.
Behold that I have not laboured for myself only,
but for all them that seek wisdom.

— Wisdom of Ben Sira 24.3-6, 9-11, 13-21, 28-34

Here is the language of the immanence of the Divine Feminine in the world. Who wrote these magnificent verses? Was he a high-priest of the First Temple whose words were preserved by the Jewish communities in Jerusalem and Alexandria and written down later by Jesus Ben Sira, whose grandson later translated them into Greek? Or did Ben Sira himself write them? Did he write down words he heard speaking to him in a manner similar to how Moses de León channeled some of the material in the *Zohar*, or did he have a vision of a great feminine being, as Apuleius had of the goddess Isis and I had in my visionary dream? The verses reveal this feminine Presence — whom we can name as Divine Wisdom and the Holy Spirit — to be the intelligence of the Cosmos, rooted in tree, vine, earth and water and active in the habitations of humanity. She is the principal of justice that inspires human laws. She is invisible spirit guiding human consciousness; a hidden presence longing to be known, calling out to the world for recognition and relationship.

Who can number the sand of the sea,
and the drops of rain,
and the days of eternity?
Who can find out the height of heaven,
and the breadth of the earth,
and the deep, and Wisdom?
Wisdom hath been created before all things,
and the understanding of prudence from everlasting.
The word of God most high is the fountain of Wisdom;
and her ways are everlasting commandments.
To whom hath the root of Wisdom been revealed?
or who hath known her wise counsels?

— Wisdom of Ben Sira 1.2-6

As a mother shall she meet him.
With the Bread of Understanding
shall she feed him,
and give him the Water of Wisdom to drink.

— Wisdom of Ben Sira 15.2-3

Come, eat of my bread
and drink of the wine that I have mixed.
Leave the simple ones, and live
and walk in the way of insight

— Proverbs 9.5, Sira 21.21

In the Book of the Wisdom of Solomon, also in the *Apocrypha*, we find further verses that still offer a message to our time:

Wisdom is glorious, and never fadeth away:
yea, she is easily seen of them that love her,
and found of such as seek her.
She preventeth them that desire her,
in making herself first known unto them.
Whoso seeketh her early shall have no great travail:
for he shall find her sitting at his doors.
To think therefore upon her is perfection of wisdom:
and whoso watcheth for her shall quickly be without care.
For she goeth about seeking such as are worthy of her;
showeth herself to them in the ways,
and meeteth them in every thought.
For the very true beginning of her is the desire of discipline;

and the care of discipline is love;
and love is the keeping of her laws;
and the giving heed unto her laws is the assurance of incorruption;
and incorruption maketh us near unto God.
Therefore the desire of wisdom bringeth to a kingdom.

— Wisdom of Solomon 6.12-20

Solomon himself prized Wisdom more highly than rubies. Wisdom was his wise and luminous guide. Tears always come into my eyes when I read these words aloud:

Wherefore I prayed, and understanding was given me:
I called upon God, and the Spirit of Wisdom came to me...
I loved her above health and beauty,
and chose to have her instead of light,
for the Light that cometh from her never goeth out....

And all such things as are either secret or manifest, them I know.
For Wisdom, which is the worker of all things, taught me;
for in her is an understanding spirit,
holy, one only, manifold, subtil, lively, clear, undefiled,
plain, not subject to hurt, loving the thing that is good, quick,
which cannot be letted, ready to do good.

Kind to man, stedfast, sure, free from care,
having all power, overseeing all things,
and going through all understanding, pure, and most subtil, spirits.
For Wisdom is more moving than any motion:
she passeth and goeth
through all things by reason of her pureness.

For she is the breath of the power of God,
and a pure influence flowing from the glory of the Almighty:
therefore can no defiled thing fall into her.
For she is the brightness of the everlasting Light,
the unspotted mirror of the power of God,
and the image of his goodness.

And being but one, she can do all things:
and remaining in herself, she maketh all things new:
and in all ages entering into holy souls,
she maketh them friends of God, and prophets.
For God loveth none but him that dwelleth with Wisdom.

For she is more beautiful than the sun,
and above all the order of stars:
being compared with the Light, she is found before it....
Wisdom reacheth from one end to another mightily:
and sweetly doth she order all things.
I loved her, and sought her out from my youth,
I desired to make her my spouse,
and I was a lover of her beauty.

— Wisdom of Solomon 7.7, 10.21-29, 8.1-2

The Aurora Consurgens [9]

There is a medieval alchemical text called the *Aurora Consurgens*, which I feel should be included with the Wisdom Texts, not only because its words are exquisitely beautiful but the commentary by one of Jung's closest colleagues, Dr. Marie Louise von Franz, is profound and illuminating. She writes:

> The *Aurora* is one of the earliest medieval treatises in which we find the nascent idea that the alchemical *opus* involves an inner experience and that a numinous content — Wisdom — is the secret which the adept was looking for in the chemical substances [in his retort]."[10] "We can understand how shattered the author of *Aurora* must have been when Wisdom suddenly appeared to him in personal form.... For an intellectual it is a shattering experience when he discovers that what he was seeking is not just an idea but is psychically real in a far deeper sense and can come upon him like a thunderclap. He is saying that she is devastatingly real, actual and palpably present in matter. [11]

This book carries forward elements from the passage attributed to Solomon quoted above and from other verses included in this chapter. The author of the book, who was believed by Dr. von Franz, to be St. Thomas Aquinas himself, is speaking of a vision and a revelation he had just prior to his passing, a revelation that was written down as he spoke by the monks sitting with him. In the first chapter he mentions a feminine figure whom he identifies with Divine Wisdom and who is the same figure who appears in Proverbs, ben Sira and the Wisdom of Solomon. He writes, "All good things came to me together with her, that Wisdom of the South, who preacheth abroad, who uttereth her voice in the streets, crieth out at the head of the multitudes, and in the entrance of the gates of the city uttereth her words, saying, "Come ye to me and be enlightened, and your operations shall not be confounded; all ye that desire me shall be filled with my riches.... I will teach you the science of God." And he continues:

She it is that Solomon chose to have instead of light, and above all beauty and health.... For all gold in her sight shall be esteemed as a little sand, and silver shall be counted as clay.... And her fruit is more precious than all the riches of this world, and all the things that are desired are not to be compared with her.... She is a tree of life to them that lay hold on her, and an unfailing light.... He who hath found this science, it shall be his rightful food for ever.... Such a one is as rich as he that hath a stone from which fire is struck, who can give fire to whom he will as much as he will and when he will without loss to himself.

And Wisdom speaks to him:

Be turned to me with all your heart and do not cast me aside because I am black and swarthy, because the sun hath changed my colour and the waters have covered my face... because I stick fast in the mire of the deep and my substance is not disclosed. Wherefore out of the depths have I cried, and from the abyss of the earth with my voice to all you that pass by the way. Attend and see me, if any shall find one like unto me, I will give into his hand the morning star.

And in words that resonate with those attributed to Jesus, and also with the work of the later alchemists:

I am that land of holy promise, which floweth with milk and honey and bringeth forth sweetest fruit in due season; wherefore have all the philosophers commended me and sowed in me their gold and silver and incombustible grain. And unless that grain falling into me die, itself shall remain alone, but if it die, it bringeth forth threefold fruit: for the first it shall bring forth shall be good because it was sown in good earth, namely of pearls; the second likewise good because it was sown in better earth, namely of leaves (silver); the third shall bring forth a thousandfold because it was sown in the best earth, namely of gold. For from the fruits of this grain is made the food of life, which cometh down from heaven. If any man shall eat of it, he shall live without hunger. [12]

The Sacred Marriage of the Mother-Father of the Cosmos

I will end this chapter on the Wisdom Texts, with Neil Douglas-Klotz's *Prayers of the Cosmos,* and his beautiful translation of the Lord's Prayer from the Aramaic language that Jesus spoke. Here, a startling image of the sacred marriage of the Father and Mother of the Cosmos, similar to that given in Kabbalah emerges. As he writes in his Introduction: "Aramaic was the common spoken language throughout the Middle East at the time of Jesus and the tongue in which he expressed his teachings.... Unlike Greek, Aramaic presents a fluid and holistic view of the cosmos. The arbitrary borders found in Greek between 'mind,' 'body,' and 'spirit' fall away. Furthermore, like its sister languages Hebrew and Arabic, Aramaic can express many layers of meaning. Words are organized and defined based on a poetic root-and-pattern system, so that each word may have several meanings, at first seemingly unrelated, but upon contemplation revealing an inner connection.... Jesus showed a mastery of this use of transformative language, which survives even through inadequate translations. In addition, the Aramaic language is close to the earth, rich in images of planting and harvesting, full of the natural wonder of the cosmos. 'Heaven' in Aramaic ceases to be a metaphysical concept and presents the image of 'light and sound shining through all creation.' Like its native Middle Eastern predecessors and like other native languages around the planet, Aramaic is rich in sound meaning; that is, one can feel direction, colour, movement, and other sensations as certain sacred words resonate in the body. This body resonance was another layer of meaning for the hearers of Jesus' words and for the native Middle Eastern mystic." [13]

Here, with his permission, is Neil's translation from the Aramaic that Jesus spoke, of the first line of the Lord's Prayer, which in the Christian Bible (KJV) is rendered "Our Father which art in heaven."

O Birther! Father-Mother of the Cosmos,
You create all that moves
in light.

O Thou! The Breathing Life of all,
Creator of the Shimmering Sound that
touches us.

Respiration of all worlds,
we hear you breathing – in and out –
in silence.

Source of Sound: in the roar and the whisper,
In the breeze and the whirlwind, we
hear your Name.

Radiant One: You shine within us,
outside us – even darkness shines – when
we remember.

Name of names, our small identity
Unravels in you, you give it back
as a lesson.

Wordless Action, Silent Potency –
Where ears and eyes awaken, there
heaven comes.

O Birther! Father-Mother of the Cosmos!

Notes:

1. see Dr Margaret Barker's latest book, *The Great Lady*, for a description of how The Great Lady was lost in the process of editing out or altering all references to her in the Pentateuch or first five books of the Old Testament. pp. 6-13
2. Wonderful artefacts from this civilization were included in a book called *The World of Old Europe: The Danube Valley 5000 to 3,500 BC* and were also shown in an exhibition in New York and the Ashmolean Museum, Oxford. They can also be found online under this title.
3. Wilson, Stuart & Joanna Prentis (2011), *Atlantis & The New Consciousness*, Ozark Mountain Publishing, Huntsville AR, p. 107
4. Barker, Dr Margaret, (2023) *The Great Lady, Restoring Her Story*, Sheffield Phoenix Press.I know this quotation is from one of Dr Barker's books but I cannot find the exact reference for it and she has been unable to help me find it. Therefore, I refer the reader to her latest book, *The Great Lady* and to her website… www.margaretbarker.com
5. Freeman, Charles (2008) *AD 381: Heretics, Pagans and the Christian State*, Pimlico, Random House, London, passim
6. Quispel, Gilles, (1973) *The Birth of the Child*, page 23. Eranos Lectures 3: *Jewish and Gnostic Man*, Gershom Scholem and Gilles Quispel. Professor Quispel was one of the four original translators of the Gospel of Thomas.
7. Griffiths, Father Bede (1976) *Return to the Centre*, Collins, London, p. 62
8. Barker, Dr Margaret, *The Great Lady*, Prologue
9. *Aurora Consurgens*, Routledge and Kegan Paul, London, 1966, Bollingen Foundation, New York
10. ibid, p. 186
11. ibid, p. 62
12. ibid, pp. 142-3
13. Douglas-Klotz, Neil (1990), *Prayers of the Cosmos: Meditations on the Aramaic Words of Jesus*, Foreword by Matthew Fox, HarperSanFrancisco, p. 12. See also *The Hidden Gospel: Decoding the message of the Aramaic Jesus*, Quest Books, 1999.

Ms. 64 (97.MG.21), fol. 11
Wisdom

probably 1170s, unknown artist/maker

Within the arc of heaven, the personification of Wisdom, flanked by David and Abraham, supports God the Creator. Below her is the priest Zechariah, father of John the Baptist, and below him the patriarch Jacob.

Chapter Six

THE GNOSTICS: PART ONE

We must close our eyes and invoke a new manner of seeing... a wakefulness
that is the birthright of us all, though few put it to use.

— Plotinus

No study of Western civilization or, indeed, of Christianity, can be complete without including Gnosticism: for Gnosticism is the Second Corner-Stone that the builders have rejected, a forgotten treasure consigned to our past, a treasure that, like the Hebrew Goddess, disappeared almost without trace. It is an essential part of the underground stream that flowed from the Mysteries of the pre-Christian world into Kabbalah, Alchemy and other spiritual movements in the later Middle Ages. Gnosticism grew out of Egyptian, Hebrew, and Greek and possibly even Indian spiritual and mystical traditions.

Gnostics were called "knowers" because they addressed the deeper questions of our existence — "Who are we? Where do we come from? Why are we here? Where do we go when we die?" — and followed an inner path of relationship with spirit. Gnostics had a complex creation story that was startlingly different from the one in the Book of Genesis. They were concerned with the nature of the universe, the origin of evil, the fall and redemption of the soul and the survival of the soul after death. Jewish Gnostics would have been aware of the role of Wisdom in the Book of Proverbs. Greek Gnostics would have known about the myth of Demeter and Persephone and the Mysteries of Eleusis, even if they were not initiates of them. They would have been aware that spiritual growth develops from inner illumination rather than by following a set of beliefs, precepts or admonitions given by an outer authority.

This vital stream of esoteric teaching which was to suffer relentless persecution at the hands of two Roman emperors Constantine and Theodosius 1, in the early and late fourth century, as well as from the growing power of the Christian Church in Rome, is the missing counterpart of the Christian story that is familiar to us. It is an important yet largely unknown aspect of our spiritual inheritance. In a patriarchal, largely extrovert civilization, it belongs to the neglected understanding of the existence and experience of the soul, and the priceless Wisdom legacy of the great civilizations that preceded the patriarchal era. We may ask what our modern culture might have looked like if the gnostic insights had not been destroyed or driven underground. Today, we can see that concerns that were of interest to the Gnostics are returning after an interval of sixteen hundred years: concerns such as the absence of the feminine in the image of God, the survival of the soul and the nature of consciousness — perhaps because many of the souls living then have reincarnated in our time. We are recovering fragments today of what was then widely known, understood and experienced.

The Importance of the City of Alexandria

The city of Alexandria, founded by Alexander the Great in 331 BCE, plays a vitally important role in the transmission of knowledge from the ancient world to future generations. In Hellenistic Alexandria, the great city founded by Alexander the Great in 328 BCE, Egyptian, Greek and Jewish traditions met and mingled for a few centuries in a climate of tolerance. Neo-Platonism, originating with the teaching of the Greek philosopher Plotinus (204-270 CE) took root and flourished there. One of its greatest teachers was the Neo-Platonist philosopher Hypatia who taught in the university for fifteen years from 400 CE until she was murdered by a Christian mob. This extraordinary city was famous for its Great Library and the unusually comprehensive curriculum of its university which drew students to it from all over the Mediterranean world.[1] The new Christian teachings fell on ground prepared by centuries of metaphysical enquiry which had been the focus of discussion among the Jewish and Greek communities in this city and in the wider Greek and later Roman Empire.

By the first century CE, Alexandria was a vibrant, tumultuous city with over a million inhabitants. Its extensive harbour was filled with people embarking and disembarking from ships loaded with goods from the many ports in the Mediterranean, from as far East as Caesarea in Palestine and as far West as Marseilles in Gaul, and the coastal cities of Spain. Its merchants traded with ports as far away as the west coast of India, for India was the greatest trading partner of the Roman Empire, importing from those distant destinations, silks, jewels, spices, ivory and a multitude of other luxuries in exchange for gold.[2]

Two of the five divisions of the city were Jewish. More Jews lived here than in Palestine and mixing freely with Egyptians and Greeks, their attitude to other religious traditions was liberal. Alexandria was *the* great city of

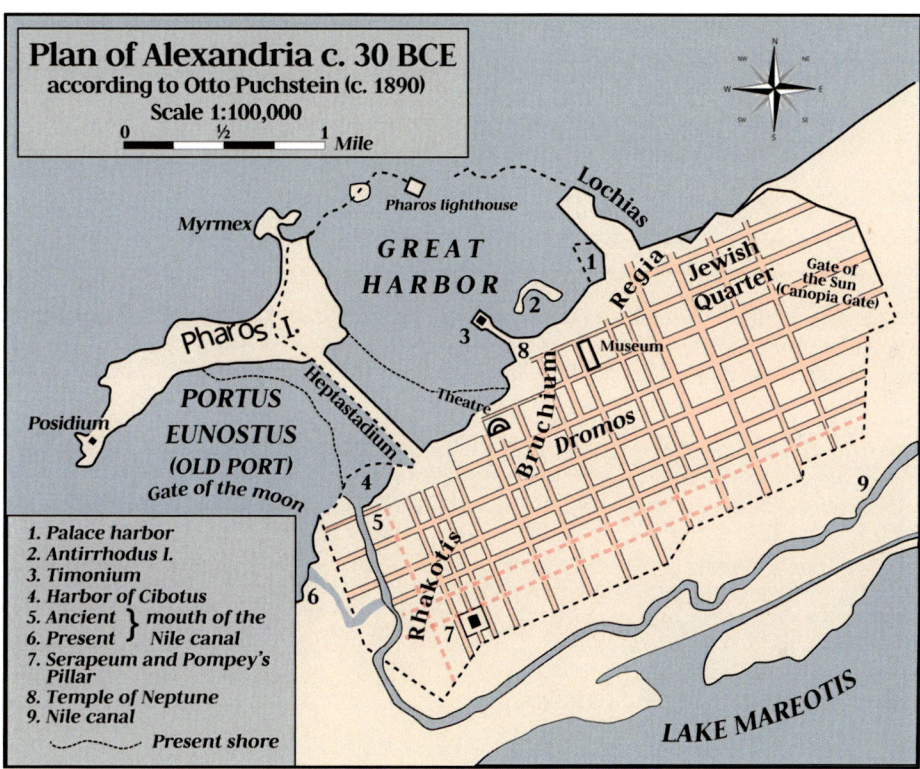

Plan of Alexandria c. 30 BCE according to Otto Puchstein (c. 1890). Scale 1:100,000

1. Palace harbor
2. Antirrhodus I.
3. Timonium
4. Harbor of Cibotus
5. Ancient } mouth of the
6. Present } Nile canal
7. Serapeum and Pompey's Pillar
8. Temple of Neptune
9. Nile canal
⸱⸱⸱⸱⸱⸱ Present shore

Gnostic teaching — the meeting place of East and West, a crucible for the exchange of ideas and teachings between Egyptians, Greeks, Syrians, Jews, and visitors from the East, bringing Buddhist and Zoroastrian teachings from India and Persia. The most highly educated of the men and women teaching in the great centres of learning throughout this vast Empire, which extended from England to the borders of Persia, "were the Gnostics, or *gnostikoi*, those who understand divine matters, knowing as the gods know." [3]

The Origins of Gnosticism: The Mysteries

No-one has defined the origin, nature, breadth, and depth of the Gnostics and the Mysteries better than G.R.S. Mead who could, I think, be described as a Gnostic. I have recently discovered that he was secretary to the theosophist, Helena Blavatsky. Anyone who wants to know the full breadth and depth of Gnosticism, should begin with his book, *Fragments of a Faith Forgotten*, written over a hundred years ago, when he wrote this:

The Institution of the Mysteries is the most interesting phenomenon in the study of religion. The idea of antiquity was that there was something to be *known* in religion, secrets, or mysteries into which it was possible to be initiated; that there was a gradual process of unfolding in things religious; in fine, that there was a science of the soul, and knowledge of things unseen. [4]

The highest praise is bestowed upon the Mysteries by the greatest thinkers among the Greeks, who tell us that they purified their nature, and not only made men live better lives here on earth but enabled them to depart from life with brighter hopes for the future. [5]

They strove for knowledge of God… wisdom was their goal; the holy things of life their study. They were called by many names by those who subsequently hailed them from their hidden retreats to ridicule their efforts and anathematise their doctrines. They are now generally referred to in Church history as the Gnostics, those whose goal was the Gnosis, although one of their earliest existing documents declares that Gnosis is not the end — it is the beginning of the path, the end is God — and hence the Gnostics would be those who used the Gnosis as the means to set their feet upon the Way to God…. Those who so bitterly opposed them, who — boasting themselves to be the only legitimate inheritors of the illumination of the Christ — stigmatised the Gnostics as the "first-born of Satan" may help us to set our feet in the direction where we shall find some materials on which to base an answer. [6]

There are three Mother Streams of Gnosticism: flowing from Greece, Egypt, and the Levant — the area closest to the shores of the eastern Mediterranean — roughly corresponding today to the area covered by modern Israel, Gaza, Jordan, Lebanon and Syria. Alexander the Great (356-323 BCE) hugely expanded the Greek Empire by conquering the powerful Achaemenid Persian Empire, then Afghanistan in 330 BCE, moving into India in 326 BCE in a campaign which lasted two years before his army withdrew. Greek was spoken throughout this vast empire. Influences and goods from these eastern areas, including India and Persia, were carried westwards, ultimately reaching Alexandria. The discovery of forgotten Gnostic texts have restored to us an essential part of our spiritual heritage. There are Jewish, Greek, Syrian and Egyptian texts, which show how diverse was the cultural background of Gnosticism.

In Greece, Mead explains, there were the Pre-Socratic philosophers, including Heraclitus, Pythagoras and Parmenides, but before them there was the earlier Orphic tradition of oracular sayings which was transmitted from Orpheus and his followers from Thrace — an area bordering the western shore of the Black Sea — to Pythagoras and Plato. Beyond the Orphic Tradition were teachings that came originally from Atlantis and the colonies established by its inhabitants before the island sank in the cataclysm that ended its existence.

"This line of transmission," Mead says, "must have been inspirational, prophetical, and oracular.... If it is difficult to form any precise notion of the evolution of popular religious ideas in Greece, much more difficult is it to trace the various lines of the Mystery traditions, which were regarded with the greatest possible reverence and guarded with the greatest possible secrecy, the slightest violation of the oath being punishable by death." [7]

These different traditions all carry the information that they were founded by men who introduced the arts of civilization. They were, as Mead says, either themselves gods or were instructed by gods and were the teachers of the infant races. This is the same message that we find in Egypt — that the God Osiris and Goddess Isis brought the arts of civilization to Egypt. "Not only did they teach them the arts, but they instructed them in the nature of the gods, of the human soul, and the unseen world, and set forth how the world came into existence and much else." [8]

Pythagoras himself is said to have been initiated into the Egyptian, Chaldean, Orphic, and Eleusinian Mysteries.[9] It is known that he spent twenty-five years with the temple priests in Egypt as well as many years in Babylon before beginning to teach in Greece and, after he was banished from Greece, at Crotona in southern Italy, where he taught until he died in 495 BCE.

In the later Roman Empire, Mead continues, "The Mithraic Mysteries represented the esoteric side of a great international religious movement, which the uniting together of many peoples into the Graeco-Roman world had made possible, and which resulted from the contact of Greece and Rome with the thought of the East." [10] We can see from all these different influences how deep and wide the stream of Gnosticism was and how it was well established and widely diffused throughout the Greek and later Roman Empires several centuries before the arrival of Christianity. It did not come into being with Christianity, as some writers have maintained, but existed centuries before.

In his book *Not in His Image: Gnostic Vision, Sacred Ecology, and the Future of Belief*, John Lamb Lash comments that contemporary ignorance of history in general, and ancient history in particular makes it difficult for us fully to understand the breadth and depth of learning in the Pagan world and the thousands of Gnostic teachers who were the enlightened educators of that world. He quotes the words of a classical scholar, Gilbert Highet, writing in the 1940's, who observed:

It is not always understood nowadays how noble and how widespread Greco-Roman civilisation was, how it kept Europe, the Middle East, and North Africa peaceful, cultured, prosperous, and happy for centuries, and how much was lost when the savages and invaders broke into it. It was in many respects a better thing than our civilisation until a few generations ago, and it may well prove to be a better thing all in all. When the Roman Empire was at its height, law and order, education, and the arts were widely distributed and almost universally respected. We can be sure that many if not most of the population could read and write. [11]

I have gone into such detail about what existed before the arrival of Christianity to show how much was lost when the Gnostics were persecuted as heretics in the fourth and fifth centuries CE, and most of their gospels destroyed. Yet there is so much more to be understood before we can comprehend the far-reaching influence and legacy of the Gnostic communities. In this chapter I can only offer the briefest glimpse of these and how, astonishingly, seventy-nine years ago, a door was opened for us to be able to hear their long-silenced voice. Many of the books I have drawn on are listed at the end of this chapter, but one chapter of this book cannot hold more than a fragment of the wisdom of the Gnostics or the extensive research on them that is contained in these books.

The Discoveries at Nag Hammadi

In 1945, the extraordinary discovery of the Gnostic texts near the Egyptian village of Nag Hammadi opened the eyes of incredulous Biblical scholars to the existence of unknown Gnostic texts, hidden at a time during the fourth century when the Gnostics were being persecuted and their many gospels destroyed. One evening, in an area honeycombed with caves, an Arab peasant named Muhammed Ali, came across a large red clay jar as he and his brother were digging around the edge of a large boulder. Thinking that it might contain gold, he smashed the jar. It is said that when he broke open the jar, a cloud of golden particles rose into the air around him and vanished into the sky.[12] To his amazement, he found several books or codices, bound in leather and written on papyrus. He took a few home to his mother who found some of them useful as fuel for her fire. Fortunately, the remainder (thirteen codices) found their way to Cairo and the Coptic Museum there and eventually, after many delays and hair-raising adventures, into publication and international awareness. A large part of the 13th codex was smuggled out of Egypt and offered for sale in America where it was bought by the Jung Foundation in Zurich. Professor Gilles Quispel who had contacted Jung to arrange the sale, saw that there were pages missing and flew to Egypt to photograph some of the pages from that codex in the Coptic Museum. To his astonishment, Quispel read: "These are the secret words which the living Jesus spoke, and which the twin, Judas Thomas, wrote down."

This is how the Gospel of Thomas came to light, a text that named itself as a secret gospel and held within it enigmatic sayings of Jesus, such as this one: "If you bring forth what is within you, what you bring forth will save you. If you do not bring forth what is within you, what you do not bring forth will kill you." (*logion* 70)

This Gospel was one of over fifty-two texts that found their way into publication as The Nag Hammadi Library in 1977, translated and with commentaries by many different scholars under the editorship of James M. Robinson. Among them were the two hitherto unknown Gospels of Thomas and Philip. John Lash comments,

> The Nag Hammadi materials provide enough insight into Gnostic teachings to explain why Gnostics risked their lives to challenge such doctrines as the supremacy of the male creator God, sin and atonement, the divinity of the Saviour, resurrection, and final judgement from on high. The remaining 50 odd fragmentary Texts in Coptic, a mere flake of a vast corpus of writings, yet so potent was the Gnostic argument that this flake still contains enough theological dynamite to shake the foundations of Christianity. [13]

Although the Nag Hammadi texts were buried during the fourth century, they are thought to be translations of Greek originals that were possibly written three hundred years earlier. Some offer a very different account of the Creation from the one in the Book of Genesis and, in certain texts, a concept of the primal Creator as both Mother and Father.[14] They also offer deeper insight into the essence of the teaching of Jesus and, in two different texts, *The Dialogue of the Savior* [15] and *The Gospel of Philip*,[16] the startling disclosure of his close relationship with Mary Magdalene. There is one missing text, the *Disposyni* Chart, that recorded the genealogy of the family of Jesus which, according to Lawrence Gardner, was removed and sold to the Vatican.[17] The explosive material in the codices reveals why the Christian Church in Rome felt so threatened by the Gnostics and why it was drawn into direct confrontation with "those who understand divine matters, knowing as the gods know," who called themselves telestai or "those who are aimed." [18] These preserved the shamanic visionary practices that existed long before, in the Neolithic Era, that were originally focussed on the Great Mother and later, on Sophia, the Wisdom Goddess.

The Primary Message of the Gnostics

There are two Greek words for knowledge. One of them — *epistémi* — means knowledge in the sense of information gathered. The other — *gnosis* —

means knowledge in the sense of insight and wisdom. The Gnostics believed that the meaning and purpose of life was to be discovered neither through belief and faith nor through knowledge about the known world, but through inner spiritual transformation, illumination, shamanic practices and insight, a process that could best be described by the Greek word *metanoia*. God was not to be found in a distant heaven, but within the soul of the one searching for Him. The focus of the Gnostic Gospels as with the entire Gnostic Tradition, was how to connect the human soul with the divine element hidden within it; how to awaken from a state, not of sin as in later Christian teaching, but of ignorance — as in the eastern traditions. This mysterious process is summed up in these illuminating words from the third century *Vision of Zosimus:* "*Hidden within man there exists a heavenly and divine light which cannot be placed in man from without but must emerge from within.*" [19]

The Gnostics divided people into three main categories. The first category (*pneumatic*) included those who were awakened to the spiritual realm, focussed on discovering the divine light hidden within their nature. The second category of people (*psychic*) applied to those who were dominated by the mind and were ignorant of the soul. The third category (*hylic*) described those who were immersed in materialism.[20] These three categories defined by the Gnostics two thousand years ago can still be discovered in our modern society.

Like the Kabbalists and the writers of the *Upanishads* in India, the Gnostics demonstrate that their focus was on how to awaken their followers to an initiatory path that led them to awareness of their immortal nature, and then to the experience of and union with the divine ground within and around them. Those who were initiates of the Greek Mysteries of Eleusis saw the natural world as transparent to the immanence of divinity. This was essentially the same teaching as that of the *Upanishads* and the Buddha 500 years before Jesus and the same as the Hermetic teaching of Egypt. It was about the inner work of integrating the soul with spirit and a conscious reunion or sacred marriage with the Divine Ground that they named 'Light'. Christian Gnostics understood that the Kingdom of Heaven was not a place but a higher, more enlightened state of consciousness.

The primary message of the Gnostics was that we are essentially spiritual beings, sparks of the Divine Light or very substance of the highest world, that they called the Pleroma. Incarnated into the material world, we have forgotten our divine origin and, like the inhabitants of the cave described by Plato, see only the flickering shadows of reality reflected on its walls. The world we inhabit is an 'underworld' where we are ineluctably focussed on our survival to the exclusion of anything else. In our ignorance of our predicament, we have become the unwitting slaves or victims of the institutions, rulers, beliefs and corrupt values that govern and control this world. We are prisoners of a situation from which we cannot free ourselves until we become aware of it. This is as true and relevant today as it was two thousand years ago.

Gnostic teaching offered a recognition of human suffering, loneliness, and bondage, but sought a luminous and courageous solution to it. The Gnostics, including the Jewish Gnostics, tried to go beyond any image of deity hitherto formulated, to one that could only be expressed as Light, and that could be revealed to people through an inward experience of their own soul, not through belief or obedience to any religious authority, doctrine, or creed. "Knock on yourself as upon a door and walk upon yourselves as on a straight road," said *The Teachings of Silvanus*.[21] The first aim of their teaching was to awaken the soul to awareness of her predicament. The salvation of the individual soul was not dependent upon the sacrificial death of a Saviour, the Son of God, but upon her 'bringing forth' or 'giving birth' to the divine element in the depths of her own consciousness, overcoming her ignorance and awakening from her sleep or, in modern Jungian terminology, from her unconscious state.

The theme that pervades Gnostic thought is not that of original sin, but of the soul's captivity or entanglement in a tragic fate that can be changed through a creative act of insight, transformation of understanding, and inner growth. So, the great Jewish Gnostic teacher Valentinus taught: "What liberates is the knowledge of who we were, what we became; where we were, whereinto we have been thrown; whereto we speed, wherefore we are redeemed; what birth is, and what rebirth." [22] As the soul awakens, she becomes aware of her indwelling divine or holy spirit who says to her: "I am thou and thou art I; and wheresoever thou art I am there, and I am sown (or scattered) in all; from whencesoever thou willest, thou gatherest Me; and gathering Me thou gatherest Thyself." [23]

The great contribution of the Gnostics to the further evolution of humanity was the emphasis on awakening through revelatory insight and experience rather than belief. Their teaching about the need of people to discover the light of the divine spirit within them, thereby effecting their own salvation, brought them into conflict with the orthodox Christians, whose teaching was (and still is) that salvation can only come through Christ's sacrificial death and through belief and belonging to the Church. The myth of the unconscious soul and the possibility of her awakening to the presence of the spirit within her may appear to be the creation of the Gnostics, yet it was directly inherited from the long-established esoteric traditions of Egypt, Greece, and possibly even India through the dissemination of Buddhist ideas and even Buddhist travellers who followed the trade routes westwards after Alexander's military campaigns in Afghanistan and India.

The Gnostic View of the World

Gnostics taught their followers to ask themselves the question: "Who are we?" and to go in search of the answer. This is the question that Plotinus (204-270 CE), considered to be the founder of Neo-Platonism, asked in the third century CE in his great work, *The Enneads*. Plotinus developed a complex spiritual cosmology involving three fundamental elements: the One, the Intelligence, and the Soul. He thought the One was the source of all manifestations of itself in separate beings, a concept that is beginning to return in our time. Gnostics did not, as certain writers on Gnosticism have claimed, regard the material world as evil, only that its institutions were controlled by the Demiurge or false god that had set himself up as the ruler of the world. They held Nature to be sacred. Like the Pre-Socratic Greek philosopher, Parmenides, they believed their origin was in the divine world that they called the Pleroma. They might have echoed his words: "We are divine beings, having a human experience."

The Visionary Experience of the Gnostics: The Mysteries

In his book, *Not in His Image*, John Lamb Lash explains that:

> The Mysteries were teleological rites intended to enhance the full range of human faculties to the optimal level. Those who advanced to the higher ranks of the Mysteries assumed the sacred commitment to guide humanity by teaching self-direction. The telestic [aimed] method both satisfied human needs and went beyond them, opening the way for each individual to realize transpersonal purpose. The guiding rule of the Revealers was that the transpersonal fulfils the personal, the personal cannot fulfil itself. The sacred commitment of the Mystery School guardians involved several initiatives that would have been common to all cells throughout the network in Europe, the Levant and Egypt: instruction by the Light, participation in the revealer cycle, the consecration of the Anthropos, the disclosure of the inner guide, and development of the guiding story, the Sophia mythos. This is the legacy of the revealers, the deathless promise of Gnosis, ultimate wisdom, knowing as the gods know. [24]

The Eight-petalled Rosette at the Temple of Eleusis

Lash explains that "fragments from the ruins of Eleusis present three images that epitomize the organization, method, and supernatural source of Gnostic illumination. The architrave frieze of the Lesser Propylaeum shows the sheaf of cut wheat "white barley," the biological source of mystic illumination. Next to it is a sixteen-petalled rosette with interior and exterior petals. Next to this is the image of an upright urn or ringed pillar, symbolizing the downloading of the

The Eight-Petallled Rosette at the Temple of Eleusis,
Photograph courtesy Rebecca Battles

Mystery Light." [25] The rosette "was the symbol of the Mystery cells, consisting of sixteen adepts, eight men and eight women. In what is known as the Orphic bowl, one of two surviving artefacts of Mystery rituals and carved from greenish-white alabaster, sixteen naked men and women, alternating with each other, lie on their backs, with their feet touching. At the center of the bowl is the winged serpent of Kundalini. [26]

On reading this, I was reminded of a similar arrangement of men and women from the Cucuteni Culture of Romania, dating to 4,200 BCE. This beautiful artefact was shown in an exhibition in New York and the Ashmolean Museum, Oxford, in 2010 and published in a book called *The Lost World of Old Europe: The Danube Valley*, 5,000-3500 BC. Princeton University Press, 2010. But in the illustration, there are twelve naked men and women, lying alternately in a circle. Was this a similar ancient ritual, one that might have been practiced in the Orphic Mysteries of Thrace?

Lash further explains that:

> "The inner petals of the double rosette at Eleusis represent the initiates dedicated to retaining and developing the instructions received by repeated encounters with the Mystery Light, while the outer petals represent the eight initiates dedicated to interpreting, translating, and externally transmitting those instructions. These two roles were periodically rotated, allowing the adepts to concentrate on different tasks in different shifts.... The roles changed seasonally and reflected the ages old initiatory techniques of guiding society by Goddess-centered rites of death and renewal." [27]

The Encounter with the Divine Light

Lash describes the Encounter with the Divine Light:

> All ancient testimony of the Mysteries attests to the sublime encounter with the Divine Light. This is a form of luminosity that does not appear to ordinary awareness, owing to the filters of human perception, including the egoic filter. The mental gloss of self-reflection is like light shining on a window pane that makes it impossible to see through the window. Once the ego melts away, the parameters of perception are shifted and the Light is there, a *substantial* presence in the world, soft, white, and shadowless. It is also sentient, animated and animating, aware of itself and what comes into contact with it. The Organic Light is everywhere and permeates all things. It does not shine *on* what is seen but *from* what is seen, emitting a soft white luminosity with the texture of marshmallow, in which matter floats." [28] Moreover, "the undulant surges of the Organic Light were sound currents as well as visible waves of pale, lustrous radiance. [29]

> This 'downloading' of the Mystery Light was depicted by the stylized pillar [on the right] of the Eleusis pediment. The shadowless Organic Light is white and visible, manifesting everywhere, although it cannot be observed everywhere at once, in a single, encompassing gaze, because it literally overflows the human capacity of seeing.... Preliminary preparation for this experience could take as long as twenty-one years, with the actual process of initiation accomplished in a matter of days.[30]

The Use of White Barley to Induce a Visionary State

Just as millennia ago in northern India, as recorded in the *Rigveda*, shamans used the plant *soma* to induce a visionary state, so the Initiates (Mystes) of

Eleusis used a concoction made from white barley — called the *kykeon* — (represented on the pediment by the sheaf of cut wheat) to enable them to move into this state. From the Palaeolithic era onwards, sacred plants were used all over the world to enable people to go beyond their normal vision and enter the visionary state. The experience of entering was to know, as an experience, that our mind or soul was not our own, but came from the life around us, the life of the plants, the trees, the earth, from the *Anima-Mundi* or Soul of the World. This vision of the Divine Light is such an extraordinary realization or revelation that it would be almost impossible for anyone who has not experienced it, to understand and explain its revelatory impact.

At the end of the initiation, the hierophant held up a sheaf of cut wheat — "a sheaf of wheat in silence reaped." This gesture was, for one initiate "the great, the marvellous, the most perfect secret into the highest mystic truths." (Hippolytus *Refutation of all Heresies.* 5.3) "This secret," Lash continues, "which could only be learned directly from the Divine Light, reveals how our perception is given externally, yet given in such a way that we are allowed to experience it as originating from us, internally." [31] This experience must have given the initiates the revelation that they were living within Divinity; the absolute certainty that they were part of Divinity, that they were part of the One Life around them. "When the initiates emerged from the inner chamber at Eleusis into the clear autumnal light, and beheld the golden grain of the Rarian fields, and on the nearby hills, the outline of the lithe poplars and cypress trees, they saw nature through the power of seeing given by nature, sacred and inviolable power." [32]

I have quoted at length from John Lash's book rather than paraphrasing his paragraphs because I believe he is describing an authentic experience that he himself has had.

The Organization of the Christian Gnostic Communities

Long before the advent of Christianity, as Mead and Lash have demonstrated, there were Gnostic communities all over the Greek and later Roman Empire. Many had their own teachings, initiation practices and gospels and did not conform to a single set of beliefs. When the Gnostic *Christian* Communities were established, they did not organize themselves on a hierarchical model like the Church of Rome. They took their teaching and their apostolic descent, not from Peter but from James, the brother of Jesus and from Mary Magdalene, whom Jesus appointed Teacher to the disciples just before the Last Supper as will be described in Chapter Eight.[33] Those who were contemplatives had, like the older gnostic communities, well-established shamanic practices of meditation, clairvoyance, clairaudience, remote viewing and lucid dreaming. Visionary experience would have been an integral part of these practices.

They repudiated the ideas expressed in the Apostolic Creed formulated at the Council of Nicaea in 325 CE that Jesus was of the same substance as God and therefore was the Son of God; they rejected the belief that Jesus was the only Son of God, whose sacrificial death on the cross had guaranteed Christians, salvation, and redemption from sin. They repudiated the Trinity and the declaration that Jesus was born of a virgin mother who was declared to be *Theotokos* or God-bearer (at the Council of Ephesus in 431 CE); that on the third day after his crucifixion, he was resurrected in his physical body; that *belief* in the Christian faith and *belonging* to the Church of Rome offered redemption and salvation. They made a radical distinction between God as Spirit, the *Anthropos*, the unknowable ground of being, and the image of the deity — the God in the Old Testament — that Christian priests and people worshipped as King, Lord, Creator, Master and Judge. They saw this God, whom they named the Demiurge Ialdebaoth, as an imposter. They saw the statements made by this God – "I am God and there is no other" and "I am a jealous God" — as issuing from the Demiurge and not the true God.

They did not accept the hierarchy of bishops, priests, deacons and laity, saying that these were serving the Demiurge and not the true God whom they called 'The Father'. Jesus was the Son of Man, not the Son of God, even though he called the Divine Ground, 'the Father'. The emphasis of their teaching was on good works and helping the poor. They welcomed women as priests, teachers and healers.

The earliest group of Gnostic Christians, called Nazarenes, was established in Jerusalem by James, the brother of Jesus, after Jesus's death. Nazarene was another name for the Essenes, a community that will be explored in Chapter Seven. When James was murdered by the Sanhedrin in 62 CE, the persecuted community in Jerusalem dispersed, some going to Alexandria, others to Syria, and to Edessa in Mesopotamia where a hundred years later, a strong Gnostic community had been established with a renowned teacher called Bardesanes (154-222 CE), who is believed to be the author of a wonderful gnostic text called *The Hymn of the Pearl*, or *Hymn of the Robe of Glory*. (see Part Two)

They saw Jesus as a spiritually advanced visionary teacher of the path to union with the divine ground, much like the Eastern teachers of Buddhism and Hinduism. Unsurprisingly, they faced increasing antagonism from, and later, vicious persecution by the Church in Rome, particularly after the year 200 CE when Christianity was becoming well established in several cities, with a hierarchy of bishops, priests and deacons.

The Resurrection

The resurrection of Jesus after the crucifixion was a foundational belief of all Christians and meant that, three days after the crucifixion, he rose from the dead in his *physical* body. The Gnostics believed that Jesus rose in what they called the 'ascension body' or 'body of light' which they saw as the luminous ground of the soul and was neither born nor died with the physical body. It was eternal. The Gnostic's vision of this 'body of light' beyond the physical form gave them, like the initiates of the Mysteries before them, the knowledge that there was no death for this 'body of light.' In certain Gnostic texts Jesus appears to his disciples after his resurrection (ascension) in his 'body of light,' and it is helpful to consider 1 Corinthians 15 together with these Gnostic texts to understand the 'resurrection of the body' in a different sense from the literal one given in Christian teaching. In another context 'resurrection' signified to the Gnostics the coming of spiritual enlightenment, awakening from the sleep of ignorance, when one could reach a higher level of consciousness or insight. "He who has not known himself knows nothing, but he who has known himself has at the same time achieved knowledge about the Depth of the All." [34]

The Gnostic Imagery of the Divine Mother

Elaine Pagels, in her book *The Gnostic Gospels*, has explained much that was obscure about the early history of the Christian Church and the many Gnostic sects that flourished during the first three centuries of the Christian era. The texts reveal many images relating to the Divine Feminine, which were lost with the suppression of these sects. By the year 200, as she tells us in Chapter III of her book *The Gnostic Gospels*:

> All the sources cited so far — secret gospels, revelations, mystical teachings — are among those not included in the select list that constitutes the New Testament collection. Every one of the secret texts which gnostic groups revered was omitted [by Irenaeus, Bishop of Lyons in the second century CE, who made the selection] from the canonical collection and branded as heretical by those who called themselves orthodox Christians. By the time the process of sorting the various writings ended — probably as late as the year 200 — virtually all the feminine imagery for God had disappeared from orthodox Christian tradition. [35]

Until 1977 when the texts discovered at Nag Hammadi in Egypt in 1945 were finally published, no-one knew that some groups of early Christians — among them many Jews — had an image of the Divine Mother whom they had named 'The Invisible within the All'.[36] One of the greatest Jewish gnostic teachers,

Valentinus, suggested that the divine can be envisioned as a dyad; consisting of the Ineffable, the Depth, the Primal Father; and, in the other, of Grace, Silence, the Womb and "Mother of All." [37] Valentinus goes on to describe how, as the 'Eternal Silence', the Divine Mother received the seed of Light from the ineffable source and how, as from a womb, she brought forth all the emanations of Light, ranged in harmonious pairs of feminine and masculine entities or energies. They prayed to her as "the mystical, eternal Silence." [38] They knew this Divine Mother as the Holy Spirit and saw the dove as her emissary.

This suggests that this gnostic cosmology may have had some distant connection with the cosmology of the First Temple described in Chapter Three. It also suggests a connection with the later mystical Jewish cosmology of Kabbalah that was called "The Voice of the Dove" and "The Jewels of the Heavenly Bride." Jewish Christians believed, as recorded in the lost *Gospel of the Hebrews*, and mentioned in Chapter Five, that at the baptism of Jesus, it was the Divine Mother — the Holy Spirit — who spoke to her son, saying "This is My beloved son, in whom I am well pleased." [39]

I find it significant that in some texts, the imagery and mythology of the Divine Mother in Gnostic texts is so similar to the imagery of the Shekinah in Kabbalah that they appear to be like two branches of the same Wisdom tradition and that is another reason why I think Kabbalah may originate in the teachings of the First Temple in Jerusalem and have been carried to Alexandria when the Temple was taken over by the Deuteronomists. Now with the research of Dr Margaret Barker confirming that three waves of Jews moved from Jerusalem to the city of Alexandria, the fragments of an incredible story come together and their relationship would seem to be more plausible. Certain texts name the Divine Mother as the Mother of the Universe but also speak of the androgyny of the divine source in imagery similar to the later kabbalistic texts. In some gnostic texts such as *The Apocryphon of John*, the Divine Mother is named as the Holy Spirit. [40] The imagery and mythology of the Divine Mother, the Holy Spirit, in certain gnostic texts is so similar to the imagery of the Shekinah in Kabbalah that they seem to belong to one and the same Wisdom tradition.

In one Gnostic text called the *Trimorphic Protennoia,* the speaker describes herself as the intangible Womb that gives shape to the All and as the life that moves in every creature:

> *I am the voice speaking softly.*
> *I exist from the first.*
> *I dwell within the Silence,*
> *Within the immeasurable Silence.*

I descended to the midst of the underworld
And I shone down upon the darkness.
It is I who poured forth the Water.
I am the one hidden within Radiant Waters...
I am the Image of the Invisible Spirit.
It is I who speak within every creature
I am the Womb that gives shape to the All
By giving birth to the Light that shines in splendour. [41]

Women as Disciples and Teachers of Gnosis

Astonishingly, in an era that regarded women as almost sub-human, the gnostic communities held men and women to be equal. This may be because they had an image of the primary creator as both Father and Mother as in a text in the Nag Hammadi Library called *The Sophia of Jesus Christ*.[42] In many gnostic groups, men and women were trained together as initiates; both could hold the position of teacher, healer, priest, bishop, and deacon and these positions were not fixed but were drawn by lot daily, so there could be no competition between them. Women in the gnostic communities could teach, heal, prophesy, and hold any rank within it that men did, including that of bishop. This was a source of great irritation to the orthodox Christians. Tertullian (ca.150-220 CE), one of the main opponents of the Gnostics, exclaimed: "these heretical women — how audacious they are! They have no modesty; they are bold enough to teach, to engage in argument, to enact exorcisms, to undertake cures, and it may be, even to baptize!" [43] Defining the way women ought to behave, he wrote, echoing St. Paul: "It is not permitted for a woman to speak in the church, nor is it permitted for her to teach, nor to baptize, nor to offer the Eucharist, nor to claim for herself share in any *masculine* function — not to mention any priestly office." [44]

Pagels observes that from the year 200 'we have no evidence for women taking prophetic, priestly, and episcopal roles among orthodox churches." [45] This, Pagels says, "is an extraordinary development, considering that in its earliest years, the Christian movement showed a remarkable openness towards women. Jesus himself violated Jewish conventions by talking openly with women, and he included them among his companions." [46]

Hypatia

I cannot leave the subject of Gnostic women without mentioning the most famous of these teachers in the early fifth century. She was the brilliant Neo-

Platonist philosopher and mathematician, Hypatia, the daughter of Theon (c. 335 - c. 405 CE), the last recorded Director of the Royal Library in Alexandria. From the year 400, when she would have been about 30, Hypatia held the chair of mathematics at the university for fifteen years.

> Her dialectical powers were exceptional, honed to a fine edge by her mathematical training. When it came to debating ideas about the divine, Hypatia eclipsed in argument every proponent of the Christian doctrines in northern Egypt. Her expertise in theology typified the pagan intellectual class of Gnostics, *gnostikoi*, those who understood divine matters, 'knowing as the gods know' but she was also deeply versed in geometry, physics, and astronomy.... Hypatia's talents were not confined to theology and didactics. She was also involved in applied science related to geography and astronomy. Working with a Greek scientist called Synesius, who was proud to be called her student, she invented a prototype of the astrolabe, a device later to prove essential in the navigation of the world's oceans. [47]

The word *philosophy* means love (philo) of wisdom (sophia). "To Gnostics Sophia was a revered divinity, the goddess whose story they recounted in their sacred cosmology. To the people of her time and setting, Hypatia would have been wisdom incarnate." [48]

There is, unfortunately, no remaining vestige of her writings, although she is known to have written at least two books on mathematics and one on astronomy. The ordinary people loved her and came to listen to her lectures. Because these challenged the power of the Christian Church in Alexandria, in 415 CE Hypatia suffered an excruciating death at the hands of an enraged Christian mob led by a man called Peter, who was possibly incited to murder her by Saint Cyril, the Christian Bishop of Alexandria.

> Imagine a time when the world's greatest living mathematician was a woman, indeed, a physically beautiful woman, and a woman who was simultaneously the world's leading astronomer.... Imagine such a female mathematician achieving fame not only in her specialist field, but also as a philosopher and religious thinker who attracted a large popular following. Imagine her as a virgin martyr killed not *for* her Christianity, but *by* Christians because she was not one of them. And imagine that the guilt of her death was widely whispered to lie at the door of one of Christianity's most honoured and significant saints.... Would her life not be common knowledge? You would think so but that is not the case.... [49]

Historians mark the beginning of the "Dark Ages" from the death of Hypatia in 415 CE. The Christian Church in Rome turned against Paganism and Gnosticism and in so doing, contributed to the collapse of an extraordinary civilization that had nourished and enlightened millions for hundreds of years.

The barbarians who subsequently poured into the collapsing Empire gave this civilization its coup de grâce.

Apart from the Gnostic Communities, the only exception to the exclusion of women from priestly office in the 1,700 years of Christianity since it was officially established under Theodosius 1 in 380 CE, was the heretic twelfth century Cathar Church of the Holy Spirit, in which, as in the Gnostic Communities, women held the rank of bishop, administered the sacraments, taught, baptized, and healed the sick. (see Chapter Nine: Esclarmonde) The Vatican's refusal to allow women to hold priestly office was and is in striking contrast to the welcome given to women by the Gnostic communities. It cannot pass without wondering how deeply this exclusion has wounded woman's soul and curtailed her trust in herself and her development as a human being. In none of the three patriarchal religions, Judaism, Christianity, and Islam, was there an image of the mother, wife, or daughter of the Father God. These images are only to be found in Kabbalah, the mystical tradition of Judaism. With no metaphysical image of woman and with no longer any 'sacred' role in society, how could women, and equally men, become aware of and relate within themselves to all the different aspects of the archetypal feminine, including their deepest feelings?

The Confrontation with Christianity

The Christian Gnostics did not believe that Jesus was the Son of God nor that he had been resurrected from the dead in a physical body. They saw him as an advanced visionary teacher of the path to enlightenment and union with the divine ground, much like the eastern teachers of Buddhism and Hinduism. They felt that what distinguished the false from the true community was the level of understanding of its members, and the empathic quality of their relationship with one another — not how closely they conformed to the teachings of the bishops and priests. These beliefs were revolutionary and offered an enormous challenge to the Roman Church trying to establish itself at the same time and in the same cities, Alexandria, Antioch, Carthage and Rome in the second to fourth centuries CE. While this doctrinal battle was going on, Christians were being atrociously persecuted by certain Emperors, notably Nero and Diocletian.

By the second century CE there was still great freedom in the early Christian Church established in Alexandria. But in Rome a different spirit prevailed, inspired by the authoritarianism of the Roman Empire, and this spirit ultimately brought about the persecution and suppression of the Gnostics in the fourth and fifth centuries. How different the history of Christianity would have been if the great Jewish Gnostic teacher Valentinus (100-180 CE), who had moved from Alexandria to Rome to teach there, had been elected Bishop of Rome in 140 CE instead of Pius I, who later became Pope. Pius was chosen, and the group that Valentinus represented and the texts his students used as the foundation of his teaching were gradually suppressed and lost. Valentinus was expelled from the Christian Church in Rome by 150 CE and returned to Egypt, but his influence endured for three hundred years, carried forward in the writings of his followers. He was an extraordinary teacher. Several texts in the Nag Hammadi Library were thought to have been authored or influenced by him, notably *The Gospel of Truth*, which has this beautiful passage about the effect Jesus had on those who listened to him:

> Light spoke through his mouth and his voice gave birth to life. He gave them thought and understanding and mercy and salvation and the powerful spirit from the infiniteness and gentleness of the Father. He made punishments and tortures cease, for it was they who were leading astray from his face some who were in need of mercy, in error and in bonds; and with power he destroyed them and confounded them with knowledge. He became a way for those who were lost and knowledge for those who were ignorant, a discovery for those who were searching, and a support for those who were wavering, immaculateness for those who were defiled. [50]

In the man we know as Jesus, we encounter someone with the same charismatic presence as the Buddha, whose powerful and radical teaching was very similar to that of the Buddha. It has been suggested that Jesus, in the 'missing years' before the beginning of his Mission, spent time in India, possibly in Taxila, one of the great Buddhist Universities there. He is also thought to have spent time in Egypt where he spent his early childhood. Like the Buddha, he was perhaps an emissary from the higher regions of the cosmos: an extraordinary individual, a shaman with the power to heal diseases, even to bring people back to life; a man whom tens of thousands of people followed and others, the Pharisees, hated and feared. He had only three short years in which to fulfil his Mission and in that time, he unknowingly laid the foundations of what would grow into a new religion whose effect on the world would be far-reaching and profound. This religion was not what he intended but it is what happened in the hands of those who within three centuries had created the myth of the Only Son of God, who, by his sacrificial death was the Saviour and Redeemer of humanity. Jesus never referred to himself as the Son of God or the Messiah, only as the Son of Man. Yet, in an extraordinary turn of events, by the middle of the fourth century, "the Jesus who *has* the message changes into the Christ who *is* the message." [51] It must have been the fusion of the Church of Rome with the Roman Empire that deflected it from the path of love to the path of power. The Gnostics saw what was taking place before their eyes, but their voice was silenced.

This gnostic saying of Jesus from the *Oxyrhynchus* manuscript is among his important sayings:

> *Who then are they that draw us*
> *and when shall come the Kingdom that is in heaven?*
> *The fowls of the air and the beasts,*
> *whatever is beneath the earth or upon the earth,*
> *and the fishes of the sea,*
> *these they are that draw you.*
> *And the Kingdom of Heaven is within you*
> *and whosoever knoweth himself shall find it.*
> *And having found it, ye shall know yourselves*
> *that ye are sons and heirs of the Father, the Almighty,*
> *and shall know yourselves that ye are in God and God in you.*

And in the gnostic Gospel of Thomas, we read:

> *I am the Light which is above everything.*
> *I am the All; from me the All has gone forth,*
> *And to me the All has returned.*
> *Cleave a piece of wood, I am there;*
> *lift up the stone and you will find Me there. logion 77*

Jung's Encounter with the Gnostics

Jung (1875-1961) once tried to buy a train ticket for Rome but was overcome with faintness at the ticket office, and never visited Rome. I think he could have lived as Valentinus, although could also have lived as Basilides, who was teaching in Alexandria from 117 to 138 CE. Basilides is said to have written twenty-four books of commentaries on the many Gnostic and Christian gospels then extant. Tragically, only a few fragments of this important body of writing survive. He was also a poet and his teachings were carried as far as Spain by his disciples.

Jung became very interested in the then extant Gnostic writings (early twentieth century), which consisted mostly of the polemics against them by early Christian writers and spent a lot of time familiarizing himself with them. In his autobiography, *Memories, Dreams, Reflections*, he recounts an extraordinary visitation he experienced when a group of discarnate Gnostics pressed him to acknowledge their presence and to answer their questions. He replied to them and in the name of the Gnostic Teacher, Basilides.

> Around five o'clock in the afternoon on Sunday the front doorbell began ringing
> frantically... Everyone immediately looked to see who was there, but there was
> no one in sight. I was sitting near the doorbell, and not only heard it but saw it
> moving. We all simply stared at one another. The atmosphere was thick, believe
> me! Then I knew something had to happen. The whole house was as if there was
> a crowd present, crammed full of spirits. They were packed deep right up to the
> door and the air was so thick it was scarcely possible to breathe. As for myself,
> I was all aquiver with the question: "For God's sake, what in the world is this?"
> Then they cried out in chorus, "We have come back from Jerusalem where we
> found not what we sought." So began the *Septem Sermones ad Mortuos*.
>   Then it began to flow out of me and, in the course of three evenings, the
> thing was written. As soon as I took up the pen, the whole ghostly assemblage
> evaporated. The room quieted and the atmosphere cleared. The haunting was
> over. [52]

> From that time on, the dead have become ever more distinct for me as the voices
> of the Unanswered, Unresolved, and Unredeemed; for since the questions and
> demands which my destiny required me to answer did not come to me from out-
> side, they must have come from the inner world. These conversations with the
> dead formed a kind of prelude to what I had to communicate to the world about the
> unconscious: a kind of pattern of order and interpretation of its general contents.
>   When I look back upon it all to-day and consider what happened to me
> during the period of my work on the fantasies, it seems as though a message had
> come to me with overwhelming force. There were things in the images which
> concerned not only myself but many others also. It was then that I ceased to
> belong to myself alone, ceased to have the right to do so. From then on, my life
> belonged to the generality. The knowledge I was concerned with, or was seeking,
> still could not be found in the science of those days. I myself had to undergo the
> original experience, and, moreover, try to plant the results of my experience in
> the soil of reality; otherwise, they would have remained subjective assumptions
> without validity. It was then that I dedicated myself to service of the psyche. I
> loved it and hated it, but it was my greatest wealth. My delivering myself over to
> it, as it were, was the only way by which I could endure my existence and live it
> as fully as possible.
>   Today I can say that I have never lost touch with my initial experiences.
> All my works, all my creative activity, has come from those initial fantasies and
> dreams which began in 1912, almost fifty years ago. Everything that I accom-
> plished in later life was already contained in them, although at first only in the
> form of emotions and images. [53]

Jung, deeply steeped in and influenced by the Gnostic texts, recorded his
experience of his descent into the Underworld of the Unconscious, described
by him as his *Nekyia*, when, from 1913-19 after his break from Freud in 1912,

he deliberately provoked a near-overwhelming eruption of visions, dreams, and fantasies. He recorded his experiences and visions in over 1000 hand-written illustrated pages which he bound together in an unpublished Gnostic text that he called *The Red Book*.[54] In this book, he recounts his meeting with his mentor Philemon who, he says, "taught me that there are things in the psyche which I do not produce, but which produce themselves and have their own life.… It was he who taught me psychic objectivity, the reality of the psyche.… Psychologically, Philemon represented superior insight.… At times he seemed to me quite real, as if he were a living personality. I went walking up and down the garden with him, and to me he was what the Indians call a guru.[55] Jung's later concept of individuation or soul growth was based on the Gnostic idea of bringing the conscious mind into alignment with the indwelling spirit that he called 'the Self' or the Spirit of the Depths.

When Nietzsche proclaimed the death of God at the end of the nineteenth century, he was describing not the literal death of God but the decay of a belief system and an image of spirit that was worn out, because it was no longer numinous and therefore relevant to millions of people. When writing *Answer to Job*, Jung saw that the God of the Old Testament was missing a feminine counterpart, whom he named Sophia.[56] He also realized that the problems of our time are rooted not only in the grip that scientific rationalism has on our culture, but above all in the loss of a living myth and the increasing polarization between the conscious mind and the unconscious, between thinking and feeling, mind and soul. He saw that the dissociation of the conscious, rational mind from what he called the primordial soul presented a growing and unrecognized danger to humanity. The more we emphasized reason and the supremacy of the rational mind, splitting off feeling, the more instinct would respond in negative ways. Ignorance of the tremendous power of the hidden energies which lie beyond the fragile conscious mind, risks our being taken over by them, and falling into collective insanity and the dissolution of our humanity — something that we increasingly see happening today.

Jung knew that conventional religious teaching had not preserved the vital knowledge that nature and instinct are an expression of spirit. In splitting nature from spirit, emptying matter of soul, and contaminating the instincts with guilt and fear, an essential part of our wholeness has been lost. He knew it was vitally important to balance the predominantly masculine character of our culture with its addiction to power, conquest and control, by integrating the less valued aspects of the feminine archetype: nature and matter, soul and body, feeling and instinct — that is, to create a conscious, healing and receptive relationship with these neglected aspects of spirit within ourselves and within our culture. What he offered was not a new belief system but a spirituality grounded in self-knowledge—particularly awareness of the shadow—leading to ethical responsibility towards life in all its aspects, seen and unseen. He knew we did not have much time to accomplish this momentous task.

Humanity faces an epochal task. We stand at a pivotal moment in our evolutionary story and, as Jung declared in *Answer to Job*, we urgently need Sophia or the Divine Feminine aspect of God that Job was seeking. Jung sensed a new encounter with Sophia was at hand. Sophia was not a bygone relic of ancient history. Her myth was alive; he experienced it first hand, and he saw it arising anew in his work and in this age.

> The years when I was pursuing my inner images were the most important in my life — in them everything essential was decided. It all began then; the later details are only supplements and clarifications of the material that burst forth from the unconscious, and at first swamped me. It was the *prima materia* for a lifetimes' work. [57]

The Christian Confrontation with the Gnostics

The religion that developed in Rome from the fourth century onwards, after the incorporation of the Church of Rome into the Roman Empire, was very different from the original teaching of Jesus who, like the great teachers of the East, had taught a path of transformation leading to union with the divine ground. What was originally a direct shamanic transmission of the Path to Union had become, by the fourth century, a faith that put its emphasis on belief and belonging to the Church of Rome as the path to salvation. The theme of inner transformation taught by the Gnostics was lost. We hear about it through the experience of the Christian and Sufi mystics but it does not appear as a spiritual path until the hidden writings of the alchemists of the sixteenth and seventeenth centuries, the Rosicrucians and, in the twentieth century, the writings of Blavatsky, Steiner, Gurdjieff, Ouspensky, and Jung.

The Closing of the Western Mind

I hope it is clear from this Chapter that Western civilization developed out of what was suppressed and repressed — the gnostic knowledge of who we really are — divine and immortal beings. Constantine's conversion to Christianity led to an alliance of church and state in the century that followed, that stifled freedom of thought and the highly developed Greek rationalism that was intrinsic to it. It led to what the historian Charles Freeman calls the "Closing of the Western Mind: The Rise of Faith and the Fall of Reason" where, on the back cover of his book with this title, he writes, "The churches enjoyed enormous patronage and exemptions from tax, and in return allowed the emperors to take on the definition and enforcement of an increasingly narrow religious orthodoxy." [58]

Timothy Freke and Peter Gandy, in their book *Jesus and the Goddess* describe how the Church authorities — whom they call the Literalists — created a distorted picture of Christian Gnosticism that still prevails today. "In a classic case of psychological projection, the Gnostics were represented as the diabolical heretics that the Literalists had actually become." [59]

The Christian Refuters of Gnosticism

This vital stream of wisdom known as Gnosticism which was later to suffer such repression and persecution at the hands of the late Roman Empire and the Christian Church under the Emperors Constantine and Theodosius 1 is a vital yet largely unknown aspect of our spiritual inheritance. It was far more advanced and enlightened as a spiritual teaching than the form of Christianity that was being developed in Rome. It was a threat to the small Christian community there because there were so many different Gnostic sects, each embracing a slightly different form of Gnosticism, some but not all of them Christian and many with their own gospels. One can understand why the theologians of the Roman Church were enraged, perplexed, and exasperated by them. This may explain but cannot excuse the violent methods they used to eradicate them.

Several Christian writers in the second century CE carefully recorded what they were able to discover about the different gnostic groups. Origen (185-235 CE), an early Christian Father and a man of immense learning, was one of these. Another was a lawyer called Tertullian (155-220 CE) who lived in Carthage and who wrote one of the most vitriolic attacks on woman that has ever been written.[60] The most prolific writer was Irenaeus (120/40-200/203 CE), bishop of Lyons in France, a city where many Christians were being martyred and dying horrific deaths. He wrote several volumes describing the Gnostics and their writings under the title of *Adverses Haeresias*. His principal aim was to refute the Gnostic teachings. These books provided the evidence used against them by the Christian Church which 'won' the doctrinal battle against them in the fourth and fifth centuries.

The Gnostics' Rejection of the Salvationist Ideology of the Christian Myth

The Gnostics were horrified by the Christian doctrine of salvation, or redemption by the sacrificial death of the Only Son of God. They saw it as a deliberately created myth, similar to earlier saviour myths, that would give overwhelming power and control to the Christian Church. They saw that the role of saviour projected onto a single individual who was named as the Son of God, was, in their view, false, and would take away the autonomy of the individual soul to accomplish his or her own redemption. They saw that this salvationist theology would lead to dividing people into those who were saved (the believers) and those who were not saved (who must be persuaded to believe or be destroyed). They also saw that it was leading to the inflation of the Christian Church in Rome, even to the point of psychosis when, in the eleventh century, believing itself to be carrying out the will of God, it launched a series of bloody Crusades against the Muslims in the Holy Land or in, the thirteenth, against the Cathar (Albigensian) 'heretics' in the Languedoc area of France.

Wherever Christianity went, it introduced the concept of original sin, guilt, and the silencing of women. It instituted a programme of polarization and conflict between different groups that would influence the seventeen hundred years that followed and would be copied by Islam in the seventh century, forcing the people it conquered to choose between conversion or death. Setting up Jesus as the Only Son of God and the Only Redeemer, made believers utterly dependent on the Church as the sole intermediary between them and the one and only Redeemer. It left them in an unconscious state, needing only to believe, waiting for the Last Judgement, when they would be raised to heaven in their physical bodies or banished to hell.

An edict of the emperor Theodosius 1 in 381 CE, introduced the concept of heresy, naming as heretics those who did not believe in the definition of the Trinity established at the Council of Nicaea in 325 CE.[61] This led inevitably to the persecution and murder of those whom the Church identified as heretics and to the utter destruction of the Gnostics who, Lash writes, "in Egypt, the Levant and the Near East held a crucial line of defence until they were destroyed by the proponents of the delusional system they tried to expose." [62] It also led to the abolition of the Mysteries, which for centuries had celebrated the revelatory bond with Nature and the *Anima-Mundi* or Soul of the World. It demolished the enlightened structure of education that had been established in cities and centres of learning throughout the Greek and later Roman Empire, as well as the many magnificent Pagan temples and the ancient mystical practices — the Mysteries — that had deeply revered and honoured Nature.

What became known as the Dark Ages, beginning in the fourth and fifth centuries CE, was inaugurated when the Christian Church, now supported by the Roman State, launched a brutal crusade to completely eradicate Christian Gnosticism and Paganism. In an orgy of violence, armies of Christian Literalists tore down the architectural wonders of the pagan world. They built infernal bonfires of books containing the spiritual wisdom and scientific knowledge of the ages. They subjected to grisly torture and a painful death philosophers, priestesses and scientists — anyone who disagreed. They did not stop until they had cut the head off Western culture, leaving it to wander like an amnesiac in an ignorant stupor. They did not stop until they had cut the heart out of Western spirituality, bleeding it dry of its mystical vitality. The corpse of a religion which remained offered nothing but hope of a better afterlife in return for blind belief in its irrational opinions and unquestioning allegiance to power-crazed popes....

Yet, despite this ruthless persecution, Gnosticism survived. It can be suppressed but never eradicated. It is the spontaneous expression of the natural inquisitiveness and enthusiastic exuberance of the human soul. It is the unquenchable thirst for truth and the undeniable urge to enjoy. It is the spirit of liberty, equality, love and insight. It is the force of Life. It always reasserts itself. [63]

The Gnostics as Knowers of the Way

The three patriarchal religions with their transcendent creator god-image, broke the umbilical cord of our relationship with a Sacred Nature, and therefore with the life of the planet. The Gnostics had honoured and kept alive the shamanic relationship with nature which had been established in the three-thousand-year period between 6500 and 3500 BCE during the Neolithic era in the area named as "Old Europe" which extended from Italy to the borders of Russia. (see Chap. Two) It seems beyond tragic that the Gnostics were destroyed by a Christian Church determined to have no rivals and given the power to eliminate them by two powerful emperors, Constantine and Theodosius I. Theodosius made it his personal mission to annihilate all traces of Pagan and Gnostic literature. He had 27,000 scrolls from the Mystery Schools collected and burned because he was told that they contained Gnostic teachings that contradicted his adopted belief system.[64] Lash writes, "Salvationism promised liberation for the immortal soul, in contrast to Pagan religion which offered liberation from selfhood through ecstatic immersion in the life force, Eros. For Salvationism to prevail, the traditions of Pagan religion and the attitude of tolerance toward religion had to be brutally eradicated." [65] "The purpose of the Mysteries was to keep us on course for our evolution as a species.... When the vision and the practices [of the Gnostics] were destroyed, we were, as he says, set on a sure course for self-annihilation.[66] As we survey the carnage of war in the modern world and the moral depths to which we have descended as a species, this prediction does not seem far-fetched.

A final word on the Gnostics comes from this channeled statement from an angel called Alariel, in a book I will return to in Chapter Eight, called *The Power of the Magdalene.*

> The true Gnostics were not only Knowers of the Truth, they were Knowers of the Way. Within them, Knowledge and Wisdom, Structure and Flow, Ritual and Process merged into Oneness, as the masculine and feminine energies are blended into the ultimate Wholeness of Being. Here all the balancing energies merge into the totality of the human experience. This was what Christianity was designed to lead towards. This was the balanced path of spiritual development which Jeshua (Jesus) worked to establish upon the Earth, and this, sadly, was what was rejected in favour of a one-sided presentation that valued the Form and rejected the Life. [67]

The Transmission of the Wisdom Tradition

The Gnostic beliefs and practices and the image of the Divine Feminine, the Holy Spirit, Divine Wisdom (Sophia), were nevertheless cherished by the Gnostic communities who, after the edicts of Constantine and Theodosius, could only survive persecution by going underground. These beliefs and practices were to emerge in Europe 800 years later in the Cathar Church of the Holy Spirit. They also seem to have survived or been paralleled in certain of the teachings of Kabbalah, particularly in its cosmology. Hans Jonas writes in his preface to his book *The Gnostic Religion*, "Our art and literature and much else would be different, had the Gnostic message prevailed."

Who treasured this Wisdom tradition and transmitted it to later generations through a thousand years? Who took the tradition of Divine Wisdom and the Holy Spirit to south-western France where it was carefully hidden and passed from generation to generation until the twelfth century when, astonishingly, it surfaced as the Cathar Church of the Holy Spirit, whose presiding Presence was Sophia or Divine Wisdom? I believe it was Mary Magdalene, or Miryam of Bethany, herself an Essene Priestess, who took the Essene (Gnostic) Wisdom tradition to France, or Gaul as it was then called. The 450 images of the Black Madonna honour the Wisdom tradition she brought with her as an Apostle to that country. [68] She took with her *The Gospel of the Beloved Companion*, her eyewitness account of the Mission of Jesus. (see Chap. Eight) This ancient Wisdom tradition of the Divine Feminine as the Holy Spirit has miraculously been kept alive for us today, when our world is crying out for re-connection with the neglected soul and the Divine Ground of our existence. Awareness of the Divine Feminine is returning to us at the dawn of a New Age. Part Two will tell the story of the Fall of Sophia and the beautiful Gnostic Hymn of the Pearl.

Notes:

1. The idea of a Great Library in Alexandria is said to have been suggested by Ptolemy I. His idea was developed further during the reign of his son, Ptolemy II (308-246 BCE). During his reign, more than 100 scholars were housed within the *Musaeon* or univer sity. Their job was to immerse themselves in scientific research, to give lectures and to collect, translate, copy and publish not only original manuscripts of Greek philosophers, poets and playwrights, but translations of multiple works from Egypt, Assyria and Persia, as well as Buddhist texts and Hebrew scriptures. (World History Encyclopaedia)
2. See William Dalrymple's latest book (2024), *The Golden Road: How Ancient India Transformed the World*
3. Lash, John Lamb, (2006, 2021), *Not in His Image: Gnostic Vision, Sacred Ecology and The Future of Belief*, Chelsea Green Publishing, Vermont, USA & London, p. 6
4. Mead, G.R.S. (1931) *Fragments of a Faith Forgotten*, John M. Watkins, London, p. 46
5. ibid, p. 49
6. ibid, p.32-33
7. ibid, p. 42, 46
8. ibid, p. 47
9. ibid, p. 51
10. ibid, p. 56
11. Lash, op. cit, p.13
12. The Nag Hammadi Library in English, (1977) editor James R. Robinson, E. J. Brill, p. 21
13. Lash, op. cit., p. 13
14. *The Apocryphon of John*, NHL, p. 98 and Pagels, Elaine (1980) The Gnostic Gospels, Weidenfeld and Nicolson Ltd., London, Chapter III
15. Dialogue of the Savior, NHL, p. 229
16. The Gospel of Philip, NHL, p. 131
17. Gardner, Laurence (2005) *The Magdalene Legacy*, HarperCollins, London. pp. 20 & 27, and index. In 318 CE, a genealogical Chart of the descendants of Jesus and his brother James, known as the *Desposyni Chart*, was presented to Pope Sylvester 1st by eight bishops, all male descendants of Jesus, one of whom was the Bishop of Jerusalem. On the order of the emperor Constantine, they had been summoned to Rome by the Pope with the aim of having their hereditary bishoprics removed. They brought with them their genealogical charts which proved their descent from Jesus and their entitle- ment to their bishoprics. The genealogical tree they presented to the Pope showed how each of these bishops was descended from Jesus and Mary Magdalene and James, the brother of Jesus. It covered 300 years and 10 generations. The Pope dismissed the visitors but kept the Chart they had brought with them. Bearing his signature, it was deposited in the secret archives in the Vatican. Some years ago, a researcher working in these archives, managed to evade the security cameras and photograph the 318 Desposyni Chart and bring the pictures back to England. These were published in 2015 by Barry Page in his book *The Historical Jesus Found.* (MPM Publication) Sylvester was Pope from 316 until his death in 335. He converted and baptised the emperor Constantine and was Pope at the time of the crucial Council of Nicaea in 325 which established the divinityof Jesus (as being of one substance with God).

18. Lash, *op. cit.*, p. xxi
19. Zosimus of Panopolis was a Greek alchemist and Gnostic mystic who lived from the end of the 3rd and beginning of the 4th century CE. He was born in Panopolis, present day Akhmin in the south of Egypt, and flourished ca. 300. He is unanimously recognized as the greatest of the Graeco-Egyptian alchemists, who was a prolific author but whose texts have survived only in tiny scraps.
20. from the Foreword by Stephan Hoeller to *The Fall of Sophia* by Violet MacDermott, 2001, Lindisfarne Books, P.O. Box 799, Great Barrington, MA
21. *The Teaching of Sylvanus*, NHL, p. 356
22. Jonas, Hans, (1958) *The Gnostic Religion*, Beacon Press, United States, p. 45
23. Mead, *op. cit.*, from The Acts of John, *The Gospel of Eve*, p. 439
24. Lash, *op. cit.*, p. 214
25. ibid, p. 216
26. ibid, p. 216
27. ibid, p. 217
28. ibid, p. 217
29. ibid, p. 218
30. ibid, p. 219
31. ibid, p. 221
32. ibid, p. 223
33. *The Gospel of the Beloved Companion*, (2010) trans. Jehanne de Quillan, Éditions Athara, Foix, France
34. *The Book of Thomas the Contender*, NHL, p. 189
35. Pagels, Elaine (1997) *The Gnostic Gospels*, Weidenfeld and Nicholson Lt., London, p. 57
36. *Trimorphic Protennoia* NHL, Invisible one within the All.
37. Pagels, p. 50
38. *op. cit.* p. 50 (Irenaeus *Adversos Heraesias* 1.13.6)
39. Quispel, Gilles, (1973) *The Birth of the Child*, page 23. Eranos Lectures 3: Jewish and Gnostic Man, Gershom Scholem and Gilles Quispel.
40. Pagels, op cit. p. 51
41. *The Trimorphic Protennoia*, NHL, pp. 461-70
42. *The Sophia of Jesus Christ*, NHL, p. 6
43. Pagels, *op. cit.*, p. 60
44. ibid, p. 60
45. ibid, p. 61
46. ibid, p. 61
47. Lash, *op. cit.*, pp. 6-7
48. ibid, p. 6
49. Deakin, Michael, (2007) *Hypatia of Alexandria*, Prometheus Books, Amherst, NY, p.13
50. *The Gospel of Truth*, NHL, p. 44
51. John Bowden in *The Myth of the Goddess*, Appendix 2, p. 686, from his book *Jesus, the Unanswered Questions*
52. Jung printed a few copies of the *Septem Sermones ad Mortuos* for friends of what he had written down in 1916. His account was published in the German edition of his autobiography but was omitted from the English edition. The English translation of *The*

Seven Sermons to the Dead is included in *The Gnostic Jung* by Stephan Hoeller, Quest Books, Wheaton, Illinois, 1982 and in the edition of his autobiography published in The Fontana Library of Theology and Philosophy, 1967 pp. 215-216

53. Jung, C.G. (1963) *Memories, Dreams, Reflections,* Collins & Routledge & Kegan Paul, London p. 184

54. Jung, C.G. (2009) *The Red Book,* The Foundation of the Works of C.G. Jung

55. M.D.R, p. 176

56. Jung, C.G. (1954) *Answer to Job,* trans. R. F.C. Hull, Routledge & Kegan Paul Ltd., London, p. 73

57. Jung, C.G. (1963) *Memories, Dream, Reflections,* pp. 190-191

58. Freeman, Charles (2003) *The Closing of the Western Mind, The Rise of Faith and the Fall of Reason,* Pimlico, London - quotation on the back cover

59. Freke, Timothy and Candy, Peter (2001) *Jesus and the Goddess,* Thorsons, London, p. 45

60. Tertullian, "By every garb of penitence woman might the more fully expiate that which she derives from Eve — the ignominy, I mean, of the first sin, and the odium of human perdition… Do you not know that you are each an Eve?... You are the devil's gateway; you are the unsealer of that forbidden tree; you are the first deserter of the divine law; you destroyed so easily God's image, man. On account of your desertion — that is, death — even the son of God had to die." *De Cultu Feminarium*

61. Theodosius surrendered his claim to be the Son of God so that Jesus could be the only Son of God. He also surrendered his Pontifex Maximus title and bestowed it on the Pope, the Bishop of Rome.

As an example of the orgy of destruction launched against both Pagans and Gnostics, in the late fourth century, Theodosius ordered the destruction of many Pagan temples and artefacts, including the renowned temple of Eleusis in Greece. In 391 he issued a decree sanctioning the demolition of temples in Alexandria. The Temple of Serapis (The Serapeum) was the most magnificent building in the ancient world. It was the storehouse for thousands of scrolls from the Great Library. In 392 a Christian mob, led by a bishop called Theophilus forced its way into the Temple and destroyed everything it could lay its hands on. Tens of thousands of priceless manuscripts were destroyed. Much of the genius and wisdom of the Ancient World perished with it. The Temple itself was left in ruins yet its basic plan can still be seen from Google Earth.

The Royal Library, also the repository of thousands of precious scrolls, suffered the same fate as the Temple of Serapis. The double catastrophe was an unimaginable loss for Western civilization. There is no final consensus as to who or what set fire to the Royal Library, but at least a part of it must still have been in existence at the time of Theon and Hypatia, even though the Temple of Serapis had been destroyed. Many archaeologists believe that the buildings that once composed this legendary seat of learning in ancient Alexandria, if not buried under the modern metropolis, could still survive relatively intact somewhere in the north-eastern part of the city. (World History Encyclopaedia)

It was not only Alexandria that had a great Library. Wherever there were temples and withdrawn communities like that of the Therapeutae on Lake Mareotis, near Alexandria, there were also libraries holding large collections of scrolls. From as early as Pre-Socratic times, scrolls from writers steeped in the Mysteries comprised an extensive treasury of writings on many different subjects. These were stored in the main centres of learning such as the Great Library in Alexandria and in other libraries situated in cities, temples, and withdrawn communities such as those of the Essenes.

62. Lash, op. cit. I regret that I cannot find the page number for this quote
63. Freke and Candy, op. cit. p. 46
64. Lash, p. 54
65. *op. cit.*, p. xxi
66. *op. cit.*, p. xix-xx
67. from *The Power of the Magdalene* by Stuart Wilson and Joanna Prentis, p. 95
68. see two books by Dr Annine van der Meer: *The Black Madonna from Primal to Final Times* 2019, and her latest book, *Magdalene's Ascension: Mary's Journey to Becoming Light* (2025) Inner Traditions

Books on the Gnostics and Gnosticism:

AD 381: Heretics, Pagans and the Christian State and *The Closing of the Western Mind* by Charles Freeman,
The Gnostics by Tobias Churton,
The Gnostic Religion by Hans Jonas
A Gnostic Anthology edited by Robert Grant
Gnosticism: New Light on the Ancient Tradition of Inner Knowing by Stephan Hoeller
Jung and the Lost Gospels by Stephan Hoeller
The Gnostic Jung and the Seven Sermons to the Dead by Stephan Hoeller
Jesus and the Goddess by Timothy Freke and Stephen Candy
The Divine Spark by Dan Morse
Gnostic Religion in Antiquity by Roelof van der Broek

Chapter Six

The Gnostics: Part Two

There is a light within a man of light, and he lights up the whole world.
When he does not shine, there is darkness.

— The Gospel of Thomas, *logion* 24

It is no exaggeration to say that the discovery of the transcendent inner
principle in man and the supreme concern about its destiny
is the very centre of gnostic religion.

— Hans Jonas, *The Gnostic Religion*, p. 124

This Chapter is about the Gnostic Myth of Sophia: her Fall and her Ascent. The Gnostics developed an elaborate cosmology, embracing many different levels or dimensions of reality and many beings inhabiting these dimensions. The Myth of Sophia, whose name means Wisdom, forms part of this cosmology. It is of great importance because it is one of the very few texts in the West that address the subject of the incarnation of the soul on this planet, even the idea of a planetary soul. In this myth, we can hear a feminine voice speaking, a rare event at any time. The myth provides a context for the subject of why we are here, what our evolutionary purpose here might be and how we might understand each other better than we do, knowing that we are all on the same evolutionary journey. Belief has not been enough to achieve this goal, as recent events in the world illustrate. We need more knowledge about where we have come from, what we are doing here and where we go when we die.

The Wisdom Texts and the Banished Goddess

Before we proceed, it would be helpful for the reader to remember the history of the Goddess Asherah, worshipped as the Queen of Heaven, Divine Wisdom and the Holy Spirit, who was deleted from Jewish cosmology in 623 BCE. And also the Wisdom texts: Chapter 8 of the Book of Proverbs and the wonderful passages from the Book of Ben Sira in the *Apocrypha* (See Chapter Five). These need to be borne in mind when reading this chapter.

This is the historical background to the story of the Fall and Ascent of Sophia in the *Pistis Sophia*, whose title means Faith-Wisdom. It is possible that in this Jewish Gnostic text, the fallen Sophia has a distant connection with the banished Goddess of the First Temple. There may be a hint, in Sophia's ascent, of her return. So there are two levels to this myth: one has to do with historical events surrounding the image of the Divine Feminine; the other with the courageous journey of the soul.

Reincarnation

Reincarnation was once part of Christian doctrine until it was removed at the time of the Second Council of Constantinople in 553 CE when the Emperor Justinian anathematised the teachings of the great Christian teacher Origen about the pre-existence of the soul. Origen, (ca 82 CE - ca 251 CE) wrote: "Every soul comes into this world strengthened by the victories and weakened by the defeats of its previous life." Justinian put an end to the teaching about reincarnation in the Christian Church. After a thousand years of its existence, Justinian also ordered the closure of the Platonic Academy in Athens, driving out its final director, Damascius. Accepting an invitation from the king of Persia, Damascius moved to a university near Basra, taking with him priceless scrolls from the Academy in Athens which eventually, via Persia and Arab Spain, reached the Schools of Chartres and Paris in the twelfth century.[1]

Through the decision of one powerful emperor, Christianity was deprived of a teaching about reincarnation that could have given it far greater depth and a more comprehensive perspective on life. The Christian West was immeasurably impoverished not only by the loss of the concept of reincarnation but also by the loss of the legacy of Platonic and Neo-Platonic teaching with all its rich insight into the nature of the soul.

There is one other very important factor in the history of Christianity which affected Christian teaching. During the ninth century, Pope Nicholas 1 (Pope from 858-67) decreed that the spirit should be removed from the nature of man, who was henceforth to be thought of as consisting of body and soul only; belief in the existence of an indwelling divine spirit in man was, from that date, to be named as heresy. After the schism between the Eastern and Western churches in 1054, the Eastern church did not follow this decree but continued to regard man as a unity of spirit, soul and body. [2]

In the West, it is only in Gnosticism and its modern relative, Theosophy, that we hear about reincarnation and the multiple times the soul descends into incarnation on this planet before she awakens sufficiently to embark on her journey of return to her 'home' in the higher regions of the cosmos. There are two Gnostic myths about the descent of the soul into incarnation and its return to its cosmic 'home.' One is the *Pistis Sophia*, a Gnostic text of the third century CE (but originally much earlier) that tells the story of the descent of Sophia to this lower world and the painful process of her release from it and her ascent through successive "repentances" or *metanoias.*

The other myth is *The Hymn of the Pearl* or *The Hymn of the Robe of Glory*, thought to have been written in Syriac by a Gnostic called Bardasanes, who lived in Edessa in the third century CE but also thought to have been written originally by the apostle Thomas who had travelled to south India, taking with him the teaching of Jesus. I have included a large part of this Hymn in this chapter, because it has been part of my life for sixty years and it never fails to move me to tears. I have also included the gnostic text of *The Wedding Song of Wisdom*, where the wedding of soul and spirit is celebrated in the bridal chamber. This was an important Gnostic ritual, mentioned in the Gospel of Philip in the Nag Hammadi Library, and will have been part of the story of Sophia.

The Pistis Sophia

In 1785, an extraordinary Coptic Gnostic Codex called the *Pistis Sophia*, meaning Faith-Wisdom, thought to date to the third century CE, but probably dating to an original Greek text of the second century or even earlier, was bought by the British Museum from the heirs of a Dr. Askew. It is the main source for the Gnostic Creation Myth — the story of the Fall and Ascent of Sophia. The other sources where the Myth of Sophia is mentioned are several gnostic texts in the Nag Hammadi Library, published in 1977: *The Apocryphon of John, Eugnostes the Blessed, The Sophia of Jesus Christ, The Exegesis of the Soul* and *The Second Treatise of the Great Seth.*

The *Pistis Sophia* was translated into English and published by G.R.S. Mead in 1921 and 1947 and in a more recent translation by Violet Mac-Dermott, called *The Fall of Sophia*, that was published in 1978 by Brill and again, in a book of that title, published in 2001 with a Foreword by Stephan Hoeller, that is unfortunately out of print.

Pistis Sophia was, Mead says, written by two hands, one in a fine, careful script; the other by a shaky hand suggestive of the writing of an old man. They used different inks and different methods of paging and correction and were probably contemporaries. The original manuscript, he believes, was written in Greek and later translated into Coptic. So far, no trace has been found of the Greek manuscript. It is a miracle that the Coptic text has survived.

The Voice of the Feminine in Gnosticism

So many of the gnostic texts and gospels were destroyed that it is not surprising that the voice of the Feminine in Gnosticism is almost inaudible. Apart from the *Pistis Sophia*, it can be heard in two texts in the Nag Hammadi Library: *The Thunder, Perfect Mind* and *The Trimorphic Protennoia*, both of which seem to have been communicated by channeling [3] I will include some verses from the latter at the end of this chapter. They are incredibly beautiful and moving. *The Thunder, Perfect Mind* [4] is written in the style of an aretalogy, a proclamation issuing from a deity, like the one spoken by the Goddess Isis to Apuleius. Elaine Pagels writes: "'The Thunder Perfect Mind' is a marvelous, strange poem. It speaks in the voice of a feminine divine power, but one that unites all opposites. One that is not only speaking in women, but also in all people.... It is a poem which sees the radiance of the divine in all aspects of human life, from the sordidness of the slums of Cairo or Alexandria, as they would have been, to the people of great wealth, from men to women to slaves." [5]

It is unfortunately too long to include in this chapter but here are a few selected lines:

> *I was sent forth from the power,*
> *And I have come to those who reflect upon me,*
> *And I have been found among those who seek after me.*
> *Look upon me, you who reflect upon me.*
> *You who are waiting for me, take me to yourselves*
> *And do not banish me from your sight.*
> *Do not be ignorant of me.*
> *For I am the first and the last*
> *I am the honoured one and the scorned one.*
> *I am the whore and the holy one.*
> *I am the wife and the virgin.*
> *I am the mother and the daughter...*
> *I am the barren one*
>   *And many are her sons...*
> *I am the one whose image is great in Egypt*
>   *And the one who has no image among the barbarians.*
> *I am the one who has been hated everywhere*
>   *And who has been loved everywhere...*
> *I am the one whom they call Life,*
>   *And you have called Death.*

The Divine Source: The Ineffable One

Gnostic cosmology is immensely complex but at the Source or Divine Ground of all Life there is what they named "The Unknowable Ineffable One." I am indebted to Dan Morse for his helpful summary of Gnostic Cosmology in his book *The Divine Spark Within*, "From this Source the Great Emanation came forth and with it a Holy Light that filled the Universe. Or, more precisely, it was the universe." [6] Sometimes the primal emanation from the Ineffable Source is male, sometimes male and female: a Mother and a Father as in *The Apocryphon of John* (The Secret Book of John) where John had a vision of the whole creation and heard a voice which said to him, "John, John, why do you doubt?... I am the one who is with you forever. I am the Father, I am the Mother, I am the Son." [7]

The Apocryphon of John also says this about the Mother, the first emanation from The Ineffable Divine Source which it wonderfully describes. I find it very moving to read these words, written down two thousand years ago:

> And his Ennoia performed a deed and she came forth before him in the shine of his light. This was the first power which came forth from his mind, that is the Pronoia of the All. Her light is the likeness of the light, the perfect power which is the image of the invisible, virginal Spirit who is perfect. The first power, the glory, Barbelo, the perfect glory in the aeons, the glory of the revelations, she glorified the virginal Spirit and praised him, because thanks to him she had come forth. This is the first thought, his image; she became the womb of everything for she is prior to them all, the Mother-Father, the first Man, the holy Spirit. [8]

In another text called the *Trimorphic Protennoia*, She says, "I am the first thought, the thought that is in the Light. I am the movement that is in all, she in whom the all takes its stand, the firstborn among those who came into being, she who exists before all.... I am invisible within the thought of the invisible one. I am revealed in the immeasurable, ineffable things. I am intangible, dwelling in the intangible. I move in every creature." [9] To me, these words suggest that she is the first articulation of the feminine Holy Spirit. Morse, in a fascinating passage, says that it was the Divine Light Mother who named the other aspect of what was emerging, Father. "This profound first creation might just be the Universe's first experience of love." [10]

The Third Element of the Great Emanation: The Son and Daughter

After the Emanation from the Ineffable Source, there was a union of the Mother and the Father and from this union came a third, their Son and Daughter. The

Son is variously named Anthropos, Logos, the Word, Son of Man, Christ, Light of Lights, First Mystery.[11] The daughter is named Sophia (Wisdom) after her Mother, or Pistis Sophia (Faith-Wisdom). In a text called *The Sophia of Jesus-Christ*, Jesus says to the disciples, "I desire that you understand that First Man is called 'Begetter, Mind who is complete in himself. He reflected with the great Sophia, his consort, and revealed his first-begotten androgynous son. His male name is called 'First-Begetter Son of God; his female name is First-Begettress Sophia, Mother of the Universe'. Some call her 'Love.'" [12] On the following page we read similar words in the same text: the perfect Savior said, referring possibly to the next level of creation: "Son of Man harmonized with Sophia, his consort, and revealed a great androgenous light. His male name is called Savior, Begetter of All Things, His female name is called 'All-Begettress Sophia.' Some call her 'Pistis.'" [13] To clarify, Pistis Sophia is the daughter of the Primal Mother Sophia, the womb of the All.

From this heavenly creative ground emanated twenty-four male and female angelic beings called "aeons" inhabiting a divine universe called The Pleroma, meaning "Fullness," which could be equated with our (Christian) concept of heaven. These aeonic beings had an important role to play in preserving the divine order of the universe. The daughter Sophia held the position of thirteenth aeon, together with her brother/consort Christ. It was the daughter Sophia's abandonment of her position and role as thirteenth aeon in the hierarchy of aeons that upset the balance of this divine order and may have precipitated her fall.

An Overview of the Pistis Sophia

The *Pistis Sophia* is about the Gnostic Myth of the Fall and Ascent of the daughter Sophia. It consists of six Books of which the first two are the most important for this Chapter. In all six books, Mary Magdalene is the disciple who asks Jesus most of the questions and who receives the highest praise from him. This is extraordinary for the time *Pistis Sophia* was written. Both translations, by Mead and MacDermott, tell the story of Sophia, who, in gnostic cosmology, is located with her male partner or brother, in the position of the thirteenth aeon. She is one of twenty-four brother and sister aeons, twelve of each gender. Wanting to reach the Light of lights above her, she confused that Light with a lesser light that drew her into a lower world where she found herself trapped in the chaos of a world that was controlled by malevolent beings called archons who were under the control of a lion-faced chief Archon called the Self-willed One, whose other name was Ialdabaoth. She not only found the archons ranged against her but also the rulers of the aeons who were outraged that she had tried to leave her appointed place and go to the Light that was higher than she was. In essence, it is the story of the soul's descent from the higher spheres into incarnation on earth, losing touch with her celestial home; her suffering, confusion and sorrow, and her many appeals to the Light to rescue her. After the thirteenth such appeal for help, Jesus [or Christ], her spiritual 'brother' aeon, descends to rescue her from the power of the archons and help her to return to a place just below that of her original 'home' in the thirteenth aeon.

As the helpless prisoner of the archons, Sophia or the human soul has no free will; no ability to determine her fate. In Gnostic texts she was called a 'poor desolate widow' and a prostitute who is defiled by many brutal men who take advantage of her and rape her. She is asleep, blind, or drunk, according to the different metaphors used in the Gnostic texts.

> *Sometimes she mourned and grieved,*
> *For she was left alone in darkness and the void;*
> *Sometimes she reached a thought of the light which had left her,*
> *And she was cheered and laughed;*
> *Sometimes she feared;*
> *At other times she was perplexed and astonished.* [14]

This Gnostic myth is the first to express the fourfold image of mother, father, daughter, and son, which offers an image of the totality of human experience in these four divine figures. It reflects the plight of the incarnated human soul, in the image of the daughter Sophia's bondage and suffering. But true to its lunar character, it is also a myth of release, for it offers an image of return to wholeness, and the possibility of transformation through Sophia's parents sending their son and her brother, Christ, to rescue her, ending with her ascent and return to the higher regions of the cosmos.

This myth describes the same tragic human experience of our separation from our source in the divine world of our origin as the Myth of the Fall, formulated by the Deuteronomist priests in 623 BCE. (see Chapter Three) But it does not carry the same sense of disobedience and guilt as the Myth of the Fall, more the sense of a response to a higher authority that was asking the daughter Sophia to undertake this journey for the sake of a higher purpose. The human soul, incarnating on this planet, makes the same mistake as *Pistis Sophia*, mistaking the light of the image of God — the Demiurge, formulated by the patriarchal religions, for the Light of the Divine Ground.

Echoes of the Greek Myth of Demeter and Persephone

Interestingly, in this Gnostic myth, we can glimpse the earlier Greek myth of the mother and daughter Goddesses, Demeter and Persephone, but the orientation of the gnostic myth is now specifically towards an inner world, an invisible cosmic world, and loses its relation to the cycle of the seasons in the Greek myth. It is as if the Gnostic myth continued the tradition of the Eleusinian Mysteries of Demeter and Kore, with their emphasis on the initiates or 'Mystes' having a visionary experience, whose nature was never revealed. Going even further back, there are fascinating echoes of the Sumerian lunar myth of the Descent of the Goddess Inanna to the underworld realm of her sister Goddess Ereshkigal, and her rescue by Enki, the God of Wisdom.[15]

As in the earlier Greek myth where Persephone, now the prisoner of Hades, God of the Underworld, cries out to her mother, the goddess Demeter for help, and Hermes, messenger of the gods, is sent to rescue her so, in this Gnostic myth, Jesus (or Christ) descends into the chaos of the "underworld" to release Sophia from the power of the Archons which are impeding her return to her home.

In Sophia's exile, we can also hear echoes of Eve's expulsion from the Garden of Eden, and this older myth can be read as a story of our losing the memory of our original home as we were expelled from the Garden of Eden and banished to earth.

The Meaning of the Word 'Metanoia'

The translations of the book by both Mead and MacDermott use the word 'repentance' when translating the Greek word *metanoia*. As I read this word 'repentance' repeated many times in the long text, I felt uncomfortable, even upset, because too much guilt or wrong-doing was being placed on Sophia, whereas what this extraordinary myth conveys is that, in compliance with an aspect of the Divine Plan initiated by a cosmic entity called The First Mystery, she had descended into incarnation for the purpose of preparing dwellings or bodies in which the sons of Light could incarnate, and became lost, frightened and confused in the chaos in which she found herself.[16] After many appeals for help to the Light, she began to ascend to her place of origin.

In her process of ascent, Sophia gave vent to her fear, sorrow, and desperate appeals for help. She experienced thirteen *metanoias*, each followed by moving appeals and songs of praise to the Light and by psalms or odes offered by the disciples who were gathered, listening to Jesus telling them the story of Sophia. The word *metanoia*, generally translated as "repentance," and suggesting 'sin' or guilt, is found in the four Gospels and is central to the Christian tradition. But its original Greek meaning suggested a transformation of a mental state, an *inner* change of attitude, understanding, values, and behaviour, not repentance for sin. I have in my library a book written in the 1950's by Maurice Nicoll, called *The Mark*, which explores the meaning of this word and offers a very different interpretation of it from the word 'repentance'. It has more the meaning of turning around to face another direction, a change of consciousness, a flash of intuitive insight into something that was not seen or understood before, thus offering release from a former belief, conviction, or less conscious state. Or, in Jungian understanding, release from destructive aspects of the personal unconscious or 'shadow' that were previously unknown or unrecognized and were controlling the psyche in a negative way.

The Inner Meaning of Pistis Sophia

Mead says that "The Gnostics regarded Wisdom as an all-encompassing [feminine] power that received and brought forth the Ideas of the Divine Mind, and manifested the Divine Laws. In brief, Wisdom was the World-Soul for the cosmos, and the individual soul for man." [17] It is important to remember this dual role of Wisdom in what follows.

In a very illuminating article published in *Quest Magazine*, the Bulletin of the Theosophical Society in Fall 2011, that is also available on Wikipedia, Raul Branco writes:

> Like the parable of the hidden treasure, the *Pistis Sophia* is ready to yield to any man or woman who works hard tilling its soil a veritable treasure hoard of esoteric teachings, hidden there by the Master for the benefit of his disciples of all times, and not only for those who followed him during his earthly life in Palestine two thousand years ago. The unveiling of the progressive passage by the soul through the different levels of manifestation by means of '*metanoias*' (progressive inner changes) provided in the text seems designed to awaken man to the reality of his divine origin and his mission on Earth. Throughout the story of *Pistis Sophia*, and in the remainder of the book, there are many teachings that might touch the soul of each reader in a different way. In this sense the text is magic. It is designed to work in every sincere heart that is looking with zest and determination for the keys that will enable him to open the Gates of the Kingdom of Heaven.

Raul Branco continues:

The Gnostic texts provide such profound insights on the inner nature of man and their psychological importance that they seem to have provided the foundation for modern psychology as presented by Carl G. Jung. Thus, a myth would have macro as well as microcosmic dimensions, although one of these would generally be the focus for the teaching provided therein. In the case of the *Pistis Sophia* the inner dimension seems to be the main focus. Almost every entity in the story, i.e., *Pistis Sophia*, Jesus, the Self-centered one, the Power with a Lion Face, the aeons, etc, can be interpreted as inner aspects of man.

While this story looks like a myth, Jesus actually seems to be recounting one aspect of his experience at the Great Initiation, which probably took place during the thirty hours that he remained at the height [see below]. His recollection of the incidents on his way up has a surprising parallel with the life review that takes place in the dying process of every human being. We learn that this rapid but thorough process at the end of each incarnation teaches us the implications of our actions in this world. If we recall that the law of correspondence tells us, "What is above is like that which is below and that which is below is like what is above," we can infer that the *Pistis Sophia* tale seems like a monumental review of the actions of the soul throughout its long journey in this world. This seems also to take place when the evolutionary process is speeded up, as in the case of adepts who reach the Fifth Initiation in advance of the majority of the race [as Jesus did].

Thus the *Pistis Sophia* myth is the story of the passage of Jesus's soul through the world from time immemorial until his final triumph. Jesus and *Pistis Sophia* are presented as a pair, the two aspects of the soul, just like the two sides of a coin. Each has its role in the mystery of life. The progressive expansion of consciousness that eventually turns Jesus into a Master of Wisdom was in fact a reflection, on a higher level, of *Pistis Sophia's* slow and relentless battle in this world against all the agents of matter that have constantly striven to take away her light. No mention is made of the great number of incarnations that Jesus must have gone through until that historical one in Palestine. During all those lives, regardless of the names by which he may have been known, *Pistis Sophia*, his soul, was the loyal heroine doing battle in this world.

It is said that *Pistis Sophia* reaches her final liberation at the exact moment when Jesus is at the Mount of Olives with his disciples in the process of being elevated to the Height in the midst of the Light. Thus, we have an indication of the Fifth Initiation, both from the point of view of the glorified individuality, Jesus or the Higher Self, and of the soul finally freed from the prison of the world. At that moment *Pistis Sophia* is finally reunited with her partner [aeon], Jesus, a parallel with the sacrament of the Wedding Chamber mentioned in the Gospel of Philip [in the *Nag Hammadi Library*] and the experience of the great mystics at the last stage of "Theosis", or Union with God.

The Transfiguration of Jesus

With this in mind, we can now turn to the First Book of the *Pistis Sophia*, where Jesus is with his disciples, his mother and Mary Magdalene on the Mount of Olives, eleven years after his resurrection. On the night of the full moon of May, he is seated slightly apart from them. Suddenly, "there came forth behind him a great light-power shining most exceedingly… and that light-power came down over Jesus and surrounded him entirely, while he was seated removed from his disciples… and there was no measure for the light that was on him." He was enveloped in light so brilliant and dazzling that the disciples could no longer see him. They saw only the light-rays "that formed one great immeasurable glory of light that stretched from under the earth right up to heaven." [18] Then Jesus ascended or soared into the height, shining most exceedingly in immeasurable light. The awestruck disciples gazed after him as he vanished into the heights of heaven and they all stayed in deep silence.

After thirty hours, he returned, accompanied by thunder and lightning and an earthquake that terrified the disciples. He hastened to reassure them and they saw that now he "shone more radiantly than at the hour when he had ascended… and the light shot forth light-rays in great abundance." They saw that Jesus was now surrounded by three robes of light — a triple Robe of Glory — of a brilliance far exceeding that when he ascended. The shaken disciples said, "Lord, if it be thou, withdraw thy light-glory into thyself that we may be able to stand; otherwise our eyes are darkened, and we are agitated, and the whole world is agitated because of the great light which is about thee." [19] He tells them that he had been given his Light-vesture or Robe of Glory by the First Mystery — the robe which he had left behind until the time had come for him to have it restored to him when he had completed his Mission on earth. Then he begins to recount to the disciples the details of what he had accomplished during his absence.

This section is very complex. In the course of it, Jesus tells the disciples and his mother that he arranged to bring to birth the souls of John the Baptist and all the disciples, as well as his own incarnation in the body of his mother, Mary, with the help of the Archangel Gabriel, so they would be all be born at the same time and be able to help him with his Mission. [20]

At a certain point, Mary Magdalene asks to speak and Jesus answers her, saying, "Mary, thou blessed one, whom I will perfect in all mysteries of those of the height, discourse in openness, thou, whose heart is raised to the kingdom of heaven more than all thy brethren." [21] Elsewhere he says to her: Well said, Mary, for thou art blessed before all women on the earth, because thou shalt be the fulness of all fulnesses and the perfection of all perfections." [22]

Having penetrated the veils of the twenty-four aeons and set them on their new courses, Jesus arrived at the thirteenth aeon and found *Pistis Sophia* "below the thirteenth aeon all alone and no one of them with her. And she sat in that region grieving and mourning, because she had not been admitted into the thirteenth aeon." [23] In answer to a question from Mary Magdalene about why *Pistis Sophia* was no longer in the thirteenth aeon, Jesus embarked on a long explanation:

"It came to pass, when *Pistis Sophia* was in the thirteenth aeon, in the region of all her brethren, the invisibles, that is the four-and-twenty emanations of the great Invisible, — it came to pass by command of the First Mystery that *Pistis Sophia* gazed into the height. She saw the light of the Veil of the Treasury of the Light and she longed to reach to that region and she could not reach to that region. But she ceased to perform the mystery of the thirteenth aeon, and sang praises to the light of the height which she had seen in the light of the veil of the Treasury of the Light."

"It came to pass then when she sang praises to the region of the height that all the rulers in the twelve aeons who are below, hated her, because she had ceased from their mysteries, and because she had desired to go into the height and be above them all. For this cause, they were enraged against her and hated her [as did] the great triple-powered Self-willed... who is in the thirteenth aeon, he who had become disobedient... in that he desired to rule over the whole thirteenth aeon and those who are below it."

"It came to pass then, when the rulers of the twelve aeons were enraged against *Pistis Sophia*, who is above them, and hated her exceedingly, that the great triple powered Self-willed [Ialdabaoth] of whom I have just told you, joined himself to the rulers of the twelve aeons, and also was enraged against *Pistis Sophia* and hated her exceedingly because she had thought to go to the light which is higher than her. And he emanated out of himself a great lion-faced power, and out of his matter in him he emanated a host of other very violent material emanations, and sent them into the regions below, to the parts of the chaos in order that they might lie there in wait for *Pistis Sophia* and take away her power out of her, because she thought to go to the height which is above them all, and moreover had ceased to perform the mystery, and lamented continuously and sought after the light which she had seen." [24]

"It came to pass then thereafter by command of the First Commandment that the great triple-powered Self-willed, pursued Sophia in the thirteenth aeon in order that she should look towards the parts below, so that she might see in that region his lion-faced light-power and long after it and go to that region, so that her light might be taken from her."

"It came to pass that she looked below and saw his light-power in the parts below; and she knew not that it was that of the triple powered Self-willed, but she thought that it came out of the light which she had seen from the beginning in the height, which came out of the veil of the Treasury of the Light. And she thought to herself: I will go into that region without my pair [brother] and take the light and thereout fashion for myself light-aeons, so that I may go to the Light of lights which is the Height of heights."

"This then thinking, she went forth from her own region, the thirteenth aeon, and went down to the twelve aeons. The rulers of the aeons pursued her and were enraged against her, because she had thought of grandeur. And she went forth also from the twelve aeons, and came into the regions of the chaos and drew nigh to that lion-faced light-power to devour it. But all the material emanations of Self-willed surrounded her, and the great lion-faced light-power devoured all the light-powers in Sophia and cleaned out her light and devoured it, and her matter was thrust into the chaos... When this befell, Sophia became greatly exhausted, and that lion-faced light-power set to work to take away from Sophia all her light-powers, and all the material powers of Self-willed surrounded Sophia at the same time and pressed her sore." [25]

"And *Pistis Sophia* cried out most exceedingly, she cried to the Light of lights which she had seen from the beginning, in which she had had faith and uttered this repentance saying, O Light of lights in whom I have had faith from the beginning, hearken now then O Light, unto my repentance. Save me, O Light, for evil thoughts have entered into me." [26]

Pistis Sophia then moves through a series of seven further repentances or *metanoias*, each time lamenting her fate and calling upon the Light for help. After each one, a disciple comes forward and recites a psalm that reflects or expands on what Sophia has just said. After the seventh repentance, Jesus says that he has not received the command from the First Mystery to save Sophia and lead her up out of the chaos. Nevertheless, without a commandment and out of compassion, he led her into a somewhat more spacious region in the chaos. This had the effect of lessening the oppression of Self-willed until he saw that she had not been finally released. Whereupon, he renewed his attacks on her. [27]

At the ninth repentance, when Sophia was being oppressed again by the Lion-faced power, she cried out to the Light: "O Light, in whom I have had faith from the beginning, for whose sake I have endured these great pains, help me." Her words seem to confirm that she had been sent on a mission by the First Mystery, a mission that involved her in great suffering and oppression by the power of the archons. At last, the First Mystery responded to her appeals for help and sent Jesus to raise her out of the chaos. "Sophia then saw me, that I shone ten-thousand times more than the lion-faced power and that

I was full of compassion for her." [28] Sophia then uttered the tenth repentance saying, "I have cried unto thee, O Light of lights, in my oppression and thou hast hearkened unto me." [29] When the lion-faced power saw what was happening, it grew more furious and emanated from itself a multitude of exceedingly violent emanations. Jesus drew near to it, to take away the light from the lion-faced power, who called for help to the Self-willed god situated in the thirteenth aeon. In great fear, Sophia uttered the twelfth repentance, pleading desperately for help from the Light. [30]

Jesus continued in his discourse and said unto the disciples: "It came to pass when Pistis Sophia had uttered the thirteenth repentance [one for each aeonic level?] that the time was fulfilled that she should be led out of the chaos. And of myself, without the First Mystery, I despatched out of myself a light-power, and I sent it down to the chaos, so that it might lead *Pistis Sophia* forth from the deep regions of the chaos, and lead [her] to the higher regions of the chaos, until the command should come from the First Mystery that she should be led entirely forth from the chaos. And my light-power led *Pistis Sophia* up to the higher regions of the chaos. It came to pass then, when the emanations of the Self-willed had noticed that *Pistis Sophia* was led forth into the higher regions of the chaos, that they also sped after her upwards, desiring to bring her again into the lower regions of the chaos. And my light-power, which I had sent to lead up Sophia out of the chaos, shone exceedingly." [31] Sophia again cried out for help to the Light, begging it not to leave her in the chaos.

And Jesus continued, saying to his disciples, "It came to pass then when *Pistis Sophia* had finished saying these words [the thirteenth repentance] in the chaos, that I made the light power, which I had sent to save her, become a light-wreath on her head, so that from now on the emanations of Self-willed could not have dominion over her. And when it had become a light-wreath around her head, all the evil matters in her were shaken and all were purified in her. They perished and remained in the chaos while the emanations of Self-willed gazed upon them and rejoiced. And the purification of the pure light which was in *Pistis Sophia,* gave power to the light of my light power, which had become a wreath around her head." [32]

And Sophia praised the wreath around her head and sang praises, saying, "The Light hath become a wreath round my head and I shall not depart from it, so that the emanations of Self-willed may not rob it from me and though all the matters be shaken yet shall I not be shaken. And though all my matters perish and remain in the chaos, — those which the emanations of Self-willed see, — yet I shall not perish. For the Light is with me, and I myself am with the Light." [33]

"It came to pass when *Pistis Sophia* had uttered the 13th repentance, — *in that hour was fulfilled the commandment of all the tribulations which were decreed for this to Sophia for the fulfilment of the First Mystery* [italics mine], which was from the beginning, and the time had come to save her out of the chaos and lead her out from all the darknesses. But her repentance was accepted from her through the First Mystery; and that Mystery sent me a great light power out of the height, that I might help her up out of the chaos. So I looked towards the aeons into the height and saw that light-power which the First Mystery had sent me, that I might save *Pistis Sophia* out of the chaos. It came to pass therefore when I had seen it, coming forth in the aeons and hastening down to me — I was above the chaos — that another light-power went forth out of me, that it too might help *Pistis Sophia*. And the light-power which had come down from the height through the First Mystery, came down upon the light-power which had gone out of me; and they met together and became a great stream of light." [34]

Mary Magdalene then interpreted the meaning of what Jesus had said and when Jesus heard her words he praised her, saying, "Well said, Mary, blessed one, who shall inherit the whole Light-kingdom." [35]

Mary Magdalene

Mary Magdalene takes the lead throughout this long description of the Fall of *Pistis Sophia* and her Ascent to the heavenly spheres from which she came, after her release from the power of the Archons. Her ascent carries a faint association with Miryam's ascension of the Tree of Life, as described in her *Gospel of the Beloved Companion* (Chapter Eight). This dialogue in the *Pistis Sophia*, is said to have taken place on the Mount of Olives. It may be the record of their final meeting before Mary Magdalene left for France. It is extraordinary that their last conversation together should have somehow been recorded, perhaps by the disciple Philip, who was the scribe for the meeting, perhaps by a later Gnostic teacher who was not present at the meeting but who had access to the original Greek text. There is no record of Jesus and Mary Magdalene meeting again. Their joint Mission had been accomplished.

The Antagonism of Peter

What becomes clear in the recounting of this myth and the comments and contributions of the disciples in the form of quoting from the psalms and the Odes of Solomon after each "*metanoia*" of *Pistis Sophia's* ascent, is the gulf that existed between Mary Magdalene and Peter — a gulf that must have been visible to Jesus and the other disciples around them. The entire volume of six chapters gives the most space to the dialogue between Jesus and Mary Magdalene. In Book Two, Mary Magdalene is mentioned 150 times whereas Peter is mentioned 14 times. Truly extraordinary for the time, Mary Magdalene is the chief questioner, asking 39 of the 42 questions put to Jesus by the disciples. Jesus addresses her as 'Thou pure in Light' and repeatedly praises her after she has spoken, saying, "Well said, Mary, for thou art blessed before all women on the earth, because thou shalt be the fulness of the fulnesses and the perfection of all perfections." [36] And later, "Well said, Mary, blessed one, the fulness or all-blessed fulness, thou who shalt be sung of as blessed in all generations." [37] One can imagine Peter's jealous rage on hearing these words. At one point Peter, exasperated, interrupts, saying, "My Lord, we will not endure this woman, for she taketh the opportunity from us and hath let none of us speak, but she discourseth many times." [38]

In the middle of Book Two, Mary says, "My Lord, my mind is ever understanding, at every time to come forward and set forth the solution of the words which she [Sophia] hath uttered; but I am afraid of Peter, because he threateneth me and hateth our sex." [39] Peter appears to be jealous of her close relationship with Jesus and even her presence with the disciples. In Book Six he again protests, "My Lord, let the women cease to question, in order that we also may question." [40] He is shown here as well as in the *Gnostic Gospel of Thomas*, to be a misogynist, when he says in *logion* 114 of that Gospel, 'Let Mary leave us for women are not worthy of life'. The dialogue is almost entirely between Jesus and Mary Magdalene. In view of her important role in this Jewish Gnostic or possibly Essene text, it makes me wonder whether she could have taken the Greek text of the *Pistis Sophia* with her when she went to France in 44 CE and whether the many statues of the Black Madonna there represent Sophia as well as the teaching of the Wisdom Tradition she brought with her. Dan Morse, in a fascinating webinar, has shown the sculptural images associated with Wisdom on the cathedrals of Notre Dame and Chartres. There can never be proof of this but it may be worth mentioning it and remembering it when we reach Chapter Eight. [41]

The Archons and the Demiurge

To the Gnostics, every institution existing in the world of humans was contaminated by evil, including religion, which was subject to error because it was the creation of the darkened consciousness of man and malevolent beings called Archons, whose aim was to block, prevent or divert humanity from awakening to its true destiny—its return to the Pleroma.

Then, as now, the Light of Wisdom within her shines in this darkness, but the soul, in her unconscious state, is not aware of it. The Gospel of John, which many Gnostic Christian sects used, expressed this in the words: "And the Light shineth in darkness; and the darkness comprehended it not." (John 1:5) It was in this way, that certain Gnostic myths explained the creation of the world and of humanity, as well as the existence of suffering. Humanity is not evil, but unconscious; ignorant rather than inherently sinful, its existence controlled by false teachings, incomplete or inadequate beliefs and flawed human institutions, including its priesthoods. Men and women are the victims of a fate they cannot control, precisely because they do not know they are controlled by it.

Christ before the Judge
Cecil Collins

There are two chapters in the *Nag Hammadi Library* called *The Hypostasis of the Archons* (Reality of the Rulers) and *The Origin of the World* which refer to the Archons. Originally, archon (from the Greek arkhon), meant ruler. But to the Gnostics the word came to represent malefic powers or beings that were actively engaged in keeping humanity in a state of bondage. Looking at the world today, as from a transcendent perspective, it is not hard to see that humans are in bondage to addictive habits of behaviour and beliefs that have been in place for thousands of years and seem impossible to change or eradicate. Driving these habits and beliefs are three primordial instincts which seem to be active primarily in men: the will to power, the will to survive and the will to avenge. All three have their origin in the fear of not surviving, of not knowing why we are here. Also involved in these habits and beliefs is an incomplete image of God which does not include the whole of the created order within it.

The Christian Gnostics saw the world, including the Christian Church, as ruled by an imposter, a Demiurge named Ialdabaoth, chief of the Archons, who was involved in the Fall of the daughter Sophia, a false god who had set himself up as the God of the Old Testament and the Creator and Ruler of the world, and who proclaimed, "Thou shalt have no other gods before me." (Exodus 20:3) This false god, whose existence and nature are described in several of the Nag Hammadi texts, had managed — as the God of the Old Testament — to gain control of the world through terrifying his followers into obedience. Morality was imposed on the people by a set of commands and rules emanating from him and rigorously enforced by his priests, instead of arising instinctively from within the natural order and within the human heart. In the passage below, we can hear the angry tone of the Demiurge's denunciations of Paganism, which would have been anathema to the Gnostics, who held nature to be sacred and imbued with divinity. Such vicious invective would have been incomprehensible to them:

> Ye shall utterly destroy all the places wherein the nations which ye shall possess served their gods, upon the high mountains, and upon the hills, and under every green tree. And ye shall overthrow their altars, and break their pillars, and burn their idols with fire; and ye shall hew down the graven images of their gods, and destroy the names of them out of that place. Deut:12:2-3

The problem as John Lamb Lash succinctly describes it is this: "The religion of the extra-terrestrial father god ruptures humanity's empathic bond with the Earth… yet it is that same religion that has given humanity in the Western world its historical and spiritual identity." [42]

Archons appear to be intermediaries between the material and spiritual dimensions, sometimes described as fallen angels or as a hybrid, not fully human race, compared to an aborted foetus that was inadvertently brought into being during Sophia's fall, or even as a malefic group of extra-terrestrials. The soul is compelled continually to reincarnate on this planet in a new body, as long as, knowing nothing of her true nature, she has no desire to return to her 'home'. Like Sophia, the soul finds herself bound and persecuted by the Archons as she descends into the chaos of the world where their influence prevails. Their aim was to hold humanity in bondage to their power and to use their power to lure humans into serving their aims, ignoring the need to look for anything beyond them. There were seven specific Archons who were said to be the rulers of the seven planets, controlling humanity through their astrological influence and barring humans from escaping from their control. But beyond these seven, there were many others. They are sometimes described as having the appearance of demonic beings or animals, reminiscent of the images in *The Temptation of St. Anthony* by Hieronymous Bosch or *The Torment of St. Anthony* by Grunewald. The chief Archon Ialdabaoth in the *Pistis Sophia* is described as having a lion's face. Lash describes them "as a freak species of inorganic composition, but they are alive and conscious in their own way. Archons present an extra-Pleromatic phenomenon, a cosmic aberration, *anomia.*" [43] In the *Pistis Sophia*, they are very clearly described as the power to bind Sophia to them until she is released from her bondage by her thirteen appeals to the Light for help and her ultimate rescue by Jesus, her aeonic 'twin' brother, descending as an emissary of the Light, to release her from their power.

What is easier to comprehend is their apparent aim, which was to prevent humanity from ascending to the higher realms and to deflect humanity from its evolutionary path and goal—its reunion with the Light of the divine ground. The methods they used to implement this aim were to lure humans to seek power and control over others, and to replace higher aims with lower ones that bind humans to the material world and its unconscious rulers. Lash writes at the end of his chapter *The Insane God*:

> Gnostics warned of the danger posed by the side effect of Sophia's plunge: humanity may be deviated from its proper course of development.... It is as if the presence of the Archons in the planetary system sets up a deviant field that distorts human thinking. "The world system we inhabit came about due to a mistake," says the Gospel of Philip from Nag Hammadi. This may be one of the strangest notions ever proposed. [44]

It was these archontic powers that Jesus referred to in no uncertain terms as Caesar, or the Ruler and Master of the World in the Gospels of Matthew 22:21 and Mark 12:17 and as the Ruler or Master of the World in *The Gospel of the Beloved Companion* (Chapter Eight). It may be that in the mysterious saying in the Gospel of Thomas, 'Blessed is the lion which the man eats and the lion will become man; and cursed is the man whom the lion eats and the lion will become man,' (*logion* 8), he was referring to the lion-faced Archon and Demiurge Ialdabaoth.

Because humans are not aware of the existence of the Archons, their power and their Plan, they have, for millennia, been the victims of them, without knowing what has happened and why. The protracted struggle for freedom, truth, justice, and democracy bears witness to the protracted battle to overcome their power, above all, the power of those who govern us. The virtual slavery of some parts of humanity under their rulers — namely women under the Taliban and the Iranian regime — bears witness to their ongoing agenda of control. The current threat from the rulers of Iran to the whole Middle East is another example of archontic power.

Knowing nothing about the reasons why we are here, on this planet, we have created all kinds of theories about malefic influences to explain the existence of evil, from the Sumerian Annunaki to the Zoroastrian Ahriman, to St. Paul's 'Powers and Principalities and the Rulers of Darkness' (Ephesians 6:12), and lately, the twentieth century theories of Rudolf Steiner about the influence of the forces of Ahriman. Looking at the state of the world and the various leaders attempting to manipulate and control it to their advantage, or the unconscious addiction to materialism and the seductive wiles of social media — an Archontic enterprise if ever there was one — it does seem as if a malefic influence is repeatedly deflecting humanity off course, drawing people into following beliefs and leaders representing them into actions that create unimaginable suffering. AI presents a huge threat to humanity if it falls into the wrong hands. That too could be seen as an archontic enterprise.

Another archontic influence has been the desire of religions to convert and control the people they conquered and to eliminate their rivals. The recent declared aims of Islamic State to achieve world dominance through terror and brute force fall into this category, but centuries ago, there were the Crusades and the brutal attempts to force the conquered to convert to the religion of the conquerors, whether Christian or Muslim. The drive for dominance over others can be traced to 3,500 BCE and the infiltration of northern tribes into the peaceful Goddess culture of the inhabitants of Old Europe (see Chapter Two). Perhaps this was the first historical example of archontic influence.

Jung might have associated the activity of the Archons with what he called the Shadow and a state of possession by unconscious instincts — often originating in childhood trauma, that can act in a malevolent, destructive, even demonic way, when they take possession of the conscious mind through fear, hatred, greed, envy, jealousy, lust, the desire for revenge and the will to power, or desire to control others. The root cause of all these can, I believe, be attributed to the long-term effects of feeling abandoned on this planet, not understanding that there is a reason why we are here and that we have an evolutionary path to follow. But it includes the horrific cruelties and devastating losses that humanity has experienced at the hand of its rulers through the millennia, as well as through natural disasters. There is also the devastating power of the inner critic in man and woman — the negative animus or anima — formed by trauma inflicted in childhood, that can lead to depression and suicide as well as to violent attacks on others. The addiction to war and the creation of our weapons of mass destruction would be two further examples of the influence of the Archons. In Chapter Thirteen, The Abuse of Power, I will return to this subject.

The Sacred Marriage of Soul and Spirit

The quest in Gnostic myth takes a dual form: the soul's longing for the Light she desires to reach and the longing of the Light to rescue her. The underlying unity of soul and spirit is expressed in the image of marriage and the bridal chamber — that originates with *The Song of Songs* in the Old Testament and is wonderfully expressed in a beautiful Syrian gnostic text called *The Wedding Song of Wisdom*.[44] At the interface between inner and outer worlds, the spirit, as bridegroom, emissary of the divine Mother-Father, comes to meet the awakened soul, his bride, and the two become one. Gnostic ritual celebrated this sacred marriage of soul and spirit. The spirit was visualized and described as the Robe of Glory, the greater Self of the soul.

The Wedding Song of Wisdom or Ode to Sophia
From the Acts of Thomas [45]

"The Maiden is Light's daughter;
in her the King's radiance is treasured.
Majestic her look, and delightsome under lights;
in radiant beauty she shineth.
Like to spring flowers are her garments:
from them streameth scent of sweet odours.
Throned o'er her head the King sitteth,
with food free from death feeding them at his table.
Truth crowneth her head; joy sports at her feet.
She openeth her mouth as becomes her;
all songs of praise she lets stream forth.
Two and thirty are they who sing praises;
... Her tongue is like the entrance veil,
moved by them who enter in only.
Her neck towereth step-like;
the first world-builder to build it.
Her hands suggest the band of blessed aeons, proclaiming them;

her fingers point towards the City's Gates.
Her bridal chamber doth stream with Light,
and pour forth scent of balsam and sweet herbs,
delicious scents of myrrh and savoury plants;
with myrtle wreathes and masses of sweet flowers t'is strewn within.
Her bridal couch is decked with reeds.
Her bridesmen are grouped round her; seven are they in number;
she hath picked them herself.
Seven too are her bridesmaids dancing before her.
Twelve are they who serve and attend her; their eyes ever look for the Bridegroom,
that He may fill them with Light.
For ever with Him will they be in joy everlasting;
and will take their seats at that feast where the Great Ones assemble,
and remain at that banquet of which the Eternal alone are deemed worthy.
In kingly dress shall they be clad, and put on robes of Light, and both shall joy in bliss
and exultation, singing praise to the Father,
For of his glorious radiance they've received;
and at the sight of Him, their Lord, they have been filled with Light.
They have received from Him immortal food that knows no waste.
They've drunk of wine that makes men thirst no more, nor suffer fleshly lust.
So with the Living Spirit they glorified Truth's father,
and sing their praise to Wisdom's Mother."

Mead comments: "This hymn looks back to the sacred marriage of Sophia with her Bridegroom, Christ. In this marriage the cosmic Sophia was received back into the Light-world and united with her heavenly spouse. This was to take place at the Great Consummation; but, mystically, it was ever taking place for those who united themselves with their Higher Selves. As in the consummation of the universe, the World-Soul was to be reunited with the World-Mind, so in the perfectioning of the individual, the soul was made one with the Self [Spirit] within."

"The Maiden is the daughter of the Pleroma of Light; she reflects the splendour of the Kings, the Lords of the Light-realm. Above her, in the light realm sits throned the King of glory, the Christos, who giveth the food of deathlessness to the Spiritual Souls who are worthy to be bidden to the Feast."

"At this high initiation the whole Pleroma (the two and thirty aeons) sing songs of rejoicing that the victory is won. It is only such perfected souls who could move Wisdom's tongue in praise to God; they alone can make the subtle substance of such lofty heights vibrate in songs of praise."

"The 'City' is the Pleroma; the bridal chamber is the shrine, the holy place, where the initiation is given. Thither the purified soul is conducted by seven pairs of powers. Rising aloft she takes with her, the twelve, her servants, no longer her rulers as in the lower world, where she has so long been chained in the bonds of desire. The twelve are now her own purified powers, whereby the Light of the Christos is reflected. In the phrase, "both shall joy in bliss and exultation," of the third verse from the end, "both" refers to the reunited soul with its "Angel" — those Angels who always behold the Face of the Father."[45]

The Hymn of the Pearl or The Hymn of the Robe of Glory

Sometimes the soul is portrayed as feminine, as the aeon Sophia; at others, it is masculine, as the *Anthropos*, or divine son, who 'fell' into matter and forgot his relationship to the world of his origin, as in *The Hymn of the Pearl*. The myth of the *Anthropos* resembles far older myths where the son-lover of the Goddess descended into the underworld for the sake of the regeneration of life, and is restored to life by his mother, the Goddess. (Myth of Ishtar and Tammuz). The rescue and redemption of the myriad parts of the sacrificed and suffering God who has poured himself into life as the 'sparks' of human souls forms the essence of this Gnostic myth. Both myths in their feminine and masculine versions tell the story of the awakening of the unconscious soul and its return to its 'home' in the higher reaches of the cosmos.

In a Gnostic myth from the third century CE, the meeting of soul and spirit who become one in one likeness is most beautifully described in a deeply moving poem known as '*The Hymn of the Pearl*' or '*The Hymn of the Robe of Glory*.' This, like the Wedding Song of Wisdom, forms part of the Acts of Thomas, said to be a brother of Jesus, who took the Gospel to India and ended his life in the far south of that country. It was written in Syriac by a Gnostic called Bardesanes, living in Edessa from 151-233 CE, who had established a School there. Like the *Pistis Sophia*, although much easier to understand, it describes the descent of the soul — who in this Hymn is masculine — into the material world, named in the poem as Egypt. Once there, the soul forgets his mission, which was to find and take the pearl guarded by a fearsome serpent. His parents, who sent him forth on his mission, become aware of his plight and send him a letter in the form of an eagle. With the help of the letter, he is roused from the spell which had entangled him in material reality, and is able to take the pearl from the serpent and return to the higher spheres from which he had been sent forth on his journey. It is interesting that he does not kill the serpent but hushes him to slumber, casting a spell on him in the manner of Medea calming the serpent guarding the Golden Fleece. I love this poem and included the whole of it at the end of my first book, *The One Work*. Here is an abridged extract from it:

When I was a little child
and dwelling in my kingdom, in my Father's house,
and in the wealth and the glories of my nurturers had my pleasure,
from the East, our home, my parents having equipped me, sent me forth.
And of the wealth of our Treasury they had tied up for me a load.
Large it was yet light, so that I might bear it unaided –
gold of Beth-Ellaye and silver of Kazakh the great,
And rubies of India, and agate from the land of Kushan,
And they girded me with adamant which can crush iron.
And they took off from me the bright robe,
which in their love they had wrought for me,
and my purple toga, which was measured and woven to my stature.
And they made compact with me, and wrote it in my heart
that it should not be forgotten:
'If thou goest down into Egypt, and bring us the one pearl
Which is in the midst of the sea, hard by the loud-breathing serpent,
Then shalt thou put on thy bright robe and thy toga, which is laid over it,
and with thy Brother, our next in rank, shalt thou be heir in our kingdom.
I quitted the East and went down, there being with me two messengers,
For the way was dangerous and difficult, and I was young to tread it.
I went down into Egypt, and my companions parted from me.
I betook me straight to the serpent, hard by his dwelling I abode
Waiting until he could slumber and sleep…
I forgot that I was a son of Kings, and I served their king:
And I forgot the Pearl, for which my parents had sent me,
And I lay in a deep sleep.
But all those things that befell me, my parents perceived
And were grieved for me;
And a proclamation was made in our kingdom,
That all should speed to our gate,
Kings and Princes of Parthia and all the nobles of the East.
So they wove a plan on my behalf, that I might not be left in Egypt,
And they wrote me a letter, and every noble signed his name thereto:
From thy Father, the King of Kings, and thy Mother, the Mistress of the East,
And from thy brother, our next in rank,
To thee, our son, who art in Egypt, greeting! Up and arise from thy sleep,
And listen to the words of our letter! Call to mind that thou art a son of Kings!
See the slavery – whom thou servest!
Remember the pearl for which thou didst speed to Egypt!
My letter flew in the likeness of an eagle, the king of birds;
It flew and alighted beside me, and became all speech.
At its voice and the sound of its rustling, I started and arose from my sleep.
I took it up and kissed it, and loosed its seal, and read;
and according to what was traced on my heart
were the words of my letter written.

I remembered that I was a son of kings,
And my free soul longed for its natural state.
I remembered the Pearl, for which I had been sent to Egypt,
And I began to charm him, the terrible loud breathing serpent.
I hushed him to sleep and lulled him to slumber;
For my Father's name I named over him,
And of my Mother, the Queen of the East;
And I snatched away the pearl, and turned to go back to my Father's house…
And their filthy and unclean garb I stripped off and I left it in their country,
And I took my way straight to come to the light of our home, the East.
And my letter, my awakener, I found before me on the road,
And as with its voice it had awakened me, so too with its light it was leading me.
And with its voice and its guidance, it also encouraged me to speed.
And with its love it was drawing me on…

And my bright robe, which I had stripped off,
and the toga wherein it was wrapped,
From the heights of Hyrcania my parents sent thither,
By the hand of their treasurers,
Who in their faithfulness could be trusted therewith.
And because I remembered not its fashion –
For in my childhood I had left it in my Father's house –
On a sudden as I faced it, the garment seemed to me like a mirror of myself.
I saw in it my whole self; moreover, I faced my whole self in facing it.
For we were two in distinction and yet again one in one likeness…
I heard the sound of its tones which it uttered to those who brought it down
Saying, 'I am the active in deeds…'

It poured itself entirely over me
And in the hands of its givers it hastened that I might take it.
And me too my love urged on that I should run to meet and receive it;
And I stretched forth and received it,
With the beauty of its colours I adorned myself
And my toga of brilliant colours I cast around me, in its whole breadth.
I clothed myself therewith, and ascended to the gate of salutation and homage;
I bowed my head and did homage
to the Majesty of my Father who had sent it to me,
For I had done his commandments and he too had done what he promised,
And at the gate of his princes, I mingled with his nobles;
For he rejoiced in me and received me; and I was with him in his kingdom…
And he promised that also to the gate
of the King of kings I should speed with him,
And bringing my gift and my pearl
I should appear with him before our King.

With this wonderful poem, we leave the Gnostics and move on to the Essenes, their near-contemporaries.

* * * * * *

The beautiful words given below from codex 13 of the Nag Hammadi Library and dated to c. 200 CE, may be descended from far older texts cherished by the Jewish community in Jerusalem and Alexandria who safeguarded the teachings of the First Temple. They are clearly related in feeling and imagery to the verses given in Proverbs and Ben Sira where Wisdom is speaking of herself, but also to the imagery of the Shekinah revealed in the *Zohar* or *Book of Splendour* that appeared in northern Spain a thousand years later. (Chap.4)

The Introduction to the text by John Turner, the translator of it, says, "The tractate proclaims three descents of the Gnostic redeemer Protennoia, who is actually Barbelo, the First Thought of the Father [The Ineffable One]. *The Trimorphic Protennoia* itself is divided into three sections, each with individual subtitles and each describing one of the descents of the heavenly redeemer.... As the tractate proclaims, Protennoia is the Thought of the Father, the one born first of all beings, the one who has three names [Father, Mother and Son] and yet exists alone, as one. She dwells at all levels of the universe; she is the revealer who awakens those that sleep, who utters a call to remember, who saves."

Listen to these selected lines where the voice of the Divine Feminine speaks:

I am *Protennoia*,
The Thought that dwells in the Light.
I am the movement that dwells in the All…
She in whom the All takes its stand. [becomes manifest]
I am Invisible within the Thought of the Invisible One.
I am revealed in the immeasurable, ineffable things.
I am intangible, dwelling in the intangible.
I move in every creature.
Those who sleep I awaken.
I am the sight of those who dwell in sleep…

I am the Invisible One within the All.
I am the immeasurable, ineffable,
yet whenever I wish, I shall reveal myself.
I am the movement of the All.
I exist before the All, and I am the All,
Since I exist before everyone…

I am a Voice speaking softly.
I exist from the first.
I dwell within the Silence,
And it is the hidden Voice that dwells within me,
Within the intangible, immeasurable Thought,
Within the immeasurable Silence.

I descended to the midst of the underworld
And I shone down upon the darkness.
It is I who poured forth the Water.
I am the one hidden within radiant waters...
I am the Image of the Invisible Spirit.
I am the Womb that gives shape to the All.
By giving birth to the Light that shines in splendour…

I cry out in everyone and they know me.
I am the Thought of the Father
And through me proceeded the Voice, that is,
The knowledge of the everlasting things.
I revealed myself within all those who know me
For I am the one joined with everyone
Within the hidden Thought…

I am the Image of the Invisible Spirit
And it is through me that the All took shape,
I am the Mother as well as the Light,
The intangible [Virgin] Womb,
The unrestrained [boundless] and immeasurable Voice…

I am the Mother of the Voice
Speaking in many ways, completing the All.
It is in me that knowledge dwells,
The knowledge of things everlasting.
It is I who speak within every creature
And I was known by the All.

It is I who lift up the Sound of the Voice
To the ears of those who have known me,
That is, the Sons of the Light.

So now, O Sons of the Thought, listen to me,
To the sound of the Mother of your mercy…
I am the Womb that gives shape to the All
By giving birth to the Light that shines in splendour.

(NHL pp. 461-70)

Two books which I highly recommend in addition to those mentioned in Part One is *The Divine Spark Within*, by Dan Morse and John Lamb Lash's exhaustive study of Gnosticism and the importance of the Myth of Sophia and its relevance today: *Not in My Image*.

Notes:

1.   Reeves, Minou, (2013) *Europe's Debt to Persia from Ancient to Modern Times*, Ithaca Press, Reading, UK
2.   Ravenscroft, Trevor, (1981) *The Cup of Destiny: The Quest for the Grail*, Rider & Co., London, p. 47
3.   *The Nag Hammadi Library in English*, (1977) Brill, Leiden, p. 271 and p. 461
4.   The Nag Hammadi Library (NHL), p. 271
5.   Elaine Pagels, from her interview in Frontline Magazine: From Jesus to Christ
6.   Morse, Dan (2022) *The Divine Spark Within*, Sophonia Press, p. 47
7.   The Nag Hammadi Library, *The Apocryphon of John*, p. 99
8.   ibid, p. 101
9.   ibid, *The Trimorphic Protennoia*, p. 461
10. Morse, op. cit. p. 48
11. ibid, p. 49
12. *The Sophia of Jesus Christ*, NHL, p. 216
13. ibid, p. 217
14. Grant, Robert, (1961) *Gnosticism, An Anthology*, Collins, London, p. 171
15. Baring, Anne & Cashford, Jules, (1992) *The Myth of the Goddess*, p. 216
16. Sophia's mission to prepare the bodies to receive the sons of Light is found in a text in the NHL called *The Second Treatise of the Great Seth*, p. 330
17. Mead G.R.S. (1908) *The Wedding Song of Wisdom*, Theosophical Publishing House, p. 54
18. Mead (1947) *Pistis Sophia*, John M. Watkins, London, p. 4

19. ibid, p. 6
20. ibid, pp. 7-34
21. ibid, p 20
22. ibid, p. 22
23. ibid, p. 33
24. ibid, p. 35
25. ibid, p. 32
26. ibid, p. 37
27. ibid, p. 69
28. ibid, p. 82
29. ibid, p. 83
30. ibid, p. 87
31. ibid, p. 92-93
32. ibid, p. 96
33. ibid, pp. 96-97
34. ibid, pp. 98-99
35. ibid, p. 100
36. ibid, p. 22
37. ibid, p. 45
38. ibid, p. 47
39. ibid, p.135
40. ibid, p. 318
41. Dan Morse webinar on images of Wisdom in the Gothic cathedrals in France https://www.youtube.com/watch?v=j_KAfAjiE2I
42. Lash, op. cit. p. 228
43. ibid, p. 186
44. Mead, *The Wedding Song of Wisdom*
45. Mead, *Fragments of a Faith Forgotten,* pp. 419-422

Chapter Seven

THE ESSENES

I am a child of earth and starry heaven, but my race is of heaven alone.

— Orphic saying

It is difficult to draw a line between the Gnostics, the Therapeutae and the Essenes. I see all three as essential for an understanding of what has been rejected, left out of our history. What has been rejected are the communities persecuted by the Christian Church, communities which were devoted to the inner life of the soul, to practices which developed our understanding of life; who were able to ask and to answer the questions put by the Gnostics: Who are we? Where do we come from? Why are we here? Where do we go when we die? All this evidence of the life of the soul comes under the heading of the neglected inner, feminine aspect of our existence, that aspect which is devoted to establishing a relationship with and an understanding of spirit.

All three were withdrawn communities and all three included women among their members, which set them apart from the social customs of the wider society in which they lived. In this Chapter, I have drawn again on *Fragments of a Faith Forgotten*, the book in which the great scholar G.R.S. Mead wrote about Philo Judaeus, the famous Jewish philosopher (15-10 BCE – 45-50 BCE), who spoke Greek and lived in Alexandria during the first century CE. Philo apparently spent three years in the community of Therapeutae or Healers who lived on the shores of Lake Mareotis, near Alexandria and described their practices in detail. [1]

> Now the purpose of our wisdom-lovers is immediately apparent from their name. They are called Therapeuts and Therapeutrides [men and women healers] in the original sense of the word.... Now this natural class of men is to be found in many parts of the inhabited world, both the Grecian and non-Grecian world sharing in the perfect goal… in Egypt there are crowds of them in every province, and especially around Alexandria. For they, who are in every way the most highly advanced, come as colonists, as it were, to the Therapeutic fatherland, to a spot exceedingly well adapted for the purpose, on a terrace overlooking Lake Mareotis immediately south of Alexandria. [2]

Each dwelling had a sacred place within it, set aside for contemplation and meditation. "Thus they preserve an unbroken memory of God, so that even in their dream-consciousness nothing is presented to their minds but the glories of the divine virtues and powers. Hence many of them give out the rhythmic doctrines of the sacred wisdom which they have obtained in the visions of dream-life." [3]

Philo describes how, for six days, the Therapeutae remain within their dwellings, studying and contemplating in silence and eating only after sundown and then, only bread with a little salt, and water. On the seventh day they come together in a general assembly with the men and women separated by a breast-high partition between them, to listen to the senior member of the community addressing them. Every seventh week [seven being a sacred number for them], men and women come together for a special meeting where they are addressed by the president who expands on the text taken from sacred scripture, ending with a hymn that he himself has composed or taken from an extensive body of such hymns. All then join in the chanting. Later, they join in a ritual dance where the men form one group and chorus and the women another group and chorus, together creating a beautiful and harmonious symphony. "So" Philo says, "the chorus of men and women Therapeuts, by means of melodies in parts and harmony — the high notes of the women answering to the deep tones of the men — produces a harmonious and most musical symphony. The ideas are of the most beautiful, the expressions of the most beautiful, and the dancers reverent; while the goal of the ideas, expressions, and dancers, is piety." [4]

Mead ends Philo's detailed description of the Therapeutae with this paragraph:

> It is therefore reasonable to conclude that there were at this time numerous communities of mystics and ascetics devoted to the holy life and sacred science scattered throughout the world, and that Philo's Mareotic community was one of these. Others may have been tinged as strongly with Egyptian, or Chaldaean, or Zoroastrian, or Orphic elements, as the one south of Alexandria was tinged with Judaism…. For the people, there were the Law and the prophets and the Gospel; for the lay-pupils, the intermediate literature; and for those within, those most highly mystical and abstruse treatises that none but the trained mystics could possibly understand or were expected to understand. [5]

The Essenes

In this section on the Essene communities, I could have drawn from contemporary sources like Josephus, Pliny and Philo but instead have decided to draw on channeled material from a book called *The Essenes: Children of the Light*, by Stuart Wilson and the late Joanna Prentis (1943-2020), who have long prepared themselves for this work.[6] I have chosen to do this because their book gives a vivid and comprehensive picture of the kind of people the Essenes were, how they lived, what their values and teachings were and how they formed a protective and supportive community to prepare for the coming of Jesus (Yeshua), to help him to achieve his Mission in many practical ways. The sources mentioned above do not place Jesus in the context of the Essenes but the source I am using places his life and his teaching at the heart of their community. It is known from other sources that his brother, James, was leader of the Essenes in Jerusalem, and that his uncle (his mother's brother), Joseph of Arimathea, was an Essene and a member of the Sanhedrin.

The two authors of *The Essenes* describe their encounter with Daniel, the Essene lay brother who, after gaining the permission of his community, agreed to speak with them. Daniel brings this distant community to life in ways that an academic study could never do. The beauty of his descriptions is often breath-taking.

The Essenes appear to have been established in Palestine around 150 BCE and remained there until 70 CE. It is not clear what happened to them after that date. They were known as Therapeutae or Healers and for their ascetic way of life. Daniel said that there were several Essene communities in Palestine: at Rama, Mount Carmel and Jenin in the north, Qumrân at the head of the Dead Sea and Hebron and Ein Gedi in the south. The community at Qumrân consisted of about two hundred people but the usual number in other communities was about seventy. Qumrân, where the Dead Sea Scrolls were originally written and discovered in 1947, was their main centre. This community was destroyed in 68 CE by a Roman Legion shortly before the Romans destroyed Jerusalem and the Second Temple in 70 CE. They had many other communities in the first century CE, several in Egypt and one as far away as Massalia [Marseilles].

According to Daniel, some Essenes lived in towns and formed an outer circle which acted as a kind of shield for the inner circle of isolated communities, where most of the Essenes lived. At the height of their movement, Daniel said that they numbered three to four thousand and the arrangement of the outer circles protecting the inner [more remote] communities "was a useful cloak and spread confusion in the minds of our enemies [the Saducees and Pharisees]. We were open and yet secret, visible and yet invisible, known and yet unknown." [7]

Some Essenes were married and had families; others were celibate and lived more withdrawn from society. They were vegetarian and were skilled in growing the grain, vegetables, and fruit they needed to sustain them, caring for the goats that gave them milk, and cultivating the herbs used for healing illnesses and wounds. Honey was a precious food and many communities tended hives of bees. For those living in the remote communities, their days were divided between the physical work needed to grow and tend their crops, the work on the different kinds of crafts needed to create the different tools and pottery vessels they used, and the study of the precious scrolls that were stored in their extensive libraries. They were experts at conserving water, for every drop was precious in the arid land they lived in. They called themselves "Sons of the Light" or "Children of the Light." [8]

Daniel said that the Essenes received their teaching from people called the Kaloo, who were originally from Atlantis and later, Egypt, where their main centre was on the shores of Lake Mareotis, which was their 'Mother House' before they moved on to Palestine, and Damascus in Syria... "Qumrân was the Father House, shedding the light of knowledge upon us all." [9] The Kaloo set up an energy system in Palestine in preparation for the coming of a great Teacher who would lead them to the Light and who would need the support of this prepared energy system. [10]

The Kaloo had already established centres in Egypt, Persia and Greece and they brought with them to Palestine the quintessence of what they had absorbed from the Mystery Schools established in these different centres of civilization. These sources of enlightened teaching were blended with Hebrew wisdom teaching so that there was a rich foundation of Teachings for the Essene communities to draw on: Egyptian, Zoroastrian, Pythagorean, Hebrew and, ultimately, Atlantean. By the time Daniel had reached maturity, these four elements had fused together to create a powerful and broad pathway to the Light. [11] He said that unless one knew the part the Kaloo played in their lives it was impossible to understand the breadth and depth of their knowledge. [12]

The Essene Communities

One of the interesting facts revealed in this book is that Joseph of Arimathea was Jesus' uncle, the brother of his mother, Mary, and that Jesus was brought up in an Essene community. Joseph, himself an Essene, was a member of the Sanhedrin in Jerusalem as well as a successful merchant, a trader in tin, and the owner of many ships in which he travelled to buy tin from the mines in Cornwall to sell to the Roman army. Cyprus was one of the bases for his ships. This trade took Joseph to Britain several times. Once there, he contacted the leaders of the Druids, whose centre was at Avalon, a centre established long before his time by the Kaloo. [13]

The Essene communities kept a balance between families with children, those working the land or engaged in a variety of essential work or study, and those who were teachers and priests. The priests were the guardians of the rules and ceremonies which governed the community, but the real authority rested with the Council, where priests and lay brothers each had an equal voice. In each community of about a dozen elders, one chosen from each area of study, played a major part in the council. These elders had the role of listening to the various views of all members of the community, and settling any dispute in a fair and balanced way, which also respected the rules and aims of the community. They were reliant on each other, and developed a complete and satisfying system. Each member contributed to the working of the whole system and this gave strength and balance to the community. [14]

The Essenes knew that they were essentially star beings. "Our wisdom was star wisdom, for we saw far out into the cosmos. We were star people, but also Earth people as human beings. We lived in Earth reality and in star aspiration and in that balance, we found the key to many things." [15]

They drew on star charts to help them to understand the life path and interests of every individual, and this eliminated a lot of jealousy. Each focused on his life path and this created a benign structure supported by everyone's consent and agreement. Everything was shared equally according to the needs of each. Families would have different needs from those of individual members. The wellbeing of the communities rested on a foundation of merit, consent, and love. All three were necessary and all three contributed to a community living in harmony. Each part of a community would choose someone to speak for them at a council and the leader chosen by each community would speak at the larger councils that took place at Qumrân. [16]

> The teachings were given out so that they would lead people on the path of love… There was simplicity in our lives, but we did not strive for it. It grew naturally from our lives as the perfume arises from the flower. We strove for good things: peace, harmony, love, truth — yes, good things. My only sadness is I wish we had been able to share this sweet fruit more widely with others. We shared as much as we could, as much as we dared, and still only a few, very few tasted of the sweet fruit. [17]

The Libraries and the Precious Scrolls Stored in Them

One of the most important roles of a few individuals in the larger communities was to go in search of scrolls that could be copied and stored in their libraries. The tracking of these scrolls was difficult and they were expensive to buy because others were also searching for ancient scrolls. Some brothers travelled to remote places by night, to be less visible.

Daniel was anxious about "the survival of all these precious things, all this knowledge. We were few, and the sons of darkness [the Saducees and the Pharisees] were many. We knew the value of these things, but there were many superstitious ones who despised all knowledge from outside the boundaries of our land, and would destroy these libraries if they could. All these wonderful truths, these most marvellous pearls of wisdom, were quite impossible [inaccessible] for them because their minds were closed." [18]

People have wondered why the four Gospels took so long to be written down after the crucifixion of Jesus. The reason was that the Pharisees destroyed every scroll recording his life and teaching that they could get their hands on.

Because it is so interesting, I am including Daniel's description of the library at the Essenes' Mother Community at Lake Mareotis, which he said was being even bigger than the library at Qumrân. "It was a large building with windows right along the south side. Outside there were awnings, so you could adjust the amount of light coming through each of the windows. And all along the south wall were tables for the scholars to sit at. It was a most practical place to study. The tables had deep half-rounded channels in them, so that the handles of the scroll were put down into these when one had unrolled it to the desired place. This was a simpler arrangement than at Qumrân and I preferred it." [19]

He said that the other three sides of the building were occupied with shelving, right up to the ceiling. "There were special ladders with broad platforms instead of rungs, so you could stand comfortably at any height. These ladders had wheels upon them so they could be moved along the line of shelving. The shelves were divided off so that five or six scrolls could be stored in each compartment. All the compartments were labelled and numbered, and a central index told you where the scroll you wanted was to be found." [20]

The Soul of the Child

The Essenes believe that we have many lives, incarnating again and again until our understanding is complete and we are one with the Light. They applied this insight to the way they brought up their children, using star charts to help parents and the community understand the life path of a child. One of Daniel's most interesting insights was about the soul of the child — insights as relevant today as they were then. He said that the child when it arrives on Earth:

is like a spirit putting a finger down into the world, to see how life is, to gently explore and see if this is a good place to be. It is only a finger-hold at that
point and there is much need of very gentle nurture so that the being is not
alarmed or frightened. It should be a most friendly, welcoming and gentle
place, hence also the emphasis on culture and beauty. Surrounding the child
with beauty so that it knows that it is entering the world where the spiritual and
the beautiful — which it sees as identical — are respected, as much as these are
respected in the spiritual realm from which it comes. [21]

The child is a spiritual being, and it will see and feel the spiritual, the beautiful,
and the harmonious as one and the same thing. And that is what the child
should be surrounded with so that it can grow in confidence and strength, and
the ability to go forward in an open state. But if there is no understanding
of the importance of this, and the child is not kindly treated and is unable to
remain open and trustful, when the time comes for it to be taught meditation,
that openness and trust will have been lost. So it is of vital importance in its
early years to nurture a child with the greatest care and gentleness.

Daniel explained that in the first seven years the soul of the child is still
becoming integrated with the new self. Any great shock within the first seven
years will impede and set back the whole process. The integration of soul
and self is what the Essenes aimed for, but life is full of shocks of one sort or
another, so it is a difficult aim to achieve. [22]

The Cultivation of Skills

The Essene communities would have practiced advanced forms of meditation
and, most likely remote vision and lucid dreaming. In Daniel's case he was
taught how to project his consciousness into past and future time, to absorb
star lore and star wisdom and the impact stars have on human consciousness.
Others were trained to look back into the past or forward into the future to
observe the effects of great cosmic cycles on the life of humanity.

These were essentially shamanic skills, passed down the generations from
the Neolithic era through many different cultures. Among these skills, taught
to the Essenes by the Kaloo, were the development of inner vision, the ability
to see the aura and to attune to the energy of angelic beings, as well as to learn
how to work with earth energies, using crystals and sacred forms. [23]

Healing Illness

They saw illness as the effect of being out of tune with the essential note of one's
being. So, although they also used herbs, crystals and other aids to healing,

they also called on the healing angels to help the sick individual to retune to the essential note of his being. Once this was done, healing followed. "In this way the sick person becomes an active participant in his own healing." [24]

Harmony and the Heart

The Essenes saw harmony as the essential law of the universe and being in harmony with the Heavenly Father and the Earthly Mother as essential for a balanced life. "Harmony, truth, peace and love are the four pillars on which we build our house, and without any of those four pillars the house would not stand."

"What is occurring in the heart is the key to how we are moving along a spiritual path, how we are moving towards the Light. The heart holds the essence of things and as Essenes we are concerned with the essence rather than the outer husk. We have found that what really moves people forward is energy experienced in the heart, not words or ideas circulating in the mind." [25]

From the Kaloo, they learned that the universe is a web of consciousness founded upon harmony and sustained by love. "It is like a great rocking stone which pivots on the single point: if you push the stone in any direction, it moves back towards the centre again to restore the balance, to restore the harmony. That is the process of it, consciousness is the intelligence of it, and the energy of it is love. The universe is sustained by love, by the great ocean of cosmic love, unconditional love." [26]

The Essenes felt it was important to teach the young these things because, if children are ignorant of everything else and yet they know these things and can use them as a guide to their lives, then they will be able to live well, as enlightened human beings, and will be happy. But if they have knowledge of a multitude of other things but know nothing of these teachings, they will make many errors in their lives, and bring unhappiness to others as well as themselves. [27]

"Every human being is a microcosm of the universe, and within our bodies and minds the forces of the universe flow and resonate. By attuning to these forces and becoming conscious of them we integrate ourselves into the universe and bring Spirit and matter ever closer together. When the universe and the human being are fully merged and integrated, we become the Living Truth, an embodiment of wholeness, harmony, Light and peace.... Through our daily Attunements, and through living anchored within these energies, we harmonize our being with the greater whole." [28]

These Attunements, also called Communions, are wonderfully described in *The Essene Gospel of Peace*, pages 67-85. Each morning, the Essenes communed with one of seven Angels of the Great Mother and each evening, with one of the seven Angels of the Great Father. In this way, through their daily Communions, they kept their lives in harmony with both Earth and Cosmos.

Daniel's Definition of God

In this section, I have quoted Daniel's words in full, because I think they are so perfectly and beautifully expressed. Here is his definition of God:

> The universe, the cosmos, the Heavenly Father, Celestial Man, Supreme Wisdom, the Totality of Knowledge, all these terms are used for the same. This is God manifested in Creation. But God is also the Infinite Source beyond manifestation, the Eternal Mystery. [29]
>
> Though there are many ways of perceiving God, I found the symbolism of Light most helpful. I saw human beings as Children of the Light, dwelling perhaps for a while in the shadow of darkness, but coming home at last into the Light which is their birthright and their destiny. For in the heart of every human being burns the Light of God's presence, and so at the deepest level we are Light, and returning to Light is returning to our own fundamental nature. Even though a human being may have fallen into error, still the essence of God within longs for the Light. And forgiveness and love are the ways in which Light expresses itself within our lives and teaches us how to grow ever closer to God.
>
> God manifests as the Light which illumines our path, and as the Spirit within which makes our inner development possible. As we live in joy and harmony and love, we live in the nature of God, and the Light steadily expands within us. This expansion of the Light anchors us in the true nature of our being. It nourishes us and allows us to unfold our talents and abilities as Children of the Light. Walking in the Spirit and inspired by the Light, we become expressions of God upon Earth. As Spirit merges with matter in us, we complete our task here, and prepare to ascend to the spiritual realms. [30]
>
> All sages are of one heart, knowing that all life is One, and that all human beings share the same origin as Children of the Light, and the same goal, to merge with that Light. We saw the Triumph of the Light as something that must come, perhaps not for many years, or even many centuries. But however long it takes, we saw the Triumph of the Light, the victory of God and of love and truth as sure and certain as the rising of the sun.
>
> All flows from the Spirit and from the Light. We are Children of the Light, Children of God, and Light is our source, our goal, and our destiny. This view of things has become central to my life, and was arrived at through study, discussion, reflection and attunement over many years. [31]

And he continues:

We enforce no common belief, no orthodoxy, and each one is free to choose their own perception of the Divine. Indeed, each one has the responsibility of finding their own pathway to God. The heart can help us, can guide us, but no conformity of belief can direct our footsteps to the Light. Yes, there are universal meeting points within the Essene tradition, the Heavenly Father and the Earthly Mother, and the over-arching Peace. That is the foundation, but what each one builds upon this foundation is an individual choice. I have made my choice. This is where I stand. [32]

Finally, he concludes what he has learnt with these words:

I see all human beings as Children of the Light, sons and daughters of God. Some have chosen to move away from the Light, and become sons of darkness, but this is only for a moment or two in the eternity of God. When these sons of darkness turn again to the Light they will fulfil their destiny as Children of the Light. And love and peace will embrace them as surely as it embraces each and every one of us. God never turns away and rejects us, even if we choose to turn our faces from the Light. And when we return to the Light there is great rejoicing amongst the angels. [33]

Reverence for the Angels

Daniel said that "All Essenes shared a great reverence for angels and especially for the Elohim, very high angelic beings who stand above the level of archangel. The Elohim we saw as filling their places by reason of merit and not through being created great. We saw them as rising upwards from lesser angels or from the equivalent of human beings, through great ages of cosmic development until they reached that high level." [34]

Preparations for the Coming of a Great Teacher

The Kaloo had begun preparations for the coming of a Great Teacher long before the arrival of Jesus. There were many things that had to be done: the choosing of communities to form a series of triangles running from the south to the north of Palestine; the precise placing of crystals to form an energy grid over the whole land, the formation of a core community to oversee these long-term and vital preparations. Daniel describes an important meeting at which he was present, that took place at night in a large cave, in a remote and hilly place.

The cave and the ways leading to it are well guarded. We are sitting in the circle, maybe about 30 people. In front of us are lamps, so that we can see the faces. The only other light is coming from the middle of the circle, where there is a huge round crystal. It's pale purple in color, and is glowing. There are people here from all the communities, as well as the core group.

This is a special place, a sacred space and we've been meditating here for some time before anyone speaks. Members of the core group are talking about Jesus and his next step forward. They either call it his ritual death experience or sometimes simply his process. So we're discussing the preparations that have to be made, the effort which has to be put in, and the possibility of succeeding. And it's a very special process he will be going through, focusing on the use of the love energies through the heart. This is a new energy, a cosmic energy which is being brought in and demonstrated so that others can see how to use it. It is capable of taking people through a process of spiritual transformation in a direct way which is quite different from the complex methods used in the past. Jesus is marking out a new path, a broad new road into the Light. It is not certain that he will be able to achieve this, but the members of the core group are optimistic. They seem to talk from much deeper knowledge than we possess. We all hope it will work. We understand that it will help human development if it succeeds but it is not certain.... We hope it will work, and will do what we can to assist, but it is not at all certain.

So the plan is being laid before us: Jesus will go forward and act out in public the climax of the mystery school teaching. He will go through a mock trial, be crucified, and bring all the energies together into a synthesis. He will need a massive amount of support to sustain him while all this is proceeding.... We will go forward with high hopes but also much anxiety.

There will be a group of leaders who lead the meditation in their communities. The meditational energy will be generated and directed to Jesus at higher levels, so he will have both this higher energy and the energy through the system with the crystals. There are crystals in patterns to hold the energy, and the energy of each of the community sites leads into the central area: triangles flowing into a central triangle to make a complete energy system. [35]

Daniel explained that there was an inner and outer energy system. "The outer energy, generated by the Earth, focused and intensified by crystals, was directed along lines of force running across the surface of the land towards Jesus on the cross. This enabled the energy levels in his body to be maintained. The inner meditational energy was fed by the communities into subtle levels for directing to Jesus. Together these two sources provided a complete system of support. The inner energy sustained the higher aspects of his being, and particularly their link with the physical body. It was essential that this link was strongly maintained until his energy process was completed." [36]

This was a vast project. Most of the basics were put in place before Daniel's lifetime. "The central triangle was formed by Jerusalem, and the crystals at Qumrân and in the cave.... The work had to be done very quietly and secretly so as not to attract the attention of the other Jews.[37] The whole operation lasted about a hundred and fifty years and the area of land covered by this grid of earth energy lines supported by carefully placed crystals extended to one hundred and twenty miles. The Kaloo foresaw what was to come and made their preparations accordingly. All their work was to prepare the ground for a great Teacher of Righteousness who was to come and all this work was to support him. The Essene communities willingly cooperated with these plans to establish this complex system of energy. [38]

During the crucifixion, the meditators could feel that those who opposed this plan were trying to sabotage it. They knew they were engaged in a tremendous battle. They could feel Jesus weakening and their energy waning and knew they had to call for help from the angelic beings — to the Archangel Michael — or all would be lost. This help was forthcoming and with it the immense project was completed and the new spiritual energy embedded in the Earth. [39]

After the crucifixion, healers were able to reach Jesus' body in the sepulchre through a tunnel that connected it to Joseph's house nearby, a tunnel that had been constructed well in advance and in great secrecy, with a false door put in place between the tunnel and the sepulchre, a door disguised on one side to look like stone. [40]

The tunnel allowed the healers to reach Jesus' body and anoint it with healing ointments and surround it with huge crystals. Jesus came back to consciousness slowly because he had gone so far out but the healers were certain that they could bring him back. He came slowly and reluctantly back into his body because the pain from his wounds was acute, despite the efforts of the healers, who included his sister, Clare. After Jesus had been revived, he was too weak to walk and so he was laid on a stretcher and carried through the tunnel to Joseph's house. Then the evidence of the tunnel was removed so no-one would know of its existence. It was filled in with earth from above, by means of a stable hastily constructed above it which acted as a cover for the work. All this was prepared far in advance.[41]

The Presence and Teaching of Jesus

The Essenes did not see Jesus as the only Son of God but as an elder brother, a great Teacher who had gone further along the path than they had and had come back to show them the Way to the Light.

Daniel gives this portrait of Jesus:

There was a great clarity, a searching in the eyes, but the love was strong and his manner so gentle. He had clear eyes, all-seeing eyes, but much love in them and he spoke with great gentleness: great strength and great gentleness: It is said that many who had been Essenes for many years and thought they knew what it was to be an Essene, when they encountered Jesus, only then did they begin to realize what it was like to be an Essene to your fingertips.... So Jesus was the ultimate Essene, the ultimate pattern of Esseneness. He was the exemplar for all of us. And when we looked at him — his power, his gentleness, the sheer radiance of this being who was nearer to God than any of us had thought possible — we could see our destiny. [42]

Some, who had sight upon very high levels, told me that when they looked at Jesus they did not see only his aura, they saw this vast vortex of cosmic energy whirling around him. They said it was like the layers of an onion, an infinite number of transparent layers of energy moving out and out into the universe. So that he was the center of all things, the center not only of our drama but of the whole drama of the planet. He was the center of all things and forces were gathered around him that made many things possible. Others who were attuned to the higher reaches of the angelic realm said that around Jesus they sense the presence of very high angels. [43]

He was the bringer of Grace — who else could be a focus for all these energies? And because all these energies were focussed together, we could move through our experience faster. It quickened everything. You could not be any-where near him and not move more quickly along your path.

We were aware that a whole vortex of cosmic energy revolved around Jesus and that anyone who encountered him stepped into that vortex. That was really the miracle for us. Not that he did this or that remarkable healing, but that his whole being was a focus of cosmic energy, and thus he could bring profound changes into the lives of all those he met who could accept these energies. [44]

His Central Theme

His central theme was the need to connect with the heart energy, the energy of unconditional love. He not only talked about this energy, but demonstrated it in his life and his being. He gathered and focused the love energy, and because his energy was so strong within him, others were able to feel it and express it in the heart. This great cosmic energy of unconditional love focusing through Jesus — and through him being made available to all. It was quite different from love as most people saw it. For many people it depended very much upon the response they got from the loved one. To love the person in front of you, however they act, whether they smile at you or snarl at you — that was quite a new idea for them. [45]

Jesus understood the nature of a human being better than any of us. He understood that we are the children of the Creator, and is it not natural to love the children of a loving Creator? He understood the nature of God because that nature is essentially love and is expressed as love, focused as love and demonstrated as love. He understood all these things, and brought them together in his teaching.

All felt that in his presence a new beginning was possible. That was his great power, because there was nothing judgemental about him. No matter how much people had complicated their lives, with his help it could now be made most simple, a turning to the Light.... We all came trailing our doubts and fears and prejudices. All these things stopped us from living in the moment. Somehow Jesus stepped out of all the rubbish of time. He had stepped into the living moment as he stepped into the Light. And he was able to convey the magic, the openness, the wonder of this to those around him. It was wonderful and moving to see the effect he had on people's lives. [46]

Jesus taught such powerful and simple things. He taught us to unite with the Spirit and go into the Light — that is all! Nothing else — no elaborate ceremonies, no building of temples, no great hierarchy of priests, no formulas to learn or doctrines to master.

So simple his teachings were: unite with the Spirit, be open to the Kingdom of Heaven that is the world of Spirit, and let the energy of the Spirit flow down into us and wash away all heaviness, all fear, all doubt, and all the littleness within us that is uncomfortable with the Light. And when we are full of the Spirit, how easy it is to step into the Light which is our Source and the very nature of our being. How easy to lay aside the body that has served us well, and in the formless world become one with the Light. And he taught us that the nature of the Spirit is Truth and Love and Freedom, and when these three are present in our hearts then indeed we may feel the Kingdom of Heaven close to us.

And he taught us always to keep these things simple, and clear, and not muddied up with elaborate words and rigid formulas, for in simplicity he said we would see the Truth of things. And when that simplicity, that Love and Truth and Freedom flowed through us and blessed us, then indeed we felt that God was with us, carrying us upwards on the wings of the Spirit. [47]

Daniel said that the main lesson he had learned in his life was the power of love working in the heart, how strong this could be, and how this love could be a blessing to all who touched it.

Our hope was to see this love spread out until it would cover the Earth like a planet carpeted with flowers. I can see now that I was born at a time when the pattern of Essene thought was about to change and develop more rapidly than any time in our history. That development increased in speed during the period when Jesus was at the height of his powers.... When Jesus changed the focus from God in the Heavens to God in the Heart, only some within our Order could fully accept this. Many of our Brothers found this too challenging, and so they clung to the traditional form of the Essene Way.

This process of change and transformation swept through our communities like a tidal wave, fragmenting and eventually dispersing the Brotherhood, but this had to be so in order for the new Way to be established. Looking back over it all, it is now clear to me that this was all part of the necessary pattern of things.

In the Infinite Garden the old always has to give way and die a little, so that the new growth can come forth and flourish. I can see that our main task is completed now. The main reason for us all coming together — to provide support for Jesus and his work — all this has been accomplished. [48]

His teachings were so simple: love, forgiveness, and seeking the truth within. When he spoke, all the complexities of the past dissolved into the simplicity of the Way of the Heart. He just loved and accepted everyone as they are, without judging them. [49]

Grace is a gift of love and healing from the highest level. God going the extra mile to meet us upon the road of life. We considered that we were living in a time of Grace and we felt that this Grace centred around Jesus. He was the bringer of our Grace because many cosmic energies focused around him, and made possible breakthroughs in consciousness, and a transformation in the lives of those who came into his presence. [50]

As his work flowered, he became more a timeless being talking about time-less things which would be relevant in any age.… But we knew that in the end, time might dilute and distort the message he came to bring. Once the Teacher is no longer physically present, the Teaching may become changed and weak-ened. What needs to go forward is the essential message that Jesus was trying to convey: unconditional love working through the heart, and the surrendering of the will to the Divine Presence within. The more one surrenders one's will to the Divine Presence, the more one merges with that Presence which is within every human being, the more the path opens and the way becomes clear and straight. Then one can go forward and rise in consciousness and ascend into new frequencies of being.

All of this was what Jesus was trying to teach the disciples and the groups around him. He was trying to teach this but many did not want to hear this message, and would much rather have rigid structures. The inner truth is of the Spirit and lives, and anything which is of the letter has its day, flowers and is gone. [51]

Remember always that Jesus lived in a difficult and troubled time. Many people were frightened, and in their fear they clung to the comforting thought of a strong Father who would protect them. They preferred a strong external perception of Deity, a strong Father rather than the Divine Presence within. They saw the within as weak, and the external forces as strong and threatening. Jesus came to show them how strong the Divine Presence could be. How it could burn like a great Light within him and illumine the lives of all those around him but many in their fear were not able to see this. [52]

Because of all the vortex of power around Jesus he was able to pull people out of an obsession with the past and into the moment. When they were in his presence, the past disappeared. They realized that nothing was important but the moment, and that they were free to act within that moment.… Nothing else is important, nothing else will exist for you. That is why Jesus excited so many people. They could feel themselves being pulled out of time and into timeless-ness, out of the past into the everlasting present which is the only place in which you have power. The past and the future, if you are entangled with guilt or with worries and anxieties, rob you of your power. Only the present gives you power, and forgiveness is the key to ensuring you stay within that focus, expanding your awareness and living fully within the moment. This is living as God intended. This is joy, this is freedom — and this is what Jesus taught. This is the most wonderful gift which he gave to us. [53]

Jesus said that if we can make this leap into the unknown all the fragments of our life will come together on a higher level and we will be transformed forever. He said that in the temple of the heart the Presence was like a Shining Angel, casting its Light into every corner of our being. And when we merge with this Angel we will enter a Light brighter than we have ever known, and catch an echo of unimaginable bliss. Then at last our pilgrimage through the realm of darkness will be over and we will have come home safely into the Light. All the scattered fragments of our being will be gathered up into wholeness, and all limitations will fall away, leaving only love and peace and oneness, and harmony, and joy. [54]

The Essenes had many prayers for different occasions in different communities. The prayer that Daniel preferred was the Foundation Prayer invoking the Divine Presence within:

> *Divine Presence within,*
> *living in wholeness,*
> *moving in joy and love,*
> *I surrender to your will.*
> *Bring the radiance of your Light*
> *into my heart and mind.*
> *and merge with me to manifest*
> *your Will upon the Earth.*

We were used to the concept of Presence. Shekinah is the Presence of God in the world. And wholeness, joy and love we saw as the nature of God and the gift of God when we manifest it in our lives. The reference to Light is important: many Essene prayers focused upon Light. The Light inspires us because it is a symbol for the Spirit. [55]

Some sense the Divine Presence as an Angel, and some like a loving Energy which enters every fibre of their being. But the simplest way of thinking of the Divine Presence is as the Spirit. Jesus saw a clear difference between the Spirit and the soul. He told us that the soul is good but limited, whereas the Spirit has no limits or boundaries, and links all beings in the greater Oneness.... Jesus came to establish a more permanent way of spiritual development, and that centered upon this knowledge of the Divine Presence, the Spirit within. [56]

The Misunderstanding of His Teaching

Daniel explained that,

compared to the spiritual traditions of the past, this connection with the Divine Presence is a simple and straitforward way of moving into the Light. The work of Jesus was like a signpost pointing to this new way but even when he taught them, many did not understand him. They could not grasp [the idea] that because the Divine Presence is within, knowing ourselves is also knowing God. I think this idea frightened them, and they would rather think of a perfect Father in the heavens, and themselves as miserable and imperfect creatures crawling upon the surface of the earth. Yet the ancient sages had always said that knowing oneself is the key. The tragedy of the average person in my day was that this was a key they were too frightened to use, too frightened even to admit that it existed. This was the root of the confusion during my lifetime, and it is likely that in future time, this confusion will only increase. Many people will not see clearly what is to be done and will not have the commitment or the courage to surrender to the Divine Presence, even if it is a gateway to the Infinite. They will be like men starving when the richest treasure in the world lies neglected under their feet. [57]

Ascension

Daniel said that when he visited the community at Lake Mareotis, near Alexandria, he studied some Egyptian texts or scrolls in its library:

Ascension was part of the esoteric tradition in Egypt, and was well understood in the inner schools there. The Egyptian texts spoke of the Merkabah, the Body of Light through which we become travellers upon the higher planes of being and citizens of the universe. The Egyptians knew that the universe was built upon sacred geometry and sought to unite this with our own inner Light-structure in order to complete our journey as star-beings. So I learnt much in Egypt, and my meetings with the Kaloo also helped to add to my knowledge.

The Kaloo said that ascension was the great Completion of which the ancient sages spoke. Spirit and matter merge and become one, and the body is raised into a higher realm. They said that a human being may attain ascension at any time, but in the Divine Plan for this planet it was intended that the great bulk of humanity should achieve it at the end of the planetary cycle. [58]

There are many levels of ascension. At the first level which is spiritual ascension you can continue in the physical body for a while, but when your task on earth is completed, you go forward into physical ascension. At that point the physical body dissolves into Light, and from then on as an ascended being you live within your Body of Light. If you are an immortal being, living an Eternal Life in harmony with God, why would you need a physical body? The whole point of ascension is to move into limitless and eternal being, beyond the constraints of physical form.... Resurrection and ascension are very different things, although they are often confused. Resurrection allows you to continue in physical form, but it does not enable you to enter eternal life, whereas ascension does. [59]

Ascension has been difficult in the past and those who achieved it did so with great difficulty and after many lives of struggle. But Jesus came to change that, and to make the way clear and straight. He told us that ascension is a transformation of the heart. A brilliant mind will not help you to ascend but a loving heart will.... As the cycle progresses it will get ever easier. When you reach the end of the cycle it will just be like stepping into the Light. Yet it is important to see ascension always as the Completion stage of our existence. Jesus said that we should aspire towards it in our lives, but from day to day, moment to moment we should focus upon our area of service, our self-appointed task. He also said that when our task upon Earth is completed, we should be ready to ascend into the realm of Light.

Jesus told us that there comes a point in the development of every human being when the soul is filled with a great longing for the Light. At that point everything that the world can offer seems hollow and worthless. The only thing that will satisfy the soul is to return to the Light from whence it came, and merge with that Light and become one with it. This state of oneness with the Light is what we call ascension. [60]

And for ascension, the heart alone can open the door. It is unconditional love working through the heart which makes ascension possible. This is a simpler and more direct way than was practised before, and will enable many to ascend who could not master the complex procedures I found described in the Egyptian texts. But to move forward in this way we will need to give up every little hatred we harbour in our hearts. In this I separated myself from many of the priests, who held that hatred of wickedness and the sons of darkness was a virtue, even a duty for the Essenes. I could not agree with this, for I saw the destructive effect hatred had in people's lives. And when I heard Jesus talk always about love and never about the need to hate, this only confirmed me in my view that love uplifts and purifies whilst any form of hatred destroys and defiles. Those who hate are denying themselves their birthright, their birthright as Children of God to ascend into a state of Limitless and Eternal Life. [61]

The joy of limitless being is the very core of what Jesus taught us, and he demonstrated it first by rising from the tomb, and later by ascending from physical form into the glory of the formless state. But Jesus knew from the beginning that many people would not be able to accept his teachings. They would cling to the outer husk and reject the inner seed which gives Eternal Life. How can life be eternal if we do not live it as ascended beings? The principle of ascension make sense of all that Jesus said, and without this key he would seem to be speaking in riddles. Yet we saw how difficult it was, even for Essenes, to accept this in this inner seed, for this teaching was so profound and subtle. It requires a great leap into the unknown, and many people would be too fearful to make this leap.

Many would prefer to think of a comforting heavenly space, a warm and homey place filled with friends and loved ones. But this Interlife state, this space between lives, always leads us back into another life upon Earth. It is part of the cycle of life and death, and for that reason cannot be an eternal state. Only through the ascension process can we move out of the cycle and know the freedom of endless life as ascended beings, dwelling in Eternal Joy.

Jesus revealed to us the limitless joy of the ascended state and turned our hearts and minds towards Heaven. Jesus opened up the way and turned a narrow and difficult path into a broad road into the Light. In doing so, he saved us from continuing in a series of limited physical lives. He saved us from spiritual poverty and spread before us all the abundance of Eternal Life for that is truly what the ascended state is. [62]

The River of Consciousness Uniting All Essenes Through Time

Daniel understood that one consciousness united all who were Essenes — flowing like a vast river of energy. He asked the Brotherhood if he might observe this river of consciousness as it flows on through time and his request was granted.

> I watched as our people came back time after time to work within the Way that our Teacher of Righteousness had established. The original simplicity of the Way only lasted for a little time. Too many minds were at work to change and codify and "improve" it — where no improvement was needed. Our people tried to keep the Way simple, but events overwhelmed them. And as I watched, the structure grew ever more complex, ever more rigid.
>
> I saw that over the centuries Jesus became misunderstood, until most people believed that he came to establish a religion in the Greek fashion, descending like the son of Zeus to save the world entirely on his own. What a lie that is! What an unjust lie, removing from the record all the work and efforts and suffering of the Essene Brotherhood in support of our Teacher! [63]

To end this chapter, I would like to repeat the words of Daniel given earlier which offer such a clear summary of Jesus' Teaching.

> Jesus taught such powerful and simple things. He taught us to unite with the Spirit and go into the Light — that is all! Nothing else — no elaborate ceremonies, no building of temples, no great hierarchy of priests, no formulas to learn or doctrines to master.
>
> So simple his teachings were: unite with the Spirit, be open to the Kingdom of Heaven that is the world of Spirit, and let the energy of the Spirit flow down into us and wash away all heaviness, all fear, all doubt, and all the littleness within us that is uncomfortable with the Light. And when we are full of the Spirit,

how easy it is to step into the Light which is our Source and the very nature of our being. How easy to lay aside the body that has served us well, and in the formless world become one with the Light. And he taught us that the nature of the Spirit is Truth and Love and Freedom, and when these three are present in our hearts then indeed we may feel the Kingdom of Heaven close to us.

And he taught us always to keep these things simple, and clear, and not muddied up with elaborate words and rigid formulas, for in simplicity he said we would see the Truth of things. And when that simplicity, that Love and Truth and Freedom flowed through us and blessed us, then indeed we felt that God was with us, carrying us upwards on the wings of the Spirit.

But there was such a contrast between the simplicity of the Way and the vast and rigid structures which I saw accumulate around it. And when I saw all the complexities that time had heaped upon this simple Way, all the doctrines and formulas and ceremonies, my heart became sad for my Brothers.... Only the Light at the very end of the planetary cycle gives me any hope for a better outcome. Perhaps then simplicity will return again, and the path of the Spirit shall shine before us and lead all humankind into the Light. [64]

In this chapter, I have focused on the Essenes because I think that what Daniel has so beautifully described gives great insight into the teaching of Jesus, a different view of our presence on this planet and how we can help ourselves to connect with the Light of the Spirit that we carry in our hearts and in all that is around us. I have always been repelled by the image of the crucifixion in Christian churches and felt that Christianity was mistaken in placing so much emphasis on the sacrificial death of Jesus on the cross rather than on his resurrection, and to emphasize belief as the path to redemption, rather than the transformation of our understanding of Life and of Spirit — an understanding that the Essenes evidently had and Daniel has so wonderfully conveyed. I would urge everyone reading this chapter to read the book: *The Essenes, Children of the Light* as what I have quoted is only a small part of what this book offers.

Stuart Wilson and Joanna Prentis end their revelatory book with these words:

The Essenes did not try to elaborate the teachings of Jesus into any kind of ceremonial or doctrinal structure. The simple and profound fellowship of lives lived close to Mother Earth had taught them the power and beauty of simplicity.

From this unique perspective, they understood that the forgiveness and love demonstrated by their Teacher could transform the Children of the Light, lifting them up in the power of the Spirit so that they could ascend into the Kingdom of Eternal Joy.

In *The Essene Gospel of Peace*, there are fourteen most wonderful Communions spoken by Jesus. He said these Communions were to be addressed each morning to the seven Angels of the Earthly Mother, and each evening to the seven Angels of the Heavenly Father. (pages 67-85)

To end, here are these timeless words from the end of the Fourth Book of *The Essene Gospel of Peace*:

> *I tell you truly,*
> *your body was made not only to breathe, to eat, to think,*
> *but it was also made to enter the Holy Stream of Life.*
> *And your ears were made not only to hear the words of men,*
> *the song of birds, and the music of the falling rain,*
> *but they were also made to hear the Holy Stream of Sound.*
> *And your eyes were made not only to see the rising and setting sun,*
> *the ripple of sheaves of grain, and the words of the Holy Scrolls,*
> *but they were also made to see the Holy Stream of Light.*
> *One day your body will return to the Earthly Mother;*
> *even also your ears and your eyes.*
> *But the Holy Stream of Life, the Holy Stream of Sound,*
> *and the Holy Stream of Light,*
> *these were never born, and can never die.*
> *Enter the Holy Streams,*
> *even that Life, that Sound, and that Light which gave you birth.*

Notes:

1. Mead, G.R.S., (1931) *Fragments of a Faith Forgotten*, John M. Watkins, London
2. ibid, p. 69
3. ibid, p. 70
4. ibid, p. 81
5. ibid, p. 86.
6. Wilson, Stuart & Prentis, Joanna, 2005, *The Essenes, Children of the Light*, Ozark Mountain Publishers, Huntsville, AR
7. ibid, p. 46
8. ibid, p. 13
9. ibid, p. 36
10. ibid, pp. 28-29
11. ibid, p. 31
12. ibid, p. 32
13. ibid, p. 222
14. ibid, pp. 53-54
15. ibid, p. 248
16. ibid, pp. 55-56
17. ibid, pp. 57-58
18. ibid, p. 109
19. ibid, p. 105
20. ibid, pp. 105-106
21. ibid, p. 63
22. ibid, p. 64
23. ibid, pp. 84-87, 90-91
24. ibid, pp. 88-89
25. ibid, p. 95, 96-97
26. ibid, pp. 96-97
27. ibid, p. 97
28. ibid, p. 98
29. ibid, p. 100
30. ibid, p. 111
31. ibid, pp. 112-113
32. ibid, p. 113
33. ibid, p. 114
34. ibid, p. 110
35. ibid, pp. 155-157
36. ibid, p. 158
37. ibid, p. 159
38. ibid, pp. 161-162
39. ibid, pp. 165-166
40. ibid, p. 170
41. ibid, p. 173
42. ibid, p. 134

43. ibid, pp. 188-189
44. ibid, p. 189
45. ibid, p. 148
46. ibid, pp. 149-150
47. ibid, pp. 335-336
48. ibid, pp. 314-315
49. ibid, p. 315
50. ibid, p. 188
51. ibid, pp. 189-190
52. ibid, p. 190
53. ibid, p. 191
54. ibid, p. 200
55. ibid, p. 196
56. ibid, pp. 197-199
57. ibid, p. 199
58. ibid, p. 259
59. ibid, p. 258
60. ibid, pp. 260-261
61. ibid, pp. 261-262
62. ibid, pp. 262-263
63. ibid, p. 335
64. ibid, p. 338

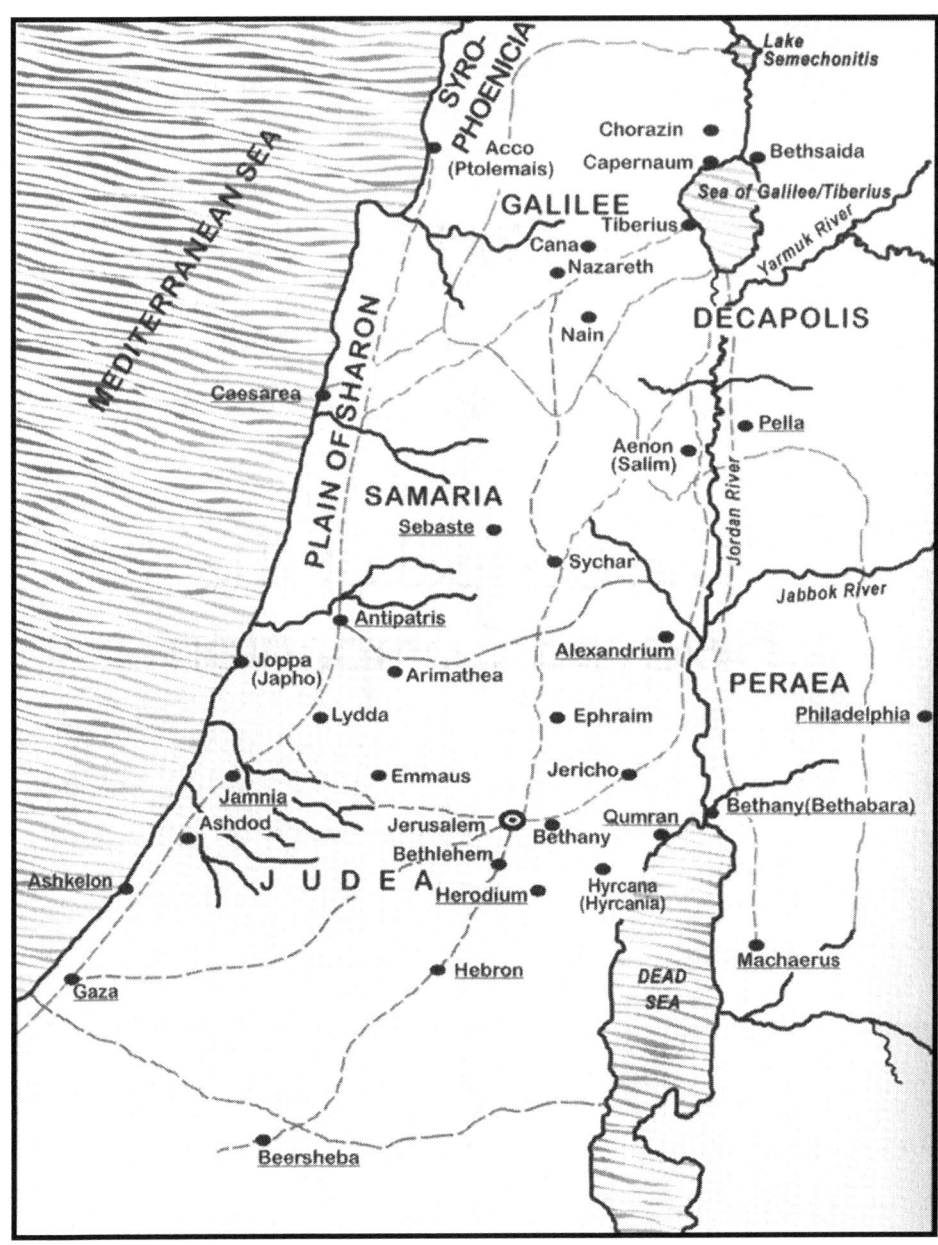

Map of the Holy Land

Chapter Eight

MARY MAGDALENE
OR MIRYAM OF BETHANY

One word of Truth outweighs the whole world.

— Solzhenitsyn [1]

I would like to say, as an introduction to this Chapter, that this transformative time we are living in is a time of metamorphosis, a time of profound change, when what was hidden is coming to light; what was lost two thousand years ago is being recovered and restored. We can hear the voices, silenced so long ago, returning to life. Profound wrongs are being righted, among them the shocking wrong done to Mary Magdalene by the Church of Rome. The lies we have been told about the flawed nature of Mary Magdalene have been refuted. Many books, restoring her true image, have been written.[2] We can now know that Mary Magdalene or Miryam of Bethany was the beloved consort of Jesus, appointed teacher to the disciples by him, and taking the Essene Wisdom Tradition to France, where she lived and taught for twenty years. She was, in the words of Tau Malachi, the Holy Bride.[3] She may also have been, as Tricia McCannon writes in her book, *Return of the Divine Sophia*, "the most important single teacher, aside from Jesus, in the entire Christian movement." [4] The growing interest in her, particularly the interest of women, reflects the activation of the feminine archetype within our soul and within our wider culture.

To begin, let us look at the map of Palestine in the first century. Look for Jerusalem and a little to the right, Bethany. Bethany was where Mary Magdalene lived, with her sister Martha and brother Lazarus. Jesus often stayed in their home after his marriage to Mary and during his Mission. Note the name Hyrcana, to the south-east of Bethany. Further to the right is Qumrân, at the head of the Dead Sea, the place that was home to an important community of Essenes at the time of Jesus and Mary Magdalene. In 1947, the Dead Sea Scrolls were discovered, their contents studied for decades by different scholars and only very slowly and reluctantly released.[5] Jesus and Mary Magdalene both belonged to a community of Essenes called Nazarenes or Nazoreans, a community to which Joseph of Arimathea, Jesus' uncle, and other members of his family, also belonged. Jesus lived in Judea, not Galilee and was not a carpenter but a leader of the Nazarenes, known as The Teacher of Righteousness. At this time Palestine or Judea as it was then called, was under Roman rule. Rome appointed a succession of kings or rulers with the overall title of Herod.

The First Temple in Jerusalem

To understand the historical and spiritual context for the sacred mission of Jesus and Mary Magdalene, we need to return again to the First Temple in Jerusalem where, as explained in Chapter Three, an enormous change in Hebrew cosmology took place in 623 BCE, when, under the orders of a king called Josiah, a powerful group of priests called Deuteronomists took control of the Temple and eradicated any trace of the Goddess Asherah, the Queen of Heaven, leaving Yahweh as the sole Creator God. They imposed their own rule, based on the Law of Moses, and banished all communication with the Angels — the Hosts of Heaven. Dr Margaret Barker, former President of the Society of Old Testament Studies, comments in her book, *Temple Theology,* that the most important result of Josiah's purge was the introduction of monotheism in Judaism.[6] The Goddess Asherah, was worshipped as the Holy Spirit and Divine Wisdom and as the Tree of Life — a cosmic Tree that connected the invisible and visible worlds, whose fruit was the gift of immortality. This magnificent Temple had an ancient, shamanic, visionary tradition where, in the great tower in the furthest courtyard of the Temple — the Holy of Holies — the high-priest climbed the stairs to commune with the Queen of Heaven, the Holy Spirit, and the angels.

This is how the Divine Feminine aspect of the god-head was excised from Judaism, and from Christianity as well because it took its image of God from the Old Testament. The Deuteronomists then created the Myth of the Fall in Genesis 2 & 3, with its message of sin, guilt, punishment and the banishment of Adam and Eve from the Garden of Eden to a life of hardship on Earth. They demoted the Goddess Asherah into the human figure of Eve, giving her the title of the former Goddess — 'Mother of All Living.' In this new patriarchal cosmology, the image of deity is the transcendent Father: divine immanence, held by the image of the former Goddess, was lost. Earth was designated a place of exile and punishment for primordial sin and was no longer sacred. Adam and Eve were exiled to a world contaminated by the Fall and subject to sin, suffering and death, introduced into the world by Eve.

From the perspective of our relationship with the planet, this new cosmology was a catastrophe. Nature, held in the image of the Goddess, was split off from spirit, and was effectively de-souled. We lost the sense of harmony and trust in the cosmos and the awareness that spirit was active and present within the world. We lost the sense of living within a Sacred Order. We lost the shamanic ability to communicate with higher dimensions. The umbilical cord between spirit and nature was severed and has remained severed until our time.

This new myth imprinted us with a negative image of our presence on this planet and placed a heavy burden of shame and guilt, particularly sexual guilt, on our shoulders. It is astonishing that this myth, received as divine revelation, was created by a powerful group of priests who deleted the Divine Feminine from the image of God. It has endured for over two and a half thousand years and has had a profoundly negative influence on Judaism and Christianity. This is the unhealed wound that lies at the heart of western civilization — the wound that split nature from spirit, since the banished Goddess had personified nature and held everything in relationship to the Whole for thousands of years in ancient civilizations. It is impossible to exaggerate the long-term negative effects of the change in the relationship between the archetypes, leaving the masculine supreme and the feminine nowhere to be seen.

As described in Chapters Three and Five, many Jews moved to Alexandria in three waves: at the time of the takeover of the First Temple, at the time of the Babylonian destruction of it, and in 70 CE when the Romans destroyed the Second Temple. I believe they took with them, probably in the first wave, the Love-Wisdom teachings, and the rituals of the First Temple. From this multi-cultural and thriving city, they found their way into many Gnostic texts, as well as, I believe, into the later teaching of Kabbalah. The extraordinarily rich cosmology of Kabbalah may have had its origin in the pre-Deuteronomic Temple in Jerusalem. This mystical tradition of Kabbalah has long been known as "The Voice of the Dove" and "The Jewels of the Heavenly Bride" — titles which seem to confirm their relationship with the banished Goddess Asherah.

Mary Magdalene as the Penitent Whore

The most significant development to take place in Christian theology was the Doctrine that Jesus was the Son of God. This Doctrine was only officially established at the Council of Nicaea in 325 CE when, amid scenes of furious disagreement between two groups of bishops, it was decided that Jesus was the Son of God because he was 'begotten of God' and of the 'same substance as God', rather than only 'like unto God'. Because of the taint of original sin, celibacy had to be an essential aspect of his divinity. All trace of his marriage to Mary Magdalene and even all trace of his brothers and sisters was eliminated. Yet something called the *Desposyni Chart*, which listed the family of Jesus and his descendants, existed until 318, when the Chart was hidden in the archives of the Vatican.[7] To eliminate the threat to this doctrine offered by his marriage to Mary Magdalene, Pope Gregory the Great in a sermon of 591 CE created the vicious calumny that she was a sinner and a whore. Countless sentimental paintings show her as 'the Penitent Whore.' This calumny was removed in 1969 by Pope Pius VI who belatedly made her a saint. Her name day is July 22nd. In 2016 Pope Francis named her Apostle to the Apostles.

The Essene Communities

Most fortunately, the traditions, rituals and teachings of the First Temple and the image of the Divine Feminine somehow survived in the Essene Communities which nurtured both Jesus and Mary Magdalene and supported Jesus during his Mission. The Essenes, as described in the previous Chapter, were a group of Jews who rejected the teachings of the Deuteronomists and who lived mainly in isolated communities.[8] They were known as Therapeutae or Healers, practising techniques of meditation and communion with the higher realms. Jesus and Mary Magdalene both belonged to a community of Essenes called Nazarenes or Nazoreans. In this Chapter, I am drawing on the remarkable information disclosed in another book of channeled messages called *The Power of the Magdalene*, received by Stuart Wilson and Joanna Prentis. They reveal important facts about the Essene men and women who provided the support system and framework for the Mission of Jesus, or Jeshua as he is called in these transmissions.

The Nag Hammadi Library

In 1945, an extraordinary discovery of Gnostic codices was made at a place called Nag Hammadi in Egypt. These Gnostic codices were a hugely important discovery for an understanding of the Gnostics and Jesus' shamanic method of teaching about the inner path to the kingdom of heaven. Among them was a hitherto unknown gospel called *The Gospel of Thomas* and the translation of a Coptic manuscript, *The Gospel of Mary*, that has vital pages missing. In a text called *The Dialogue of the Saviour*, Mary Magdalene is described as 'The woman who knew the All'[9] In the same Library, the Gnostic Gospel of Philip tells us that 'There were three who always walked with the Lord... his sister and his mother and his companion were each a Mary.'[10] And in another longer passage in the same Gospel: 'And the companion of the Saviour is Mary Magdalene. Christ loved her more than all the disciples, and used to kiss her often on her mouth.' [11] The scholars commissioned to translate these texts translated the Greek word *koinonôs* as 'companion', when describing the relationship between Jesus and Mary Magdalene, disregarding the fact that this word can also mean consort or wife, no doubt because it was inconceivable to these scholars that Jesus and Mary Magdalene could have been married. Discovering these intimate references to Mary Magdalene changed the whole picture of her relationship with Jesus, although it has taken fifty years to assimilate this new evidence about her.

There is another important aspect to their relationship. The teaching of Jesus offered the revelation of a direct relationship with spirit rather than collective worship of God. His love for and marriage to Mary Magdalene restored in the mythic sense the sacred marriage and the lost relationship between the two archetypal principles carried in the images of Yahweh and Asherah that had been broken 600 years before their time. Dr Margaret Barker in her book *The Great Angel* writes, "The Jesus who walks with the feminine is the *redemption* of the Yahweh of the Deuteronomists who had abandoned Wisdom. For these mystics who were the early Christians [who wrote the Nag Hammadi texts], redemption meant allowing Wisdom, the exiled part of God, to return as the beloved of God." [12]

I agree with Dr Margaret Barker, Dr Annine van der Meer and Dr Betty Kovács that the joint Mission of Jesus and Mary Magdalene was to restore the teachings and practices of the First Temple, to embody together a new incarnation of the pre-Deuteronomist sacred marriage of Yahweh and Asherah.[13] No wonder the priests of the Temple and the Pharisees, who followed the literal interpretation of the Law of Moses laid down by the Deuteronomists in 623 BCE, hated and feared him and wanted to kill him.

The Power of the Magdalene

Now, I will turn to the passages in a remarkable book called *The Power of the Magdalene* by Stuart Wilson and Joanna Prentis. I consider the information they received through their contact with an angelic being called Alariel, one of twelve angels who work with the Order of Melchizedek, to be authentic and a much-needed contribution to our knowledge of the Essenes and the character and contribution of Mary Magdalene as well as for the teaching of Jesus or Jeshua as he is called in these transmissions. (See Part 15 of *The Essenes* by the same authors for an explanation of this Order)

Interestingly, Alariel said that former Essenes who have incarnated now were contributing to a reassessment of what happened 2000 years ago, particularly in the group of Essene disciples who were close to Jeshua. They are encouraging Christians to take another look at the whole narrative of Jeshua's life. Change, he said, has always been part of the Christian experience, and there are aspects of Christianity that bring the promise of renewal and a fresh beginning. What is emerging now is interest in the female disciples and the central role of Mary Magdalene, whose story could help people to understand the important role played by the women disciples at that time.[14] This vital information about Mary Magdalene and the women disciples around Jesus given through Alariel could never emerge through the discovery of new documents from that distant time because all evidence of their role was effectively and deliberately destroyed two thousand years ago.

> He (Jeshua) was trying to establish a new spiritual path, a new way of living in relating to people and to God. Using the Cosmic Energy of Love which he was anchoring into Earth reality, he was encouraging people to focus that energy through the heart centre. This energy is profoundly transformative. It moves through the dry forest of the heart like a cleansing fire, sweeping away the deadwood of past experiences and all the anger, fear and hurt that people cling to. When all that has gone, it empowers the individual in expanding awareness and rising into higher frequencies of consciousness. All this re-establishes the Children of the Light in a new relationship with God. [15]

Alariel said that the Essenes viewed consciousness as One, and as evolving towards the One again, but in between these points of Oneness going through an apparent separation, which confirms the theme of Owen Barfield's important book, *Saving the Appearances: A Study in Idolatry* that Jules Cashford and I used for the tripartite plan of *The Myth of the Goddess* and I used in *The Dream of the Cosmos*. "There is a Divine Plan, a blueprint for the whole of creation, and the angelic host works to manifest that blue-print, first in creation and then in sustaining what is created and in assisting in the spiritual evolution of manifested beings." [16]

He explained that the Great Spirit Beings called the Elohim can be regarded as "the Architects of the Universe, planning and supervising creation and working to bring it back into the Greater Harmony. As the Universe is linked together in one vast Web of Consciousness and Being, the whole system must move as One. Your galaxy is now beginning to return to Source by ascending into the Light, and to keep pace with this a good deal of help is being given to the planet Earth at this time under the direction of the Elohim." [17]

In response to a question put to him by Joanna Prentis: "What element of human consciousness that we have lost is it important for us to bring back now?" Alariel replied, "Undoubtedly it is the Goddess element: the Sacred Feminine is the source of the highest and most subtle wisdom, and the most profound Knowing. Shamanic cultures have always recognized the primacy of feminine wisdom, and it is time that this primacy — symbolized by Mary Magdalene — is more widely acknowledged in the world. It is only by acknoowledging the primacy of feminine wisdom that conflicts will be resolved and the deep wounds that humanity has inflicted upon itself over the centuries will finally begin to heal." [18]

The Balance of Female and Male Disciples

Alariel said that it is one of the great tragedies of Western culture that all knowledge of the female disciples of Jeshua has been lost. And it is now time to restore that knowledge.

> It is important to understand that the discipleship system that Jeshua set up was designed to mirror the greater symbolism of the Universe. The balance of Father-Mother God was mirrored in the balance of male and female disciples. So there were six circles of 12, making 72 male disciples, and six circles of 12 female disciples, making 72 female disciples — a total of 144 disciples in all. The names of the first circle of 12 male disciples are well attested and known to you. However much less is known about the first circle of female disciples. First of all we have two advanced initiates who were frankly head and shoulders above the rest, and these were Mary Anna, the mother of Jeshua, and Mary Magdalene. These were initiates who had reached high levels of spiritual attainment long before that time. They arrived in Israel as fully qualified adepts, both very advanced in their own way. So they were head and shoulders above the rest of the group and were respected as such. [19]

Alariel continued:

> The whole point about the balanced male and female system of discipleship, as set up by Jeshua is that it reflected the central balance of Father-Mother God. Father-Mother God is completely balanced, completely integrated and completely whole. If you try to take either the Father or Mother element out of this equation, the result is a major imbalance in perception. Any system that honours the Father energy and neglects the energy of the Divine Mother will lack flexibility, sensitivity, compassion and wisdom. It would tend to become rigid and brittle and will fragment into competing elements.... It is one of the great tragedies of western culture that all knowledge of the female disciples of Jeshua has been lost and it is now time to restore that knowledge. [20]

The Role of the Female Disciples

The role of the second circle of female disciples was to support the first circle of women, by covering family and community duties which made it possible for the first circle to spend much of their time with Jeshua. "Jeshua regarded the help of generous, open-hearted sharing amongst the female disciples as a model of Unconditional Love, and brought this to the attention of the male disciples, amongst whom it was not widely understood or very well received. The male disciples regarded themselves as teachers and leaders, and saw the role of women as listening and following. So it was hard for them to accept that the females had anything at all to teach them." [21]

> As Jeshua put Unconditional Love at the very centre of his teaching this made it all the more irritating to the men, who would have preferred that he had taught some more intellectual philosophical doctrine based upon reason rather than upon heart-energy. They felt ill at ease in matters of heart-energy, and longed to elaborate or structuralize Jeshua's teaching in some way, to make it more intellectually challenging and therefore more impressive to the male mind. They saw heart energy as much too vague and insubstantial, and longed for a set of logical and profound concepts that would seize the high ground of intellectual debate.… Bear in mind that the male disciples were brought up in the Jewish culture that still believed in "an eye for an eye and a tooth for a tooth." The leap from that position to turning the other cheek and even loving your enemy was simply too big a step for them. [22]

Alariel explained that the female disciples were bound to have a more difficult task than the male disciples because they were living in a society that was rigidly patriarchal. To survive that and still be able to work and teach was going to be very difficult. The women encountered males who, though they believed generally in the teachings of Jeshua, found it difficult to accept a woman in a teaching role.

He compared the group of male disciples with the very different group of female disciples, explaining that this was a very close-knit group, a group which had been working towards this moment for many incarnations when they had been gaining experience at various spiritual levels.

> The women had been meeting at different Mystery Schools, coming together and planning what they would do. Because this group of female disciples had been working on this project for a long period of time, they chose to incarnate in a very close-knit extended family group, many of them being born about the same time. Their families were closely connected, so there was an instinctive trust and solidarity amongst the female disciples that simply wasn't there with

the male disciples. The women were all telepathically linked, and formed one complete telepathic unit. [23]

The first circle of women disciples was a close-knit team with one undoubted leader, totally different to the first circle of male disciples. And indeed, the close-ness of the team — and they obviously were a team — did not please the male disciples, who were wary and suspicious from the beginning. They just did not react well to a group of twelve women all moving with one intent; they found that quite eerie, quite frightening. They didn't understand it, and so that was another motivation for them to marginalize the women disciples, and another reason to write all this out of history. [24]

So the story of the female disciples is a big story, and its time has come. Various members of this close-knit team will be stepping forward quite soon to tell their part of the story. It is not only the first circle of female disciples, but the second, and to some extent, the third circle as well. Many of these pioneers of the Way are now ready to tell their story, and it is a remarkable and inspiring story. Many things will flow from the information about the female disciples as they come forward. It is time for a shift in human consciousness. And the empower-ment and leadership role of women is an essential element in leaving the past behind and beginning to access the full potential and creativity available within the human race as a whole. If you ignore or belittle the skills and creativity of half your population, many of the problems of the Earth will remain unsolved and insoluble. [25]

A great deal of information was suppressed and marginalized but now, after all these years, its time has come to go out into the world. Also, it strengthens the recognition that God is balanced: masculine and feminine. And that if we attempt to perceive God in a very narrow masculine way — or even a narrow feminine way — that only leads to imbalance, and no good ever comes from that. So all this is going in one direction now, the direction of balance. [26]

The Mother of Jeshua

One of the most interesting aspects of Alariel's information is about the mother of Jesus:

Mary Anna was a person of quiet and calm authority. There was a great sense of clarity about her, and her dedication to the Light shone forth in everything she did. She acted as the spiritual anchor and foundation for the group of first circle female disciples, being well qualified to do so as she had been a high initiate since the days of the [Pharaoh] Akhenaten in Egypt. She was one of the brightest jewels in the main Egyptian Mystery School of that time and achieved a balance in spiritual empowerment that made her the ideal leader for the first circle of female disciples. [27]

Mary was an impressive speaker, but it was the energy she carried — the quality and sheer power and vastness of that energy — which really impressed those who met her for the first time. Here was a Master-soul, an Initiate who had reached the very highest levels of attainment within the Isis system of Egypt, a system that was widely respected throughout the Middle East as the mainstream Mystery School tradition at that time. So to be in the presence of a high Isis Initiate was something that many people would have seen as a great blessing. [28]

Some people mistook the quietness of Mary's manner for docility or weakness, but when they looked into her eyes, they saw a quality of steely and unmovable determination that surprised them. A few might be foolish enough to start arguing with Mary Anna, but that look of determination made them change their minds very quickly. When you look into the eyes of a being that steady, that integrated and that dedicated you know all argument is useless.

When she led the meetings of female disciples, Mary Anna would start off the discussion, but from that point onwards said very little. She let everyone have their say and express themselves fully, and only when a matter had been thoroughly discussed, would she round this off with a balanced and moderate summary which acted as a fair consensus for the whole group. [29]

In the Christian tradition, almost nothing is known about the character of the mother of Jesus. What a contrast this image of Jeshua's mother offers to the traditional image of the Virgin Mary. In Alariel's words, she comes to life as an exceptional woman of great authority, wisdom and power.

Mary Magdalene

Mary Magdalene had a very different temperament. "Powerful, eager, enthusiastic, the fire of her total commitment to the Light burned within her like a bright flame. She was a passionate advocate for truth and justice, but in her zeal, might occasionally overstate the case, something that Mary Anna would never do. If Mary Anna's empowerment expressed itself in her poise, her restraint, Mary Magdalene's empowerment manifested in a confident and joyful outpouring of her energy and her love." [30]

"Peter, who had trouble dealing with any empowered woman and who had real difficulties with Helena Salome [Jeshua's aunt, his mother's sister], had problems with Mary Magdalene from the very beginning. Her free and powerful expression of opinion, which might have seemed frank, open and engaging in a man, grated upon Peter's patriarchal nerves. Whilst he would never dare to question Mary Anna — one look from those eyes would have silenced him — questioning, and indeed criticising Mary Magdalene was something that Peter did often." [31]

He deeply resented her closeness to Jeshua, and wished to promote the interests of the male disciples and diminish the importance of the women. He could not bear the thought that Jeshua could be telling Mary Magdalene things that he, the obvious leader (in his eyes at least) of the male disciples, needed to know. Above all, Peter could not accept the basic structure through which the Way would be spread: that after Jeshua left them the teachings would be given out in two ways. The outer teachings would be spread by most of the male disciples, led by Peter who was to be the rock, the foundation, of this new movement. Whilst the inner teachings (the Inner Mysteries of the Way) would be taught by John, James, Thomas, and Philip, this group being led by Mary Magdalene. [32]

Mary, trained in the initiatory mystery schools of Egypt, was thoroughly familiar with this pattern of teaching because it was a method that was much used in Mystery Schools throughout the region. She saw the two teaching arms as mutually supportive because the outer group would be open and public and would deflect attention away from the inner, which in any case needed a quieter environment to do the sort of work along esoteric and Gnostic lines. In her view of things, the most advanced followers of the Way would naturally gravitate over time from the outer to the inner group, and this would give the whole movement a fluidity, a pattern of development, and a richness of potential experience that one level alone could never provide. [33]

Alariel mentioned another outstanding woman leader who was Helena Salome, an aunt of Jeshua and sister of Mary Anna, who took the matronymic name of Mary. Outside the family group she was often called Mary Salome. In the biblical account of the crucifixion, he said, she was called Salome. [34]

The Rift Between Peter and Mary Magdalene

Alariel explained that after the crucifixion, "James, the brother of Jesus, together with Mary Magdalene, tried to explain this dual role of the male and female disciples to Peter, but he at once dismissed this plan as impractical. He saw the followers of Jeshua as an embattled army, and regarded any kind of division as a splitting and weakening of their forces. Peter could not tolerate the idea of a rival leader, and a rival leader who happened to be a woman was quite unthinkable for him." Alariel continued:

Peter began the rift that developed between the mainstream teaching of the Way (which in time became the Catholic and Orthodox Churches) and its Gnostic counterpart. This led to the final persecution and elimination of all Gnostics as heretics — a persecution which paradoxically was carried out by the outer Church, which had been designed to nourish and protect it. Thus the clash of personalities between Peter and Mary Magdalene had profound implications for the future development of Christianity, implications whose effects are felt right up to the present day. Although the outer aspect of the Way might develop (as it did) along religious lines, and become a Church, the inner aspect was never truly a Church, but rather a spiritual movement of free kindred souls. A movement in which spirituality and not religion was the principal focus and driving force. As Islam has the Sufi movement and Judaism the mystical Kabbalah, so Christianity should have had its own mystical and Gnostic core. The loss of this core has left it with a permanent wound from which spiritually it has never recovered. [35]

He explained further that if Peter and Mary Magdalene had gone forward united (after the crucifixion) the history of the West might have been very different, and the leadership role of women within Christianity might have been accepted from the beginning...

Christianity was damaged so deeply that it could not fulfil its purpose as Jeshua had planned. Without its inner Mystery School counterpart, the Church is like a clock with some of its mechanism missing. In a sense, you have not really experienced Christianity yet, only the incomplete fragment that Christianity has handed down to you. This incomplete fragment has helped and inspired countless people since its foundation, but it could have been infinitely more effective as a way of treading the spiritual path that leads to the Light. A balanced system is always to be preferred to an imbalanced system, and only a balanced system can help human beings realize their full potential. [36]

The balance between the outer Church and the inner Mystery School was designed to provide a practical and effective system of spiritual development, but it was also a reflection of the essential nature of the Universe. The outer Church represents Father God, and also the Sun, Knowledge, Structure, Ritual and Form. The inner Mystery School represents the Mother Goddess, and also the Moon, Wisdom, Flow, Process and Life. Neither is complete without the other and together they manifest the wholeness of the Way. [37]

The true Gnostics were not only Knowers of the Truth, they were Knowers of the Way. Within them, Knowledge and Wisdom, Structure and Flow, Ritual and Process merged into Oneness, as the masculine and feminine energies are blended into the ultimate Wholeness of Being. Here all the balancing energies merge into the totality of the human experience. This was what Christianity was designed to lead towards. This was the balanced path of spiritual development which Jeshua worked to establish upon the Earth, and this, sadly, was what was rejected in favour of a one-sided presentation that valued the Form and rejected the Life. Is it too late now to heal the rift, to embrace both the Form and the Life within a two-fold balanced system of Church and Mystery school? Will Masculine Structure acknowledge the importance of Feminine Wisdom, and will the Heir of Mary Magdalene stand forth to balance the Heir of Peter? We shall see. [38]

The Gospel of the Beloved Companion

Having explained the arrangement of the disciples around Jeshua in the words of Alariel, and the vital role played by Mary Anna, the mother of Jesus, and Mary Magdalene, I can now come to an extraordinary text called *The Gospel of the Beloved Companion*.[39] Whoever is reading this book may be aware that the four gospels of the New Testament were only written down two generations after the crucifixion, mainly because earlier existing texts or scrolls written by the Essenes were destroyed by the Pharisees. This manuscript, which has long been in the possession of a Cathar Community in the Languedoc or south-western France, is written in Alexandrian Greek. Tests on the original manuscript confirm both its origin in Alexandria and its approximate date to the first century CE. It was and is the most closely and carefully guarded treasure of this Community from the time it came into their possession until the 12th century, when it was translated from Greek into Occitan, the language of the Languedoc. Both manuscripts continue to be held by this Community, whose name and location are not revealed, to protect them from the long arm of the Vatican. A little over a decade ago, it was decided by this Community that this was a pivotal time in our evolution and an appropriate time to release this Gospel. It was translated from the Alexandrian Greek, with an extensive commentary by Jehanne de Quillan, a member of this Community, and published in French and English in 2010 by Éditions Athara in the town of Foix. It is available from Amazon.

Prior to this publication there were three copies of a Gospel of Mary, one of which, written in Coptic and forming part of the Berlin Gnostic Codex, was included in the Nag Hammadi Library.[40] All three are missing the same vital pages which appear to have been deliberately deleted because of their significance. These missing pages are restored in *The Gospel of the Beloved Companion*. They give extraordinary insight into the teaching of Jesus and his close relationship with Mary, or Miryam as she is called in this Gospel.

It was astounding for me to discover in this Gospel — following everything I have written in *The Dream of the Cosmos* and subsequent webinars about the Shekinah and the original feminine gender of the Holy Spirit — these words of Jesus or Yeshua — his Aramaic name in this Gospel: '*My words are the Way, the Truth and the Life. For my words are given of the Spirit, and no one comes to the Kingdom except through Her Teachings.*' (35:12)

Yeshua speaks of the Holy Spirit as His Mother throughout this Gospel. The feminine gender of the Holy Spirit is itself a startling and welcome revelation. It recalls the banished Goddess — called Holy Spirit and Divine Wisdom — of the First Temple, as well as the later image of the Shekinah of Kabbalah who is also called Divine Wisdom and the Holy Spirit. This newly revealed Gospel is of immense importance in my view, because it establishes the fact of Mary Magdalene's marriage to Jesus and the fact that, knowing that he would be arrested and executed, he appointed her as Teacher to the disciples in her house in Bethany just before the Last Supper took place, giving her the title of 'The Migdalah' or The Tower. It also demolishes the Christian myth of the celibate Son of God and the edifice of a celibate male priesthood built upon it. This Gospel, unquestionably written by Mary Magdalene, is the only extant *eye-witness* account of Jesus' Mission, crucifixion, and restoration to life. Its value is beyond price.

Mary Magdalene Unveiled

Before I come to the words of this Gospel, I need to mention a most interesting and ground-breaking book on Mary Magdalene called *Mary Magdalene Unveiled* by Dr Annine van der Meer, published in the Netherlands in 2021 and in English in 2023. Dr van der Meer is an academic who trained in Gnosticism under Professor Gilles Quispel, one of the four translators of *The Gospel of Thomas*. She is also the author, among many other books, of a remarkable book called *The Black Madonna from Primal to Final Times*, published in English in 2020 that I highly recommend. In the massive and minutely detailed study of her latest book, she compares *The Gospel of the Beloved Companion* with the Gospel of John, showing where the author of the latter redacted words and clauses to give a different meaning to the original content.

According to Dr van der Meer, a copy of *The Gospel of the Beloved Companion* came into the hands of the author of the Gospel of John, known as John the Elder, who wrote his Gospel at a much later date ca 90-100 CE in Ephesus. He copied Chapters 1-20 from *The Gospel of the Beloved Companion* but redacted many of them to accord with the doctrinal tenets of the Christian Church and the leadership of Peter. He cut out all mention of the marriage of Mary Magdalene and Jesus and changed the feminine Holy Spirit or God the Mother into God the Father, and the words 'Beloved Companion' into 'Beloved Disciple', leaving commentators to ponder for centuries the identity of the beloved disciple. Chapter 21 was added at the end of the Gospel, after John the Elder's death. There were, therefore, two much later redactions of Mary's original Gospel that became known as the Gospel of John. This is truly an astonishing and significant discovery. To see the discrepancies between the two Gospels, one would need to read Dr van der Meer's minutely detailed comparison of them.

The Wedding at Cana

The Gospel of John is the only one to describe the wedding at Cana — but John the Elder deliberately made no mention of the fact that Mary Magdalene and Jesus were betrothed or married to each other there. According to *The Gospel of the Beloved Companion*, this ceremony, took place at Hyrcana near Bethany, not Cana in Galilee as the Gospel of John describes it. Since Bethany was where Mary Magdalene lived, it makes sense that Hyrcana was not too far away, certainly not in Galilee.

The Gospel of the Beloved Companion as well as Dr van der Meer's new book shows that Mary Magdalene, whose Aramaic name was Miryam, was the beloved wife of Jesus (Yeshua). At their first marriage ceremony which followed their betrothal ceremony at Hyrcana, Miryam as an Essene or Nazarene priestess and his lawful wife, anointed Jesus' head with the precious oil of spikenard — a costly and exquisitely fragrant oil that came from a plant in the Himalayas. She did not anoint his feet and wipe them with her hair as described in the Gospel of John.

Sculpture depicting Jesus and Mary Magdalene seated at supper.
Church of St.Volusien, Foix, Ariège, France

It was an Essene custom to have a second marriage ceremony when the bride was three months pregnant and the second anointing took place at the marriage ceremony which was held in Miryam's house in Bethany in 33 CE. It was at this event that Yeshua appointed her Teacher to the disciples and bestowed on her the title of 'Miryam the Migdalah' or 'Miryam the Tower' — which he said would stand by his in the future. The image of the Tower recalls the great

Tower in the furthest courtyard of the First Temple that was destroyed by the Babylonians, the Holy of Holies where the high-priest once communed with the Holy Spirit and the Hosts of Heaven. Only as a Messianic bride and an Essene priestess in her own right could Miryam have anointed Yeshua's head with the precious oil.

Shortly after this, Miryam was seated next to him at the Last Supper where she laid her head on his breast. There is unique sculpture, reproduced in Dr van der Meer's book (p. 285), which is in a church in the town of Foix, in south-western France and shows Mary Magdalene seated next to Jesus at the Last Supper, (previous page). I do not know the date when it was created but it is a miracle that it still exists and shows that in this south-western part of France, the truth of their relationship was known.

The Last Supper – Leonardo De Vinci

I believe certain of the painters of the Renaissance in Italy knew the truth of their relationship, including Leonardo. In his painting of *The Last Supper*, he painted a feminine figure in pink sitting on the right of Jesus and leaning away from him with an I-shaped column between them. I am sure Leonardo knew that this feminine figure was not the beloved disciple, John, but the beloved wife of Jesus — the 'Holy Bride', (above).

At the Last Supper Yeshua announced that Mary Magdalene would be the leader and the 'Mother' of the disciples and he appointed her his successor, the leader of the Nazarenes, as his followers were called. Then followed the terrible ordeal of his arrest and her accompanying him to Pontius Pilate and then to the crucifixion, where she stood with his mother and sisters at the foot of the cross — all of which is described in *The Gospel of The Beloved Companion*. We have to imagine her feelings as the helpless witness of what was happening to her beloved husband. However, she would have known that the crucifixion was part of the planned Mission of Yeshua, as described in Chapter Seven.

The Meeting in the Sepulchre Garden

The famous scene of the meeting of Mary and Jesus in the sepulchre garden after his resurrection is only recorded in the Gospel of John (20:1). Mary Magdalene would not have been allowed access to the sepulchre, either alone or with other women accompanying her unless, as his wife, mother or sister she had come to wash and prepare his body for burial with spices, as was the custom of that time — a custom to which Mark (16:1) testifies. She may have even been present when Essene healers worked on the body of Jesus to keep alive the flickering flame of life in his exhausted and pain-wracked body. Let us therefore, turn to the text of *The Gospel of the Beloved Companion*.

> *Now on the first day of the week, Miryam the Migdalah went early, while it was still dark, to the tomb and saw the stone taken away from the entrance. Stooping and looking in, she saw that the tomb was empty and the linen cloths scattered where the body had been laid. Yet she did not enter in, but remained standing outside the tomb, weeping. And hearing a noise, she turned around and saw a figure standing close by. Because of her weeping, she did not know that it was Yeshua. 40:3 – 40:4*
>
> *Then Yeshua said to her, "Woman, why are you weeping? Who are you looking for?" She, supposing him to be the gardener, said to him, "Sir, if you or another have carried him away, tell me where he is laid, and I will go and take him away.*

Who recorded this scene in the sepulchre garden? It certainly wasn't Jesus, so it must have been Mary in her original *Gospel of the Beloved Companion* before it was copied much later by John the Elder for his Gospel of John. She was in the sepulchre garden because she was his wife, come there to say a last farewell. But there was no farewell, only a radiant dawn. At first, she did not recognize him, now restored to life, because she was blinded by her weeping. Then, overcome with joy, came her ecstatic greeting: "Rabbouni".

In the words of *The Gospel of the Beloved Companion,* Yeshua said to her,

> *Miryam, do not hold to me. For I am not yet of the flesh, yet neither am I one with the spirit; But rather go to my disciples and tell them you have seen me, so that*

all may know that my words are true and that any who should choose to believe them and keep to my commandments will follow me on their last day. (40:6)

Then Miryam went back to her home in Bethany and to the group of family members and close friends who were anxiously gathered there and who are all named in her Gospel. She told them about the miracle that had taken place.

And her Gospel says, "*they knew the truth of her and were all filled with great joy and believed.* (40:8)

A week or so later, Miryam, now the appointed leader of the disciples, convened a meeting of them at her house in Bethany to decide what to do next. Some, including Peter, had fled in fear to Galilee before the crucifixion and took some time to return. When they had come together, she told the disciples what she had seen and what Yeshua had said. The disciples told her that they were worried about going forth into the world and asked her to impart the hidden teaching that Jesus gave to her.

Peter said to her: *Sister, we know that he loved you more than any other among women. Tell us the words of the Rabbi, which you remember, which you know and understand, but we do not, nor have we heard them.* (41:5)

In this precious *Gospel of the Beloved Companion*, we can at last hear the words that Miryam spoke to the disciples in answer to Peter's request. It fills in the pages of text that are missing from the other three Gospels of Mary, including the one in the Nag Hammadi Library. Here, the startling focus is the Tree of Life, which at once takes us back to the First Temple where the Goddess Asherah was worshipped as the Holy Spirit and Divine Wisdom as well as the Tree of Life, bestower of the fruit of immortality.

Raising her right hand, Miryam then speaks to the assembled disciples, telling them about the ascent of her soul that she experienced with Yeshua. What Miryam is describing is, according to Dr van der Meer, the Ascension Experience that would have been part of Essene as well as Egyptian temple initiatory ritual. According to Dr Margaret Barker, the Tower is itself the symbol of the Ascension Experience that was a shamanic practice of the high-priest [or possibly high priestess] in the Wisdom Tradition of the First Temple.

I have Jehanne de Quillan's permission to quote the following passages. These are the words that Yeshua spoke to Miryam, his beloved wife:

Miryam, blessed are you who came into Being before coming into being and whose eyes are set upon the Kingdom, who from the beginning has understood and followed my teachings. Only from the truth I tell you, there is a great tree within you that does not change, summer or winter, and its leaves do not fall. Whosoever listens to my words and ascends to its crown will not taste of death, but will know the truth of eternal life. (42.2)

He then shows her in a vision a great Tree whose roots are in the earth, which is her body. The Tree has eight boughs which represent the levels of initiation that have to be passed before the Kingdom of the Spirit is reached, each with its own fruit which, Yeshua tells her, *"will grant her the light of the Spirit that is eternal life."* Between each bough is a guardian who challenges those who are unworthy to pass.

The leaves at the bottom of the tree are thick and plentiful, so no light penetrates to illuminate the way. But fear not, for I am the Way and the Light, and I tell you that, as one ascends the tree, the leaves that block one from the Light are fewer, so it is possible to see all the more clearly. Those who seek to ascend must free themselves from the world. If you do not free yourself from the world, you will die in the darkness that is the root of the tree. But if you free yourself, you will rise and reach the Light that is the eternal life of the spirit. (42.5)

The following passage describes the initiatory ascent of Miryam's soul through the boughs of the tree. At each level she has to overcome the Archon, the guardian spirit or shadow aspect of that level. The first bough holds the fruit of love and compassion, the second of wisdom and understanding.

And then my Master showed me the third bough, which bears the fruit of honour and humility. Only when free of all duplicity and arrogance may you partake of its nourishment. And arrogance called to me, saying, 'you are not worthy.' Go back. But my soul was deaf to him, and so moved onward and upward into increasing light. (42.8)

And then there came the fourth bough, blossoming with the fruit of strength and courage. And I heard him tell me that to eat of this fruit, you must have freed yourself from the weakness of the flesh and confronted and conquered the illusion of your fears. And the Master of the World stood before me and claimed me as his own, but I denied him and he had no part of me. (42.9)

[The Master of the World is the most powerful and deceiving of all the Archons, the one that Jesus called Caesar and The Deceiver.]

Only then, my Master told me, when you have rejected the Deceiver, can you pass through the hardest gate of all, to attain the fifth bough and the fruit of clarity and truth. Only then will you know the clarity and truth of your soul, and, know-

ing yourself for the first time, understand that you are a child of the living Spirit. And as my soul moved upward, I realized that I could no longer hear the voice of the world, as all had become as silence. (42.10)

Miryam then sees the sixth bough bearing the fruit of power and healing that can only be eaten when she has acquired the clarity and truth of the fifth bough, giving her the power to heal her own soul and make it ready to ascend to the seventh bough, '*where it will be filled by the fruits of light and goodness.*' (42:11)

Then comes this wonderful passage:

And I saw my soul, now free of all darkness, ascend again to be filled with the light and goodness that is the Spirit. And I was filled with a fierce joy as my soul turned to fire and flew upwards in the flames from whence my Master showed me the eighth and final bough, upon which burned the fruit of the grace and beauty of the Spirit. (42:12)

And I felt my soul and all that I could see dissolve and vanish in a brilliant light, in a likeness unto the sun, and in the Light, I beheld a woman of extraordinary beauty, clothed in garments of brilliant white. The figure extended its arms, and I felt my soul drawn into its embrace, and in that moment, I was freed from the world and I realized that the fetter of forgetfulness was temporary. From now on I shall rest through the course of the time of the age in silence. And then, as if from a great distance, I heard the voice of my master tell me, 'Miryam, whom I have called the Migdalah, now you have seen the all, and have known the truth of your self, the truth that is I AM. Now you have become the completion of completions.' And thus, the vision ended. (42:13)

Then Miryam turned to the disciples and said,

This is what my Master has told and shown me. And only from the truth I tell you, that all that have revealed to you is true. (42:14)

The disciples, in the previously known Gospels of Mary and in this translation of *The Gospel of the Beloved Companion*, appear baffled and offended that Yeshua imparted this teaching to a woman and not to them. It is evident that the disciples listening to her revelation had no idea of what she was talking about or what her vision meant. Peter and Andrew said they did not believe what she said and their words made her cry. Peter (Shimon Kefa) said:

Did he really speak privately with this woman and not openly to us? Are we to turn about and all listen to her? Did he prefer her to us? (43:3)

Then the Migdalah wept and said to him,

> *My brother Shimon Kefa,what do you think? Do you think I have thought this up myself in my heart, or that I am lying about Yeshua? Only from the truth again I tell you that what I have said is the truth* (43:4)

Levi, another disciple, defends her, saying that surely Yeshua knew her better than all the others:

> *Shimon Kefa, you have always been hot-tempered Now I see you contending against this woman like the adversaries. But if the Rabbi made her worthy, who are you indeed to reject her? Surely as his companion, Yeshua knew her better than all others. That is why he loved her more than us. Rather, let us be ashamed and do as she says. Let us put on perfect humanity and acquire it as she has done, and separate as he commanded us and preach the testimony of the Son of Humanity, not laying down any other rule or other law beyond that which he gave us.*

And so, baffled and uncomprehending, and arguing among themselves, they went their separate ways. (43:5-6)

The Joint Mission of Yeshua and Mary Magdalene

Returning to the channeled transmissions received from Alariel in *The Power of the Magdalene*, he explained an unknown and very interesting aspect of the relationship between Jeshua and Mary Magdalene, saying that their joint Mission was to anchor the Cosmic Energy of Love — Unconditional Love — upon the Earth.

> The energy required to initiate a big breakthrough needs to be balanced before it appears in full manifestation upon the Earth. Anchoring the Cosmic Energy of Love — Unconditional Love — upon Earth was a major project and needed powerful and balanced energy. No single human being could have accomplished that task. The crucifixion process was part of this, but just one part of it. Another part was the life which Jeshua and Mary shared, blending and aligning their energies and forming a single Star of Oneness, an energy vortex that created a portal through which this Love Energy could descend fully and anchor itself upon the Earth. This Energy had long been available to the advanced few, but humanity as a whole could not access it until Jeshua and Mary anchored it through their balanced focus. Jeshua and Mary Magdalene worked upon this project together, they achieved this together and should be honored together. [41]

Jeshua and Mary Magdalene, through their high intent and by invoking major angelic aid, were able to create a vortex of energy which functioned as a portal through which the Cosmic Energy of Love could descend into the vibrational conditions of the Earth and anchor securely within Earth-reality. If this energy had not been securely anchored on Earth, those who came after Jeshua would not have been able to lock onto it in their consciousness, and so could not have applied this energy in their lives. The vibration of Cosmic Love would then have been too subtle for their consciousness to sustain and hold. If that had happened, Jeshua would have been become a mystical and legendary figure that no later generation could understand, and therefore no one could follow effectively. He would have passed into the world of myth and legend and his teachings would soon have been forgotten. [42]

The great outpouring of the spiritual energy of Love affected the whole evolutionary process of human development. If you look at the arc of human history, there was a steady increase in the density of physical existence starting in Lemuria, accelerating through the Atlantean period and reaching a high point of physical density (and a corresponding low point of spiritual sensitivity) during the Roman Empire. The point at which Jeshua was born was the very nadir of spirituality on the planet, the lowest point of the devolutionary arc. Because Jeshua and Mary Magdalene moved human consciousness forward into an upward spiral, this opened up many new opportunities for human beings to rise in vibration and access higher levels of consciousness, subtler frequencies of Light and being, that would not have been possible within the previous downward spiral. [43]

By turning the devolutionary spiral into an upward evolutionary one, Jeshua and Mary saved humanity from a long period of experience at a much lower level. Had this Love Energy not been anchored in Earth reality at that time, you would still be living now under the world-wide domination of a Roman Empire so depraved that you could scarcely begin to imagine the depths to which it would have sunk. Instead of turning round and moving up into Light from that time on, your planet would have plunged ever more deeply into darkness and despair. [44]

The collaboration of Jeshua and Mary Magdalene saved humanity from all of that — and in this aspect of their work the whole world has reason to be grateful to them. Jeshua and Mary Magdalene saved humanity from the possibility of future sins, not the burden of past Karma. They saved you from all the sins that would have been committed if the darkness had continued to spread and the downward arc of devolution had not been turned into the upward arc of spiritual evolution. Jeshua and Mary Magdalene are the combined saviours of humanity and should be honoured as such. [45]

At the present time (2024) humanity seems still to be transfixed in old patterns, yet a new era is dawning, a new astrological Age. All over the planet, the old tectonic plates are shifting: we are awakening to a new relationship with it, realizing how deeply we have injured it. Many people have come together who are trying to challenge the pattern of war in online gatherings that are intensely moving.[46] (World Beyond War; Unity Earth and many others) Changing a pattern that has existed for four thousand years is a mammoth task, yet progress is being made, both to counter the existence of nuclear weapons and the ongoing addiction to war itself. Young people are waking up to the world they will inherit if war continues and they are seduced into becoming a genetically altered species (see Chapter 13: Part Two). Without the Internet, this coming together of millions would have been unthinkable.

The absence of the image of the Divine Feminine in the god-head may still have a considerable influence on that part of humanity that continues to adhere to the old patterns, the old beliefs. But this new insight into the role of Mary Magdalene as the spiritual partner of Jeshua — both teachers of Wisdom — working with him to anchor the Energy of Unconditional Love into the energy field of the Earth is to me, one of the most wonderful aspects of their close relationship and also their karmic responsibility and achievement. Without these channeled communications, and those who are on a high enough spiritual level to receive them, we would never have known this. It is for this reason and because I am deeply grateful that they exist, that I am including so much of this material in my final book.

The Church's Efforts to Efface the Evidence of Mary Magdalene

It is not difficult to understand why the Church of Rome had to efface all evidence of the relationship of Jesus and Mary Magdalene as well as all evidence of her influence. Alariel looked deeper into the antipathy towards Mary:

> Mary Magdalene has been a profound problem for the Church over the centuries. In the early days of Christianity, it was not understood that the whole Universe is balanced from Father-Mother God downwards. Because this was not understood, the role of women as leaders and wisdom-bearers could not be understood, and a powerful woman seemed to be a threat to the whole patriarchal structure of the Church. So how do you deal with an empowered woman? You marginalize and malign her. You say she is a prostitute and hope that no one will pay attention to her. [47]

The Church of Rome and the Eastern Orthodox Church are the two Christian institutions that are the most resistant to the idea of women priests. The Protestant Churches have moved on in this respect. In November 2016 Pope Francis published a letter that said that "ordaining women was not possible because Jesus chose only men as his apostles."

The testament of Alariel in *The Power of the Magdalene*, challenges this belief.

> Let us be clear about what is involved here: that Jeshua had a partner of great spiritual attainment. And that Mary Magdalene achieved a level of understanding that went far beyond that of all the male disciples, with the sole exception of John. Consider what effect this might have upon the Churches. Will they be able to adapt to these new ideas, or will they retreat into a time-warp of self-imposed irrelevance? How can they turn the clock back when the time for change is upon them? Out of all this one central question emerges: How can any Christian organization deny leadership roles to women when one woman was the spiritual partner, closest collaborator, and chosen companion of its Founder? [48]

The Christian Church and the Denigration of Mary Magdalene

In answer to a question from Joanna: Was the marginalizing of women part of the changes that were made in the early Church? Alariel replied:

> Yes. The tendency to disempower and marginalize women had been present since the time of Peter, but it intensified as the Church structure developed and became more complex. The image of Jeshua's mother Mary as a humble, faithful and docile female was promoted, and the image of Mary Magdalene as an empowered woman and a pioneer of Christianity in her own right was attacked and denigrated. The implications for female Christians were obvious: the Church wanted women as compliant followers, not as empowered leaders. [49]

Alariel continued:

> The early Church Fathers could not tolerate the idea of a woman who was a teacher in her own right. And they wished to move the Church in a direction which, over time, would consolidate patriarchal control. They had already started to develop Christianity from its beginnings as a God-centered presentation, steadily changing it until it became a Saviour-centered presentation focusing on a Divine Savior Hero. The concept of a Divine Hero was familiar to all those brought up in a Hellenic or Roman culture, but quite alien to the Judaic tradition. The Jews perceived their long-awaited Messiah as king of the Davidic line, a great prophet and the restorer of independence and glory to Israel, but NOT as the Son of God. Jewish tradition was quite different from Hellenic culture in this respect, a Greek could aspire to become a God but the Jews perceived God and humanity as being distinct and strictly separate. [50]

> The early Church Fathers were not held back by any constraints of this kind, and they were starting to blur the boundaries that separated the humnan Jeshua from the Divine Jesus. Within that context, Mary Magdalene was a major obstacle to Church ambitions. Mary's role as the spiritual partner of Jeshua

drew attention to his humanity at a time when the Church leaders wanted to emphasize his Divinity as a way of increasing their power and authority. They reasoned that the more powerful the founder of a religion was, the more power and respect his priests would be able to command. [51]

The Church leaders viewed the growing veneration of Mary Magdalene as a direct threat to their power-base, and to the concept of a Divine Jesus that they wished to present. Rather than risk their presentation and their power being undermined, the early Church Fathers were prepared to revile Mary Magdalene, and falsely accuse her of being a prostitute.

    The Church's treatment of Mary Magdalene is not only a great paradox but one of the great injustices of the Western world. It is only now, after all these years that this injustice is being exposed. [52]

The Power of the Magdalene does not diminish or wither with the passing of time: she is the Wayshower, embodying the energy and wisdom of the Sacred Feminine and inspiring others to do the same. She held a unique position among the disciples of Jeshua and demonstrated in her life the transforming power of the Spirit. It was Mary Magdalene's ability to attune to the power of the Spirit that gave her the most complete understanding of the All. Whilst the disciples of Jeshua might be able to grasp the All intellectually, she absorbed the All into every level of her being and thus became the ideal living pattern of what discipleship should be. [53]

The Importance of the Partnership of Jeshua and Mary Magdalene

Alariel summarizes the importance of the Partnership between Mary Magdalene and Yeshua:

Mary Magdalene and Jeshua demonstrated a new kind of partnership between two Advanced Beings. Their work on anchoring the energy of Love into the matrix of the Earth laid the foundations for all future expansion of the Light on this planet. And their partnership provides a new model to inspire human beings to reach up into higher frequencies of understanding and collaboration.

Through this model, you begin to glimpse a better way forward, with man and woman working together in a greater harmony where each respects the different talents and abilities of the other. When you begin to absorb and act upon this principle, it will inevitably lead to it rethinking of the whole basis of relationships. So the partnership of Jeshua and Mary Magdalene was both real in itself and yet also deeply symbolic. [54]

The partnership of Jeshua and Mary Magdalene reflects the ultimate balance of Father-Mother God which lies at the heart of the Universe. This is why the image of Jeshua and Mary Magdalene, as partners going forward hand in hand, has such power to move hearts and minds. They embody a higher partnership between me and women, but they also point towards a fundamental truth about God and the Universe.

This is the message which the partnership of Jeshua and Mary Magdalene sends out into the world.

This is the truth which your civilization has so long repressed and denied.

This is the reality which you are now challenged to acknowledge and accept. [55]

I will end this section on the channeled treasures from Alariel with this prophetic paragraph:

In the West, you are experiencing a time of re-evaluating and rebalancing. What started as a rebalancing within relationships is now culminating in a rebalancing of your whole belief system. The increasing interest in the Sacred Feminine, the female disciples of Jeshua, and the role played by Mary Magdalene, are all part of this rebalancing process. Rebalancing your belief system is an essential precondition for moving out of your past limitations and into the very different energy conditions of the New World, a World in which all aspects of the Divine will be valued.

The whole process of transformation and rising in consciousness, supported by the New Children, will open up the possibility of living in a post-conflict, post-competitive world in which collaboration and forgiveness replace the destructive patterns of your past.

This is the New World in which you are no longer the dependent children of Creation, but spiritually-adult Beings, standing in the Light of your own Consciousness. [56]

The Sea-Journey to Gaul

We do not know how, when, or why Mary Magdalene travelled from Judea to Alexandria or how long she lived there before travelling to south-western Gaul (France) in 44 CE, where she lived and taught for twenty years. She may have travelled in one of the many ships belonging to Joseph of Arimathea, the uncle of Jesus, whose main base was in Cyprus. She may have had to leave Palestine because of the assassination of the ruler of Judea which was blamed on the Nazarenes, or possibly to escape the virulent antagonism of the followers of Peter towards her, arising from their jealousy of her appointment by Jesus as leader of the disciples instead of Peter.

Mary Magdalene, who would have worn the black robe of a Nazarene or Essene priestess, took with her the Essene Wisdom Tradition. She travelled with her sister Martha and brother Lazarus. It is probable that she took with her precious Essene scrolls relating to the teachings that she and Jesus shared with a close group of disciples, including the Gospel she had written. She is said to have founded The Order of the Blue Rose, perhaps a symbol of the Essene Wisdom Teaching she brought with her to France.

The Journey to France
Painted by Giotto. Lower Church Assisi

Mary is thought to have landed either at Marseilles or at a tiny port called Saintes-Maries-de-la-Mer, not far from Marseilles. To this day gypsies gather here once a year to commemorate her arrival, landing with a woman called Sarah who was said to have been black. But this may be a distant memory of the black robe of a Nazarene priestess.

Mary travelled widely in Provence and the Languedoc and taught there for over 20 years until her death in 68 CE. There are many legends about her in this region and there is even a village called Les Labadous near Rennes-le-Chateau in the Languedoc where she is said to have lived. There apparently was an Essene community there. It is possible that the widespread cult of the Black Madonna, of which according to Dr van der Meer, there are 450 statues in France, developed after Mary's arrival and reached its height in the Middle Ages. The origin of these statues may have been the cult of the goddess Isis who was worshipped in France as late as the sixth century CE but it is possible that they became the symbol of the Wisdom Tradition brought to France by Mary Magdalene, which may have included the text of the *Pistis Sophia.*

In his thirteenth century *Golden Legend*, Jacob de Voragine writes: "When the blessed Mary Magdalene saw the people gather by the temple to offer sacrifices to the idols, she stepped forward: her demeanour was calm, her face was serene, and with well-chosen words she advised them to abandon the veneration of idols and preached passionately to them of Jesus. All who heard her admired her beauty, her eloquence and the sweetness of her message."

She is said to have spent the last years of her life in a cave on the Sainte-Baume mountain in Provence. Sainte-Baume refers to the Holy Balm or oil of spikenard with which she anointed Jesus' head on two occasions. Her brother Lazarus, who had become bishop of Marseilles, buried her in a small church called Saint Maximin-La-Sainte-Baume. There, her remains were guarded for centuries by Cassianite monks. To this day the Basilica of that name holds her relics including her skull, in a shrine devoted to her memory. In the twelfth century a magnificent Basilica was built in her honour at Vézelay.

Think what it would have meant for the development of Western civilization if the union of Jesus and Mary Magdalene had been celebrated by the Church founded in his name. Had their marriage been recognized at the inception of Christianity, the emphasis on celibacy as the path to spirituality would never have existed, nor would the celibate priesthood of the Catholic Church and the tragic sexual abuse of boys. We might have been spared the disastrous association of sin with sexuality and the misogyny that pollutes our culture to this day. We would have had a living image of a sacred marriage right at the heart of Christianity. This may be the time to restore the image of Mary Magdalene as the Holy Bride and undo the harm that has been done to her by the Christian Church.

Tau Malachi writes in *The Gnostic Tradition of the Holy Bride*: "From the Sophian perspective, the idea of Christ consciousness being revealed exclusively in a male form, apart from the female form, is considered incomplete and goes against the very nature of our experience, for the Life-power is equally in men and women, and Christ consciousness is essentially the same whether embodied in a man or woman." [57] We surely need to know that each of us — male and female — carries the Divine Light within us that is variously called Christ Consciousness or the Holy Spirit or Cosmic Consciousness. The quintessence of the Ascension Experience was the experience of that Consciousness, as recounted in *The Gospel of the Beloved Companion.* In this Gospel the banished First Temple tradition of Love and Wisdom and direct shamanic communion with the Divine Ground, was restored through the Mission of Jesus and Mary Magdalene. We only know this because of her Gospel, which is her priceless legacy to us, and through the channeled communications given in this Chapter.

For nearly eighty years I have treasured these words received by my mother in a channeled message in the late 1940's which are more relevant than ever today:

> The Divine Mother is the Holy Spirit who presides over the New Age. Inspired by her, women, through their love and understanding, have been given the task of awakening in humanity the compassion and devotion to life taught by Me at the beginning of the Piscean Age. Man, through woman, will realize in himself the sense of his mission on earth and see clearly as in a mirror, the law of the universe. [58]

Notes:

1. From Aleksandr Solzhenitsyn's Acceptance Speech for the Nobel Peace Prize, October 8th, 1970
2. The first of these books was *Holy Blood, Holy Grail* (1983) by Michael Baigent, Richard Leigh and Henry Lincoln. Then came Dan Brown's *The Da Vinci Code* in (2005). Both these books sold millions and brought Mary Magdalene to the awareness of the public. There was also *Bloodline of the Holy Grail* 1996, *The Magdalene Legacy* (2005) and *The Grail Enigma* (2008), all written by Laurence Gardner and all full of interesting material about Mary Magdalene. As well as these books, there were several books about her by Margaret Starbird and the highly acclaimed *The Meaning of Mary Magdalene* by Cythia Bourgeault (2010). There was also the classic *The Gospel of Mary Magdalene* by Jean-Yves Leloup (2002). All these books and many more, have brought Mary Magdalene to life.
3. Tau Malachi, (2006) *St. Mary Magdalene, The Gnostic tradition of the Holy Bride*, Llewellyn Publications, Woodbury, Minnesota. Tau Malachi is the founder of the Sophia Fellowship and the author of several books in the Gnostic tradition.
4. McCannon, Tricia, (2015) *Return of the Divine Sophia: Healing the Earth through the Lost Wisdom Teachings of Jesus, Isis, and Mary Magdalene*, Bear & Co, Vermont
5. Vermes, Geza, (1991) *The Dead Sea Scrolls*. Baigent, Michael & Leigh, Richard, (1991) *The Dead Sea Scrolls Deception*, Jonathan Cape, London.
6. Barker, Dr Margaret, (2004), *Temple Theology*, SPCK, p. 7
7. Gardner, Laurence, (2005) *The Magdalene Legacy*, HarperCollins, London. pp. 20 &

27, and index. In 318 CE, a genealogical Chart of the descendants of Jesus and his brother James, known as the *Desposyni Chart*, was presented to Pope Sylvester 1st by eight bishops, all male descendants of Jesus, one of whom was the Bishop of Jerusalem. On the order of the emperor Constantine, they had been summoned to Rome by the Pope with the aim of having their hereditary bishoprics removed. They brought with them their genealogical charts which proved their descent from Jesus and their entitlement to their bishoprics. The genealogical tree they presented to the Pope showed how each of these bishops was descended from Jesus and Mary Magdalene and James the brother of Jesus. It covered 300 years and 10 generations. The Pope dismissed the visitors but kept the Chart they had brought with them. Bearing his signature, it was deposited in the separate inner archive of the secret archives in the Vatican. Some years ago, a researcher working in these archives, managed to evade the security cameras and photograph the 318 *Desposyni Chart* and bring the pictures back to England. These were published in 2015 by Barry Page in his book *The Historical Jesus Found*. (MPM Publication) Sylvester was Pope from 316 until his death in 335. He converted and baptised the emperor Constantine and was Pope at the time of the crucial Council of Nicaea in 325 which established the divinity of Jesus (as being of one substance with God).

8. See Chapter Seven.
9. *The Nag Hammadi Library in English*, (1977), Director James M. Robinson, Brill, Leiden, p. 235. Pagels, Elaine, (1979), *The Gnostic Gospels*, George Weidenfeld & Nicholson Ltd., London, p. 22
10. ibid, NHL, pp. 135-6
11. ibid, p. 138
12. Barker, Dr Margaret, *The Great Angel, A Study of Israel's Second God*, p.3 and p.51.
13. van der Meer, Dr Annine, (2023), *Mary Magdalene Unveiled*, p. 148. Kovács, Dr Betty J. (2019) *Merchants of Light: The Consciousness that is Changing the World*, The Kamlak Center, Claremont CA, pp. 186, 187, 194, 170-71, 205
14. Wilson, Stuart & Prentis, Joanna, (2009), *The Power of the Magdalene*, Ozark Mountain Publishing Inc., Huntsville, AR, p. 18
15. ibid, p.19
16. ibid, p. 22. Barfield, Owen, (1965, 1988) *Saving the Appearances: A Study in Idolatry*, Weslyan University Press, Middletown, Connecticut
17. ibid, p. 21
18. ibid, p. 24
19. ibid, p. 78
20. ibid, p. 85
21. ibid, p. 80
22. ibid, pp. 80, 81
23. ibid, p. 83
24. ibid, p.84
25. ibid, p. 84
26. ibid, pp. 84-85
27. ibid, p. 90
28. ibid, p. 40
29. ibid, p. 90

30. ibid, p. 91
31. ibid, p. 91
32. ibid, p. 92
33. ibid, p. 92
34. ibid, p. 79
35. ibid, pp. 92-93
36. ibid, pp. 93-94
37. ibid, p. 94
38. ibid, p. 95
39. Quillan, Jehanne de, (2010). Éditions Athara, Foix, France
40. The Nag Hammadi Library, p. 371
41. *The Power of the Magdalene*, p. 98
42. ibid, p. 98
43. ibid, pp. 98-99
44. ibid, p. 99
45. ibid, p. 99
46. World Beyond War, Unity Earth and many others.
47. *The Power of the Magdalene*, p.100
48. ibid, p. 102
49. ibid, p. 105
50. ibid, p. 145 Alariel does not make it clear that Mary Magdalene was the *wife* as well as the spiritual partner of Jeshua and that she was Mary of Bethany, the sister of Martha and Lazarus. Dr. Annine van der Meer noticed there was confusion about this in *The Power of the Magdalene* and pointed it out to me. She said that their marriage was definitely proven by the text of *The Gospel of the Beloved Companion*, written by Mary Magdalene.
51. ibid, pp. 145-146
52. ibid, p. 146
53. ibid, p. 146
54. ibid, p. 146
55. ibid, pp. 147-148
56. ibid, p. 198
57. Tau Malachi, (2006) *St. Mary Magdalene: The Gnostic Tradition of the Holy Bride*, p. xvi
58. Baring, Anne, (2023), *Messages from a Transcendent Dimension*, Archive Publishing, Shaftesbury, Dorset

I should add here the important research of Marguerite Rigoglioso Ph.D., whose book about the training of priestesses in the Egyptian and Greek cultures, discovered that high-priestesses were trained to be able to have immaculate conceptions, drawing into incarnation exceptional souls. "There once existed mystery schools of the priestess in ancient times, in ancient lands, that engaged in the practice of miraculous conception. Through ceremony, meditation and initiation they were able to draw in specific souls to incarnate on Earth through their womb portals." She has published four books of great interest:

The Cult of Divine Birth in Ancient Greece 2009; Virgin Mother Goddesses of Antiquity 2013; The Mystery Tradition of Miraculous Conception: Mary and the Lineage of Virgin Births 2021 and *The Secret Life of Mother Mary: Divine Feminine Power for Personal Healing and Planetary Awakening.*

Scholar and author Marguerite Rigoglioso, Ph.D., has unveiled a worldwide lineage of women engaged in this sacred practice. Learn about the mystery tradition that surrounded it and get to know [the Virgin] Mary as the empowered priestess she actually was.
Source: Portal to Ascension 11/10/25.

There is a channeled book called *Anna, the Mother of Jesus*, by Claire Heartsong, that details the way Anna and her husband prepared to receive the soul of Mary as an Immaculate Conception. And how Mary, in turn, was prepared to receive the soul of Jesus in the same way.

The Black Virgin
from Beaulieu-sur-Dordogne

Notre Dame de Saint Gervasy

Interlude

THE WISDOM TRADITION

Now I move on to a later phase of this story, which will be told in greater detail in Chapter Nine. As the Christian Church became more and more fused with the Roman model of Imperial power during the fourth century CE and more and more intent on consolidating its power through the eradication of 'heresy,' the beliefs and practices of the Gnostic communities, together with the image of the Divine Feminine as the Holy Spirit and Divine Wisdom, had to go underground for many centuries. We do not know how these were transmitted to France and preserved there for seven hundred years, but astonishingly, they re-emerged in the twelfth century, in the region of the Languedoc, the very region where Mary Magdalene had taught for 20 years. They re-emerged as the Cathar Church of the Holy Spirit, or Church of Sophia, established there in 1167. This Church claimed to have the true teachings of Jesus descended directly from the Apostles, from James, the brother of Jesus, and Mary Magdalene. It had Gnostic texts — most importantly — *The Apocryphon of John* (The Secret Book of John) and possibly, through Mary Magdalene, the *Pistis Sophia* and other Gnostic texts.

The new Cathar Church repudiated the control of the Church in Rome. Naturally, this aroused the enmity of that Church and in 1209 Pope Innocent III launched the Albigensian Crusade. After a hundred years of relentless persecution and genocide, the Cathar Church of the Holy Spirit was destroyed, together with the people of the Languedoc who supported it. Up to a million perished by murder, torture or starvation at the hands of the Papal armies and the Inquisition. To me, this is one of the most horrific and scandalous chapters in the history of the Christian Church.

The Black Madonna

In many of the cathedrals and churches of France are found the magnificent wooden statues of the Black Madonna whose numinous, hieratic presence holds their fascination and their healing power to this day. There are some 450 sculptures of the Black Madonna in France alone.[1] The finest examples of these were carved in the Auvergne region of France from the eleventh century but some may be related to far older statues of Isis who was worshipped in France as late as 600 CE. All show Mary as *Theotokos* or 'Mother of God,' some crowned, and all seated on the Throne of Wisdom, holding her son on her lap. The colour black signifies the presence of the Wisdom Tradition which descends, ultimately, from the Egyptian Mysteries. But it also returns us to the Shulamite — black but beautiful — of the Song of Songs, to the lustrous black robe of Isis as seen in Apuleius' famous vision, and to the Shekinah whose black veil hides the radiance of her glory. These images of the Black Madonna also stand for Nature — Mother and Womb of all.

The Extraordinary Twelfth Century

The twelfth century saw the return of the Wisdom Tradition that had gone underground in the calamitous fourth century with the eradication of the Gnostics, when we began to lose touch with our soul. The twelfth century was an extraordinary century which saw the rise of the magnificent Gothic Cathedrals in France, situated in different towns of the north of France in such a way as to reflect the shape of the constellation Virgo. It saw the founding of the Courts of Love by Eleanor of Aquitaine in Poitiers and her daughter Marie de France in Troyes which had a huge influence on raising the status of women. It saw the dissemination of the Grail Legends — a new mythology that was expressed in stories, poetry and song and carried the length and breadth of Europe by the troubadours. It saw the founding of the Schools of Chartres and Paris which drew enlightened men to teach in those cities, to create and develop what might be called civilization. It saw the rise of the Order of the Knights Templar and the streaming of pilgrims across Europe to sacred sites like Santiago de Compostela in northern Spain. It saw the spread of the mystical Jewish teaching of Kabbalah in northern Spain and south-western France. It saw priceless manuscripts translated from Arabic and Greek into Latin, carried from Toledo in Spain to the cathedral of Saint Denis in Paris. It saw the Cathar Church of the Holy Spirit established in south-western France, whose teaching spread rapidly over the whole region of the Languedoc, threatening the power of the Church of Rome, the Church that had, in 1096, inaugurated the First Crusade. Finally, it saw the activation of the shrines of the Black Madonna, particularly along the pilgrim routes where dozens of these majestic statues had existed for centuries as renowned centres of healing.

The Significance of the Grail

In twelfth-century Europe, the Feminine Archetype was secretly reborn in the image of the Holy Grail. In the twelfth century when the Grail legends were becoming known in the royal courts of Europe, carried there by the troubadours, the Holy Grail was the secret symbol of the banished feminine aspect of God — the sacred feminine womb or vessel eternally overflowing with Life, Light and Love. Her name then was Sophia or Divine Wisdom. The Grail knights were her devotees.

The Grail was also the secret symbol of the Cathar Church of the Holy Spirit. An unknown group of people must have secretly transmitted the Essene Wisdom Tradition in France for seven hundred years before it surfaced during the twelfth century, inspiring the building of the great Gothic Cathedrals that were financed by the Knights Templar. These were all dedicated to 'Our Lady.' To the people, this dedication meant the Virgin Mary but to the initiates of the Wisdom Tradition, including the Master-Masons of Chartres, it meant Mary Magdalene whom they saw as the embodiment of Sophia or Divine Wisdom. The cathedral of Chartres could be mystically understood to embody the lost First Temple and to restore the forgotten image of the Queen of Heaven — Divine Wisdom and the Holy Spirit — who was banished from it. The cathedral itself is a Holy Grail.

The Quest for the Grail as a Spiritual Journey

The Holy Grail is one of the greatest symbols we have of the spiritual quest. It opens the heart to the Quest for the lost feminine aspect of the Divine. As the image of sacred vessel or precious stone, it changed the face of Europe in the twelfth century, spreading the concept of courtly love, chivalry, and a profound change in men's attitude towards women and towards the existence of a higher dimension of reality. Bringing together the invisible and visible realms, the Above and the Below, it invited men to enter the *mundus imaginalis* of the visionary realm where, after many tests, they would be granted a vision of the Grail.

Betty Kovács writes in Chapter Thirty-One of her superlative book, *Merchants of Light: The Consciousness That Is Changing The World*,

> The Quest for the Grail itself was a quest for direct experience and communion with the Otherworld through love, respect, and loyalty to the Queen of that world, the Sovereign of the Land, *Our Lady*, the soul of the world. Out of the European wasteland emerged an incredible blossoming of soul. There must have been a profound longing for spiritual meaning that was ignited by contact with the great intellectual and sophisticated cities of Muslim Spain and through contact with the Sufis through the Crusades. And this new focus, in turn, ignited the underground traditions in Europe.... The Grail stories reveal that the wasteland of Europe had come about because we had lost contact with the Otherworld, the spirit realm.
>
> This incredible awakening prepared the way for the later Italian Renaissance. It is now clear that the various creative periods in Europe were powerful waves of this first renaissance during the High Middle Ages. What amazes me is that after hundreds of years of repression by the Church of the ancient mysteries of death and rebirth — our true wisdom — the soul knowledge reemerged into the consciousness of Western culture along with a clear image of the damage done to the Western psyche during these years of repression. [2]

One of the greatest of the Grail stories, called Parzival, was written between 1200 and 1210 by a German knight, Wolfram von Eschenbach, living at the time of the Christian Crusades against the Muslim Infidel. It has been retold in our time by Lindsey Clarke in his book, *Parzival and the Stone from Heaven*.[3] It tells the story of how a knight from King Arthur's Court, called Parzival, reaches the Grail Castle — situated in the region of the Pyrenees — and is presented to the Grail King, who lies dying in the great hall, wounded in the groin. Parzival is given a vision of the Grail — a glorious procession of women passing through the great hall, led by a beautiful woman, the Grail Bearer. However, awed by this vision, nervous and inarticulate, Parzival fails to ask the question of the king that would allow him to die and his kingdom — that had become a Wasteland – to be restored to fertility. The next morning, in disgrace, he leaves the silent castle and distraught, wanders through the Wasteland until he meets a hermit, who is the brother of the wounded king and his own uncle, his mother's brother. After spending a year, humbly learning from his uncle, he is ready to return to the Grail Castle.

But before he can enter it, there is a great battle fought before the Castle, between the Christian knight, Parzival and a Saracen knight, Feirefiz, Parzival's sword breaks and he faces death but Feirefiz throws away his sword and, removing his helmet, says he will not kill an unarmed knight. Embracing each other, they learn that they each had the same father but one had a Christian, and the other a Muslim mother. Arm in arm, they enter the Grail castle and, speaking from his heart, Parzival asks the question he was too immature to ask on his first visit — "What ails thee, Sire?" — allowing the old king to die, leaving Parzival, his nephew, as his heir and the Wasteland restored to life and fertility. Parzival and Feirefiz see the Grail, carried into the hall of the castle by a procession of women led by the beautiful woman called Repanse de Joie whom Feirefiz falls in love with and marries, while Parzival marries his true love, Blancheflor, whom he had previously rescued from a man who was persecuting her. In today's world, ethnic and religious rivalries compound the suffering of our collective estrangement from the holy mystery at the core of life. This Grail story shows the miracle that can take place when enemies are reconciled, and we address the question to ourselves: "What ails thee?" thereby healing both the Wasteland around us and awakening our darkened consciousness.

Betty Kovács writes in the same Chapter thirty-one of her book,

> The Grail stories flourished for fifty years, from 1175 to 1225, and then they ceased to be written. The awakening during the High Middle Ages manifested on so many different levels that many of its goals and accomplishments are yet to be discovered on a scale that could bring about their integration into Western culture. What is important for our purpose is the recognition that it was the underground shaman-mystic-scientist tradition, developed and enriched by Mystic Christianity and its relationship to Islam, that gave birth to this new consciousness in Europe. [4]

She quotes the medieval scholar, Jessie Weston, who wrote, "The fountain of inspiration, seems suddenly to have run dry.... May it not be that it was because the origin of the Grail... bore the impress of a body of thought and ideas which, known by the name of Gnosticism, was already under the Church's ban?" Even as early as 1913, Weston understood that "There is a stream of tradition, running as it were underground, which from time to time rises to the surface, only to be relentlessly repressed."" [5]

Chartres Cathedral

Chartres cathedral was and is a revelation: a Hymn to the Divine Feminine. The building of Chartres was part of the stupendous effort of constructing eighty cathedrals as well as many abbeys, monasteries, and churches in less than a hundred years. Chartres was designed to be a revelation by the brilliant Master-Masons who planned, built and completed it within the space of twenty-six years. All this focus on a spectacular programme of building required the collaboration of hundreds, if not thousands of people. The inhabitants of Chartres and many thousands of pilgrims helped to draw the wagons transporting the huge quantities of stone and wood required for building the cathedral. But think of the number of builders, stonemasons, carpenters, stained-glass window makers required to erect even one cathedral. Where did they come from? Who trained and supervised their work? How were they fed daily and through the years of building work? It is known that Muslim artisans contributed to the marvellous blue of the stained-glass windows. Who arranged for their transportation from Palestine to France? Did they come voluntarily or as prisoners of the Knights Templar? All this required vision, organization, and huge amounts of money, which would have been provided by the Knights, some of whom had spent several years in Jerusalem in the century before Chartres had begun and could have come into contact with Islamic geometry and architecture as well as Sufi teachers and poets. Gordon Strachan suggests they may have overseen the building of the Al-Aqsa Mosque there.

In his fascinating book, *Chartres: Sacred Geometry, Sacred Space*, he writes,

> It is difficult for us in the West to realize that in those times, Islam had reached a far higher level of civilization than north-western Europe, in almost every field of the arts and sciences. However, the historical evidence clearly indicates that it was only through contact with Islam that the full works of Plato, Aristotle and Euclid, which had been largely lost in the West, were rediscovered. It was only after these, and other classical works had been fully translated from Arabic into Latin, and added to the curriculum of Paris, Laon, Chartres and other centres of learning, that a renaissance of culture was triggered in northern France. The rise of Gothic architecture was the most spectacular result of this. [6]

Later in his book, which I urge everyone to read, he says the hexagram is the key to the geometry of Chartres and writes, "Without the genius of Islam, it is doubtful that there would have been any Gothic cathedrals. Without the Sufis, how could the Templars have learnt about the universality and ultimate oneness of truth? Yet without the militant, if misguided zeal of the Crusaders, how would they have ever rediscovered and entered into their own lost Gnostic heritage?" [7]

La Belle Verrière – Chartres Cathedral

Chartres cathedral was built as the dwelling place on earth of the Virgin Mary, the Queen of Heaven. It is also a Grail — a container of the Mysteries and the numinous Presence of the Holy Spirit. The rose itself has long been a symbol of Divine Wisdom and the whole cathedral, with its three sublime rose windows, is a hymn to Mary who is herself a Grail. What more wonderful image of the Wisdom Tradition is there than the great rose windows of Chartres and what connection did these have with the rose in the Sufi poetry of Islam? The Way of the Rose was and is still the Way of the Heart, the Way of the shamans and visionaries who preserved this ancient Wisdom Tradition that had from time immemorial connected us to transcendent levels of reality and opened our soul to the awareness of our divinity and immortality as well as to the Sacredness of the entire cosmos.

Betty Kovács writes,

> From the megalithic builders to the builders of the great cathedrals, there appears to be a continuum of knowledge rooted in the great mysteries and sacred geometry. Nothing was more important to the builders than knowing and understanding the laws of nature — of the earth, the human being, and the cosmos — *so that they could create structures in harmony with those laws.* Keith Critchlow tells us that from megalithic times, the square symbolised the stability of the earth and our experience in the physical world; the triangle symbolised the human being 'as the harmonizing human consciousness;' and the circle/hexagon symbolized the cosmos. These archetypal forms and their many manifestations continue to exist in cathedrals and temples around the world. *What is so important for us to know is that human consciousness is the mediator between the cosmos and the earth and that the builders had the knowledge of how to enhance this ability to mediate through the geometric structures themselves.* [8]

> Our ancestors understood that losing this relationship will result in the very wasteland that the Grail stories so vividly depict. The consciousness behind these stories knew what the West had lost — and they knew what had to be re-done to regain it. *So they created structures for our transformation. In the words of Sir Ronald Fraser, the cathedrals are "an instrument of high initiation.* [9]

> Keith Critchlow in "*Sacred Geometry,*" his DVD of Chartres Cathedral, explains how, with the use of sacred geometry, the cathedral was constructed according to cosmic laws in proportion to the human body. This creates the possibility for the human being to experience a sense of eternity, timelessness, spaciousness, unity and grandeur — that is, to experience the depth within and without. And in this way says Critchlow, we can begin to experience our own sacredness. Once we experience our own sacredness, he says, we are much less likely to destroy life. The cathedral is designed to open us up. It is the *Opener of the way.*[10] Beginning around a thousand CE, even before the final construction of the cathedral at Chartres between 1194 and 1250 CE, much of the wisdom that would be expressed in the new architecture was already being taught and experienced. René Querido in *The Golden Age of Chartres, the Teachings of a Mystery School and The*

Eternal Feminine, says that the master teachers at the famous School of Chartres sought to bring together in their teaching the major streams of thought that from early on had met and mingled at Chartres. There was, he says, "an ancient Greek stream penetrated with Platonism" that brought "a profound knowledge and practice of esoteric Christianity." For two hundred years, Querido tells us, the master teachers of Chartres "sought to reconcile Celtic and Greek mysteries, Arthurian and Grail streams, with a Christianity based not on belief but on the possibility of man's direct experience of Christ and the spiritual hierarchies. [11]

At the core of all the streams was the knowledge of Christ consciousness and how to achieve it. And this is why, says Querido, the emphasis at Chartres has always been on birth, "the birth of the higher self." This birth of higher consciousness was called "The Mary Mysteries." The child that is birthed at Chartres "is the potential in each of us of the higher self, seeking to emerge so that we may become co-creators with the gods. This is the image of the Virgin bearing the Child that imbues the entire cathedral." [12]

The master teachers at Chartres made it clear that the questions that I asked in my book, *The Dream of the Cosmos*: How do we heal our soul, our culture and our planet? are answered by entering the path of *direct inner experience* where we discover our inherent harmony with the cosmos, with the earth, and with the deepest core of our being. Querido tells us that during the 200 years that the School of Chartres was blessed with these great teachers, they and their students "practised a path of initiation leading to an active communion with the world of the spirit."
"These masters," Betty Kovács continues,

were intellectual giants, but they were not content with knowledge alone. While they taught the Seven Liberal Arts as the path of inner development, they knew that healing could only be achieved through the direct inner experience of soul — gnosis. Everything at Chartres, Querido says, was rooted in the mysteries of gnosis — the birth of the new consciousness, the new human being. And it was the path of these great masters that paved the way for the full manifestation of the cathedral of Chartres. [13]

Querido writes,

Nothing is comparable in any of the great French cathedrals to the sublimity of Chartres' western rose window and three lancets. They express iconographically an apotheosis. Taken together with the Royal Portal's splendid statuary on the outside, they present the beginning and the end, the Alpha and the Omega, of human development, encompassed in one great sweep of astonishing variety yet harmonious unity. Here, past, present, and future appear to be lifted into an eternal dimension. Time is held fast in majestic, sculptural form and brilliant stained glass. Great beauty and deep religious aspiration come together. By contemplating the inner and the outer, the soul is lifted to a crossing of the threshold between the physical and the spiritual, where true imagination is born of a deeper seeing; a beholding that is not simply of the senses. [14]

Betty Kovács continues,

These shaman-mystic builders were Masters of Light who knew how to construct magnificent alembics for the distillation of our darkness into the light of cosmic consciousness. For two hundred years at the school Chartres the master teachers "practised the path of initiation that opened the world of spirit for themselves and their students. While they engaged the intellect, the ultimate goal was gnosis—direct experience of Christ/cosmic consciousness." [15]

Labyrinth — Chartres Cathedral, France

The labyrinth was a symbol of this path. I had not known that twenty-two of the eighty Gothic cathedrals built in France had labyrinths. I had only known about the one at Chartres. Unfortunately, many of these beautiful labyrinths were later destroyed by the Church clergy during the seventeenth and eighteenth centuries, but the labyrinth at Chartres remains today in all its beauty and symbolic significance. As we have seen, the labyrinth reaches deep into our ancient spiritual history as a symbol of our individual path to higher consciousness. As we enter Chartres Cathedral, a great womb itself, we immediately see yet another womb; the great labyrinth. [16]

　　What happened during the high Middle Ages is one of the most phenomenal events in the history of the West. Christianity began as do all great religions, in an experience of higher consciousness—gnosis. This is precisely what the Church had denied and what it had spent so much of its time, energy, and money to destroy — and seven hundred years later, this knowledge emerged like the great Phoenix out of the fire of its destruction within the very heart of the Church itself! [17]

Here at last we see the true story of Christianity. Scholars today often say there were many different streams of early Christianity and this is true. But that does not prevent us from knowing that the *origin of Christianity*, as in all religions, was in gnosis — direct experience of a higher consciousness. And it is *this consciousness* that is the Saviour of our species. It is this consciousness that gives us the answers to the healing of soul, culture, and planet.[18]

The Troubadours

The Grail Legends were rapidly carried all over Europe by the troubadours, welcomed by the courts of Eleanor of Aquitaine in Poitiers and her daughter Marie de France in the city of Troyes, east of Paris. Surprisingly, women as

Women and men as troubadours
from a Renaissance painting

well as men were troubadours. The place where many of these troubadours were trained was a tiny town in the south-west, called Saint Guilhelm-le-Desert, not far from Montpellier, whose abbey held a relic of the true cross. At their forest meetings, they are said to have worn red cloaks, embroidered with a dove, ageless symbol of the Holy Spirit. The troubadours carried the Grail Legends and the hidden tradition of the Church of the Holy Spirit or the Church of Sophia all over Europe under cover of the Quest for the Holy Grail. They called Mary Magdalene 'Notre Dame' and 'The Grail of the World.' At the same time, the more familiar Grail stories that we know, spread from the Court of Queen Eleanor in England. Married to Henry II, the king of England after she was granted a divorce from the king of France, she invited Chrétien de Troyes to come to her Court and write his stories about King Arthur and his Court, and the Quest for the Grail undertaken by his knights. He died before he could complete this work, yet enough survived to inspire and enchant future generations.

The Knights Templar

The Knights Templar held Mary Magdalene in the highest honour as the patron of their Order. They secretly guarded the heretical knowledge that she was the wife of Jesus and the mother of his children. They called her 'Our Lady of Light' and 'Light of the World' because they saw her as the embodiment of Sophia (Wisdom) or the Holy Spirit. The story of how this association came about is told by Lawrence Gardner in his book, *The Magdalene Legacy*.[19]

In the eleventh century, a small group of Templar knights set out from the town of Troyes to travel to the Holy Land. They spent several years in Jerusalem, exploring the area beneath the ruins of the Temple Mount. No-one knows whom they contacted while there or what they learned, but on their return, the building of the Gothic cathedrals began, financed by them. At the beginning of the fourteenth century their immense wealth and extensive power aroused the enmity and greed of the king of France.

In 1307, in a minutely planned military operation extending to every part of France, 5,000 members of the Order of the Knights Templar were arrested overnight without warning and charged with heresy and magical practices. After confessions extracted under torture, many were burned at the stake while others were sentenced to perpetual imprisonment. All their lands, castles and possessions were confiscated by the king. In March 1314, Jacques de Molay, the Grand Master of the Templars, was burnt to death in Paris. Before he was executed, he had prepared 40 Templar boxes, each containing the facts about the life of Jesus. He distributed two of these boxes to each of the senior surviving *Desposnyi* families — the name given to the descendants of Jesus and Mary Magdalene, and James, the brother of Jesus.[20] The Templars knew the true story. That is why they had to be destroyed.

The Transmitters of the Hidden Wisdom Tradition were:
The Gnostics, The Essenes, The Builders of the Gothic Cathedrals — The Black Madonna, The Templars, The Alchemists and Kabbalists. The Wisdom Tradition is the hidden thread connecting all of these.

Notes:

1. see van der Meer, Dr. Annine (2015), *The Black Madonna from Primal to Final Times*, Pan Sophia Press
2. Kovács, Dr Betty J. (2019) *Merchants of Light: The Consciousness that is Changing the World,* The Kamlak Center CA United States of America pp. 351-352
3. Clarke, Lindsay, (2001) *Parzival and the Stone from Heaven*, HarperCollins, London
4. Kovács, op. cit. p. 354
5. ibid, p. 354
6. Strachan, Gordon, (2003) *Sacred Geometry, Sacred Space*, Floris Books, Edinburgh, p. 17
7. ibid, p. 72
8. Kovács, op. cit. p. 356
9. ibid, p. 358
10. ibid, p. 360
11. ibid, p. 360 quoting René Querido, pp. 14-15
12. ibid, p. 360 quoting Querido 16-17, 37
13. ibid, P. 362 quoting Querido 16, 18, 71
14. Querido, René (1987) *The Golden Age of Chartres: The Teachings of the Mystery School and the Eternal Feminine*, Floris Books, Edinburgh, p. 67
15. Kovács, op. cit. pp. 364
16. ibid, pp. 364-65
17. ibid, p. 365
18. ibid, p. 365
19. Gardner, Lawrence, (2005) *The Magdalene Legacy,* Element, London, for *Desposyni* (see index in that book)
20. see Gardner op. cit. for Templar references under Knights Templar and pp. 89-101

Dan Morse, in a fascinating webinar, has shown the sculptural images associated with Wisdom on the cathedrals of Notre Dame and Chartres.
https://www.youtube.com/watch?v=j_KAfAjiE2I

Apart from the mystical Jewish teaching of Kabbalah, the only place where the image of the Divine Feminine survived was in Alchemy, where she was known as Sophia or Wisdom. The alchemists called themselves Sons of Wisdom.

Chapter Nine

Esclarmonde de Foix
and The Cathar Church of the Holy Spirit

There are some individuals who stand out like supernova from the starry background of history. They are remembered for their achievements but also for their contribution to a quality of being that infuses a whole culture and lifts it to a level it might not have reached without them.

The twelfth century has given us an abundance of such individuals: Dante, Heloise and Abelard, Bernard of Clairvaux, Chrétien de Troyes, Francis of Assisi, to name only a few.[1] Esclarmonde de Foix (1155-1240), like Hildegarde of Bingen (1098-1179) and Eleanor of Aquitaine (1122-1204), is one of the three outstanding women of the Middle Ages.[2] She was what Jung would have called an '*Anima* figure' at the highest inspirational level. It is fascinating that their lives to some extent overlapped with each other. Eleanor of Aquitaine would certainly have known about Esclarmonde de Foix and vice-versa although it is unlikely that they ever met.

The word Esclarmonde means 'Light of the World, the same title that was given to Mary Magdalene by the Templars. It may be that her name came from the Visigoth '*Is Klar Mun*' meaning 'Moon of Cristal' that in time became 'Esclarmonde'. What a strange name to give one's daughter, and what a strange destiny she had, born into one of the most revolutionary, creative and secretive of all centuries. Why was she remembered in the remote part of France where she was born, the part that borders Spain and that has a fascinating and largely unknown history? What vision did she incarnate that led to the discovery, eight hundred years later, of the role she played in one of the greatest tragedies of European history; a role that was treasured by the people of the Languedoc, as this region of France was called, and enshrined in stories that were passed from generation to generation until at last they have reached us?

Esclarmonde was one of the leaders of a group of men and women who were called Cathars or Albanenses after the white robes they wore. The word 'Cathar' means pure and Albanenses comes from the Latin word 'alba' which means 'white'. They were members of a secret church which served the Holy

Spirit and the Divine Feminine — imaged as the Holy Grail and presided over by Sophia or Divine Wisdom. The mystery of the Grail infuses the Middle Ages with the image of the sacred quest for the lost feminine element hidden within the outer forms of Christianity. As the Christian Church became more and more fused with the Roman model of Imperial power and more and more identified with the masculine archetype, the feminine element had to go underground. It survived as an underground gnostic movement after the suppression of the Gnostics in the fourth century CE under the emperors Constantine and Theodosius 1, surfaced in an extraordinary flowering in the twelfth and thirteenth centuries in south-western France and northern Spain, was driven underground again through persecution and genocide, and is once more surfacing in our own time as men and women respond to the need for a different understanding of life and of themselves.

Throughout these two thousand years, it has been kept alive by individuals, drawn from different European countries and from a Jewish as well as a Christian background. This underground stream of secret teaching was hidden in the elaborate code of symbols known as Alchemy, as well as in the mystical Jewish tradition of Kabbalah. This secret teaching nourished not only those designated as heretics by the Catholic Church but other groups of individuals within the Order of the Knights Templar, as well as Jewish and Islamic mystics. It was woven into the symbolic imagery of the Grail legends and was spread all over Europe by the troubadours, many of whom were initiates of this teaching. It is carved into the soaring masonry of the Gothic Cathedrals, every stone of which proclaims it.

The twelfth century has much in common with our own time which demands from us a creative response as great as the challenge of the immense problems confronting us. The twelfth century offers an image of a gigantic cauldron in which men and women, ideas and institutions were thrown together in a process of transformation that must have seemed almost apocalyptic in its intensity. It was the age which saw the surge of devotion which built the great Gothic cathedrals, which sent thousands of men on Crusades to the Holy Land and hundreds of thousands of pilgrims streaming along the roads that led to the shrine of Compostela in northern Spain. It saw the founding of the Cistercian Order and the rapid expansion of the Order of the Knights Templar. It witnessed the rise of the universities and the impact of Aristotelian thought on European philosophy and of the works of Plato and other Greek philosophers, reaching France from Arabic Spain via translators working in Toledo. It nurtured the Grail legends which at its beginning were virtually unknown, and by its end were so well known that there can have been hardly a soul in Europe who had not heard of them. It was dominated by two images: the image of the Quest and the image of the Divine Feminine as the object of the Quest. 'Notre Dame', as she was called by troubadours, Cistercians, Knights Templar and pilgrims, was the focus of adoration. The three hundred or so Cistercian monasteries built in this century were dedicated to her. Many of the Gothic Cathedrals, built in a miraculously short time, were called Notre Dame. Some, like Chartres, were built on Celtic or Druid sites that had long been sacred to the Earth Mother. But the title 'Notre Dame' described not only the Virgin Mary, but also her daughter-in-law, Mary Magdalene.

In the twelfth century, the image of woman was transformed in the culture of the Languedoc although it has taken eight hundred years for that local transformation to bear fruit in the gradual ascent of woman and the slow rehabilitation of the feminine principle that is now taking place. But it was followed by a century that witnessed a horrific act of genocide: the destruction of a people, a culture and a religion which set a fearful precedent for future centuries — of tyranny, slaughter and barbarism that was justified by both Church and State and never acknowledged by them to be the atrocity it was. A shadow fell over Europe that has not been lifted even now, because we are the unconscious inheritors in the twentieth century of the intolerance, cruelty and fanaticism of that one.

France was the cultural centre of Europe at this time and the most cultur-ally advanced part of France was precisely the south-west, the Languedoc, where Esclarmonde was born in 1155. She was born in the castle of Foix, a fairy-tale castle perched high above the town, clinging to an enormous rock that looked out onto the snow-capped mountains of the Pyrenees. Her father, the count of Foix, was a vassal of the count of Toulouse. Her mother was called Zebelia Trencavel, daughter of the count of Carcassonne. We know that she had a brother and a sister, that the family was close and devoted and that her parents welcomed both troubadours and Cathar priests to their renowned and cultured court.

The History of the Region

I think it is helpful to know a little bit about the history that made this region of France so culturally advanced and so fascinating. To go back a long way, it seems that there may have been Egyptian colonies here before there were Greek or Roman ones. The cult of the Egyptian goddess Isis was established here and, indeed, in other parts of France, and may date from this early period. Secondly, there were the Visigoths who, moving from East to West through Europe, conquered Rome in the early fifth century and moved on to establish their own kingdom in the area between the Rhone and Garonne rivers. In

418 CE this area was recognized by Rome as the kingdom of Toulouse. One tiny detail is fascinating: each Visigoth warrior carried a pouch containing tweezers, a comb, scissors and an ear and tooth pick. They may have inspired terror but at least they took care of their personal hygiene! Moreover, many of them were scholars and welcomed other scholars, particularly the Jewish and Moorish ones who had established themselves in Toulouse and other southern towns, like Narbonne and Béziers as well as Girona in northern Spain. Eventually a Visigoth princess whose ancestors had intermarried with the Jews, married a Frankish King and started the short-lived Merovingian dynasty of French kings.

The third influence in this area were the Jews who had a particularly strong community in Toulouse and Narbonne and who, in the late eighth century, established a kingdom called Septimania that extended over northern Spain as well as south-western France. Even after the disappearance of this kingdom, the Jewish community never lost its links with Spain, particularly the towns of Cordoba, Toledo, Seville and Girona until the time when the Jews (as well as the Moors), at the instigation of the Inquisition, were expelled from that country in the late fifteenth century.

The Arab or Moorish influence was also strongly established in this area, particularly in Toulouse. The fascinating thing about these three different cultures is that they all got on well together. All were viewed as heretical by the Church of Rome. The main point to remember is that the Hermetic philosophy that scholars and mystics of all three cultures embraced derived ultimately from Egypt and may have flourished here before Roman, Visigoth, Jew or Muslim set foot on this land. There were many unsolved mysteries connected with this area, not least the whereabouts of the Visigoth treasure from the sack of Rome which was said to have been hidden here and which was said to include the Emerald Table from the Temple of Solomon in Jerusalem that had been seized by the Romans when they sacked the city in 70 CE.

The Visigoths loved Toulouse and in the sixth century built one of the most beautiful of all churches — the Basilica of La Daurade — on the site of the temple of the Roman goddess Minerva. They dedicated it to the Virgin Mary, covered it in gold mosaic and gave it a circular form and round dome like Haghia Sophia in Constantinople. The magnificent sculptures that decorated it were fortunately preserved when it was dismantled in the eighteenth century and can be seen in the museum in Toulouse. Toulouse had been a university in Roman times and the tradition of learning was continued by the Visigoths who intermarried with the Jewish community and welcomed Jewish scholars to their great city.

By the twelfth century, Toulouse, or Tolosa as it was called then, was the most prestigious city in Europe after Venice and Rome. The counts of Toulouse ruled over a huge area that was not subject to the laws of the kingdom of France. Toulouse made its own laws. Here scholars from three different cultures — Jewish, Muslim and Christian (the Visigoths had converted to the Arian form of Christianity) — met to learn from each other and lived together in harmony and friendship. Here was the centre of a prosperous, thriving economy that drew merchants and traders from all over the Mediterranean; that was so rich that it increasingly aroused the envy of the north, and so spiritually independent that it drew the enmity of the Papacy in Rome. The feudal lords of this region, among them the counts of Toulouse, Foix and Carcassonne, fostered an extraordinary culture where the cult of beauty, philosophy, poetry, courtly manners and the appreciation of woman flourished.

Poetry was the sap of life. We have records of over five hundred troubadours who lived and thrived in this culturally fertile atmosphere, who contributed to its creation. They travelled from court to court all over Europe, carrying with them a secret, hermetic knowledge which they embodied in the Grail legends and which they called "La Gaie Science" or "Le Gaie Savoir". 'Gay' or 'Gau' in the Provençal dialect meant 'cock' and the cock was one of the main symbols of the Hermetic teaching, partly because it announced the coming of the dawn and partly because it recalled the denial of Christ by Peter on the eve of His Crucifixion — Peter who became the founder of the Christian Church. The historical role of the troubadours was not only to create through their poetry a cultural climate in which a derogatory attitude to woman could be transformed, but which could reanimate the idea of the Quest: the Quest for the spiritual as opposed to the material vision. This idea took root in France, England, Germany and Italy. The troubadours were at once theologians, musicians and poets. They had wonderful voices and prodigious memories. The centre where they were trained was a small town called St. Guilhem-le-Desert, not far from Montpelier, which held a relic of the True Cross in its abbey. At the special meetings of their fraternity, held here or in remote woods and valleys, they wore red cloaks embroidered at the shoulder with a white dove. The dove, timeless messenger of the Great Mother or Goddess, was also a primary symbol of the hidden church of the Grail or the Holy Spirit.

Esclarmonde grew up in this remarkable culture. In her parents' castle, she would have missed nothing of the visits of these wandering minstrels and also the quiet, black-robed priests who accompanied them, who were called Cathars and whose teaching spread like wildfire from court to court and village to village in this part of France. It is possible that she was taught by individuals from both groups. Certainly, by the time she was in her teens, she

was celebrated in poetry and song for her beauty, her intelligence and learning. As one troubadour wrote: "Love, I sing your praises for you have made
me love Esclarmonde, the most beautiful, and by that, I am lifted so high that
to die is a privilege, so great is her nobility. My heart is consumed with love
for her."

Castle of Foix, France

The Courts of Love

The image of woman presented through the poetry of the troubadours was in
stark contrast to that which was in common usage among the people — whatever their social rank — at that time. The famous Courts of Love, established
by Eleanor of Aquitaine and her daughter, Marie in Poitiers and Troyes,
nourished this new image of woman. Eleanor was a daughter of Duke
Guillaume of Aquitaine, a renowned troubadour, and these Courts established by her, gave women for the first time a social position and a role apart
from that of wife or mother. Here women were queens presiding over the
Courts where philosophy, poetry and literature could flourish; where the
relationship between man and woman, and between man, woman and God
could be explored in a context that celebrated life and the aspirations of both
genders. Husbands who listened to troubadours singing the praises of the
beauty and intelligence of their wives began to look at them with new eyes
and paid more attention to their own appearance and their manners. The code

of values that grew up here is summed up in the words *Pretz e Paratge* which can be translated as high ideals, the courage to honour and serve them, a gracious presence and impeccable courtesy, particularly towards women, as well as the ability to compose poetry and play an instrument.

Courtly Love — from a contempory illustration

Until these Courts appeared to offer a different view of her, woman was presented to society by the Church as a lewd, wicked, treacherous creature, fatally flawed by the sin of Eve, whose destiny was to be ruled by her husband and to serve him in the same way and on a similar contractual basis, as the medieval vassal served his overlord. How different is the image of woman seen through the eyes of the troubadours and indeed, in the Grail legends, where the Divine Feminine is portrayed as the actual goal of the Quest, as well as the guiding spirit of it. What a contrast there is between woman as a chattel to be disposed of by her husband, or woman as temptress and sinner, and woman as the inspiration of a renaissance of spiritual devotion and the celebration of art, poetry and beauty and rejoicing in the marvel of life. The troubadours freed sexuality and eroticism from guilt and invited both man and woman to follow a spiritual path without renouncing the body or the enjoyment of life and human relationships.

Tragically, their vision and their culture died with the Papal Crusade against the Albigensian or Cathar heresy which virtually wiped out an entire civilization and ended the cultural flowering of the Languedoc. It was, however, preserved in their poetry and in the Grail legends, written down at the end of the twelfth and beginning of the thirteenth century by two great poets: Chrétien de Troyes and Wolfram von Eschenbach. Wolfram set the Grail castle, its knights and its treasure precisely in this area of France where the Grail tradition was already centuries old. Even the name of his hero Parzival resembles the hero-prince of Carcassonne, Raymond Trencavel, who was Esclarmonde's nephew. The name of the Keeper of the Castle in Wolfram's story, Raymond de Perella, is identical to that of the man who defended the Cathar stronghold of Monségur which belonged to Esclarmonde. The coat of arms of the Sabarthez area ruled by the Counts of Foix shows the motto "Custos Summorum": "Guardians of the Heights". The device is strange and interesting: a sixteen rayed sun with a winged cup at its centre, surrounded by a crown of thorns and backed by a pair of crossed spears. It is impossible not to connect it with the cup of the Grail.

For the troubadour, a chosen beloved woman such as Esclarmonde herself, was the earthly image of Divine Wisdom or Sophia. His one desire was to serve her. With his poetry and his music, he invoked not only the image of Sophia herself, Holy Spirit and consort of God, but also the wisdom of his own soul — the wisdom of the archetypal feminine within every human being. He strove to awaken his own soul to the hidden wisdom of the Feminine, seeing it reflected in a chosen woman whose beauty and gifts seemed to incarnate the qualities of Sophia. Sophia was the image of the wisdom of God inherent in Nature, the immanence of God in creation. The *Gaie Savoir* the troubadours taught was the result of years of initiation into the way the soul could be awakened, like the Sleeping Beauty, to awareness of itself as the hidden but luminous ground of life. The effigy of the Black Madonna was found in churches and cathedrals all over Europe, but particularly in France, where four hundred and fifty statues existed.[3] The Black Madonna represented Divine Wisdom and the hidden teachings associated with her. In the Basilica of La Daurade in Toulouse stood the same image of the Dark Lady beloved by so many who called themselves the fidèles d'amour or devotees of love, and served her under the many different images that concealed the secret science of the Church of the Holy Spirit: the star, the rose, the lily and the dove; and the Grail images: the cup, the silver vessel and the stone. As Bernard de Ventadour, one of the greatest troubadours wrote: "Lady, I am yours and will be yours; I have been yours for so long as time. You were my first joy and will remain my joy until the end — so long as my life endures". This 'Lady' may have been the Virgin Mary but could also have been Mary Magdalene, the consort of Jesus, appointed Teacher of the disciples by him, who travelled from Alexandria to southern France in 44 CE and taught there for twenty years.

So, when a troubadour wrote: "Beloved, rise up, for in the East I see the star that heralds the day. Soon dawn will break. Sleep no longer, for I hear the bird singing in the woods and fear you may be taken by surprise," we can understand that he is speaking to his soul to awake from its sleep. Three centuries later, Shakespeare, the last of the troubadours, was to echo the same theme in *Romeo and Juliet*. The star that heralded the Day, the same star that guided the wise men to the Holy Child, was the symbol of Sophia herself and also of the secret teaching of the Cathar Church of the Holy Spirit that, it was hoped, would usher in a new age where man would serve the principle of love and wisdom instead of the principle of power. The bird was sometimes a nightingale, sometimes a dove, immemorial symbol of the Great Mother and the feminine principle. The dove was one of the primary symbols of the Cathar Church and with it I think we can return to Esclarmonde who, after her death, came to be identified with the image of the dove.

Esclarmonde

The Cathar Church was already well established when Esclarmonde was born in 1155. When she was twelve an event took place that changed the orientation of her life path. This was the visit in 1167, possibly arranged by the Knights Templar, of Nicetas, the Bulgarian bishop of Constantinople and Patriarch of the Cathar Church. He appointed three Cathar bishops to organize the growing numbers of converts to the Church of the Paraclete or Holy Spirit: one for the Languedoc, whose capital was Toulouse; one for the rest of France; and one for Lombardy, with its centre on Lake Garda. He consecrated many children of the Cathar nobility to the Holy Spirit at the great synod that was organized to receive him. Esclarmonde and her brother Raymond-Roger — later count of Foix — were two of these children. She decided then, at the age of twelve, that she wished to become a member of this church.

But first, at twenty, there was marriage to a man called Jordan de Jourdain-des-Isles. It lasted twenty-five years until his death. Little is known about Esclarmonde during these years, except that she had six children, three girls and three boys, all of whom survived to be adults and to marry in their turn. She lived in a city called Pamiers, not far from Foix. Her husband was Catholic and it was believed that the marriage was difficult because of their different religious allegiances but her husband respected her beliefs and even defended her against the charge of heresy that was repeatedly made against her.

In 1163, a Catholic Council called at Tours, had condemned the Cathar heresy and in 1180 persecution began in earnest in the region around Pamiers. People were killed, their crops burned, their houses sacked. For the first time we hear of Esclarmonde playing an active role when she was about twenty-six years old. She gathered the homeless people in the territory ruled by her husband — who was away at the time — and led them to the wild region of the Corbières to safety and then returned to her children at Pamiers. In 1204 her husband died. Esclarmonde was now fifty. Her children were grown up and married. She decided to return to her childhood home at Foix. With her work as wife and mother accomplished, she was able to dedicate herself to the Cathar Church. She was ordained an 'Ancient' as the Cathar priests and priestesses were called and as an arch-deaconess — equal in rank to a Bishop. It is interesting that, alone among the Christian sects, the Cathars were the first group since the Gnostics in the second and third centuries, to ordain women as bishops, arch-deaconesses and priestesses. This may be one reason why the movement was so popular with women and why so many married women, once they had reached middle age, asked their husbands to release them from their marriages, so they could become active members of the Church. The Cathars evidently succeeded in giving women a respected and active social role as teacher, priestess and healer. There were even women surgeons, for the Cathar Ancients were, like the Essenes, trained above all in the arts of healing.

We know that Esclarmonde was an expert herbalist as well as an arch-deaconess and that she was allowed to administer the supreme Cathar rite of the *Consolamentum*, given usually at the point of death. We know that together with other women, she lived at various periods a semi-hermetic life in the mountains and wooded valleys around Foix, caring for the sick, teaching in special schools established by the Cathars for both children and adults, and administering the Cather rites.

The Training of a Cathar Ancient

The training to become a Cathar Ancient was long and arduous and made more difficult by persecution. First there was a two-year period during which they were taught to gather herbs and learn their application to different illnesses, how to store them and to make decoctions of their essential oils. They were taught to observe the stars and the ways of animals and insects: in short, to observe nature with a trained eye. They learned practical skills: how to weave, how to sow and reap crops, how to build simple houses. They did not eat meat, milk products or eggs but could eat fish. They were celibate once they had embarked on the training for priesthood. After this two-year apprentice-ship, they had to survive a forty day fast on bread and water before being accepted into the second state of preparation during which they were taught the secret lore of plants, metals and stones as well as mathematics, astronomy and music — all this in addition to a thorough knowledge of Cathar texts. During this period, they wore black or dark blue robes. As the final part of their training, they were prepared as priests and taught how to administer the supreme rite of the Cathar Church — the *Consolamentum* — usually given on the point of death. They administered the rite of baptism to adults, not to infants, following the ritual they claimed to have been established by Christ's Apostles. For these ceremonies, they wore white robes.

They travelled round the countryside in pairs, helping people in whatever way they seemed to need it: assisting the peasant with his harvest, the weaver with his cloth, the children with their education, the sick and dying with healing and comfort. They were known as the "*Bons Hommes*" or "*Bonnes Femmes*" and were welcomed by peasant and lord alike because they were gentle and trustworthy and because their presence brought relief from suffering, whether physical or mental. Their aim was to put each man in touch with his own soul, to help him to trust the inner guidance of the spirit rather than the outer authority of the Catholic Church, but they also taught people to develop new skills, to read the scriptures and to improve the physical conditions of their lives. They believed in reincarnation and in the soul's progressive enlightenment after death. They discouraged the procreation of children, believing, like the Gnostics, that the world as it was, was a prison for the soul. They rejected the feudal system where authority rested with the Church and the feudal overlord. They rejected war and killing. They rejected the patriarchal system which debased and devalued women and could even raise the question of whether they had a soul. Not surprisingly, they were a powerful threat to the institution of the Papacy. Yet, even Bernard of Clairvaux, founder of the Cistercian Order, when he was sent by the Pope to preach against the heresy, could find no fault with their way of life.

The Cathar Church of the Holy Spirit

It seems necessary at this point to say something about the Cathar Church that aroused the bitter enmity of Rome. To understand what it taught, as well as its ceremonies, we need to go back to the Gnostic Communities in the early centuries of the Christian era. The Nag Hammadi Gnostic texts, discovered in Egypt in 1945 but only released to the public in 1977, have thrown great light on both Gnostic and Cathar beliefs. There is extensive research still to be done to connect the Cathar texts with those of the Nag Hammadi discoveries. I only know of one scholar of Gnosticism, the late professor Gilles Quispel from the University of Utrecht (one of the translators of the Gospel of Thomas) who has done this. In a lecture he gave in London some decades ago that I attended, he said that traces of certain Gnostic texts were clearly discernible in Cathar teachings, and that he believed that the Cathars possessed copies of the secret Gospels used by some of the Gnostic sects. They certainly had one sacred book called "*The Secret Book of John*" [4] and their teaching was based upon this book and the Gospel of John, copies of which they always carried with them.

I have gone into the Gnostics at some length to give some idea of the roots of the Cathar Church of the Holy Spirit which became established in the area north of the Pyrenees known as the Languedoc. Like the Gnostics, the Cathars, took the dove as the symbol of their teaching — image of the ancient Gnostic church of the Holy Spirit. This teaching was carried in their Secret Book of John (The *Apocryphon of John*), and possibly in another book which may have been in circulation among the Cathars at this time and which was said to have been written by Mary Magdalene.[5]

There were several Gnostic communities established in France, notably at Lyons, in the third century CE. There is no reason to suppose that this teaching was completely eradicated with the persecution of the Gnostic sects under the emperor Theodosius 1 in the fourth century. The Visigoths in their Pyrenean kingdom offered, from the fifth century, a haven from persecution, being heretics themselves because they had embraced the Arian doctrine rather than that promoted by Athanasius, and because their kingdom was, at that time, beyond the reach of both Emperor and Papacy.

The Cathars, like the Gnostics, conceived of God in feminine as well as masculine imagery. They did not believe that Jesus was the Son of God, nor in His bodily resurrection. They taught that Jesus was a great teacher, not the only Son of God. They envisaged Christ as the indwelling divine spirit in man, the light shining in darkness: "the true Light which lighteth every man that cometh into the world." (John 1:9) "There is a light within a man of light and it lights up the whole world. If it does not shine, he is in darkness." (Gospel of Thomas, *logion* 24) They had a book called the *Liber de Duobus Principiis* (Book of the Two Principles) which explained that there was a Principle of Darkness, called the Demiurge, which controlled the world, infiltrating and contaminating the concept of God and all established institutions, including the Christian Church in Rome. They believed the world and human consciousness were ruled or controlled by this Demiurge but that their Church taught the way for men and women to free themselves from him and awaken to the divine light present within their souls. They claimed their teaching was descended from the Apostle James and the early Church, before it became a powerful institution in the fourth century during the reigns of the Emperors Constantine and Theodosius 1. As in the former gnostic groups, all members of the Gnostic Church, male and female, were equal and drew lots to take on the temporary role of bishop, priest or prophet. They taught the need for progressive *gnosis* or insight into the inner kingdom of the soul.

The image of Sophia as the Holy Spirit is a Gnostic concept that goes back to certain Wisdom texts in the Old Testament (Book of Proverbs, and the later Books of Ben Sirah and The Wisdom of Solomon which are now in the *Apocrypha)*. It can also be traced to the worship of the Goddess Asherah in Alexandria that survived in the Jewish Community in that city. Sophia (Divine Wisdom) and her messenger, the dove, became the symbol of the hidden Gnostic Church, the Church of the Paraclete or Holy Spirit, that had to go underground in the fourth century to escape persecution by the Christian Church in Rome. The leaders of that Church deplored the individualistic approach of these teachings, the emphasis on the Divine Feminine and the freedom of Gnostic women to preach and heal with absolute equality with men. By the year 200, As Elaine Pagels wrote in her book, *The Gnostic Gospels*, "virtually all the feminine imagery of God had disappeared from orthodox Christian tradition and every one of the secret texts which Gnostic groups revered was omitted from the canonical collection, and branded as heretical by those who called themselves orthodox Christians." [6]

The Cathars, like the Gnostics, believed that Christ personified the divine spirit in man and that men and women could redeem themselves from the sleep of ignorance where the principle of darkness ruled their soul. As long as they were unaware of the inner dimension of their soul, they would be unable to discover the secret treasure of the spirit or light principle hidden within it. If sought with the devotion of the lover for his beloved, this inner light would deliver the seeker from a state of imprisonment to the experience of eternal life while still living in a physical body. This, the Cathars taught, was the real meaning of the resurrection — an experience of awakening to the light of wisdom within. Their essential message was: "Follow the star of the Holy Spirit, the star that guided the wise men. Transform your understanding. Become a son or daughter of God. Free yourself from the principle of darkness by recognizing where you are serving the debased values that govern the darkened consciousness of man rather than those that belong to the invisible world of the Spirit." For the Cathars, like the Gnostics and Pelagius (in the fourth century), the world was imperfect because of human ignorance, not because of original sin. God needed man's help to redeem it by redeeming himself. The reward of the quest for enlightenment was the experience of *gnosis*, or insight into the mystery of his own nature and of nature as a whole, and the Hermetic axiom: "As Above, so Below". They believed in reincarnation, were celibate once they had become members of the priesthood and spoke of their Church as "The Cup that gives out manna" and as "The Precious Stone." It is impossible not to connect these images with the Grail.

Persecution

For a long time, all that could be discovered about the Cathars was drawn from the documents left by the Inquisition which was established in the Languedoc in 1233. These confessions, like those of the Knights Templar who were destroyed as an Order in France in the early fourteenth century, were wrung from people by torture and the terror of being burnt at the stake. They give an image of Cathar beliefs which is very much at variance with the image I have drawn above. If they had believed the body to be corrupt and the material world ruled by an evil principle, as the confessions suggest, would they have bothered to heal the sick? They showed no fear of death, believing as they did in the soul's immortality and ultimate redemption, but would they have served life as they did if they had believed it to be irredeemably evil? It was not the natural world that was evil but the structures and institutions of power, whether religious or secular, that they deplored. I think their vision and their dedication is best expressed in these words: "We lead a life hard and wandering. We fly from town to town like sheep among wolves. We suffer persecution like the Apostles and Martyrs, yet our life is holy and austere. These things are not difficult, for we are no longer of this world."

The Papal Crusade

The Papacy in the early years of the thirteenth century felt itself increasingly threatened by the Cathar heresy. In 1204, Pope Innocent III sent a brutal Cistercian legate called Pierre de Castelnau to combat the heresy. At the same time, Esclarmonde, foreseeing a time when a refuge might be needed by her people, started to rebuild the ancient fortress at Montségur, which belonged to her and had previously been a Roman, then a Visigoth citadel. With a sense of great urgency and with the help of a brilliant architect who was familiar with the teaching on Astronomy of the Cathars, it was rebuilt in the short space of five years, with a defence system of three concentric walls and a huge bastion. It was thought to be impregnable and was built not only as a fortress but also as the stronghold of the Cathar Church and perhaps as a solar temple. Emissaries travelled to it from all over the Mediterranean and were received by Esclarmonde.

Meanwhile, a conference was held at Pamiers between Catholics and Cathars to discuss the heresy in as amicable a spirit as possible. St. Dominic, soon to be appointed by the Pope to set up the organisation of the Inquisition in this area, was present. Esclarmonde spoke often, sometimes on matters of theology, sometimes about women having the right to be heard, at least in a local conference. This was fiercely resisted by the Cistercian Order whose spokesman said to her in words that have come down to us from nearly eight hundred years ago: "Woman, return to your distaff and don't meddle with affairs that don't concern you." What a boor she must have thought him, unused as women had been for a generation at least, to be spoken to in that way.

As persecution increased, the Cathars began to go underground, into the vast subterranean caves of the region that had been inhabited by Magdalenian man, some 20,000 years earlier. Their known underground temples or churches were at Lombrives, Ornolac and Ussat. In one of them, red crosses, a lance, a platter and a Grail cup emblazoned in a sun and surrounded by a black crown have been found, which recalls the heraldic shield of the Sabarthez. At Ussat, the cross of the Grand Master of the Templars is inscribed on the walls. In these secret places, the Cathar novices were trained and rituals celebrated among small groups of people. The relationship between the Cathars and the Templars has not been sufficiently researched but it is known that many Cathars were given sanctuary by the Templars, that Templars were sometimes secret Cathars, and that some Cathars were disguised as troubadours.

In 1207, Pope Innocent 111 ordered the King of France to invade the territories of the heretics. Esclarmonde withdrew to Montségur with the principal Cathar clergy, among them the Cathar Bishop appointed by Nicetas on his visit from Constantinople in 1167. She was followed there by a mass of people, fleeing in terror from the northern barbarians. In 1208, the Papal envoy, the hated and feared Pierre de Castelnau, was assassinated and the Count of Toulouse, held responsible by the Pope, was tried and condemned. The Crusade instigated by the Pope was now under way and in 1209 it broke like a tsunami upon the poorly defended territory of the Languedoc. 20,000 knights, leading a rabble of 200,000 men in search of plunder invaded south-western France. The war began which was to last forty-five years and to leave the Languedoc in ruins, both economically and culturally, with over a million people murdered by fire, sword and starvation. Those who took part in it were offered remission for their sins and assured a place in heaven, as well as any booty they could lay their hands on. The first town they attacked was Béziers and the pattern was set for the remaining years. The townspeople resisted and 15,000 were slaughtered, many in the cathedral where they had taken refuge. When the Crusaders asked the papal legate how they were to distinguish heretics from Catholics, he replied with the infamous words: "Kill them all. God will recognize his own".

Simon de Montfort was the commander-in-chief of the Crusade and, sincerely believing, like so many others, that God would welcome the death of the heretics, spared no-one in the execution of the Papal brief. In 1211, he led the destruction of the town of Lavaur where he personally saw to the death by burning of 400 Cathars. In 1214 the castle of Foix and the cities and lands of Toulouse and Carcassonne, were given to him by the Pope. The most beautiful towns of the Languedoc now lay in ruins, their populations murdered or dispersed; the countryside around them ravaged by marauding soldiers. A surviving fragment of a manuscript says it all: "In these calamitous times of cruel anguish, he who resisted was considered an enemy of God; he who defended his lands and goods, an enemy of the true religion; he who fled before the enemy was regarded as a rebel and guilty. They massacred all those who wished to protect innocents from the hands of Inquisitors and executioners".

The Siege of Monségur

In 1240 Esclarmonde died at the great age of eighty-five. It says a lot for the Cathar way of life that so many of them lived to a great age — those, that is, who escaped the sword and the stake. No trace of her body has ever been found but it was believed that she was buried in a cave beneath Montségur or possibly in one of the caves of the Sabarthez. She was without doubt the inspiration of the Cathar Heresy and the heart of its resistance. She has been immortalized in the memory of the people of the Ariège — where the ruins of the fortress of Monségur still exist — as the dove that was the symbol of the Cathar Church of the Holy Spirit.

Fortress of Monségur

The siege of Monségur began in 1243, three years after her death. The fortress was surrounded by an army of 10,000 men. In it were 500 Cathars, many of them Ancients, together with their Bishop. In March 1244, the castle sur-rendered but asked for two weeks before complying with the terms of the besiegers. There is much conjecture as to why these two weeks were needed. Was it in order to comply with an astronomically significant date? Was it in order to give the defenders more time to arrange for the transfer into safe hands of the remaining important treasure — perhaps the sacred texts of their Church or, perhaps the precious text of the Gospel written by Mary Magdalene. Two hundred and ten individuals of those remaining in the fortress chose to die rather than to give up their faith and be pardoned. Among these were the sister-in-law, daughter-in-law and grand-daughter of Esclarmonde, who had the same name as her grandmother. Watched in anguish by the remainder in the garrison, they were chained together, dragged down the steep slope, penned into a huge stockade and burned to death. That same night, four men who had been hidden in a cave while this was taking place, were lowered on ropes down a cliff on the far side of the fortress, taking with them the precious treasure. They made their escape to a neighbouring mountain and lit a fire to signal that their mission had been safely accomplished.

After the siege of Montségur, the Inquisition redoubled its efforts to hunt down the remaining Cathars who had taken refuge in the remote caves and castles of the Languedoc. One of the last and most remote castles to be attacked was Quéribus, where every single Cathar was put to the sword. Early in the fourteenth century, not long after the 5,000 members of the Knights Templar were arrested in a minutely planned military operation all over France, Jacques de Molay, the Grand Master of the Templars, was burnt to death in Paris. At the same time the remaining known Cathars were walled up in the cave of Lombrives and left to die.

One of the most remarkable aspects of this terrible story is that the Cathar Church did not vanish completely. It lived on, of all places, in the printing trade where, from 1282 and for the next three centuries, there appeared in the books printed in the Languedoc and also in the Auvergne region, an extraordinary coded system of watermarks: a secret language whereby members of the Church of the Holy Spirit could stay in touch with each other and keep their faith alive for the day when it could emerge without fear of persecution.[7]

Before he was burnt at the stake, one of the last Cathars, Guillaume de Bellebasse, spoke of the day, 700 years in the future, when "the laurel would be green again". On that day, the guardians of the Grail could rejoice. A new age would dawn, heralded by the symbol of the dove: emblem of Esclarmonde, Cathar, Troubadour and Templar Knight, who served the Church of the Holy Spirit and Sophia, image of Divine Wisdom and the Holy Spirit.

Notes:

1. St. Francis (1181-1226) who was known as "God's Troubadour", had a French mother who was born in Provence and an Italian father who frequently travelled there as a trader in cloth. St. Francis knew about the Cathars and the Troubadours through either of them or through the troubadours he encountered as a young man in Assisi. His ascetic way of life, his deep respect for nature and his devotion to the poor reflect absolutely the Cathar way of life. The present Pope Francis has taken St. Francis as his mentor and has re-animated the enlightened essentials of his teaching in his Encyclical of May 2015.

2. Eleanor of Aquitaine was married first, to Louis V11, the king of France and secondly, after a divorce from him was granted by the Pope, to Henry 11 of England, who imprisoned her for 18 years in the castle of Waverley, in Surrey. One of her daughters by Henry 11, Joanne, was married to Count Raymond of Toulouse. Eleanor lived to be well into her eighties and was still formidable at that great age, still travelling from England to her lands in Aquitaine.

3. Dr van der Meer, Annine PhD., (2019), *The Black Madonna: from Primal to Final Times*, English edition transl. Catriona O'Daly

4. *The Apocryphon of John* in the Nag Hammadi Library, p. 99

5. *The Gospel of the Beloved Companion: The Complete Gospel of Mary Magdalene*, translated and with a commentary by Jehanne de Quillan and published by Éditions Athara, Foix in 2010. It is believed to have been brought from Alexandria to the Languedoc in the early to middle part of the first century and to have been translated into Occitan, the language of the Languedoc, in the early part of the twelfth century. Since then, it has been closely guarded and passed from hand to hand, generation to generation until the present time. It gives the passages that are missing from the Gospel of Mary that is included in the Nag Hammadi Library.

6. Elaine Pagels, (1979), *The Gnostic Gospels*, Weidenfeld & Nicholson, London, p. 57

7. Bayley, Harold, *A New Light on the Renaissance*, J.M. Dent & Co., London MCMIX

As I reworked this article in September 2015, I realized that the alchemists were entirely familiar with the teaching of the Church of the Holy Spirit and must somehow have absorbed its basic tenets and developed them in later centuries. They took Divine Wisdom — Sophia, as their guide.

There is a wonderful Cathar Hymn, Song or Chant, posted on YouTube, together with other videos on the Cathars. The Hymn is deeply moving and trance-like, evoking the spirit of the Cathars — perhaps even the hymn sung by the Cathars of Montségur as they left their physical bodies and took the pathway to the stars.

https://www.youtube.com/watch?v=ED4AYD2gZ7k

Chapter Ten

CINDERELLA
AN INTERPRETATION

The best-known version of Cinderella is based on the Perrault story of 1697 called *Cendrillon* and that of the Brothers Grimm of 1812. Cinderella is the daughter of a widower who marries a woman with two daughters of her own, as proud and bad-tempered as she is. Cinderella is reduced to the level of a drudge in her father's new family. She is dressed by her step-mother in rags or a grey cloak and, after her work is finished, sits by the chimney-corner among the ashes of the fire, her face, hands and clothes blackened by soot.

One day it is announced that the king's son is to give a ball and he is to invite all the young women of the kingdom to it so that he may choose his bride from among them. Cinderella's step-sisters are invited and she helps to dress them for the ball, while they taunt her about her dirty clothes and the impossibility of her going to the ball with them. The step-mother and her daughters leave and Cinderella sits weeping by the ashes of the fire.

Suddenly, her fairy God-Mother appears, finds her crying and says "You *shall* go to the ball". She sends Cinderella into the garden to fetch a pumpkin, hollows it out, and striking it with her wand, transforms it into a golden coach. Cinderella finds a trap with six white mice in it which are changed into white horses. Her God-Mother suggests a rat for coachman and selects one of three she finds in a trap. It is transformed in a similar manner. Six lizards are found behind a watering pot and become footmen. Cinderella's God-Mother then transforms her blackened rags into a sumptuous dress of silver and gold which glitters with jewels and gives her a pair of glass slippers, warning her to leave the ball before midnight, when chariot, coachman, horses, footmen and her-self will all resume their original forms. Cinderella promises to remember the warning and sets off for the ball in the golden coach. She is greeted by the prince who has been advised of the arrival of an unknown princess. Her beauty amazes everyone at the ball and the prince falls deeply in love with her and will dance with no one else. Cinderella leaves the ball before midnight and returns to her God-Mother, asking to go again the next night. The two sisters return and tell her of the beautiful princess who has enchanted the prince. The following night, Cinderella goes to the ball in a dress more splendid than the one she wore the previous night. Again, she leaves before midnight.

On the third night however, she leaves too late, and as she hurries away from the palace, midnight strikes, and she finds her dress has once again become soot-covered rags. She makes her way home without coach or footmen. The prince rushes after her, but she eludes him. However, in her haste, she leaves a glass slipper on the steps of the palace and this the prince is able to retrieve. Questioned as to the path of her flight, the palace guards say they have seen no-one save a poorly clad girl with one glass shoe. The prince declares he will only marry the girl whose foot fits the shoe he holds. He comes eventually to Cinderella's home where the step-sisters try to fit their feet into the slipper. In some versions they cut off their heel and toe to squeeze their foot into it. Cinderella asks to be allowed to try the shoe as the step-sisters mock her. When the prince places the slipper on her foot, she draws the other from her pocket and puts it on. Her God-Mother appears and transforms her rags into a beautiful dress, whereupon she is recognized as the princess at the ball. Her step-sisters beg to be forgiven for the way they treated her. Cinderella forgives them and is taken to the palace for her marriage to the prince. So runs one version of the fairy tale which never fails to enchant.

Fairy-tales speak with the immemorial wisdom of the soul to provide the elements which have been ignored or devalued by the cultural tradition. They tell the story of what has happened to the missing elements and what still needs to happen for the balance in archetypal imagery to be restored. They may therefore conceal within their symbolic language both an historical record and a prophecy. The story of Cinderella has many possible interpretations, including the modern feminist one, but Harold Bayley, in the early years of the last century, was the first to see it as a story of the soul's transformation, and to connect it with Gnostic, Egyptian and Sumerian myth. Included in this 'story of the soul' is her bondage to a cruel step-mother, the mysteries of her transformation with the help of her 'true' mother, God-Mother or fairy God-Mother, the quest of the prince to find his bride, and finally the celebration of the royal marriage.

With masterly economy, the story of Cinderella reflects at the archetypal level the soul's perennial plight and need, and bears witness at an historical level to her experience during the many centuries of her sojourn in this material reality. Bayley's interpretation seems to me to be one of the most relevant and interesting contributions to the questions being raised today with regard to the nature of consciousness and the neglect of the soul. Now, because of what I have written about the story of Sophia in the Chapter on the Gnostics, it is possible to recognize the presence of Sophia, both Mother and daughter, in the God-mother and Cinderella.

At the beginning of the last century, in his book *The Lost Language of Symbolism*,[1] Bayley traced the historical transmission of many different stories and symbols centred around the image of light hidden in darkness, a light which had to be rescued, redeemed and recovered. Through a profound knowledge of the etymology of words, and an equally profound knowledge of European paper-making and water marks which were the medium of transmission of Alchemical and Gnostic ideas during an era of cruel persecution, he drew an astonishing picture of the relationship between mythology and the fairy tales that found their way into many different centres of European culture. Some 345 versions of the story of Cinderella from all over the world were gathered together and published by the Folklore Society sometime before he started his book,[2] and he drew on a wealth of material from these to show the relationship between Sumero-Babylonian mythology, the Song of Songs, Gnostic imagery and this fairy tale. The interpretation which follows is based on his associations.

Cinderella personifies both the exiled human soul, cut off from Paradise and her Mother and Father in heaven, and also from the 'light' of the Holy Spirit of Wisdom which is hidden within her, unsought and unrecognized until events are set in motion by her God-Mother's appearance and help in going to the ball. The word 'God-Mother' subtly introduces the idea that there is a Mother aspect of deity as well as a Father aspect. The story of Cinderella reveals the faint outlines of the great Bronze Age lunar myth of the sacred marriage. In the fairy tale, the ancient myth is given a human context, instantly reflecting human experience and human emotions, although the archetypal structure is present throughout. The images of the radiant fairy God-Mother, together with the motherless daughter, Cinderella, and the prince who chooses her for his bride, suggest that the story belongs to the mystical Wisdom tradition enshrined in the marvellous poetry of the Song of Songs, which was derived from the texts of the sacred marriage rituals between goddess and god that were celebrated in the temples of Egypt, Sumer and Babylonia and in Syria and Palestine. In the fairy-tale, the Mother Goddess of the pre-Christian and Gnostic past has become the fairy God-Mother, mistress of the art of transformation and of all the 'disguises' worn by the eternal life-spirit. Cinderella (the soul), in her servitude and despair, and her blackened rags, knows nothing of this God-Mother — her true mother — or her power to transform sorrow into joy, darkness into light. Her tears call to mind Sophia's lament in the Gnostic *Pistis Sophia*, which in turn echo the words of the Shulamite in the Song of Songs:

> And I was in that place, mourning and seeking the Light that I had seen on high. And the watchman of the gates of the Aeons sought me, and all those who stay within their Mystery mocked me.… Now, O Light of Lights, I am afflicted in the darkness of the chaos.… Deliver me out of the matter of this darkness, so that I shall not be submerged in it.… My strength looked up from the midst of the chaos and from the midst of the darkness, and I waited for my spouse that he might come and fight for me. [3]

Cinderella, like Sophia and Persephone in earlier myths, cries out in her distress to her mother in the invisible, 'transcendent' world. As in the Greek myth where Hermes descends to rescue Persephone, so in the Gnostic one, the Mother Sophia, in response to her daughter's cry for help, sends her son, Christ, to rescue his sister. Her son is the embodiment of Light and Wisdom, who descends into the darkness of his parents' furthest creation to awaken his sister to remembrance of her true nature and divine origin. In the fairy tale, the God-Mother responds to the call for help with her gift of the power of transformation, which brings Cinderella to the meeting with the prince, and after the lunar three days 'trial' or 'darkness' to the royal or sacred marriage.

What echoes there are in this myth of the descent of the Sumerian goddess Inanna into the dark underworld of her sister goddess Ereshkigal, her three days' 'death' or severance from the light, starry world of her origin, and her 'resurrection' after her rescue by Enki, the god of wisdom. In Sophia's exile, there is also the resonance of Eve's expulsion from the Garden of Eden, and suddenly this Biblical myth becomes transparent to the image of the soul's 'fall' into unconsciousness or separation as, responding to the urging of the serpent — the primordial image of wisdom and immortality — she chooses to leave the paradise of the Garden of Eden and embark on her evolutionary journey.

In the Gnostic myth of Sophia, the soul is personified as the daughter of the Mother Goddess and Father God. In one of several versions of the myth, Sophia is the Mother Goddess, named as the power of Wisdom through which life brings itself into being; the womb which generates as her child, all worlds and levels of being. Like the Shekinah of Kabbalah — the Holy Spirit — she personifies and radiates Light as the informing energy of these higher worlds. The Mother Sophia gives birth to a daughter, the image of herself, who descends into these worlds, but loses contact with her heavenly origin, and in her distress and sorrow brings the earth into being, at the same time becoming lost or entangled in the realm of darkness that lies beneath the realm of light. A curtain or veil comes between the worlds of light and darkness, making it impossible for her to return to her Mother and Father. She is condemned to wander in this dark labyrinth, "labouring her passion into matter, her yearning into soul".[4] The imagery of this late creation myth is very similar to that of the Shekinah and the emanations of the Sefiroth, and there is a close parallel between the exiled Sophia and the exiled Shekinah, who are both cut off from the divine world of their origin. There may even be a Kabbalistic source for certain elements of the story, for the 'widower' in Kabbalah was Yahweh himself, deprived of the radiance of his wife, the Goddess Asherah, who was once worshipped as Divine Wisdom and the Holy Spirit.[5] The myth of Sophia was used by the Gnostics as a metaphor to explain how the soul, the divine 'spark' of the cosmic soul, her Mother, is lost in her creation — the material world — retaining no memory of her pleromatic home. There is hardly to be found a more graphic image of the human experience of the separation of consciousness from the source, or ground of its being:

> Sometimes she mourned and grieved,
> For she was left alone in darkness and the void;
> Sometimes she reached a thought of the light which had left her,
> And she was cheered and laughed;
> Sometimes she feared;
> At other times she was perplexed and astonished. [6]

So much has been lost with the passage of the centuries, and only now, in this century, can it be recovered and the fragments pieced together. The familiar Cinderella of the fairy-tale may seem far removed from this Gnostic myth of Sophia weeping in her exile from her Mother and Father in the heavenly realm. The figure of Cinderella does not immediately suggest the black Shulamite of the Song of Songs, nor does her God-Mother evoke the Mother Sophia of the starry heavens or the shining radiance of the Shekinah. Yet a knowledge of cosmology, mythology and history suggests that a relationship between them cannot be fortuitous. In this tale, as in that of The Sleeping Beauty, the Gnostic myth and its antecedent Sumerian and Egyptian ones shine through the images and connect the psyche receptive to their numinosity, with these mythic roots.

The imagery of light is common to the iconography of the goddess in Sumerian, Egyptian, Hebrew and Gnostic cosmologies and to Cinderella as well. Bayley discovered that etymologically, the syllable 'Cin' connects Cinderella with Sin, the Babylonian moon god, father of the goddess Ishtar, whose symbol was the crescent moon. The word 'Sinai' is derived from the same root. El in Babylonian was the 'light' element in the sun god Bel (Marduk) and in El, the Canaanite father god whose name survives in the Hebrew Elohim. 'Ella', as Bayley pointed out, also comes from the Greek 'ele' which means shiner or giver of light. 'Ele' is the root of Eleusis, as also of Eleleus, one of the surnames of Apollo, the god of light, and is also present in Helios, the sun, and in Selene, the moon.[7] The word 'Cinderella' suggests both fire and light, cinders being an earthly analogy of the stars, the fiery sparks glowing in the blackness of the night sky. Jung's passages on the *scintillae* [8] come to mind here, as does the *lumen naturae* of the alchemists, and the starry ground of the soul — the meaning of the word Compostella — which was the goal of pilgrimage in the Middle Ages.

Fire, light and the dazzling luminosity of the starry dimension are all images that were associated through the ages with the radiance of Wisdom which, as a fusion of love and insight or *gnosis*, represents the union of Queen and King, the highest feminine and masculine qualities of the soul. In the fairy-tale these are personified by Cinderella and the Prince. Cinderella's particular quality of sustained devotion to whatever she was asked to do is stressed in every version of the story. The Prince's capacity for insight is shown in his recognition of Cinderella, and in the tenacity and single-mindedness of his search for his 'true' bride.

Paradoxically, Wisdom as Light may wear the cloak or disguise of black-ness, the blackness of the night sky in which the moon shines. Isis wore a black robe and it is Wisdom, "black but beautiful", whom the bridegroom in the Song of Songs seeks out as his bride in the ancient recital of the sacred marriage rite. So too did Solomon himself, for to him Wisdom was the "bright-ness of the everlasting light, the unspotted mirror of the power of God, and the image of his goodness". (Wis. of Sol. 7:26) Wisdom could do all things, "For she is more beautiful than the sun, and above all the order of stars: being compared with the light, she is found before it". (Wis. of Sol. 7:29) Like the "Wise Men" or alchemists who followed the Wisdom tradition which originated in Egypt and was transmitted to Hebrew culture, Solomon loved her, and sought her out from his youth: "I desired to make her my spouse, and I was a lover of her beauty", (Wis. of Sol. 8:2).

Like Solomon, the Prince in the story of Cinderella, once having seen her, is consumed with love for her and will have no other as his bride, and she is equally drawn by her love for him. The brother and sister imagery of the Song of Songs as well as the Gnostic myth of Sophia rescued by her brother, Christ, is carried through to some versions of the story which are known as "The Brother and Sister". The imagery of light associated with the bridegroom so dramatically portrayed in the Gnostic myth is discovered in the earlier Babylonian one where Ishtar is rescued by Uddushu-Namir, whose name means "his light shines".[9] It appears also in the Classical myth of Eros and Psyche for there Eros has "hairs of gold that yielded out a sweet savour, his neck more white than milk, his hair hanging comely behind and before, the brightness whereof did darken the light of the lamp".[10]

As far back as there is knowledge of myth there is the story of the mother/son, sister/brother, wife/husband pair, whose sacred marriage sustains and renews heaven and earth. Separated, they must seek each other. Together they form the image of the whole: dark and light, earth and heaven, moon and sun, mother and father, sister and brother, bride and bridegroom. All these form the tapestry of human experience which is the foundation of myth, fairy-tale and religion. One without the other was once inconceivable. The Song of Songs, like the marriage incantations spoken by 'goddess' and 'god' in the temples of Sumer and Egypt, celebrated the ecstatic union of the goddess with her bridegroom, who was at once her son, her brother and her lover, and who incarnated the life of nature, her *visible* creation. In Sumer, the goddess 'descended' to the temple, and the ritual of her union with the king ratified his rule by divine sanction. The union of the king, who personified the son-consort, with the high-priestess or queen, who personified the goddess, guaranteed the continued fertility of the earth during the coming year. The perennial story of their separation during the 'dark' phase of the year, and reunion at the time of the return of the Earth's fertility, is told in the myths of Isis and Osiris in Egypt, Ishtar and Tammuz in Babylonia.[11]

Over some two thousand years, the imagery of the sacred marriage was gradually transformed and interiorized. From being a fertility rite associated with the sacred marriage, as well as the ritual sacrifice of the king or his substitute, whose death gave life to the people, it became, in the Mysteries of Egypt, Greece and Rome, the celebration of the union of the soul with the divine ground of being. The ground was personified variously by a feminine or masculine deity, depending upon the culture in which the imagery took root.[12] The darkness of the time of separation was associated with the darkness of the soul's sorrow during the time of 'exile', and the time of reunion with the idea of return to the source. The sacred marriage and ritual sacrifice were both central to the Mysteries. In Cinderella they manifest as the royal marriage at the end of the story, and as the bloody amputation of the ugly sisters' toes or heel.

In many versions, apples and honey connect Cinderella with the Song of Songs and with the temple rituals of the sacred marriage. Inanna "knelt by the sacred apple tree" in the marriage ritual of Sumer.[13] In Greece, the golden apples of the Hesperides were Hera's gift, bestowing eternal life. In the Song of Songs there is the passage: "As the apple trees among the trees of the wood, so is my beloved among the sons". (Song of Songs 2:3) In one version of Cinderella, an apple tree takes the place of the fairy God-mother and shakes

down from its branches the beautiful dresses which Cinderella wears to the
ball. Cinderella, talking to the tree in another version, says:

> *Little gold apple tree*
> *With my vase of gold have I watered thee*
> *With my spade of gold have I digged thy mould*
> *Give me your lovely clothes I pray*
> *And take my ugly rags away.*

Honey has been associated as far back as Sumer with the sacred marriage
ritual and in Crete with the gift of insight or prophecy, and the revelation
of the invisible dimension behind the forms of life.[14] It is perhaps the most
ancient symbol of Wisdom and Truth, belonging specifically to the rituals
associated with the mysteries of creation and regeneration.

The fairy God-Mother can be recognized as the Great Mother of the pre-
Patriarchal, pre-Christian past. In relation to Gnostic myth, she personifies
Wisdom herself who, as the Mother Sophia, comes to the rescue of her
daughter, as Demeter comes to the rescue of Persephone. Cinderella, like the
daughter Sophia, is the 'image' of her beautiful mother. As the Mother Sophia
sends Christ, her son, to help his sister, so the fairy God-Mother arranges
everything so that the prince will fall in love with her 'daughter', the human
soul, and rescue her from a life of drudgery and misery. She is variously
described as Queen with a star on her brow which connects her with Ishtar and
Astarte; a cow with golden horns which recalls Inanna-Ishtar and Isis-Hathor;
a wise old woman; a mermaid or a sea-serpent who lives in the abyss, which
evokes the Babylonian Tiamat and the Sumerian primordial serpent goddess
Nammu. In Brazil she was called "Donna Labismina". Cinderella herself is
often called Mara, Maria, or Mariucella, all derived from the root mare, which
means sea; and the sea whose distilled essence is the salt of Wisdom, is one of
the perennial images of the soul.

Transformation is the theme of the story and the God-mother presiding
over it is Sophia or Wisdom herself who, with a wave of her wand, transforms
mice into snow-white horses, lizards into footmen, a pumpkin into the golden
(or crystal) coach, and a rat into the coachman and, of course, Cinderella
herself into a vision of beauty arrayed in dresses which reflect the radiance
of the stars, moon and sun. Cinderella has to do the work of going in search
of the animals and vegetable named by her God-mother, which suggests that
the soul has to respond to Wisdom's guidance by identifying the elements to
be transformed; once identified and 'brought' before the greater insight and
power of transformation personified by the God-Mother, the work of trans-

formation is accomplished in a flash, although the 'twinkling of an eye' of the fairy tale may extend over a life-time in this dimension. Mice, the animals that scurry about the house in the darkness of the night suggest unconscious thoughts; lizards, unconscious instincts. Mice, as the most fertile of animals, were sacred to the great Goddess as well as to the solar gods Horus and Apollo, and were associated with the healing of disease. The lizards — serpents who slough their skins — share this lunar imagery of regeneration with the milk-white colour of the horses, but they also suggest the fiery image of the salamander, one of the alchemical symbols of transformation most promnent in fifteenth and sixteenth century treatises. The pumpkin's golden colour suggests harvest and, the glow of the harvest moon. The conjunction of the images of gold and harvest perhaps reflect the last stage of the alchemical task of transformation, leading to the royal marriage and the re-union of the soul with the spirit.

The chariot, fiery or golden, is a very ancient symbol which, in Kabbalistic legend, was an image of the Shekinah as the vehicle of Yahweh, and was described by Elisha in his vision of Elijah taken up into heaven in a fiery chariot. It was also an image of the 'Ascension ritual' practiced by the high priest or priestess in the tower of the First Temple in Jerusalem. The earliest image of the heavenly chariot appears in Bronze age Crete (the Haghia Triada sarco-phagus), where the goddess drives a chariot drawn by griffons, conveying the soul of the deceased to the other world. The arduousness of the work of transformation is stressed in some versions of Cinderella more than others: for example, in the one where her step-mother throws a heap of seeds onto the ground for the girl to sort into piles. This is identical to the scene in the story of Eros and Psyche, where Psyche is given the same task by her mother-in-law, the goddess Venus, who in this context sets the harsh task which the soul has to accomplish on her journey back to the realm of the gods, and her reunion with her husband, Eros. In the Classical myth, as in the Gnostic one, the bridegroom is the son of the goddess. Doves and birds, whose association with the Goddess goes back to the Neolithic era, help Cinderella to sort the seeds and also, in some versions of the story, point out to the prince that a false bride wears the slipper destined for Cinderella, by drawing his attention to the blood flowing from the injured feet of the ugly sisters.

Cinderella's dresses, her 'robe of glory', are described as "blue like the sky", woven of the stars of heaven, of moon-beams, sun-beams, or made of all the flowers of the world. Sometimes the metaphor of the sea appears and her dress is "sea-coloured" or "like the waves of the sea, or "as the sea with fishes swimming in it", and as the "colour of sea covered with golden fishes". Sometimes, like Isis, she is robed in jet black; sometimes her dresses shine like the sun or gold, covered in diamonds and pearls, 'of splendour passing description', and giving forth the tinkling sound of bells. In one story, Cinderella's dress 'rings like a bell as she comes downstairs', which recalls the sistrum of the goddess Hathor and also the bells that rang out at the approach of the Shekinah. [15] But it also reminds one of the wondrous robe to be worn by the initiate in the Gnostic poem *The Hymn of the Robe of Glory*: "I heard the sound of its music which it whispered as it descended". [16] Cinderella "lets down her hair and shakes out showers of pearls". She is clothed from head to foot with necklaces of brilliants and precious stones, and gems fall from her lips when she speaks. At times she wears a "diamond dress, or a gold dress trimmed with diamonds, or a robe of silk, thread thick with diamonds and pearls". [17] In other versions, Cinderella's dresses are hidden beneath the furry disguise of an animal. In the variation known as *Catskin*, the king tears off the furry cloak made of a thousand animal skins to reveal the shimmering dress hidden beneath it. These marvellous dresses which, in the best-known version are given to Cinderella by her God-Mother, seem, as Bayley suggests, to symbolize the awakening and growth of Wisdom which clothes the soul in ever greater radiance.

"How beautiful are thy feet with shoes, O prince's daughter!" says the bridegroom in the Song of Songs. (Song of Songs 7:1) Cinderella's shoes or slippers are described as made of crystal, or gold or blue glass, or embroidered with pearls. Sometimes they are different on each of the three nights, ending up as gold. Without her glass slipper, Cinderella would not have been recognized, and it could only fit her whose standpoint had been so transformed that it had become translucent to the light of Wisdom.

Cinderella is instructed by her God-Mother to leave the palace before midnight or risk being transformed back into her former state. What could this mean? Could it be that midnight marks the interface between the dimensions of eternity and time? To fail to hold the balance between them is to risk being 'fixed' in one, unable to relate to or remember the other dimension of experience. To stay at the ball beyond midnight is to forget human relationships, losing touch with material reality and everyday life. Not to ask to go to the ball is to remain in bondage to material existence, without awareness of the 'other' place, the palace. The balance between time and eternity must be kept if the sacred marriage is to take place. The hardest task of all is to live in this dimension in the knowledge that it is also 'the other', yet cannot be fully experienced as such until consciousness is so transformed that it sees through the veil of appearances.

The contrast between the two 'Mothers' in Cinderella may reflect a Gnostic viewpoint. The God-Mother and the step-mother may describe the

Gnostic and Roman Churches. The Gnostics, both in the early centuries when the Christian doctrine was being formulated, and in the later Middle Ages when the Cathar Church of the Holy Spirit was founded in 1167 in the Languedoc region of France, contrasted their 'true' teaching with the 'false' teaching of the Church in Rome which did not rescue the soul but prolonged her suffering and exile, keeping her in ignorance of her divine nature and the way to recover her knowledge of herself. In the early centuries of Christianity, the Church in Rome was named by the Christian Fathers as the 'Virgin Mother' of the faithful, and the 'Bride' of Christ. The Church therefore assumed the imagery of the former Goddess, as well as the mantle of Wisdom which had once belonged to the Holy Spirit, Sophia — the feminine aspect of deity who was with God "from the beginning."

> As Virgin and Mother the Church... is represented as undefiled by false doctrine and ever loving and watchful of those who come within her affectionate embrace, sanctifying them as children of God, training them on earth and so preparing them to attain to citizenship in heaven. [18]

During the centuries of persecution, both in the early centuries of Christianity and later, in the Middle Ages, although claiming to be the 'Mother of the Faithful', the Catholic Church became the very antithesis of the true Mother, Wisdom, whose image was associated with the secret Gnostic Church. No-one who has studied the history of religious persecution can fail to be aware of the Church as the 'Terrible Mother,' and the horror of the five centuries when one's neighbour could not be trusted for fear of betrayal to the Inquisition.

In the tale of Snow-White there is the same contrast between the 'true' mother who dies, and the 'false' mother, the wicked queen who transforms herself into an old hag, and brings Snow White the poisoned or death-bringing 'gifts,' including the poisoned apple that sticks in her throat and causes her to fall into a death-like trance. The prince who awakens her with a kiss and restores her to life evokes the image of the Gnostic Christ who is sent to rescue his sister from her trance-like 'sleep' in the world.

So many elements from earlier cultures are present in this story, that it is impossible to say when and where it may have originated. One thing is certain: its importance to the psyche is shown by the universality and duration of its appeal. Cinderella tells the story of a single theme which runs from the mythology of Sumer and Egypt to the Mysteries of the Pagan world and the Wisdom literature of Judaism. It can be followed through Gnosticism and mystical Christianity to Alchemy, the Grail Legends, and the most cherished fairy tales. It was nurtured by the mystics of the Jewish, Christian and Muslim religions. It is the story of the soul's descent into the manifest world, her loss of memory of her divine origin, her quest for understanding of herself and her relationship with the divine source or world from which she had emanated and to which, in full knowledge of who she is, she might return. The figure of Sophia, the Shekinah, Divine Wisdom, the Holy Spirit — mother, source and womb — is the image of the light and wisdom hidden *within* the soul as, with the help of her God-mother, she is changed from soot-blackened drudge into radiant bride.

The image of the soul's journey weaves like a golden thread through mythology and literature that spans five thousand years. It first appears in Sumer, when Inanna, Queen of Heaven and Earth, surrenders her glorious apparel at each of the seven gates on her way to the underworld kingdom of her sister, Ereshkigal, resuming them after her three-day 'crucifixion' in darkness as she re-ascends to the light. The soul, as Eve, is banished from the Garden of Eden and goes into exile, as does the banished Goddess Asherah and the Gnostic daughter Sophia. The Cinderella of the fairy-tale personifies all these earlier mythic figures who in turn image the human soul and the predicament of the light which shines in darkness and has no knowledge of itself. As in the stories of the Sleeping Beauty and Snow White, the soul awakens to the kiss of the Prince who, as the solar bridegroom, consort of the moon goddess, personifies the divine life principle and, in these stories, the highest potential of human consciousness.

The ancient imagery of the sacred marriage is concealed in the many Renaissance paintings of the Coronation of the Virgin where Christ crowns his mother as his bride, and is developed in the transformative process of Alchemy whose aim was the reunion of the soul with spirit. It infuses the poetry and legends of the Middle Ages with the urgent beauty of the soul's quest for Wisdom — 'Notre Dame' — in whose honour the magnificent cathedrals of Europe arose. The theme pervades the Grail Legends and Dante's great allegory of the soul's awakening and return to God. The artists of the Renaissance, steeped in the Hermetic knowledge of Marsilio Ficino, proclaim Mary as the awakened soul seated in the midst of the garden, fragrant with the lilies and the roses which are Wisdom's timeless symbols. Impregnated by the Divine Spirit, she has brought forth her 'son.' So also, the Alchemist laboured to transform himself, as lover of Wisdom, into her son, the *filius philosophorum*, or *filius Sophiae*.

What is the cultural relevance of the story of Cinderella in the new age that is dawning? The image of the sacred marriage between Nature and Spirit, Goddess and God, has been notably absent in the Judeo-Christian tradition and this has inflicted a deep wound on the psyche which has yet to be healed.

The fairy-tale restores the image of union between the two primary archetypes and has, so to speak, 'carried' it for our culture until the time was ripe. The slow emergence in human consciousness of the plight of the feminine value embraces the image of the soul's suffering and ignorance of herself, and of an Earth and Nature which are also suffering, and in need of rescue. Cinderella personifies these three aspects of the feminine value so long relegated to the role of servant. The 'resurrection' of this archetype has been prepared for many centuries by those who often sacrificed their lives to the transmission of the Wisdom Tradition — 'black but beautiful' — so that it would not vanish into oblivion. It may even have been one of them — whether Jew or Christian — who first imagined this fairy tale, drawing on the repository of myth inherited by the mystical tradition of all three cultures from their Sumerian, Egyptian, and Gnostic past. This tradition taught the immanence of divine spirit in nature and human nature. It emphasized the need to embark on a quest to discover the presence of the radiant spirit hidden within the forms of life and the darkness of unreflecting human consciousness. They would each have recognised that Cinderella:

> the bright and shining one, who sits among the cinders and keeps the fire alight... is the personification of the Holy Spirit dwelling unhonoured amid the smouldering ashes of the Soul's latent, never totally extinct, Divinity. [19]

Notes:

1. Published by Williams and Norgate, London, 1912.
2. *Cinderella* by Marian Roalfe Cox, The Folk-Lore Society, 1892.
3. *Pistis Sophia*. Compare the passage in the *Song of Songs* "The Watchmen that went about the city found me, they smote me, they wounded me; the keepers of the walls took away my veil from me. I charge you, O daughters of Jerusalem, if ye find my beloved, that ye tell him, that I am sick of love". (5:7,8)
4. Hans Jonas, *The Gnostic Religion*, Beacon Press 1958. Introduction.
5. See the account of what happened in 623 BC when the Deuteronomists destroyed all evidence of the Goddess.
6. Robert M Grant, *Gnosticism: An Anthology*. Collins, London 1961 p.171
7. Harold Bayley, *The Lost Language of Symbolism*, Vol.1. p.192
8. C. Jung, *The Structure and Dynamics of the Psyche*, pp.190-192
9. M. Jastrow, *The Religion of Babylonia and Assyria*, p.142
10. From Adlington's translation of Apuleus' tale in *The Golden Ass*.
11. See *The Myth of the Goddess*
12. From 3500 BC, the incursion of warrior tribes worshipping sky gods into the territory of Old Europe, led to the Goddess gradually losing her ancient association with the heavens. However, this still survived in the lunar mythology of the Neolithic eras. (see Gimbutas, *The Civilization of the Goddess*)
13. *Inanna* by Diane Wolkstein and Samuel Noah Kramer, Rider & Co 1984, p.40
14. The priestesses of Apollo and of Artemis, Demeter and Aphrodite were known as *melissae* — bees — and the chief oracular priestess at Delphi, the *Pythia*, was called "The Delphic Bee".
15. See Patai, *The Hebrew Goddess*, Chapter 1V, for the Exile of the Shekinah, and also the Talmudic saying, p.145: "The Shekinah rang before him like a bell".
16. Trans. By G.R.S. Mead in *Fragments of a Faith Forgotten*.
17. All descriptions are taken from *Cinderella*, and quoted by Bayley, Vol.1, Chapters VIII and 1X.
18. E.O. James, *The Cult of the Mother Goddess*, p.197
19. Bayley, Vol 1, pp.194-95.

Originally included in *The Myth of the Goddess: Evolution of an Image*, by Anne Baring and Jules Cashford.

Re-published 1991 in *Psyche's Stories: Modern Jungian Interpretations of Fairy Tales*, Vol. 1. Edited by Murray Stein and Lionel Corbett, Chiron Publications, Wilmette, Ill.

Chapter Eleven

THE SACRED WAY OF THE ROSE

Oh no man knows through what wild centuries roves back the rose

— Walter de la Mare

The rose is the greatest mystic symbol of the West, just as the lotus is of the East. Like the thousand-petaled lotus of the Eastern traditions, the rose came to symbolize not only the love radiating from the Divine Ground but the awakened soul who has been reunited with it. It is above all an image of love, perfection, and beauty.

In the Christian tradition, the rose was associated with the Virgin Mary and, in the gnostic and alchemical tradition, with Sophia, Divine Wisdom and the Holy Spirit. As an initiatory path, the Sacred Way of the Rose symbolizes the hidden feminine Wisdom Tradition and the Way of the Heart. The rose represents love, wisdom, beauty, and mystery. Its exquisite beauty, its fragrance, the soft velvety feel and symmetrical disposition of its many petals, and its golden centre made it a symbol of perfection, not only earthly perfection, but heavenly perfection.

Drawing on ancient Mystery Traditions originating in Egypt and Persia, the rose was a central symbol in both European and Islamic alchemy: a symbol of the opening of the heart to the revelation and experience of divine love. It was immortalized as the white rose at the end of the *Divine Comedy*, in Dante's great vision of Paradise. The sublimely beautiful rose windows of Chartres could be seen as a vision of Divine Wisdom and the Holy Spirit, holding at their heart Christ and the Virgin Mary. I believe the Rose Windows of Chartres offer us an image of the blazing vision of the awakened soul and its union with the Divine Ground. The magnificent Rose Window over the western façade and Royal Portal depicts the Last Judgement and holds the figure of Christ at its centre. If this window were laid upon the floor of the nave, the rose window would fall almost exactly over the labyrinth. So, the person emerging from his or her journey through the labyrinth would, looking up, face the West Rose window with its promise of eternal life after the Last Judgement.

The Association of the Rose with Venus

The origins of the sacredness of the rose might be traced to the beautiful eight-year orbital pattern made by the planet Venus. Eight was the number associated with Venus in Sumer, addressed as 'The Radiant Star and 'The Great Light' in a Sumerian poem. Astronomers and mathematicians noticed the geometric connection between the orbit of Venus and the distribution of the petals of the rose with its hidden golden centre. From ancient times Venus as the bright morning and evening star was associated with the Great Goddesses of the ancient world, particularly with Isis and Inanna, but also the Greek Goddess Aphrodite and the Roman Venus. So, the association Venus — rose — Great Goddess was very ancient.

The Rose as the Primary Symbol of the Divine Feminine

From as long ago as Egyptian times, the rose has been the primary symbol of the Divine Feminine — the supreme image of love and beauty — sacred for millennia to the Great Goddesses of Egypt, Greece and Rome and the Christian Virgin Mary.

The rose was always associated with the Goddess in the ancient world. This is why the two griffins guarding the throne room in the Minoan palace of Knossos have stylized roses placed at their heart. Look carefully at these griffins (above). For the people of Crete, they symbolized the triple domains of the Great Goddess — sky, earth and underworld — represented here by the bird, the lion, and the serpent as the curved tail of the lion.

Friezes of stylized roses also adorned the frescoed walls of the Mycenean palaces built near the coasts of Greece, but this throne room was a sacred place where a priestess presided over the rites of the Goddess.

There is an eight-petalled rose at the centre of the four-thousand-year-old disk (above) from the Minoan palace of Phaistos, in Crete, whose meaning has only recently been tentatively deciphered. The disk is covered with a total of 241 "picture" segments created from 45 individual symbols and is thought to be a prayer or invocation to the Cretan Mother Goddess. It may also represent the labyrinthine path connecting this world with the other, invisible one, the path souls took as they journeyed from one to the other, into and out of the womb of the Goddess.

Roses were painted on early terracotta vases and strung on gold necklaces, now lying in the museums of Athens and Heraklion. They are found on the exquisite gold diadem and funeral wreath (previous page) found in the tomb of Philip of Macedon (382–336 BC) at Vergina, near Thessaloniki in northern Greece. The funeral wreath rested on the head of the person laid on the funeral pyre and was removed just before the flames consumed it, which may be why it has survived intact to our time. I think roses may have been an emblem of immortality.

It is beyond doubt that wherever the rose grew in the ancient world, it was associated with the Great Mother or Great Goddess. Roses may not have looked like our roses today but maybe temple gardeners knew how to grow different and more beautiful varieties to adorn her statues, decorate her shrines, and strew on the processional way of the great ceremonies in her honour, such as the celebration of the sacred marriage. Millennia later, roses still cover the heavy chariots holding the image of the Virgin Mary that are carried by men through the streets of Mediterranean cities on the day dedicated to her memory.

We know that roses were associated with the Goddess Isis through a dream that a man called Lucius Apuleius, an initiate of the Mysteries of Isis, recounts in his book, *The Golden Ass*. [1] It is a fascinating story of metamorphosis, brought about by the process of awakening or, in Jungian terminology, of individuation. Apuleius tells the story of his transformation into the form of an ass — a punishment for profaning the Mysteries of the Goddess Isis — and how, after much suffering and remorse, the Goddess came to him in a dream and told him to attend a public ceremony held in her honour. She would send the high priest a dream instructing him to carry a garland of roses in her procession. She told Apuleius, still in his ass form, that he was to push through to the front of the crowd, come up to the high priest as if he wished to kiss his hand, then pluck the roses from his garland into his mouth and eat them. He would then be transformed from an ass back into a man. Apuleius found himself intently watching the procession until he saw the high-priest approaching, holding up the promised garland. Carefully, he worked his way through to the front of the crowd until he came level with the high-priest. "My heart trembled," he said, "and my heart pounded as I ate those roses with loving relish; and no sooner had I swallowed them then I found that the promise had been no deceit." [2]

To his amazement and joy as well as the astonishment of the high-priest and the bemused crowd, he found himself miraculously changed back into his human form, covering his private parts in embarrassment until a cloak was thrown over him. Later he had an extraordinary vision of the Goddess where she spoke to him, revealing who she was. It is well worth reading this story in the original text and translation by Robert Graves. The apparition of the goddess in his vision of her is so vividly described that we could be seeing her ourselves.

In Greece, the rose was sacred to Aphrodite, Goddess of Love and Beauty. Her priestesses wore wreathes of white roses in their hair and scattered white rose petals over the approach to her temples. When, in Roman times, Aphrodite was transformed into Venus, roses were still sacred to her and would have embellished her shrines. Her priestesses would still wear wreathes of roses in their hair. We also know that in Rome, the statues of the Goddess Cybele, the Great Mother of Anatolia, who was brought to Rome in the form of a black meteorite in 204 BCE, were adorned with roses, and that once a year her effigy was covered with roses and carried through the streets of Rome on a chariot. It may be at this time when her Mysteries were celebrated, that the rose began to evolve into an image of resurrection, and the rose garden as the sacred world or hidden dimension of the Goddess.

The sacredness of the rose and its association with the Divine Feminine was transmitted to medieval Europe, where it was enshrined in the sublime rose windows of Chartres and other Gothic cathedrals in France that were all dedicated to the Virgin Mary. It is possible that the sacredness of the rose may have been introduced into France by Templar knights who travelled to Palestine and Syria with the Crusades and brought back elements of the Sufi tradition which was well established in Syria and Persia at that time. The exquisite blue colour of certain of the stained-glass windows in Chartres is thought to have been created by Muslim craftsmen who were specifically brought to France by the Templars to do this work.

There is a six-petalled rose at the centre of the labyrinth of Chartres (above). Whoever has walked or will walk the path of the labyrinth is treading the Sacred Way of the Rose from circumference to centre and the return journey from centre to circumference, taking with him or her, the experience of the central circle which holds the direct communion with the energy and frequency of Divine Love.

In the twelfth and thirteenth centuries, when these magnificent cathedrals were built, the rose was associated with the Holy Grail, a synonym or cover for the feminine Holy Spirit. It was also a synonym for the Church of Sophia or Church of the Holy Spirit, founded in 1167 in the Languedoc area of France. This Church claimed direct descent from the teaching of Jesus and Mary Magdalene. The secret teaching of this Church, as well as the many legends of the Quest for the Holy Grail, were carried all over Europe by the troubadours, many of whom were initiates of the Church. It had much in common with Sufism because its emphasis was on the transmission and practice of Love.

The Sacred Way of the Rose

What is the Sacred Way of the Rose? It is the Path of Longing that connects us to the invisible ground of the soul. It is the Path of Wisdom that fills the rose garden of our heart with the fiery power of love and connects us with each other, with the soul of nature and the soul of the cosmos. The Sacred Way of the Rose is the Way of the Heart, the Way of visionaries who, from time immemorial, have nurtured the inner Wisdom tradition which connects us to deeper levels of reality and opens our soul to awareness of our divinity and immortality and to the realization that Love is our origin, our guide and our destiny.

It was Mary Magdalene, the beloved consort of Jesus, who, with her sister Martha and brother Lazarus, brought the Essene Wisdom tradition to southern France in 44 CE, establishing there the Order of the Blue Rose. She lived and taught there for twenty years and her relics are still preserved in a Basilica in Provence which is the third most holy shrine in Christendom after the Holy Sepulchre in Jerusalem and St. Peter's in Rome. The Gospel she wrote and brought with her to France was the most precious possession of the Cathar Church of the Holy Spirit and has been secretly preserved for two thousand years in the Languedoc area of France. It has recently been translated from Alexandrian Greek into English and restored to us as *The Gospel of the Beloved Companion*. In it, Jesus or Yeshua — his Aramaic name — speaks of the Holy Spirit as his Mother. [3]

The Rose in the Christian Era

In the Christian era, the rose came to be associated with the Virgin Mary and with the rosary which assumed great importance in the late Middle Ages. Mary was named 'The Rose Garden' and the *Rosa Mystica*. The rise of the Virgin Mary to fill the place once occupied by the former Goddesses is one of the most fascinating aspects of the story of the Rose.

Drawing on ancient Wisdom or Mystery Traditions originating in Egypt, Palestine and Persia, the rose was a central symbol in European and Islamic alchemy: a symbol of the opening of the heart to the revelation and experience of Divine Love.

As an inner initiatory path, taught by the teachers of the great mystical traditions, the Rose symbolized this Wisdom Tradition and the Way of the Heart, leading to union with the Divine. In the hidden stream of the Gnostic, Alchemical and Kabbalist traditions, it was associated with Divine Wisdom and the feminine Holy Spirit. In the twelfth and thirteenth centuries, with the rise of the Feminine Archetype in the building of the great cathedrals and the Quest for the Holy Grail, the rose was the secret symbol of the dawn of Wisdom's Reign. But this great spiritual impulse that could perhaps have prevented the future blood-soaked history of Europe, had to go underground because of persecution by the Church of Rome in the thirteenth century and the devastating impact of the Black Death in the fourteenth. It was only secretly kept alive by Alchemists, Kabbalists and Rosicrucians — whose very name carries the rose within it.

Angels and the Scent of the Rose

Angels are out of fashion nowadays but in the Middle Ages, and for centuries before that people had visions of them and received messages from them. Anyone familiar with Kabbalah will know that angels and archangels are represented in the diagram of the Tree of Life. People have reported smelling the fragrance of roses after prayers for help addressed to the Virgin or to angels. I found this interesting passage on Google, written by a woman called Whitney Hopler: "People regularly report smelling the fragrance of roses while communicating with angels in prayer or meditation. Angels use rose scents as physical signs of their spiritual presence with people because roses have powerful energy fields that vibrate at a high electrical frequency — the highest of any flower on Earth. Because angelic energy also vibrates at a high rate, angels can connect more easily with roses than with other flowers that have lower vibrational rates. Rose essential oil vibrates at a rate of 320 megahertz of electrical energy. In comparison, essential oil from lavender (one of the next highest frequency flowers) vibrates at a rate of 118 megahertz."

For millennia, women in Bulgaria, Turkey, Iran and India, have gathered rose petals in preparation for them being dried and pressed to yield their exquisite fragrance, or divine perfume — the attar of roses.

The Rose Arbour of the Heart

So now, I invite you to enter the rose arbour of your heart as I go deeper into the mystery and beauty of the rose. We are the inheritors of an incredibly rich spiritual tradition — from India, from Palestine, from Persia — which speaks of Love as the pulse of the cosmos and the secret pulse of our own being. The exquisite poetry of this tradition — the poetry of the *Upanishads*, the Song of Songs, and the Essene and Sufi mystics — speaks of the longing of the human heart for reconnection with its Divine Source or Ground but also the longing of that Source for communion with us. "I was a treasure longing to be known; that is why I created the world," says a famous saying of the Prophet, who loved the rose so dearly that poets named him "the nightingale of the eternal garden".

The greatest spiritual teachers affirm that love is the fundamental principle of the universe; that the universe is brought into being by love and sustained by love; that we participate in, and are embraced by this fathomless sea of love. To know that we belong to this divine ground, that we are part of it, is the secret longing of the life that lives us. All mystic traditions say that the doors of our perception need to be cleansed so that we can see with new vision and open our hearts to the Presence of the Divine Ground. The eye of the heart and the eye of the mind have to be prepared for the revelation that we are, in essence, living within the embrace of that Light and Love. Here is one eloquent testimony:

> *The Light seemed to breathe me in even more deeply. It was as if the Light was completely absorbing me. I entered into another realm, more profound than the last, and became aware of something more, much more. It was an enormous stream of Light, vast and full, deep in the Heart of Life.* [4]

Turning to the East, to Persia, the rose held particular significance for the creators of its marvellous gardens which were the earthly expression of Paradise. We can only imagine the gardens of Persepolis and Isfahan. As an initiatory path, the Sacred Way of the Rose symbolizes the hidden Wisdom Tradition and the Way of the Heart, the way of longing and love that is so beautifully described by the poets of the Sufi tradition who were shamans, able to enter higher dimensions of reality — the *mundus imaginalis*. In Islam the rose symbolizes the Prophet Muhammad and is known as the flower of heaven. The ancient and marvellous city of Shiraz was called 'The City of the Rose.' The rose was the exquisite flower used by Persia's Sufi poets to describe the relationship between the lover and the Beloved. The most famous poem of Saadi, the great Persian poet who lived in Shiraz, was called 'The Garden of Roses.' In 1317, the Persian poet Mahmud Shabistari, a pupil of Ibn Arabi, wrote his poem *The Secret Rose Garden*. So East and West, we have the same imagery of the profound spiritual meaning of the Rose and the Rose Garden.

But it is Rumi (1207–73) whom the West knows best and who wrote so many beautiful verses about the rose and the rose garden: 'Love is the infinite rose garden; Eternal life the least of its blooms.' For lovers of the rose like Rumi, this flower was and is an epiphany or manifestation of the divinity at the heart of life.

> *I am created from the ecstasy of love and*
> *When I die, my essence will be released*
> *Like the scent of crushed rose petals.*

I found these words of a scientist and physicist called Suresh Emre on the Internet. Because his words give such an exquisite rendering of the significance of the Rose in Sufism I will quote them at some length. He says:

> Rumi used the 'rose and nightingale' symbolism of Persian literature to explain the central theme of Sufism: Divine Love. In Persian literature the rose symbolizes beauty and the nightingale the lover of beauty. The Sufi loves God as a nightingale loves a rose. The lover wants to be one with the Beloved. The soul yearns for the ultimate union with the Divine Ground… For me, he says, "the rose is the symbol of the soul. The seat of the soul is the heart which is not the physical organ but the subtle life-giving centre of our being — the soul. The Rose symbolizes the path of Divine Love." [5]

The great Sufi Sage, Hazrat Inayat Khan (1882-1927) wrote this: "Just as the rose consists of many petals held together, so the person who attains to the unfoldment of the soul begins to show many different qualities. These emit fragrance in the form of a spiritual personality. The rose has a beautiful structure, and the personality which shows the unfoldment of the soul also has a fine structure, in the manner of relating to others, in speech, in action. The atmosphere of a spiritual being pervades the air like the perfume of a rose".

There are other great Sufi mystics, among them Prince Dara Shikuh (1615-1659), the eldest son of Shah Jehan and his beloved wife, Mumtaz Mahal for whom he built the peerless Taj Mahal. Prince Dara was a poet, scholar and mystic who had the *Upanishads* and the *Bhagavad Gita* translated into Persian. Wanting to show the close relationship between Islamic and Vedic texts, he wrote a beautiful and profound treatise called *The Confluence of the Two Seas*, also known as *The Mingling of the Two Oceans*. In 1646, he wrote one of the most profound Sufi treatises, called *The Compass of Truth*, a detailed guide to the transcendent realms of the soul. But Prince Dara incurred the wrath of the mullahs by challenging the mainstream orthodoxy of Islam. He also aroused the jealousy of his younger brother, Aurangzeb, who defeated his army and executed him, sending his severed head to his father, whom he had imprisoned in his own palace. Tragically for India, Prince Dara never became the rightful heir of the Mughal Empire. These are his words that I deeply cherish, which echo those spoken earlier by Moses de León in his *Zohar*:

> All that you see as other than God is one with God in essence, though separate in name. When you transcend ordinary consciousness, you will realize that everything is God and it will inevitably follow that you will know yourself as you are in reality. [6]

Several years ago, I bought a book called *Rose of the World*. It was written by a Russian visionary called Daniel Andreev who, owing to the effects of the persecution he experienced in the former Soviet Union, died young, aged 57. He foresaw calamities for the world culminating in a Golden Age that he called the reign of Rose of the World. This he described as an international movement, unifying the teachings of all religious and philosophical traditions in a worldwide Federation, harmoniously regulating the life of the planet in the interests of all life on it and abolishing poverty, tyranny, war and violence. These are his words:

> Rose of the World can be compared to an inverted flower whose root is in heaven, while the petals are here, among humanity on earth. Its stem is the revelation through which the spiritual sap flows, sustaining and strengthening its petals — the fragrant core of all religions. But it also has a pith — a specific teaching which embodies a new attitude towards Nature, towards the role of humanity, towards creativity, love and the path of cosmic ascension.... This will be a time when Womanhood in humanity will reveal itself with unprecedented strength, in perfect balance and harmony with the male principle. The current state structure will be transformed into a Fraternity working for the benefit of all humanity.

I thought this statement was so extraordinary that it belongs here, at the end of this offering of the Sacred Way of the Rose. I think we could look upon the planet of whose life we are a part as a Rose Garden.

Notes:

1. Apuleius, Lucius, *The Golden Ass*, trans. Robert Graves, Penguin Books Ltd., Harmondsworth 1950, p. 234
2. Ibid, pp. 227-29
3. *The Gospel of the Beloved Companion*, translated and with an Introduction by Jehanne de Quillan, 2010, Éditions Athara, Foix, France
4. from the after-death experience of Mellen-Thomas Benedict, quoted at the end of *The Dream of the Cosmos*
5. Suresh Emre https://medium.com/@sureshemre/rose-symbolism-64bf66a79fc5
6. see *The Dream of the Cosmos*, p. 526

Madonna de la Misericordia
Piero della Francesca – Museo Civico di Sansepolcro

Chapter Twelve

HEALING THE HEART

We are all migrants from the invisible worlds — Hazrat Inayat Khan [1]

Le Livre du Cueur d'Amour Épris,
written and illustrated by the Roi René, Count of Provence from 1434 to 1480 [2]

This Chapter is about healing the wounded human heart, the quest for an alchemy which could transform our perception of life from base metal into gold, transform it from something that is cut off from the profound depths of our soul into something that is consciously in touch with them. Such an alchemy would attune us to resonate ever more finely with the sublime symphony of the Cosmos.

There has been an amazing discovery about the heart made by the Heart-Math Institute in the United States and shown in a recent video made by that Institute. The video says that the heart connects us to the quantum field that is beyond the boundaries of time and space, acting as a portal to a deeper intelligence than the mind. Through the heart we are connected to everything in existence. Amazingly, the video shows how a blindfolded child, connecting to her heart, can read the words of a text *without seeing them with her physical eyes*. This discovery is mind-blowing, opening our understanding to a different way of perceiving and experiencing the world and a totally different relationship with our heart.

The heart is like an umbilical cord which mediates between the life within us and the life around us. It connects us to the life of the whole, the greater life of the divine ground. The heart is our creative imagination, born of our instinct for relationship with this greater life. The heart generates all our quests, all our hopes and longings and will ultimately reunite us with the source from which we have come. Without the heart, without the instinct to feel, to imagine, to hope and to love, life is meaningless, sterile, dead. When we are in touch with our heart, when we are connected to our deepest feelings, it comes alive, it vibrates, it sings.

The life-bearing energy of the heart rises like a fountain within us to nourish and irrigate the soil of soul. As with the physical heart, if the psychic heart is not in a healthy state; if one or more of its arteries is blocked; if the circulatory system is not in good order, then we cannot function at a level of optimum health. Our heart carries many wounds, and these, like blocked arteries, can restrict the flow of energy through the psychic circulatory system, leading to the impairment of psychic and physical health. Where do these wounds come from and how are they inflicted?

To answer this question, we need to understand that the kind of consciousness we now have has evolved infinitely slowly out of the matrix of nature. Once we were contained by it as a child within its mother. Self-awareness, the ability to reflect on our actions, to think, to reason, to focus our thought is a very recent development in relation to the thousands, even millions of years of human evolution. The potential for consciousness was buried within us, like a seed buried with the earth. Once, we lived unconsciously, purely instinctively, without the self-awareness we now have. The evolutionary development of the differentiation of consciousness from the matrix of nature has inflicted on us the same kind of psychic wound that a child experiences when it is born because we have come to experience ourselves as separate from the matrix that once contained us.

This long process of differentiation has been experienced by us as an exile, a fall, a state of disharmony and disunion. From it has come our present still fragile consciousness and the fears and anxieties which torment us. But the memory of fusion or union with the ground of being we once knew, albeit unconsciously, lives on in us as a longing for reunion, for the ecstasy of belonging once again to the greater Other. We have created all kinds of myths to assuage the loneliness and terror of separation and to re-connect us with the whole. The great sages and mystics of all cultures have tried to teach us how to dissolve the illusion of our separate existence so that we would experience ourselves in full consciousness as the divine ground, as divine being. But only a few individuals, so very few, have understood their message.

The sacred image, whether Goddess or God, is essential to us because it mediates between our present awareness of ourselves and the deepest dimension of our psychic life. It relates us through our heart to this ground. Looking back beyond the image of the Father God who has been worshipped by patriarchal cultures for some three to four thousand years, we find that for some twenty thousand years before this, the Mother Goddess was the image of that ground. She stood for the whole invisible matrix of relationships that we call life. She was divine life, both transcendent and immanent. She was the divine presence within her manifest form, continually renewing and regenerating it in a cyclical process of waxing and waning as immutable as that of the moon. The whole of life was experienced as an epiphany of her being. Through her image, people were held in a state of instinctive participation with the whole. We could think of this as the first phase in the evolution of consciousness.

Then, about 2000 BCE, there was a profound change in mythic imagery which suggests that about this time a new phase in the evolution of consciousness was initiated. The image of a Great Father began to replace the Great Mother. In the earliest myth — a Babylonian one (the *Enuma Elish*) — the mother goddess was murdered by the god and her corpse was split in half, one half making the heavens and the other the earth. Later, the Goddess became the void, the deep, and in the Book of Genesis the spirit of God (*ruach*) moved upon these waters and brought life into being. The new image of deity reflected the idea of creative spirit bringing life into being as something separate from itself rather than emanating from itself, invisibly present within the forms emerging from itself. Creation was from the Word of the Father rather than from the Womb of the Mother. This change of imagery reflected a profound change in the way we perceived life. An older, participatory kind of consciousness that connected us with nature was replaced by one that increasingly emphasized the need to control and dominate nature. From now on the head rather than the heart becomes the focus of consciousness. With this change of emphasis in the sacred image, there is both an accelerated development of mind, or intellect, and a tremendous advance in technology and control of the environment but, at the same time, a loss of relationship with it.

During the last 4000 years a fundamental dualism has permeated human culture, a dualism that has split spirit from nature and divided mind from body, intellect from instinct, thinking from feeling. As human consciousness evolved further away from its instinctive ground, fear was constellated: fear of the instincts, fear of the unknown, fear of death, fear above all, of nature as the Great Mother who was the root of all these fears. Over thousands of years and quite unconsciously, this fear has led to the situation where the greater part of life has been emptied of spirit. Nature, soul, matter, body, and sexuality were gradually desacralized and the sense of life as a sacred totality from which nothing could be excluded was lost.

From this time on the emphasis was on the development of power and control over nature, mythically reflected in the image of the hero killing the dragon. The human mind, unconsciously identified with spirit, was imperceptibly elevated to the posture of a god. In our efforts to control and direct life 'from above,' and shape it to our defined goals, we have assumed the mythic position of the deity we have worshipped. The idea that life is created and controlled by a power outside and above nature originates in Babylonian mythology and was transmitted to later cultures: Persian, Greek, Roman and Judeo-Christian. This paradigm of control underlies our theological and scientific concepts. We are utterly unconscious of the fact that the structure of our religion, philosophy, and science rests on the foundation of a belief system which divided life into light and dark, good and evil, male and female and associated nature, matter and woman with darkness, chaos and sexual temptation.

Once, long ago, when spirit and nature were not yet sundered, life was sacred. The Great Mother as the womb from which life emerged and to which it returned was an image that expressed the mystery of relationship between all aspects of life, hidden and manifest. Sexuality was sacred because it led to the creation of new life. With the loss of the image of the Great Mother, the realm of the heart, the source of the creative imagination, was repressed into the unconscious. It has had to function subliminally, unconsciously, and more and more negatively, so long as nothing was done to reunite it with consciousness. No healing could take place, no fundamental shift in human values or human understanding because everything related to the heart, to the instincts and the imagination, was gradually devalued in relation to the rational, conscious mind. Because of the loss of the image of the Divine Feminine life came to be seen as mere mechanism, without meaning or purpose. Modern materialist science has emptied nature and cosmos of divinity.

I remember a dream I once had of a gigantic Eiffel tower straddling the dead, parched surface of the moon. At the time I had this dream, it referred to the sterility of my own consciousness, and the rigid control I had over my instinctual life, but I think it may also apply to the cultural paradigm that we have accepted today. Identified with this iron construction of our control over nature, unable to trust or listen to our deepest instincts, we no longer know how to love life as divine life, how to listen to its voice or enter into communion with its harmony within ourselves and the life around us. We no longer know how to value or create beauty, how to stand in awe of life, how to wonder. Everything has to pass the voice of the stern judge: 'Can it be scientifically proven?' before it is acceptable to us. So much of immense value to us has been and is lost through this censorship. To sum up, because we have lost the feminine image of the divine, we have lost touch with the instinct for relationship with life and this has deeply wounded our heart and our culture.

The Myth of the Fall

Adam and Eve, the Serpent, and the Tree of Knowledge
William Blake

In this chapter, I need to revisit the myth which stands at the root of Judeo-Christian civilization, a myth that has also wounded the heart because it has ratified the split between spirit and nature as something divinely ordained. The Myth of the Fall or of Exile from the Garden of Eden draws an image of humanity as essentially flawed, expelled from the divine world, blamed and punished by God for a primal sin or fault committed long ago. The myth was interpreted literally, as what really happened at a specific historical time, not as a myth about the great evolutionary step of the separation of consciousness from the matrix of nature. It has imprinted the Judeo-Christian psyche with a fundamental dualism and a deep sense of guilt. On the one hand there is God in the Garden of Eden, the higher, divine world. On the other, there are Adam and Eve — us — exiled from the Garden and condemned to a life of toil and suffering on earth — the lower world emptied of divinity. This image of exile and punishment has made us look for the divine beyond rather than within life, beyond rather than within ourselves, longing to get back into the Garden but forever unable to do so.

Because of the influence of this myth, active since 623 BCE, nature, matter, body, sexuality, and the instincts in general have all been dissociated from spirit and desacralized. Woman also, by her association with Eve, was included in this process. The image of exile from the Garden, inflicted on Eve and Adam as a punishment for their disobedience, infuses the story with a melancholy tone that offers a tragic view of human existence on Earth.

How has this myth formed our image of ourselves? It seems to me that there is a shadow aspect to Christian teaching, an unconscious sado-masochism in the belief that human existence and the created order are intrinsically flawed; that suffering and death are a punishment for a primal sin and that sin has been transmitted like a fatal disease through the sexual act from generation to generation. At the root of our culture there is the image of a punishing Father who inflicts abandonment and suffering on his children. The negative imagery of the myth has deeply undermined our trust and delight in life, setting us against ourselves and against our instincts.

With this myth as a divine model for human existence, how could we not blame other people, to shift the intolerable burden of sin and guilt from our own heart onto another's? How could we protect ourselves from the belief that everyone, including children, is born sinful? Imagine the effect of this myth on generations of children and how evil was beaten out of them. Imagine the effect on children of seeing a bleeding, crucified Christ hanging in every church and having the idea of sin and guilt introduced to them. Imagine the effect of this myth on generations of husbands and fathers whose subjugation of their wives and daughters was ratified by it. Consider how negatively it has structured man's perception of himself, his relationship with woman and his own feelings and instincts and how deeply it has undermined woman's trust in herself, her sense of her value as a woman. In the image of Adam blaming Eve and her bringing sin, suffering and death into the world we have the root of the deep distrust of woman in Judeo-Christian culture. In the image of the angry father punishing his errant children, we have the justification for punishing all those who seem to err — including our enemies. It was to be expected that we would divest ourselves of our sense of sin and guilt by blaming and punishing others. The myth itself has given rise to great evil, compounding human suffering, splitting nature from spirit, body from mind, creating negative habits of thinking and feeling which have profoundly affected the lives of generations of human beings.

Who knows whether the atrocities we are currently witnessing may not have their distant origin, like all our hatreds and cruelties, in a fundamental flaw in our patriarchal religious beliefs which have set us against ourselves and, therefore, ultimately, against others. It might be truer to believe, as Matthew Fox does, that we are a supremely blessed species instead of a flawed one.[3] Perhaps leaving the Garden (separating from the matrix of nature) was a privilege, a sacred trust, something life asked us to undertake for its sake, with all the bewilderment, suffering and search it entailed. Perhaps our life, together with all life on this planet participates in that divine life we have wrongly been taught to believe is something different from us, beyond and above us.

The Loss of Soul

Jung called attention to the devaluation and loss of the soul, showing how the extraverted emphasis of our religious beliefs (with divinity outside and beyond us), and the brutality of our rationalist philosophy did violence to our instincts: how our instincts or feelings were so devalued in relation to our intellect, our heart in relation to our head, that a deep chasm has developed in the psyche between the conscious mind and the unconscious. When the realm of instinct is dissociated from consciousness, the injured instinct is increasingly focused on power and the need to achieve it. When psychic injuries are not acknowledged and healed, when the creative imagination is denied expression, when the flow of life is blocked, instinct becomes compulsive, ruthless, even demonic. Eventually, the waters dammed up behind the fragile wall of consciousness burst through it, destroying everything in their path. It is not because human beings are intrinsically evil that they create evil, but that they cannot survive such injuries to their soul. Everything we call evil, the huge aggression surfacing in current wars comes from the wounded heart of the culture and the unrecognized soul-suffering of billions of individuals.

Jung saw that our consciousness has become one-eyed — a monolithic consciousness that sees only the surface of life and takes that for the only reality. He saw that the neglect of our inner life, our deep instinctual needs and wisdom, had led to the situation where, as in the Grail legend, the territory of the soul is in the grip of a terrible drought. No-one understands any more what the landscape and the language of the soul are like: no-one can read the images. They are like hieroglyphs whose key has been lost. He saw that there was an immense work to be done in recovering the soul and that time was very short.

He saw that the decay of the old god-image and the disintegration and barbarism of our time heralded a new phase in the evolution of consciousness, one which would recover the feminine value and the dimension of the soul. This transitional phase of the loss of the old god-image is dangerous. In our fear and confusion, we may lose the priceless attainment of the level of consciousness and insight we have struggled for millennia to achieve. Because of the polarization of rational mind and instinct within us, everything around us is increasingly polarized: on the one hand there is the impulse to overthrow authority; on the other, repressive authoritarian tendencies, fundamentalism of all kinds, which resist any impulse for change; censorship where the truth is not allowed to be told; cruel "cancelling" of others which masquerades as improving society.

In its fear and confusion and in its archaic habits of response to danger, the instinct may turn demonic, threatening the delicate fabric of civilization with disintegration and descent into barbarism. Rage accumulates in the unconscious and bursts forth in a tidal-wave of violence and cruelty. Religions that did so much to create civilization, are powerless to prevent this regression, perhaps because they are unable to recognize their authoritarian shadow and because they cling to an image of the divine which projects divinity beyond human existence. Belief will not sustain us through this perilous phase. We need insight into why this situation has arisen, knowledge of our nature, understanding of our instinctive habits of behaviour, above all, the integration of thinking and feeling, mind and soul and the left and right hemispheres of the brain. [4]

The twentieth century was a century of concentration camps, hydrogen bombs, human sacrifice on an apocalyptic scale and theologies of power which aim to manipulate and control both mind and body. The twenty-first century brings the risk of totalitarian control of people by their governments — a risk already applied in China, Iran, North Korea and Afghanistan and gaining ground in the United States. Where does the pathology of the split psyche reveal itself? How is the creative imagination perverted and used to destroy life? Prisoners of archaic tribal responses, we spend trillions of dollars a year on weapons and wars. Prisoners of fear, we justify the invention of weapons of mass destruction that can exterminate millions of human beings by remote control. If we knew that life is one and indivisible, would it be so easy to destroy our enemies since in essence, they are ourselves? If religion had taught us that the body was sacred and had not itself tortured and murdered in God's name, would it be so easy for us to atomize it? We seem, in a state of unconscious identification with deity to have assumed the power of the godhead itself, using the elements of life to destroy life. This malignant aggression (Erich Fromm's phrase) begins at the point where the heart is paralyzed, frozen, where our psychic life cannot grow and begins to wither and die. At this point the attraction to sadistic behaviour and death begins and with it the addiction to the power to inflict suffering and death on others.

Healing this Pathology

How could we heal this pathology? Once, long ago, we felt contained within the ground of being in the image of the Great Mother. Then we learned to fear and obey the image of the Great Father and to sacrifice the flesh to the spirit. Now we are asked to restore the feminine dimension of life to its former sacredness, so we may heal the dissociation in the soul. This means loving and honouring and valuing human existence on this planet, undoing the negative imagery of the Myth of the Fall, becoming aware of all the rigid patterns of belief which block the flow of life in the individual and in society, dismantling the edifice of bureaucratic control over everything and everyone. It means restoring matter and the physical body to the realm of spirit, understanding that they are sacred because they are the manifestation of divine life. It means learning to cherish them instead of trying to manipulate and control them, learning to cherish ourselves as an infinitely precious vehicle of life. This focus on healing our inner life is not introspective selfishness, as we have been taught for so long. It is loving and serving the divine life that we are.

Only in the last century and this one has our attention been directed towards healing the suffering hidden beneath the surface of the conscious mind. The new insights offered by psychology are a great advance or increase of consciousness because they offer us the opportunity of freeing ourselves from unconscious habits of behaviour, personal habits as well as collective tribal habits. Now, as the old paradigm fractures and dissolves, a new conception of reality is struggling to be born. A new holistic approach to the Earth and to the body as the manifest aspect of divinity reflects this new vision. New discoveries in science and medicine, new and experimental forms of healing are part of this impulse. Where religion has judged and condemned negative patterns of human behaviour as sinful, our growing insight into our nature can understand them as symptoms of trauma, of psychic injuries, deep injuries to the heart. This new impulse is grounded in compassion for life, compassion for ourselves as participants in a divine drama and the realization that the healing of the culture begins within ourselves. It is helping us to see that people are not bad but sad and that sadness can lead to badness and even to madness and to all the patterns of evil that are so resistant to our efforts to eradicate them.

This descent into the realm of the instinct is not without danger. Psychology that offers itself as a redeemer can easily degenerate into authoritarianism or facile technology. As we penetrate deeper and deeper below the surface of consciousness into the neglected dimension of the soul, we reach the molten lava of long-buried emotions, the hidden turmoil of individual and collective suffering that is carried in the collective soul of humanity. Healing comes with the recognition, acceptance, and transformation of powerful and frightening feelings. This is the direction which could lead us to the further evolution of consciousness. Where religion has emphasised repression and sacrifice, conformity to collective beliefs, guilt and punishment, the new approach does not judge or condemn but seeks to listen and to heal. Instinct is the tumultuous creative energy of life. It can never be controlled by consciousness; but it can be transformed through insight and compassion. If you tell someone he or she is bad, sinful, you will not heal the heart. You will compound the pain and rage in the unconscious. Compassionate insight can offer release for intolerable pain buried beneath years and centuries of repression. Slowly, it can free us from bondage to the collective habits of belief and behaviour that have blocked our true response to life. With infinite care, it can dissolve the false self — the defence we construct against suffering and fear and regenerate the lost true self, the treasure of the heart.

Creating a relationship between consciousness and the deeper instinctive dimension of the soul works an alchemy within us. The goal-oriented consciousness we know and live by encounters the mysterious dimension of the soul. This encounter brings into being a different relationship to life, a different attitude to it, a different way of living which one might call the Way of the Heart. It takes many years and infinite patience and trust to bring into being. It is about becoming aware of oneself as *innately divine instead of innately flawed.* It is about becoming the humble servant of life, devoted to caring for it, healing it and freeing it from our archaic fear and violence towards it. It is about attuning ourselves so that we begin to resonate with life, harmoniously.

The Child

This brings me to the child, for the child is our future and it is only through our understanding of the child's needs that we can hope to change the present and so, the future. What wounds the heart of a child? There is a general belief that children are resilient, tough, able to survive the most atrocious experiences. But my experience with my patients suggests that this is not true. The child may survive physically and intellectually, may be able to hold its own in the world, but the wound to the heart will show in its close relationships, in the way, as an adult, it treats its partner or its children, and in depression, mental illness, obsessions and compulsive behaviour of all kinds. It will develop a defensive carapace, a false self to survive the pain of its experience and may believe this false self is its true individuality.

The false self in league with the superficial goals of our culture, will drive the person to seek greater and greater power, wealth, or success, for to be at the top or in control of other people or influencing other people, is to be beyond the reach of the child's sense of powerlessness and worthlessness. Or else it will drive a person into depression because he or she cannot achieve the goals set by social media. The widespread depression or mental illness of children and adolescents today is not only the effect of the Covid Lockdown but also our educational system and the deficient goals presented to children by the culture and the media. It is due, above all, to a loss of meaning.

The psyche of the child is like warm wax. Its sense of self is barely formed by the time it reaches adolescence. It is impressionable, fragile, sensitive, vulnerable. What it absorbs from the atmosphere of the home and the wider environment of school and society, is imprinted indelibly on the memory. Children without a stable and happy home, children who struggle to survive in a brutal or depraved environment, often witnessing the emotional or physical cruelty inflicted on one parent on another, children who are exposed to the anger, lust, cruelty or the rigidly imposed belief system of their parents or step-parents or their teachers, or the recent attempts to indoctrinate children with transgender ideology, are like a baby thrown into an abattoir. They have little hope of psychic survival. Indeed, as someone has written, they are the victims of soul murder. [5] As they grow up, the memories of intolerable pain are repressed into the deeper levels of the unconscious, and into the muscles and nervous system of the body where they may manifest as illness. There may be no recall of the actual circumstances or traumas which wounded them. Later these repressed memories are re-enacted in destructive or self-destructive scenarios which are a kind of code language telling the story of what happened to them decades earlier.

The tragic fact is that in every case, the child unconsciously blames itself for what has happened in the same way that humanity in the Myth of the Fall blamed itself for the experience of suffering and death — believing it must have angered the heavenly father to have been so punished. Children depend absolutely on their parents for their survival. A child has not yet developed reflective consciousness. In a situation of terror, bereavement, punishment, sexual abuse, or abandonment, or if it is the helpless witness of the cruelty of one parent towards another, or the cruelty of an adult in any form of abuse, it feels unbearable fear and pain. But it can neither flee nor fight, so the instinctive response to danger is suppressed. There may be no witness to its suffering, no-one to confirm its feelings of distress, to say, "this is terrible, this is wrong. I will help you." To explain the situation to itself, it says, "I must be bad for this thing to be happening to me." It takes the guilt upon itself. The deep conviction that in some way it is responsible for any of these disasters and therefore guilty, establishes itself in the soul as an internalized inner critic, a persistent negative voice — even a demonic voice — which undermines and destroys its feeling of value and may destroy its life. 6

This deeply unconscious negative internal voice is the root cause of depression and other compulsive patterns of behaviour such as alcoholism, anorexia and bulimia, drug-taking and promiscuity, and the violence, cruelty and depravity that are increasingly seen in our society. All these are symptoms of original pain, not of original sin. All are patterns of self-destruction. Because soul and body are essentially one matrix of energy, the unacknowledged suffering of the heart may place great stress on the immune system of the child, preparing the way for illness and disease later in life. Yet, as many people are discovering, the breakdown of the body or the nervous system may lead to healing the heart of the child they once were.

When the child enters the wider world of society already damaged by the home situation, and finds an impersonal, frightening environment and a school curriculum that awakens neither delight nor wonder, where there is no beauty or poetry or mystery, no welcome for the heart, nothing that gives meaning or value to life, it will again be traumatized and the neglected imagination will be distorted into negative fantasies. The pathology of destructive violence presented on television, film, and video increase the sense of fear, self-doubt and powerlessness. Addiction to social media can ruin a child's life, taking them away from the ability to form human relationships. What boys watch in the sadistic behaviour towards women shown in pornographic videos, is really a rape of their soul, programming them to try and copy what they see in their relationships with girls who are becoming increasingly traumatized by the way they are treated. Neither gender can behave towards the other in the way it used to before social media came on the scene. What children watch, night after night, in scenes of sadistic violence, is the spectacle of the dese-cration of the soul. Consciously, they may say they do not copy the negative mythology they see, but unconsciously the instinct sees violent, threatening images and it *identifies with the aggressor, as the only way to survive.*

Children whose feelings did not matter to their parents will, as adults, ignore their own feelings and those of others. Compulsively, in addictive or manipulative behaviour of all kinds, they will repeat or re-enact the origi-nal trauma by attracting to themselves situations or relationships that punish them, re- traumatize them. They may also, by unconsciously identifying with the aggressor who wounded them, wound their own chosen victims — always someone weaker than themselves, making *them* suffer the intensity of the pain they once had to endure themselves. The recent case of the QC John Smyth is a horrific example of this. [7]

The work of healing and transforming the wounded heart is what in Alchemy is called 'drawing the dark matter out of the sea.' It is creating a relationship with the shadow side of ourselves, the part that is hidden from our rational consciousness, the part we are frightened or ashamed of acknow-ledging because it has been named as evil or sinful and because it has the power to control us. If this work is not done, if we fail to understand and heal the wounds that lie behind the violence in society, there is a real danger that the instinct will indeed overwhelm us. The more dissociated this wounded side of ourselves becomes, the more dangerous and uncontrollable it is when it breaks through as some violent or depraved act. The life of the planet and the continuation of our own life on it depend upon the growth of our consciousness and our ability to understand and heal the wounded aspect of our own nature.

Healing the Heart

How can we heal our heart? The child is our conduit to the heart. We can seek out this child in ourselves who was abandoned, rejected, terrorised, tortured and paralysed with fear or left bereft by a catastrophe like the loss of a parent which broke its heart. The child is the key to healing all our habits of aggres-sion. If we can heal the child in ourselves, if we can melt the long-frozen capacity to feel, if we can transform fear, rage, grief and guilt into trust and delight, the heart will begin to heal. The soil of soul, so long parched and dry, is watered by the flow of released feelings. Regenerated, it becomes rich and fertile. The imagination begins to function creatively instead of destructively. Ideas appear, take root, grow, and come to flower in creative work that

Tobias and the Angel
Andrea del Verrochio (1435-1488)

nourishes both oneself and the community, so returning transformed pain as compost to the psychic earth of humanity. Life then becomes the companion who is a constant help and support and guide. Like Tobias with the Archangel

Raphael, (opposite) we can discover how to trust and communicate with life as with a guiding and directing presence, above all, as a friend. [8]

The child who is the artist, the poet, the musician and the mystic at the heart of each one of us, the child who is the true creative nucleus of the individual, who is our vital connection to the ground of being, begins to feel, begins to come to life, begins to trust life and, no longer fearing catastrophe, begins to feel happy. Then a miracle takes place. The person imprinted with guilt, whose internal voice said "I hate myself" and whose actions said "I hate life, I hate other people" begins to say "I love myself, I love life, I love other people." The love flowing from the healed wound in the instinctual life, the life of the heart, grows and spreads and expands. And so it happens that the lead of a blocked and tortured heart is transformed into the gold of a loving and compassionate one. This is alchemy, the recovery of the heart's capacity to love — the most precious treasure of the soul.

Resurrection is about a slow transfiguration of consciousness, a gradual experience of revelation offered by a deeply compassionate relationship with life, lived at all levels of our being. Healing brings transfiguration. Healing is discovering how to live life in a different way, in trust rather than in fear, learning how to relate to life as partner and lover. It is about falling in love with life, about 'following our bliss' — Joseph Campbell's phrase which describes the rapture of being alive, following the longing impulses of the heart in whatever direction they lead because these alone guide us to realize life's intention for us. In following the impulsion of the joyous heart, we are doing life's will. The happiness of the heart is released when the fear, guilt, anger, envy, and self-hatred originating in childhood suffering are redeemed. The feeling of happiness grows as one begins to experience the revelation of the miracle that life is, and begins working consciously and deeply with it, as a contribution towards restoring the whole damaged fabric of life both within and without.

Healing the heart is about raising everything to do with the rejected feminine principle to consciousness, re-sacralizing it, crowning it with our insight and understanding. It is about learning to love and understand ourselves and therefore others at the deepest level. It is about transforming our darkness instead of projecting what we fear and reject in ourselves onto someone else. Healing is about cherishing in every sense: cherishing the heart, cherishing and healing the once and future child within us; using our compassion and insight to become our own redeemer; cherishing the time given to us as our life to discover our true direction and who we truly are; cherishing the body which has been sacrificed for so long to our distorted image of spirituality; cherishing the lives of the people who have been given into our care; cherishing the planetary life which is the greater field of all our endeavours.

A culture grounded on extraversion alone will not survive because its values are too shallow to sustain it through the kind of crises we now face. But there is a new consciousness coming into being. I will call it quantum consciousness — prepared and mediated by many thousands of individuals in different parts of the world. With it, all things are possible. With its help, we can change our image of reality and the crystallised habits in which we are imprisoned because we do not know how to trust the heart and the imagination. The answers to our questions cannot come from the incomplete consciousness of the intellect but from a deeper revelation which may be born in our hearts, a new mythology of the whole of life as a divine unity. There is, in this new myth, no essential distinction between transcendent and immanent life; as the mystics have always told us, the distinction and the duality are in our distorted perception of reality. The divine is what we are. We are eternally in the divine. This revelation above all others may heal our heart.

Notes:

1. Hazrat Inayat Khan, from *Immortality: A Traveller's Guide*, Pir Zia Inayat Khan, p. 69
2. The National Library, Vienna. Thames and Hudson, London 1975, Folio 2
3. Fox, Matthew (1983), *Original Blessing,* Bear & Co. Inc.
4. McGilchrist, Dr Iain (2009) *The Master and his Emissary: The Divided Brain and the Making of the Western World* and his recent two-volume work: *The Matter with Things* (2021) which show how the too-great emphasis on the faculties of the left hemisphere of the brain has shut down the right hemisphere.
5. The indoctrination of children in Primary Schools in the UK with the agenda of the LGBTcommunity (Stonewall) has been deeply harmful and confusing for the child's psychic development. I would call this indoctrination Childhood Abuse or Soul Murder. See Shengold, Leonard (1989) *Soul Murder: The Effects of Childhood Abuse and Deprivation,* Yale University

    The Cass Report in the UK (10/4/2024) has thankfully introduced sanity and scientific rigour into the whole subject of changing children's gender by medical means. For years, doctors at the gender clinic at the Tavistock and Portman NHS Foundation Trust in London had supported this ideology, offering hormonal treatment, and operating on children to alter their gender, without sufficiently exploring the lives of these children and finding out why they were so distressed that they wished to change their gender. The Cass Report warned that puberty blockers could harm brain development, bone density, fertility and the development of sexual function.

    This ideology could only have taken root in a materialist society where the body is viewed as a mechanism and consciousness is seen as an epiphenomenon of the brain. It could not have been widely communicated without children having access to social media where ideas spread like wildfire and where, disgracefully, there is still no control over harmful content reaching children's eyes and ears.

The introduction of trans ideas to five-year old children in English schools, inexcusably permitted by the Conservative Government's Department of Education, can only be described as a disgraceful interference with children's freedom and integrity, their being indoctrinated by ideas imposed by adults that have nothing whatever to do with the word 'education.' To interfere with hormones and mutilate the body of a child, to encourage it to change its gender in response to the child feeling unhappy in the body it was born with, to tell children that gender can be 'assigned' at birth rather than originating at conception, and that there can be multiple genders, is a hubristic act that is off the scale in arrogance, as well as abysmal ignorance of how fragile and malleable the psyche of a child is. Thankfully, puberty blockers have been banned by the Labour Government (December 2024).

The way an organization like Stonewall was able to infiltrate government departments, the Civil Service, the NHS and schools was without precedent. The fact that so many people succumbed to its "Woke" agenda can only be explained as a state of psychic possession whereby, acting as a group, they were driven into the state of mind described by Mattias Desmet — Mass Formation or Mass Hypnosis — possessed and driven by an unconscious will to power that originates in their own unhappiness with their gender, and deeper wounds to their heart that are buried in their unconscious psyche. To view the mutilation of children's immature bodies and hormonal systems as a 'compassionate act' is a travesty of the truth.

In their attempts to be inclusive, the Conservative Government opened the door to the evil of manipulating the innocent minds of very young children into believing that they can change their gender if they felt uncomfortable or unhappy in their bodies, confusing them by giving them the idea that there can be any number of genders, not just two. As a psychotherapist and Jungian Analyst, I regard this attempt to influence the minds of very young children as Soul Murder, as Leonard Shengold describes it in his book of that name. It is a crime and should be regarded and treated as such. Since this initiative was encouraged by government, teachers were confused and were persuaded to acquiesce in this agenda, feeling they were not able to challenge or resist it. They were co-opted (sometimes willingly) into keeping parents in ignorance of their children's decision to change their gender and their name. Children were encouraged to believe that they could be any one of dozens, even hundreds of genders and any form of life — a cat, a lion, a bird etc., that they chose to be, creating pandemonium in the classroom. They were also told they could call themselves female if male and male if female and make the teachers call them by their new name in class.

The other area that has led to the acute distress of women in the UK, is allowing men who have changed their gender to access toilets and other places, such as changing areas for nurses in hospitals and refuges sheltering women who have been abused by men. The NHS went to ridiculous lengths to change terms or descriptions of specific activities that previously applied only to women, such as vagina, breast-feeding and giving birth. Women were described by the NHS as 'Breast-feeding People.' There was to be no safe space for girls and women in schools, hospitals or even prisons. the 'Woke' Transgender ideology has spread its tentacles through our health system, the civil service, our primary schools, and our culture in the name of Diversity, Equity, Inclusion (DEI).

Transgender Issues in Sport

As was shown in the Olympics in Paris, July 2024, males who have changed into females were permitted to take part in women's sports even to the point of risking the life of their opponent, as we saw in the boxing match between an Algerian 'woman' and her Italian opponent who had to retire because of the threat to her life that was apparent in the first blow she received from her opponent. That cannot be called 'sport' but licensed aggression.

A report to the United Nations reveals that 600 female athletes have lost almost 900 medals across 29 sports to transgender rivals. The study, "Violence against women and girls in sports," as reported by *Toronto Sun* writer Dan Bilicki, was presented by Reem Alsalem, the UN special rapporteur on violence against women and girls. In the report, Alsalem noted that biological men have various physical advantages over women and artificially reducing their testosterone levels does not change that.

> *Alsalem stated that male athletes had specific attributes, including higher strength and testosterone levels, that are advantageous in certain sports and can result in the "loss of fair opportunity" for female competitors. She also argued that treatments to artificially suppress testosterone will not put transgender competitors on equal footing with females and may only harm the athlete taking the treatment… pharmaceutical testosterone suppression for genetically male athletes — irrespective of how they identify — will not eliminate the set of comparative performance advantages they have already acquired."*

In her report, Alsalem urged the UN to provide "stronger protections for women and girls in sports" and believes that an additional open category should be created for sports and that "non-invasive, confidential and simple sex screenings" are necessary to guarantee fairness for women."

6. The revelation of the number of young girls groomed, raped, beaten and terrified by groups of Pakistani men in certain cities in the United Kingdom is a current example of this pathology.

7. See my article about Sadism and Christianity on my original website: https://www.anne-baring.com/anbar59_sadism.html
The appalling details of how a QC called John Smyth, who was an active member of the Evangelical Church in the UK and later Rhodesia, mercilessly 'beat sin' out of over a hundred boys and young men, including his seven-year-old son, until they bled, have recently been brought to light in November 2024 by Kathy Newman on Channel 4 Television. His son Peter has spoken publicly about the effect on him of his father's cruelty, and his distress at learning what he had inflicted on so many other boys and young men whose lives had been deeply affected by what they had suffered. The scandal of the Anglican Church's inability to recognize this appalling behaviour and its failure, over many decades, to intervene to bring it to an end, has led to the resignation of the Archbishop of Canterbury and possibly other bishops and church leaders in November 2024.

8. The story of Raphael and Tobias is in the Book of Tobit in the *Apocrypha*.

Chapter Thirteen: Part One

THE ABUSE OF POWER:
COVID-19 AND THE CRIME AGAINST HUMANITY

*The world is a dangerous place to live, not because of the people who are
evil, but because of the people who don't do anything about it.*
— Albert Einstein

Power corrupts and absolute power corrupts absolutely.
— Lord Acton, 1887

*Do not offend Nature. Do not offend God by tampering with the laws of Nature,
trying to bend them to your destructive purposes. Every act of a human
being must be judged according to the rule: Does it offend Nature?
Does it offend God? Does it injure Life?*

— Messages from a Transcendent Dimension

*The liberties of a people never were, nor ever will be, secure, when
the transactions of their rulers may be concealed from them.*
— Patrick Henry 1787

*Once the herd accepts mandatory forcible vaccination, it's game over! They will
accept anything — forcible blood or organ donation — for the 'greater good.'
Control sheep minds and you control the herd. Vaccine makers stand to make
billions, and many of you in this room today are investors. It's the big win-win!
We thin out the herd and the herd pays us for providing extermination services.*

— Henry Kissinger, in a speech to the WHO
Council on Eugenics, February 25th, 2009

The function of the Feminine is to protect. I have a longing to protect
people and the life of the planet from the shadow aspect of human
nature which develops from a belief that our lives have no transcendent meaning or purpose — a belief that is a direct effect of the ideology of
Scientific Materialism and offers an open invitation to totalitarianism and
transhumanism.

Because my desire is to warn and protect humanity, I have included
two Chapters about the Abuse of Power in my final book. I have done this

because I do not think it is possible to exclude what is happening in the world — The Great Below — from the Transcendent Reality — The Great Above. Because everything in the universe is connected, what is done in this dimension of reality affects the Whole. These two Chapters will bring evidence of a crime committed against the people of this planet, a crime that has been many decades in preparation by a small group of immensely wealthy and powerful men whose intention is to gain control of the planet through reducing the human population, and frightening people into obedience and conformity through the dual threats of pandemics and climate change. Presumably they reason that it is acceptable to kill, injure and sterilize people because it is for the greater good of the planet — a reduced population. But I believe it is not our job to bring this about, because in doing so, we are arrogating to ourselves the role of God and are in danger of becoming so intoxicated with our power that we could ultimately invoke a terrifying nemesis.

In my view, this despicable crime is an assault on the Divinity of all Life on this planet, and that is why I am including it in this book on the Divine Feminine. I am drawing on the testimony of courageous men and women who have followed the guidance of their conscience in exposing this crime and countering the flood of propaganda and lies, saying that the "vaccines" were safe and effective when they were neither. Jung said that no-one stands outside the collective shadow of humanity. Each of us has a role to play in becoming aware of our individual shadow and how we project aspects of it onto others, blaming them for behaviour that we cannot see in ourselves. He said that this tendency unconsciously to project our shadow onto others lies at the root of almost all conflicts. But this does not mean that we should close our eyes to evil and fail to speak up about it when we become aware of it, as indeed, he did.

A Personal Story

This Chapter on the Abuse of Power begins with a personal story, a story of suffering, immense courage, and the determination to survive and overcome. So effective was the censorship during the Covid years, that I doubt whether I would have found out the truth of what was happening in this country and the wider world if my housekeeper who had been with me for twenty-five years had not become ill immediately after the first AstraZeneca vaccination in March 2021. Within half an hour of the injection, she had tingling all over her body, tingling that continued for two years day and night and nearly drove her mad as it was painful as well as frightening and exhausting. Investigating her symptoms in authoritative sources, she found that the tingling and pain she was suffering from were comparable to the symptoms of Guillain-Barré syndrome, a condition where the body's immune system attacks the nerves. It can cause weakness, numbness, and ultimately, paralysis. Weakness and tingling in the hands and feet are usually the first symptoms. Inexplicably, no doctor in our local NHS surgery would offer her an appointment, listen to her description of her symptoms or investigate the connection between them and the vaccine she had received. Her letters to AstraZeneca went unanswered. This was deeply upsetting and confusing for her. Where could she turn to for help?

Driven by her anger arising from the doctors' indifference, she began to research on the Internet whether other people had been injured by the vaccines. She soon uncovered facts that indicated that serious effects from the vaccines were being concealed by the NHS and the government, as well as by the US government. In the UK Parliament, there were only two courageous MPs, Andrew Bridgen and Sir Christopher Chope, who took seriously the many accounts they were hearing from their constituents about vaccine injuries. Only a tiny handful of MPs bothered to attend Parliament when the debates about these injuries were held. Andrew Bridgen was cold-shouldered as a trouble-maker and expelled from the Conservative Party.

Finding a Cure

Searching for a treatment for her symptoms, she found the website of a retired chiropractor, a Dr. Bryan Ardis in the United States, and discovered that he was helping thousands of people with symptoms of injury from the vaccines as well as from Long Covid symptoms caused by the virus. She found out from his website (www.theardisshow.com) and later, his book, *Moving Beyond the Covid-19 Lies*, that through the work of Chinese, French and Italian scientists, he had found that snake venom from the Chinese King Cobra and the Chinese krait snake was the ingredient in the so-called 'virus' that gave rise to the symptoms of COVID — symptoms that were mistakenly diagnosed as a respiratory illness.

Dr Ardis found that a group of French scientists had discovered that venom from the King Cobra and bungarotoxin from the Chinese krait snake were almost identical to the "spike proteins" of SARS-CoV-2 (COVID-19) (p. 97)

> These two venom proteins are known as neurotoxic venom proteins and, as published in this paper, can easily penetrate the blood-brain barrier because of their small size. Once these venom neurotoxins reach our brain and spinal cord, the venom spike proteins bind to specific nerve cell receptors called nicotine receptors found on every cell in the human body. (p. 98)

The diaphragm and spinal column are affected by these two toxic venoms; venom causes paralysis and a slowed heart rate when it reaches the brain stem. These venoms, in all prey, are designed to trigger respiratory arrest and hypoxia, making it difficult for the prey to breath and escape. These were the exact symptoms that people worldwide were complaining about during their battle with COVID.

Snake venom had made its way to their brain and spinal cord, and it suppressed the brain's control of the person's heart and diaphragm. The minor but very real paralysis was enough to cause them to struggle to breathe. And the bodies of humans often developed fever and chills when the venom was introduced. These neurotoxic venoms were mimicking the symptoms of a respiratory virus! The [French] scientists' work to decipher this diabolical weapon is truly amazing.

The primary receptors that the snake venom neurotoxins targeted were ones I had never heard of before: the alpha-7nACHR receptor, or nicotine receptor for short… When snake venom neurotoxins and nicotine confront any cell in the human body, the human body will always gravitate and bind to the nicotine and release the venom proteins. And if the snake venom can't bind to the nicotine receptor, it can't hurt you or cause symptoms! Such a groundbreaking discovery!

Dr Ardis said that this snake venom neurotoxin "spike protein" discovery also answered a second question regarding the success of Ivermectin, whose use against Covid had inexplicably been banned by the FDA (Food and Drug Administration) in hospitals in the United States. In their concluding remarks, the French scientists said that both nicotine and Ivermectin are antidotes to COVID-19 spike proteins because both bind and protect the specific nicotine receptors that the two venom spike proteins target, thus preventing COVID-19 symptoms. When Ivermectin was administered, the nicotine receptors released the venom spike proteins, resulting in improved breathing ability when they latched onto the Ivermectin instead. Concluding their study, the French scientists suggested that although Ivermectin was effective, nicotine agents should be used to treat the symptoms of COVID-19. (p. 99)

Chapter 14 of Dr Ardis' book compares the symptoms of snake venom with the symptoms of Long Covid and shows how they mirror each other. "There are, he says, hundreds of thousands, possibly millions of people still suffering from the symptoms that started during COVID-19 and are now given the name of LONG COVID." He recommended nicotine chewing gum or patches as an antidote to the venom in the virus and the vaccines. His own wife, who had suffered from severe dizziness and tinnitus since she had had the vaccinations, was completely cured of both within a few days of chewing nicotine gum. I have been cured by nicotine patches of the dizziness that was an effect of my two Astra-Zeneca vaccinations in 2021.

After suffering for two years after the AstraZeneca vaccination, my housekeeper cured her symptoms within a week with nicotine chewing gum, together with certain supplements that Dr Ardis recommended. The week during which she undertook to cure herself of her symptoms was difficult and frightening to begin with but she had enough trust in Dr Ardis to persevere and at the end of the week was delighted and amazed to find that her disturbing tingling symptoms, as well as long-standing tinnitus, had completely disappeared and did not return. Ordering his book, *Moving Beyond the COVID-19 Lies* from his website in the US, which was the only place that it was available at the time, she found these words on page 46:

> Never has modern medicine so egregiously misinformed and betrayed the people of the world. Never has humanity been so egregiously betrayed by those we trust to heal and save lives. Never has there been so much disease, harm, and sudden death.

> The COVID-19 pandemic will go down as one of the most ruthless acts of genocide in history. And it doesn't end there. What disturbs me is the fact that medical journals are publishing and will continue to publish the same misleading information that many people around the world have come to believe about COVID-19. [1]

While we do not yet know the full details of the content of the vaccines, what Dr. Ardis discovered should be given consideration because of the discovery that nicotine is a cure for many of the symptoms created by them. If it were not for my housekeeper's illness, her courage, and her determination to find a cure for her symptoms, I and my family would still be trusting the government and taking NHS boosters.

A Window of Opportunity

We are living through a crucially important time — a time when institutions are breaking down and when governments are betraying the people they were elected to govern. There seems to be no end to conflict and war. Over a million young Ukrainian men have died in the war in Ukraine. As of January 15, 2025, Russian combat losses amount to 812,670 troops, according to the General Staff of the Armed Forces of Ukraine. These numbers do not include the number of civilians killed, with their homes and livelihoods destroyed. Helpless people, including thousands of traumatized children, continue to suffer and die in the hell of Gaza and Sudan. Following the cease-fire, thousands are moving back to the North where their homes once were, only to find a wasteland of ruins. A well-planned coup in Syria has driven Assad from power and has revealed his monstrous crime of ordering the torture, murder, and mass burial of hundreds of thousands of his fellow Syrians.

For millennia, in every civilization, there have been crimes against the people. In this book, I have detailed some of them and have shown that at the root of each was an addiction to power. There were crimes committed by rulers over the people they ruled or the people they conquered; unspeakable crimes committed by religions; crimes of war when one group slaughtered another with or without cause; crimes of men against women in the unfor-givable assault of rape. But there has never until now been a crime against humanity itself — the root cause of which is the same addiction to power or abuse of power. This is the unrecognized shadow aspect of our civilization that Jung, among others, drew attention to many decades ago. But the shadow he observed in his lifetime has now grown to gigantic proportions.

The Influence of Scientific Materialism

For the origin of the abuse of power in our time, we need look no further than the belief with which we have been indoctrinated for several generations by the ideology of Scientific Materialism, now called Physicalism: We live in a lifeless universe that is without consciousness, intelligence, purpose or meaning. The spiritual world does not exist; only the material world is real and technocratic man is master of the material world. These beliefs are lead-ing to Transhumanism and the delightful prospect of an "improved species" envisaged by Ray Kurtzweil. [2]

I remember the wise words of the artist, Cecil Collins who, teaching at the Central School of Art in London, saw the growing decadence of modern society:

> Our civilization is the only one in the whole history of mankind, not to be based upon a metaphysical reality, that is, a reality which transcends biological man and that of the vested interests of the ego; a metaphysical reality which is unknowable, absolute, and yet a reality which can have a relationship with us, and we with it. [3]

Long indoctrination by the beliefs of materialist science have encouraged governments, immensely wealthy individuals, giant corporations, pharma-ceutical companies, and international organizations like the WEF to treat the Earth and our human lives as subject to their plans and directives. They are acting as if they have the right to rule and direct the planet. None of them appears to acknowledge the existence of a transcendent authority. They exhibit the classic symptoms of inflation — called *hubris* by the great Greek play-wrights. Out of this pathology have come geo-engineering (attempts to alter the planet's climate) and chemtrails or chemicals distributed by airplanes that veil blue skies with streaks of cloudy vapour that release harmful elements, such as aluminium. These interfere with the earth's atmosphere, pollute and degrade the soil, and infiltrate our bodies and our food. Then there is the genetic engineering of crops advocated by Bill Gates, who has bought up huge tracts of land in America; agri-business, dangerous pesticides (Monsanto and Bayer) and the many chemicals added to our ultra-processed food; the prospect of synthetic food, again promoted by Bill Gates; the dangerous radiation emitted by 5G masts, that interferes with the electro-magnetic fields of our bodies and suppresses the immune system. Even cows cannot be left in peace to belch or fart but are to be given injections to reduce the methane they emit.

All these activities trigger effects that may harm us and the life of the planet. People are right not to trust the reassurances of governments and their agencies because we do not know enough about the effects of all this interference with the environment which sustains our lives. Just because technology has given us the power to do these things does not mean that we need to accept governments doing them. The problem we face is how to prevent them doing so.

In another category of harm there is the ongoing manufacture of ever more powerful weapons of mass destruction by China, Russia, Iran, North Korea and America. The Doomsday Clock, symbolising how near humanity is to destruction, has been moved (29/1/25) one second forward to 89 seconds to midnight — the closest it has ever been. But there are other kinds of weapon that are of concern, including the unspeakable evil of the bio-weapons currently being created in hundreds of gain-of-function laboratories in many different countries, including the US and China, with many of them situated in Ukraine.

The Deaths and Injuries caused by the "Vaccines"

Included in this list are the so-called mRNA "vaccines" which, as this Chapter and the next will show, are not vaccines but bio-weapons, designed to kill, injure, and sterilize millions of people so that the end-result is a much smaller population that can be manipulated and digitally controlled by a group of immensely powerful "managers." Each of these could be described as an example of totalitarian behaviour: clandestine and covert courses of action which affect millions of people, without any consultation or warning.

The Data Analyst Edward Dowd in an exhaustive interview with Bret Weinstein, (https://www.youtube.com/watch?v=Trjv7-eUqt4 November, 2024) concluded that fifteen million people have died suddenly or unexpectedly from the effects of the Covid mRNA vaccines. These figures tally with the seventeen million estimated to have died from the vaccinations by Denis Rancourt, former professor of physics at the University of Ottawa.

Looking at the next category — Disabilities — Dowd continued: "Disabilities, when you look at the ratio of four to one, you multiply the 7 million and the 15 million times four, you get a range of 29 to 60 million disabled globally.

"And then the third category — Injuries — if you take 18% of the vaccinated, just using the Pfizer [trial data], we get a range of at the high end, 900 million, 500 million at the low end injured. 500 million to 900 million who have had an injury that has not disabled them."

Turning to the UK, Dowd produced shocking data showing that excess child deaths are still surging higher, long after the Covid mRNA vaccines were first released almost four years ago. He made the discovery while ana-lysing the official data from the UK government's Office for National Statis-tics (ONS). Dowd's data shows that excess deaths for children aged one to fourteen have surged higher each year since the Covid mRNA vaccines were rolled out in 2021. According to Dowd, excess deaths for children aged one to fourteen spiked by a staggering 22% in 2023 — the last full year of data.

While these deaths were identified in UK data, he said the trend is most likely reflected in other nations with a similar mass vaccination protocol, including the United States, Canada, Australia, and much of Europe. Although the data for 2024 are not yet complete, Dowd reveals that, so far, the official figures show that the surging death trend has continued through this year.

Bret Weinstein ended the interview with the words, "Although it is painful to face these facts, people need to make sure that this never happens again. [4]

If anyone reading this list dismisses it as 'conspiracy theory,' I would draw attention to the use of this term as an example of weaponized language, designed to shut down discussion and debate about important, even criminal activities which affect all of us. The term was introduced by the CIA in the 1960's in the context of trying to stifle dissenting opinions over the assassi-nation of President Kennedy. (https://archive.org/details/CIADOC1035960) It is another example of the so-called 'cancelling' or "woke" culture that, with co-ordinated government cooperation, has taken over social media, the universities, and transgender ideology. I feel that the abuse of power exhibited in each of these is a direct assault on the Feminine, on the Earth, on our bodies and, above all, on our souls. They are manifestations of a corrupt and power-hungry patriarchy.

The Fight with the Dragon – Lambsprinck

NATO as Puppet-Master?

Before he retired in 1961, President Eisenhower warned us about the Military/ Industrial Complex in the United States. In November 2024, that warning has been justified in the revelation that NATO or the military arm of governments has been the Puppet-master manipulating the whole Covid scene from behind the stage as it were. It is as if a dam of concealed information has burst and we are at last able to access some of the truth that was denied us during the Covid years. The revelation by a whistleblower who downloaded 10gb of unredacted pages of the minutes of meetings held in the prestigious Robert Koch Institute in Berlin during the Covid years, proves that the response to the 'pandemic' was not about science and looking after the health of the people, but about testing people's obedience to government orders—ultimately NATO's orders. An address by journalist Aya Velasquez and Professor Dr. Stefan Homburg, of Leibnitz University, in Hanover, Germany on the 23rd July 2024, revealed the facts and discussions disclosed in the unredacted pages. A more cynical and disgraceful example of an attempt at totalitarian control could not be found.

Then, on the 9th of November 2024, the Dutch Minister of Health, Fleur Agema, announced in the Dutch Parliament that the pandemic was a military operation. The Netherlands was taking orders from NATO and from the NCTV (Netherlands National Coordinator for Security and Counter-terrorism and Defence). Dutch pandemic policy was formulated under the direction of the NCTV and was complying with NATO instructions. The Health Ministry had to comply with orders from the NCTV. Presumably, every other government that was part of NATO, had also to comply. But who was directing NATO?

Shortly afterwards, Robert F. Kennedy Jr. made the disclosure (November 15th, 2024) that NATO was behind the Covid Plan to depopulate the planet and that the so-called mRNA "vaccines" were created and fabricated in an army laboratory, then distributed through Pfizer and Moderna. He has provided extensive and explicit documentation on the origins of the Covid virus and the bio-weapons arms race in his recent book *The Wuhan Cover-Up*. [5] The virus did not come from a bat or a pangolin in a wet market. It was deliberately created in a laboratory, as will be revealed later in this chapter.

The Psychology of Totalitarianism

If we want to understand how easily we can be controlled and manipulated by our governments, and by international organizations like the United Nations (UN), the World Economic Forum (WEF) and the World Health Organization (WHO) and acquiesce willingly in this controlling, one book: *The Psychology of Totalitarianism* by Mattias Desmet, a Belgian Professor of Clinical Psychology, explains what happens when we are driven by deliberately engineered fear and propaganda into a state of collective hypnosis, or what he calls "mass formation", where we unthinkingly obey or are compelled to obey what we are instructed to do by governments and the international organizations controlling them. Loneliness, the meaningless of many of our lives, the tedium of our jobs together with inadequate education, the need rapidly to adapt to social media and the digitisation of our methods of communication, together with centuries of programming to obey and trust authority, whether of church or state, can drive us to fall into a state of mind where we unthinkingly trust the propaganda that conditions us to accept the controls imposed on us. Desmet writes:

> Whenever a new object of fear arises in society, there is only one response and one defense in our current way of thinking: increased control. The fact that the

human being can tolerate only a certain amount of control is completely over-looked. Coercive control leads to fear and fear leads to more coercive control… Society falls victim to a vicious circle that inevitably leads to totalitarianism, which means to extreme government control, eventually resulting in the radical destruction of both the psychological and physical integrity of human beings. [6]

He quotes Hannah Arendt in her book *The Origins of Totalitarianism*, where she says:

Totalitarianism is ultimately the logical extension of a generalized obsession with science, the belief in an artificially created paradise: Science [has become] an idol that will magically cure the evils of existence and transform the nature of man. [7]

And one final quote from her essay *Truth and Politics* (1967)

The result of a consistent and total substitution of lies for factual truth is not that the lie will now be accepted as truth and truth be defamed as a lie, but that the sense by which we take our bearings in the real world — and the category of truth versus falsehood is among the mental means to this end — is being destroyed.

Mass formation, as Desmet calls it, results when an ideology takes hold and spreads through the mass of the people, as happened — to give only a few examples that I am familiar with — the Crusades, the Inquisition and the witch-burnings of the fifteenth to seventeenth centuries, the French Revolution, Communism under Stalin and Mao, and Fascism under Hitler.

As the centuries go by, larger and more durable patterns emerge… With the coronavirus crisis, we have, for the first time in history, reached a point where the entire world population is in the grip of a mass formation over a prolonged period of time. [8]

Fear was the driver of the most recent example of mass formation — the Covid 'Pandemic.' Fear, Desmet says, is more dangerous than the virus. Since autumn 2020, the world population was manipulated into conformity and obedience by fear — fear that was deliberately generated and promoted by governments, the WHO (World Health Organization), and the government-censored media, as well as by individuals and groups espousing whatever served their interests. An exaggerated estimate by epidemiologist Neil Ferguson at Imperial College, London, of the number likely to die from the virus, prompted governments to impose Lockdown. No public debate was allowed on any number of important issues, among them, the safety of the vaccines, the unprecedented and dangerous speed with which they were created, and the draconian measures (Lockdown, masks, and PCR tests) that were imposed to contain the virus.

It has been acknowledged in the publication on December 2nd, 2024, of the Congressional Report of the Select Subcommittee on the Coronavirus Pandemic, that Lockdown has had catastrophic effects, particularly on the lives and mental health of children and adolescents. A two-year investigation into lessons learned from the Covid pandemic, concluded that everything done was based on false premises, with no scientific evidence supporting masking, social distancing, or lockdowns. In the US, lockdowns generated devastating effects, particularly on young people, with a 51% increase in suicides among American girls aged 12-17. In the UK the lives of a million young people under 25 are on hold, waiting for mental health support that they are unlikely to get.

The devastating lockdowns were a political weapon designed to instil fear and obedience, whose effects have been described by Naomi Wolf in her book *The Bodies of Others.* [9] Only the Swedish government had the intelligence and common sense not to be driven into taking panic measures that resulted in masks and lockdowns. It had the freedom to act in this way because it was not yet part of NATO, having only joined it in March 7th, 2024.

In our heavily censored culture (2020-2024) where no public debate was allowed on such crucially important issues as the impact of the lockdowns, the use of masks, the PCR nasal swab testing for evidence of Covid, the too-rapid roll-out of the so-called "vaccines" and the excessive control exercised by governments, the voices which dared to challenge the need for this control were censored, attacked, and silenced. Hannah Arendt describes in detail exactly how totalitarianism can be imposed, step by step.

Further Examples of Totalitarian Control

America has emerged from the Covid years as a country exhibiting totalitarian behaviour, silencing all dissent. Its control and censorship of the media during the pandemic was absolute. To some doctors' bewilderment in hospitals there, drugs of proven value like Ivermectin and Hydroxychloroquine were banned by the FDA (Food and Drug Administration) and the drug Remdesivir ordered to be used instead as part of hospital protocol. Remdesivir killed thousands who died in hospitals of kidney failure — one of the known effects of this drug — although Covid was put down as the cause of their death. In 2020 in the United Kingdom, people in care homes were given two drugs, Midazolam and Morphine, at the same time and in unprecedented quantities on the orders of the Health Secretary Matt Hancock, which led to the deaths of thousands, who again had Covid wrongly put down as the cause of their death. Because of these methods of censorship and control, millions worldwide died unnecessarily, from the virus, from the drugs administered to them in hospitals and care homes, and from the effects of the bio-weapons concealed in the so-called vaccines. For three years, the fear generated by governments and the censored media was focussed on responding to the 'pandemic.' Now, the truth is slowly coming out, like pus oozing from a gangrenous wound.

Those individuals, including distinguished scientists and members of the medical profession in different countries, who courageously spoke out against this indoctrination and control were silenced, even losing their right to practice. These include Dr Peter McCullough, Dr Aseem Malhotra, Dr Paul Marik, Dr Pierre Kory, Prof Didier Rouault, the late Dr Vladimir Zelenko, Dr Simone Gold and Dr Mary Talley Bowden. Fortunately, their voices and warnings have been heard and are still being heard, as what was hidden emerges into the public eye and what was presented as 'truth' is seen to have been lies. Demonizing those who challenge the *status quo* is a control mechanism repeatedly employed in the past, as I hope I have shown in earlier chapters.

We need to pay the utmost attention to the danger of being drawn into another state of mass hypnosis generated by fear, media propaganda and government methods of control, lest we find ourselves in a future situation from which there is no escape. Specifically, we need to beware of a future attempt by governments to control the population by digital means, for instance through vaccine passports and central bank digital currencies (CBDC), as well as by the WHO generating fear once again through announcements of new pandemics, such as Bird-Flu (which will have been deliberately created in a laboratory), or even an invasion by aliens. On the 8/1/25, there were huge headlines in the Daily Telegraph Features Section: Is HMPV (a new wave of respiratory illness in China) the New Covid? In this way we are programmed by the media to expect and fear a new pandemic.

Mis-placed Trust

We have implicitly trusted governments and the medical profession because it is instinctive to look for protection from people who are more powerful than we are. We have been encouraged to trust science and scientists and to look up to them as impartial experts because they seem to know more than we do. We live at a pivotal time when we need to wake up; when we need to become capable of recognizing, challenging, and exposing evil, as courageous doctors and scientists have recently done. We need to stop believing what we are told by our governments and the censored media. The so-called pandemic has revealed the abuse of power in the criminal, even psychopathic behaviour of certain pharmaceutical companies, and their financial collusion with governments, international organizations, the medical profession and the media. But beyond these, there are institutions and individuals controlling all of these with enormous sums of money.

Recently published books, videos and films as well as webinars by distinguished scientists and doctors, have disclosed the presence of malpractice in institutions that we, in our ignorance, have trusted. Life is fragile and the fragility we feel can lead us blindly to look for support — from religions, from governments, from science and from medicine. Evil is largely fuelled by greed: greed for power above all, followed by greed for wealth; even greed for absolute control of the planet and all our lives. The saying "Follow the money" has a lot of truth in it. But another saying might be: "Follow the desire for power."

Pharmaceutical companies originally came into being to relieve suffering. Governments ostensibly exist to serve the people. Doctors take the Hippocratic Oath "First Do No Harm" when they qualify. All three have become so deeply enmeshed with the criminal mRNA vaccination programme that they have betrayed their mission and their role. In the UK, it is now known that Imperial College, The Royal College of Physicians accepted large sums of money from the Pharmaceutical Companies. The MHRA (Medicines and Healthcare Products Regulatory Agency) did the same, drawing 75% of its funding from the same companies — companies that it was supposed to regulate. The MHRA insisted on Lockdown which has had such devastating effects on young people and children as well as ruining thousands of small businesses. This bribery of offices of State by the Pharmaceutical Companies occurred in the US in the NIAID (National Institute of Allergy and Infectious Diseases) and the FDA (Food and Drug Administration).

Many doctors in the NHS have followed government orders and have not had the time or the desire to investigate the nature of the vaccines they have been instructed to inject into the arms of the people of this country. They received a payment for every person they injected. They ignored the Nuremberg Code (1949) of 'informed consent' which was designed to protect us from crimes like those of the Nazi Regime. [see end notes for the first article of the Nuremberg Code]. But, in mitigation of their behaviour, if they had not followed NHS orders, they would have lost their jobs and their livelihoods.

The recent public Covid Inquiry in the UK has barely addressed (January 2025) the injuries caused by the mRNA "vaccines" and, specifically, the lethal effects of the spike protein they carry as clearly explained by Dr Bret Weinstein in many online interviews. Censorship has prevailed here as elsewhere, with the government-controlled media giving out only what it was permitted to. By the fourth of November 2024, 489,991 people have reported an adverse reaction to the vaccines. (speech to UK Parliament 21/01/25 by MP Rupert Lowe). The Covid Inquiry has heard that 17,500 people have applied for compensation for injuries from the vaccines (18/1/25), most of these from the AstraZeneca vaccine. Injured people have told the Inquiry that the process for obtaining payment for severe injuries was inadequate and inefficient, with the amounts paid out insufficient and the injured having to wait years for a decision. The vaccine damage payment scheme offers a one-off sum of £120,000 but only to people who have such serious adverse reactions to the vaccines that they are at least 60% disabled.

Many people affected by vaccine injuries have told the Inquiry they did not get the help and financial support they deserved. All this is heart-breaking to hear and an absolute disgrace coming from a government that forced these vaccines on us and gave indemnity to the vaccine producers. We still do not know the long-term effects of the vaccines on the health of the people who were injected with them. This reminds me of the Thalidomide catastrophe of 1959 when tens of thousands of children (in the US and Europe) either died or were born appallingly crippled by the pills their mothers took to avoid nausea when pregnant. Like the vaccines, Thalidomide was declared to be "safe and effective." It was withdrawn in 1961 but in the UK reparation for the calamitous injuries it had caused took decades.

The whole issue of excess deaths and injuries caused by the mRNA vaccines since the roll-out of the vaccinations has been hidden and obfuscated, as the analyses of Dr John Campbell, Edward Dowd and Denis Rancourt have shown. Now NATO has been exposed as the power manipulating the so-called pandemic and the response to it from behind the scenes, even apparently being responsible for manufacturing the vaccines.

'Conspiracy Theories' and 'Anti-Vaxxers'

There are millions of people who implicitly trust what they have been told. They feel deeply threatened by so-called 'anti-vaxxers' and 'conspiracy theorists' and will attack them on social media by any means available — even to the point of issuing death threats against them. It is understandable that they would find it inconceivable that government, science, and medicine would betray and harm them. Self-preservation is perhaps the most ancient instinct in the human species. In a dangerous situation, anyone who does not agree with us threatens our sense of security. Instinctively, we try to silence or eliminate them. Governments try to silence anyone who challenges their policies. This creates a schizoid situation in society where no-one can trust his neighbour or those in authority. Corruption at the top seeps down into every level of society.

The Paralyzing Power of Fear

From 2020, the constant barrage of propaganda issuing daily on television from the government-censored media, urging us to have the vaccine, to stay at home and avoid contact with others, gave rise to an acute state of fear: fear of the virus; fear that if we did not comply with a series of draconian government orders to lock down, to wear masks, to acquire vaccine passports for showing when travelling or entering a restaurant, we could be arrested and charged with the crime of not obeying government orders, fined and even imprisoned. Vaccinations were given to children and even babies (May 2023) when there was no need for either. They were also given to pregnant women who were told they were safe when they were not, as extensively documented by Naomi Wolf in her book *Facing the Beast, Courage, Faith and Resistance in a New Dark Age*.[10] Fear, more than any other factor, can undermine the balance and strength of the immune system.

The media was used by governments to stir up fear of a killer virus that we could only be protected from by vaccinations that were created and man-ufactured in criminal haste. In the climate of fear engendered by the media, those pharmaceutical companies who rushed to create the vaccines and those in government who helped to facilitate their rapid distribution among the population were hailed as heroes. Anyone who challenged this precipitous descent into mass conformity, was censored, demonized, and banished from civil society.

One example of this is the fate of a distinguished international lawyer, Dr. Reiner Fuellmich, who has been wrongly imprisoned in solitary confinement in Germany since 2022, the victim of accusations brought against him by a colleague whom he trusted and with whom he appeared on videos. His 'mistake' was to reveal too much about the harm the vaccines were causing. A trap was set for taking him into custody and he fell into it, not anticipating such an event.

Experienced and respected physicians in the US, the UK, and Europe who spoke out, urging caution and querying the dangerous speed with which the 'vaccines' had been created, lost their right to practice. For example, Prof Jay Bhattacharya of Stanford was attacked by the CDC (Centers for Disease Control and Prevention) and NIH (National Institutes of Health) as a 'fringe epidemiologist' when, with Prof Martin Kulldorff of Harvard and Prof Sunesh Gupta, he created the Great Barrington Declaration, calling for focussed protection and signed by tens of thousands of scientists and physicians. In a signal development, Dr Bhattacharya has been nominated Director of the NIH by the incoming Trump administration. In this way, not realizing what was happening, billions of people were manipulated through the fear generated by their governments and the media into the state of mass conformity or mass hypnosis described by Mattias Desmet.

The Shocking Revelation of the Vaccine Injuries

However, the revelation of the harm done by the Pfizer vaccine was disclosed in the US in January 2022 when a federal judge in Texas ordered the FDA (Food and Drug Administration) to make public the data it relied on to license Pfizer's vaccine and to reveal the details of its clinical trials. Pfizer said it did not want to release these details for 75 years but the Court forced them to begin to release them immediately. The result was a month-by-month revelation of the serious, even lethal injuries the vaccines had inflicted during the trials, including injuries to pregnant women who lost their babies. Full details of this data are given in Naomi Wolf's recent book, *The Pfizer Papers*.[11] The book shows that Pfizer's mRNA COVID-19 vaccine clinical trial was deeply flawed and that the pharmaceutical company knew by November 2020 that its vaccine was neither safe nor effective. On December 6th, 2024, the FDA was ordered by judge Mark Pitman to produce one million additional pages from Pfizer's dossier by June 30th, 2025. The case was litigated by Aaron Siri of ICAN (Informed Consent Action Network). Judge Pittman ended his order to the FDA by quoting Patrick Henry during the Constitutional Convention of 1787: "The liberties of a people never were, nor ever will be, secure, when the transactions of their rulers may be concealed from them."

In July 2024, when the NHS (National Health Service) in the UK was still promoting the vaccinations and boosters, a Petition was initiated in the UK by a group of concerned doctors, saying that the mRNA injections must be stopped immediately. In the same month, July 2024, hundreds of doctors and scientists from around the world signed an Accord calling for the suspension and investigation of mRNA vaccines, due to serious concerns about their safety and efficacy. *Governments ignored both the Accord and the Petition.* Their health services have continued to promote and distribute these vaccines to a trusting population.

The Power of Survival Instincts

There is nothing more powerful than survival instincts. When a threat to our survival is presented to us, we respond blindly, instinctively, to what we are being told because we are programmed to trust authority and conditioned to fear-induced conformity, so that we can offer no challenge or resistance to orders we are instructed to obey. We have seen how the propagation of fear and guilt by the media and governments is the perfect tool to enforce conformity, acquiescence, and obedience. "Don't kill Granny," we were told. The result was that 'Granny' died from the loneliness and grief of her family being forbidden to see her or from the midazolam and morphine she was given in UK care homes.

The Confrontation with Evil and the Fight with the Dragon

Evil has its origin in the immense power of these largely unconscious survival instincts: fear of attack; fear of being subjected to another's power, fear of being the victim of things we cannot control, fear of viruses, fear of the unknown — above all, fear of death. In response to these fears, which may be deliberately generated by governments and International Organizations like the UN, the WEF and the WHO, we take steps to protect ourselves, to arm ourselves with ever more terrible weapons, to anticipate danger and prepare for defence against future attack, whether by enemies, viruses, or climate change. The antidote to fear is to increase our awareness of how we are being manipulated and controlled and free ourselves from the lethal power of fear.

In the imagery of Alchemy and Myth, these powerful unconscious survival instincts have been named the 'Dragon.' The dragon is an appropriate name to represent our primordial instincts — instincts that originate in our reptilian brain system. From the story of Jason and the Golden Fleece to the Gnostic Hymn of the Pearl, to the Great Work of Alchemy, the hero's task is to fight and overcome the dragon or to lull it to sleep and seize the treasure — golden fleece, precious pearl, or gold — from it. The treasure guarded by the dragon then becomes available to the hero. The treasure is an enhanced or higher level of consciousness that enables us to resist the overwhelming power of an instinct such as fear. Enhanced insight into the truth of a given situation where evil masquerades as good and the Lie has replaced Truth is one of the rewards of freeing oneself from the power of the dragon, or the paralyzing power of fear.[12]

What is being divulged by the events described in this chapter is that our human species is threatened by the Plan of a small coterie of very powerful men who aim to take control of the planet by reducing our numbers and

Geryon, the 'tamed' Dragon, from Dante's Inferno — Gustav Doré

minutely directing and controlling our lives, using climate change and the threat of ongoing pandemics announced by the WHO as the driver of the necessity for this control. There now exists so much evidence for the existence of the Plan that it cannot be dismissed as a conspiracy theory. One aspect of the Plan which concerns the origins of the virus and the vaccines is explored in this Chapter. The wider Plan will be discussed in Part Two of this Chapter.

The Plan

Now I can turn to the Plan to depopulate the planet as described by Dr David Martin in his Presentation to the EU Parliament during the International Covid Summit that took place there on 3rd May, 2023.[13] At this Summit, more than 30 international experts and EU Parliamentarians testified, exposing different aspects of the Covid pandemic.

Dr Martin began his 20-minute address, illustrated with slides, by telling his audience that ten years ago, he had sat in the very chair he was sitting in today. He warned the world then of what was coming. The discussion then was on whether Europe should adopt the United States policy of allowing patents on biologically derived materials. At that time, he told the European Parliament and people round the world that the weaponization of nature against humanity had dire consequences. Tragically, he had now, ten years later, to say, "I told you so." He paid tribute to his wife Kim Martin who, he said, had urged him to disclose to a wider audience, the information he had been sharing with small groups.

He told his audience that the Plan to depopulate the planet was formulated as long ago as 1913-1914, although it was not developed until 1965.

> Coronavirus was identified in 1965 as one of the first infectious, replicable viral models that could be used to modify a series of other experiences of the human condition… It was immediately identified as a pathogen that could be used and modified for a whole host of reasons… In 1966 the very first COV coronavirus model was used as a transatlantic biological experiment in human manipulation in a data-sharing experiment between the United States and the United Kingdom. And in 1967, the year I was born, we did the first human trials on inoculating people with modified coronavirus.

"Where were we," he asked, "when we allowed a violation of biological and chemical weapons treaties? Where were we as a human civilization when we thought it was an acceptable thing to do to take a pathogen for the United States and infect the world with it? Where was that conversation?"

Dr Martin went on to explain that the very first spike protein vaccine for Coronavirus was created by Pfizer in 1990. But it was found that there was a problem with these vaccines because Coronavirus modifies and mutates too quickly for vaccines to be effective. From 1990 to 2018, thousands of publications confirmed that coronavirus vaccines did not work.

However, in 2002, he said, there was an interesting development. In that year, the University of North Carolina Chapel Hill patented "an infectious replication defective clone of coronavirus. 'Infectious replication defective' means a weapon. It means something meant to target an individual but not have collateral damage to other individuals. That is what infectious replication defective means."

> And that patent was filed in 2002 on work funded by NIAD's (National Institute of Allergy and Infectious Diseases) Anthony Fauci from 1999 to 2002. And that work, patented at the University of North Carolina Chapel Hill, mysteriously preceded SARS 1.0 by a year. SARS is the research developed by humans weaponizing a life system model to attack human beings, and they patented it in 2002. I'm telling you the facts. We [the US] engineered Sars… Sars is the research

developed by humans weaponizing a life system model to attack human beings. And they patented it in 2002.

And in 2003 — giant surprise — the CDC (Centres for Disease Control and Prevention) filed the patent on Coronavirus isolated from humans, in violation once again, of biological and chemical weapons, treaties, and laws that we have in the United States, and I'm very, very precise on this. When the CDC, in April of 2003 filed the patent on SARS Coronavirus, what did they do? They downloaded a sequence from China, and filed a patent on it in the United States. Any of you who is familiar with biological and chemical weapons treaties knows that is a violation. That is a crime. The United States Patent Office went as far as to reject that patent application on two occasions *until the CDC decided to bribe the Patent Office to override the patent examiner to ultimately issue the patent in 2007 on SARS Coronavirus.* [my italics]

It turns out that the RT-PCR, which was the test that we allegedly were going to use to identify the risks associated with coronavirus, was identified as a bio-terrorism threat by me in the European Union sponsored events in 2002 and 2003, twenty years ago. Here in Brussels and across Europe. In 2005, this particular pathogen was specifically labelled as a bio-terrorism and bio-weapon platform technology. In 2005, it was actually described as a bio-weapons platform technology. And from 2005 onwards, its official classification was a bio-warfare enabling agent—that's official classification from 2005 onwards.

Biological warfare enabling technology—that does not feel like public health. That does not feel like medicine. That feels like a weapon, designed to take out humanity. *That is what it feels like, and it feels like that because that's exactly what it is.*

There was supposed to be a moratorium on gain-of-function research. Conveniently, in the fall of 2014, the University of North Carolina, Chapel Hill received a letter from NIAD saying that while the gain of function moratorium on coronavirus in vivo should be suspended, because their grants had already been funded, they received an exemption. Did you hear what I just said? A biological weapons lab facility at the University of North Carolina Chapel Hill received an exemption from the gain-of-function moratorium so that by 2016 we could publish the journal article that said SARS coronavirus is poised for human emergence. And what was the coronavirus poised for human emergence? It was WIV-1. Wuhan Institute of Virology Virus One. Poised for human emergence in 2016 at the proceedings of the National Academy of Sciences. [see Robert F. Kennedy Jr. — *The Wuhan Cover-up and the Terrifying Bio-weapons Arms Race*, which covers the planning and unfolding of this crime in minute detail, naming those involved].

Such that by the time we get to 2017 or 2018, the following phrase entered into common parlance among the community, "There is going to be an accidental or intentional release of a respiratory pathogen." And lo and behold, we got SARS Cov-2. 'Accidental or intentional release of a respiratory pathogen' was the terminology used.

And four times in April of 2019, four patent applications of Moderna were modified to include the term "accidental or intentional release of a respiratory pathogen" as the justification for making a vaccine for a thing that did not exist.

If you have not done so, please make sure that you make reference in every investigation to the premeditated nature of this, because it was in September of 2019 that the world was informed that we were going to have an accidental or intentional release of a respiratory pathogen, so that by September 2020 there would be a worldwide acceptance of a universal vaccine template. *The intent was to get the world to accept a universal vaccine template, and the intent was to use coronavirus to get there.* [my italics]

Reading aloud the words shown in a slide on the screen (from Dr Peter Daszak of the Eco-Health Alliance), he said, "Until an infectious disease crisis is very real, present and at the emergency threshold, it is often largely ignored. To sustain the funding base beyond the crisis, we need to increase the public understanding for the need for medical countermeasures (MCM's), such as a pan-influenza or pan-coronavirus vaccine. *A key driver is the media and the economics will follow the hype. We need to use that hype to our advantage to get to the real issues. Investors will respond if they see profit at the end of the process.*" [my italics]

Sounds like Public health? Sounds like the best of humanity? No, Ladies and gentlemen, this was premeditated domestic terrorism stated at the proceedings of the National Academy of Sciences in 2015, published in front of them. This is an act of biological and chemical warfare perpetrated on the human race, and it was admitted to, in writing, that this was a financial heist and a financial fraud:

"Investors will follow if they see profit at the end of the process."
Let me conclude by making five very brief recommendations:

Nature was hijacked. This whole story started in 1965 when we decided to hijack a natural model and decided to start manipulating it. Science was hijacked *when the only questions that could be asked were questions authorized under the patent protection of the CDC, the FDA, the NIH, and their equivalent organizations around the world. We didn't have independent science. We had hi-jacked science.*

And unfortunately, there was no moral oversight, in violation of all the codes that we stand for. There was no independent, financially disinterested review board ever empanelled around Coronavirus. Not once, not once, not since 1965. We do not have a single independent IRB ever empanelled, around Coronavirus. So, morality was suspended for medical countermeasures, and ultimately humanity was lost because we decided to allow it to happen.

Our job today is to say: no more gain-of-function research. No more weaponization of nature. And most importantly, no more corporate patronage of science for their own self-interest unless they assume 100% product liability for every injury and every death that they cause.

It is clear from Dr Martin's Presentation that the aim of both the virus and the mRNA vaccinations was to depopulate the planet. The virus was deliberately engineered. The results of this 'Plan' are now emerging. In many countries, people are suing governments for the injuries and deaths they and their family members have sustained from the so-called mRNA vaccinations. Unsurprisingly, the pharmaceutical companies were given immunity from prosecution (this has been the case in the US since 1986), so the compensation for injuries or deaths sustained rests solely with governments and is minimal, the least amount they can get away with. It is not easy to recognize that we have become the unwitting victims of evil that arose from the temptation of power, wealth, and the total control over populations exercised by a few individuals in positions of immense, unchallenged power. Dr Martin's two presentations to the EU Parliament as well as his many videos have fortunately been seen by millions of people world-wide. These have been warned of the dangers of the so-called vaccines and the duplicity of their governments. In a second talk to the EU Parliament in September 2023, he called for the dissolution of the WHO, calling it a criminal cartel since its inception in 1947.

> We did not have a pandemic. We had a genocide.… "Until we treat this as a criminal conspiracy of criminal racketeers resulting in global terrorism for the purpose of profiteering and murder, until we have that conversation we're having the wrong conversation, because we are not here to debate the merits of a modified agreement for a criminal racketeering organization. We are here to end the criminal organization itself. This is my call to every single person on this planet: don't just limit the power of the WHO. Destroy the WHO.

The mRNA Vaccination Injuries

The cardiologist Dr Peter McCullough was a speaker at the same meeting of the EU Parliament, hosted by five members of that Parliament in September 2023 and organized by MEP Christine Anderson. The Hearing was called to discuss the terms of the new WHO Pandemic Treaty. Dr McCullough gave evidence of the enormous amount of harm caused by the Covid "vaccines" and warned his audience not to be taken in by the narrative that it was the Covid virus rather than the vaccines that was causing a wave of serious illnesses. He advised his audience not to take any more vaccines or future boosters.

"At the outset of the pandemic, there was an investigation by the WHO on the origins of SARScov 2. That's when the beginning of the cover-up began. We knew at that time that Anthony Fauci, Francis Collins, Jeremy Farrar who was at the Wellcome Trust and who is now the chief scientist at the WHO, Kristian Andersen at Scripps, Eddie Holmes in Sydney, Peter Daszak at Eco-

Health Alliance… they all conspired in January of 2020 to cover up what they knew: that the virus was engineered in a joint US-Chinese collaboration in the lab in Wuhan, China. And they deceived the world with 12 subsequent fraudulent papers in the peer-reviewed literature."

"The vaccines have ravaged the populations of the world. Worldwide, two-thirds of people took a vaccine. The mRNA vaccine is the code for the potentially lethal spike protein part of the virus. It was the worst idea ever to install the genetic code by injection and allow the unbridled production of a potentially lethal protein in the human body for an uncontrolled duration of time. Everything we have learned about the vaccines since they came out is horrifying. The spike protein is proven in 3,400 peer-reviewed manuscripts to cause four major domains of disease:

> One is cardiovascular disease, heart inflammation or myocarditis… The cardiovascular domain of damage in the human body from the vaccine is substantially more than anything we've ever seen with cholesterol, high blood pressure or diabetes…. We've seen cardiac arrests two years after these shots.
>
> The second major domain is neurological disease. Strokes. Strokes, both ischemic and haemorrhagic, Guillain-Barré Syndrome, ascending paralysis that can lead to death and which has led to death with messenger RNA vaccines, small fibre neuropathy, numbness and tingling, ringing in the ears and headaches. These are common.
>
> The third major domain is blood clots… blood clots like we've never seen before… The spike protein is the most thrombogenic protein we've ever seen in human medicine… The spike protein causes blood clots.
>
> The fourth and last domain is immunologic abnormalities. Vaccine-induced thrombotic thrombocytopenia and muscle system inflammatory disorder are early acute syndromes.
>
> *73.9 % of the deaths after vaccination are due to the vaccine… when it is suspected Myocarditis it is 100% due to the vaccine, not Covid respiratory illness — the vaccine.*

The first false narrative was 'The virus is unassailable. We have to stay in lockdown and be fearful.' The second false narrative is 'Take the vaccine. It is safe and effective.' The third false narrative now is, 'It is not the vaccines causing these problems. It is Covid that we saw back in 2020 that is causing all these problems in 2023.' Don't fall for the false narrative… the vaccines are causing this enormous wave of illness.

Summarizing, he said, *The path forward is, clearly, for no-one to take another shot — no-one. The Covid-19 vaccines and all their progeny and future boosters are not safe for human use… I implore you to apply all pressure and due urgency to remove the Covid-19 vaccines from the market… The WHO is standing behind these vaccines. It is my belief that the European Union, the United States and all major stakeholders should actually completely pull out of the WHO.* [14]

In this Chapter, I have given you proof of a crime against humanity, planned over many decades and executed by means of first creating a virus, then developing the mRNA vaccines and forcing people in every country to be vaccinated against the so-called virus. The future prospect of mRNA technology being applied to every medical condition is a horrifying prospect because this new technology threatens the integrity of our immune system and alters our DNA. It is already being deployed for the treatment of cancer and suggested for the treatment of other diseases.

While this Plan may seem inconceivable in its evil intent, there are fortunately enough people on this planet capable of seeing through it and disclosing their findings to those they are able to reach. But there are countless millions who are still oblivious of the crime committed against them and who do not know that their governments have betrayed them.

More evidence of this crime will be brought in the Addendum between Part One and Part Two of Chapter 13, which offers the evidence given by Dr Mike Yeadon on the harmful content of the mRNA bio-weapons. As if that is not enough, we are now told that future vaccines are to be delivered by "Aerovax" needle-free Covid mRNA vaccine.

Notes:

1. Ardis, Dr Bryan Ardis, (2024) *Moving Beyond the COVID-19 Lies*, Harvest Creek Publishing. His book is now available from Amazon UK.
2. Kurzweil, Ray, (2024) *The Singularity is Nearer*, Bodley Head, London
3. Collins, Cecil (2004) Angels, Fool's Press, London. see also *The Vision of the Fool and Other Writings*, Edited and with an Introduction by Brian Keeble, Golgonooza Press, Ipswich
4. An article published by The Institute for Pure and Applied Knowledge (IPAK) in *Science, Public Health Policy, and the Law* Volume: v6.2019-2025 January 2025, Peer Reviewed, calls for the withdrawal of all vaccines.
   Review of Calls for Market Removal of COVID-19 Vaccines Intensify: Risks Far Outweigh Theoretical Benefits. Nicolas Hulscher, Mary T. Bowden, Peter A. McCullough

Abstract: COVID-19 vaccination campaigns around the globe have failed to meet fundamental standards of safety and efficacy, leading to mounting evidence of significant harm. More than 81,000 physicians, scientists, researchers, and concerned citizens, 240 elected government officials, 17 professional public health and physician organizations, 2 State Republican Parties, 17 Republican Party County Committees, and 6 scientific studies from across the world have called for the market withdrawal of COVID-19 vaccines. As of September 6, 2024, the CDC has documented 19,028 deaths in the United States reported to the Vaccine Adverse Event Reporting System (VAERS) by healthcare professionals or pharmaceutical companies who believe the product is related to the death. The total number of COVID-19 vaccine deaths reported to VAERS (37,544 among all participating countries) have far exceeded the recall limits of past vaccine withdrawals by up to 375,340%. The criteria for an FDA Class I recall, which applies to products with a reasonable probability of causing serious adverse health consequences or death, have been far exceeded. Excess mortality, negative efficacy, widespread DNA contamination, and a lack of demonstrated reduction in transmission, hospitalization, or mortality have undermined the rationale for continued administration. These unified requests for regulatory action underscore substantial shortcomings in data safety monitoring and risk mitigation. Immediate removal of COVID-19 vaccines from the market is essential to prevent further loss of life and ensure next steps are taken for accountability of the harm incurred.

5. Kennedy, Robert F, Jr, (2023) *The Wuhan Cover-Up and the Terrifying Bioweapons Arms Race*, Skyhorse Publishing, New York
6. Desmet, Mattias, (2022) *The Psychology of Totalitarianism*, Chelsea Green Publishing, London, p. 7
7. ibid, p. 48. (see the Chapter in Hannah Arendt's book — *Totalitarianism in Power*)
8. ibid, p. 93
9. Wolf, Naomi (2022) *The Bodies of Others: The New Authoritarians*, Covid-19 and the War Against the Human, All Seasons Press, Port Lauderdale, Florida
10. Wolf, Naomi (2024) *The Pfizer Papers,* Simon & Schuster, New York & London
11. Wolf, Naomi (2023) *Facing the Beast, Courage, Faith and Resistance in a New Dark Age.* Chelsea Green Publishing New York and London
12. Names of Men who have faced the dragon of fear:
    the historian Neil Oliver has consistently drawn attention to censorship on his own channel Patreon, and on GB News. Dr John Campbell has, throughout the Covid years and beyond, given out essential information that was not covered by the media. The oncologist, Professor Angus Dagleish, has spoken about the risk of cancer from the vaccines and has recommended treatments for cancer. John O'Looney, who carried out autopsies on people who had died of Covid, has courageously drawn attention to the unusual blood clots found in their bodies. The Cardiologist, Dr Aseem Malhotra, following the sudden death of his father from a heart attack after a vaccination, has repeatedly drawn attention to the danger of the vaccines and the excessive use of other drugs, such as statins. In the US The Highwire and Children's Health Defense have consistently reported on the abuse of power in that country. Mikki Willis created The Plandemic Series and the film 'Plandemic.' In the UK, The Exposé has consistently exposed the lies we have been told and the details of the WEF Great

Reset Plan. There are many more names to add to this list of courageous individuals who have spoken out about the lies we have been told.

Women who have courageously spoken out about the danger of the vaccines:

Dr. Tess Lawrie, Founder of The World Council for Health. Dr Clare Craig has written an excellent book called Expired: Covid, The Untold Story. Polly Tommey, Karen Kingston, Anna de Boussonet, Dr Jane Ruby, Dr Meryl Nass, Professor Dolores Cannon, Dr Christiane Northrup and Dr Judy Mikovits, biochemist and molecular biologist and co-author of *Plague, One Scientist's Intrepid Search for the Truth about Human Retroviruses and Chronic Fatigue Syndrome (ME/CFS), Autism, and Other Diseases*.

13. Dr David Martin, in his own words, states: "I happen to be for the USA government in the early part of the 2000s and the latter part of the 90's, a person who was sent around the world to look at the proliferation of biological and chemical weapons. I am familiar with the definition of what a biological warfare agent is in the 18 US Code — the Criminal Code — of violations of biological and chemical weapons. And so, my assessment is in fact professional and correct. The reason for that is that I have been credited to make that determination for the USA government for many years."
Dr Martin is the founding CEO of M-CAM Inc. M-CAM is the international leader of intellectual property-based financial risk management. From auditing patent quality for governments and patent offices to providing state-of-the-art actuarial risk management systems and solutions to the largest banks and insurance companies, M-CAM has established a global standard in patent quality and commercial validity assessment and management.

14. written by Rhoda Wilson and transcribed from the website of '*The Exposé*', September 19th 2023. The WHO Treaty is undergoing amendments in reply to queries and comments raised by different countries. It will be re-presented in 2025. President Trump, immediately after his inauguration 20/01/25, removed the United States from the WHO.

The first article of the Nuremberg Code 1949 states that:
The voluntary consent of the human subject is absolutely essential. This means that the person involved should have legal capacity to give consent; should be situated as to be able to exercise free power of choice, without the intervention of any element of force, fraud, deceit, duress, over-reaching, or other ulterior form of constraint or coercion, and should have sufficient knowledge and comprehension of the elements of the subject matter involved as to enable him to make an understanding and enlightened decision. This latter element requires that before the acceptance of an affirmative decision by the experimental subject there should be made known to him the nature, duration, and purpose of the experiment; the method and means by which it is to be conducted; all inconveniences and hazards reasonably to be expected; and the effects upon his health or person which may possibly come from his participation in the experiment.

Cosmos
Painting by Robin Baring

Covid-19 Addendum

Dr Mike Yeadon: The Danger of the mRNA Vaccines

I would like to include here a talk by Dr Mike Yeadon, a scientist and biologist who explains in detail why the mRNA bio-weapons are a danger to our immune systems and how the biological technology on which they are based can alter our DNA, interfering with and degrading the immune system of our bodies.

Dr Mike Yeadon is a career research scientist and biologist who has worked in the pharmaceutical industry and in biotech for over 30 years — all his adult life. His first degree included a training in toxicology, which is an understanding of how materials can injure human beings at a molecular level, and what the relationship is between their structure and their toxicity. In his second degree, a Ph.D., he did research in respiratory pharmacology, control of breathing and control of respiratory reflexes. He joined the pharmaceutical industry in 1988, and worked until very recently on new medicines for allergic and respiratory diseases. In his corporate career, he was for a long time responsible at Pfizer — then the biggest research-based drug company in the world — for everything to do with allergic and respiratory diseases in the research field. He left Pfizer in 2011 as Vice President and worldwide Head of Respiratory research. He was responsible for everything from idea to clinical proof of concept. In the ten years after leaving Pfizer, he has worked as an independent and as a consultant to 30 biotech companies. He sold his own biotech company, Ziarco, to Novartis, then the largest biotech company in the world. He is probably the most qualified former pharmaceutical company research executive in the world to be speaking on this subject, because he has spent his entire career in the business of working with teams designing molecules to be new potential medicines. Three years before Covid started, he was very well regarded in the industry. Since he has spoken out about what he knows about the so-called "vaccines," he has been attacked and smeared, becoming *persona non-grata*.

Applying his experience and knowledge to the contents of the Covid mRNA injections, Dr Yeadon was able to work out the intentions of the mRNA 'vaccine' designers. He explained how he was able to do this, and what the only conclusions that could be drawn from what he discovered, during the recorded presentation to a private session of the United Kingdom Parliament on December 4th, 2023, which was mysteriously unable to be transmitted owing to a "technical failure." On the 9th November, 2024, he spoke to the Impfopfer Resistance Conference in held in Vienna, Austria. Impfopfer (Vaccine Victim) is Austria's largest association for those who have suffered or are suffering from vaccine harm. Among many other talks, is the one below, given to the vaccine injured in the Northern Irish Parliament, 25th November 2024.

Address to the Northern Ireland Parliament 25/11/24

Hello, my name is Dr Mike Yeadon, and in the next 15 minutes or so, I would like to address those of you who have been vaccine injured or bereaved, and also those of you who are involved in the political process in Northern Ireland, as well as anywhere else in the world who might hear me. At the end of this process, I hope you will believe what I am going to tell you, which, shockingly, is that the materials masquerading as vaccines were designed intentionally to harm the people who received them.

I will also have some suggestions for what we can do together to fight against the global crime which is ongoing. I am well qualified to comment on the toxicological principles, properties of molecules, and the kind of effects you might see from certain structures. Very briefly, before I talk about the so-called vaccines, what happened in 2020? It has taken me a long time to get there, and I haven't made everybody happy with the decision I've reached, but there was not a pandemic or a public health emergency. I don't think there was anything at all, apart from lies, propaganda, fear-based information, fake diagnostic tests called PCR, and then, as it were, mis-attribution of real illnesses that people did have, which were called COVID when there was no such thing. But what happened, shockingly, was that the World Health Organisation's chairman called a pandemic, which was not true. There has never been a pandemic. There won't be pandemics. They are immunologically impossible. But after he called them, many countries in the world changed radically their medical management practises for people in hospitals, in care homes, and in the community.

Very briefly, in hospitals, many people were sedated, had a plastic tube put down their airway, and when unconscious, were put on mechanical ventilators. I can assure you that is not ever an appropriate treatment for someone with an influenza-like illness, whatever you might think COVID was. But that would not be something you would do, and if applied to frail and elderly people, they will die in large numbers, which they did.

So that was the first crime. It was not a mistake. There are no mistakes here. Mistakes were not made. They were told to do this by figures at a supranational level. We don't know exactly who, but we know this because these mad procedures changed in many countries all at the same time — in hospitals, in care homes, assisted living, old-age people's homes, and so on. *Many people were given drugs like Midazolam, which is an injectable form of a drug like Valium, a sedative. But they were also given injections of pain-relieving drugs like Morphine, even if they weren't in pain.*

My PhD was in the field of understanding what opiate drugs like morphine do to the respiratory reflux, and I can assure you it suppresses and suppresses it and depresses it. *So if you give an elderly person an injection of midazolam, they will become sedated and sleepy, and if you give them an injection of morphine, their breathing will slow. I can tell you, it is absolutely forbidden to give a person those two drugs together, those two drug classes together, unless they are under intense ongoing medical monitoring.* [my italics] And the reason for this is that they are likely to fall asleep and stop breathing. That, of course, is what happened.

Your relatives were killed by the medical procedures that were imposed. Now, it is quite possible early on that not everybody involved knew what was happening, but I am afraid that after a few days, you would have to be a blockhead not to realise that it was what you were doing to your charges, your patients, that was resulting in their deaths. So I have completely lost any trust in the medical profession because virtually no-one has spoken up four and a half years later.

… If you listen to the recordings, heartbreaking recordings given to the Scottish COVID Enquiry, I think that is probably the only place where there has been an official taking of evidence from people. And what I just described is exactly what happens to lots of people's relatives and no doubt happens to some people in Northern Ireland as well. It certainly happens in England. There were worse things as well. People in the community were deprived of medical care that would have saved their lives.

And there is plenty of evidence to say that not being given antibiotics when they had incipient bronchial pneumonia also killed thousands, possibly tens of thousands of people. And there, ladies and gentlemen, was your pandemic. All of those deaths were attributed to COVID and you were told this is this terrible pandemic, you need to lock down, wear masks, do what you're told. Nothing was happening at all apart from *medical murder and propaganda from the television and the newspapers, politicians and many well-known public figures who are doing what they were told.* So one conclusion I'm going to come to later is to stop listening to liars. The people who have lied to you — you shouldn't listen to them ever again. Stop listening to them today.

The Bio-weapons

But for me, I think the worst thing — because it comes out of my [biotech] industry and because it is so deliberate, it requires such a lot of forethought — are the so-called vaccines. Now we were told there was this new infectious disease, so far so good ladies and gentlemen, but then they said don't worry we'll rustle up a vaccine. And they did so in about 10 months, something like that.

I can tell you after spending a career in this industry, you can no more make a baby in one month with nine women than you can make a complicated biological product in 10 months. It cannot be done. It was not done. They did something else. *They created materials which were essentially injected poisons. They were not vaccines. There was never anything to vaccinate against.* And when you have listened to what I have just told you, you know that must be true because you can't do something in 10 months that normally takes 6 to 12 years. Medicines are not put together randomly. They are built. And they are built by people who are discussing with colleagues, working out what kind of materials, what kind of structures, what kind of formulations, what kind of doses you would need to add in order to hit a particular molecular target, to have a chance of a particular therapeutic goal being reached without unaccept-able side effects. That is called rational design. And that is my whole career, Ladies and Gentlemen, from my undergraduate days to today.

So when I look at the design of the medicine, whatever kind it is, and look at the design on paper and its composition structures and so on, it is as if I'm looking over the shoulder of the designer, someone like me, someone with my qualifications who designed these things. So when I look at them, I'm looking over the shoulder of the designer and I can discern something of what their objectives were, what were they trying to do. *And I came quickly to the conclusion that they wanted to bring about toxicity that would injure, kill and reduce fertility.* There aren't any other alternatives. And remember, there was no public health emergency. So I will just give you three examples. I am not going to be too scientific, but three things so you can check them.

The objective of these so-called *gene-based vaccines was to inject you with a genetic sequence for something called spike protein.* Now, it doesn't really matter what spike protein is, if it's real, where it came from. *The point is, it's a genetic sequence for a protein that doesn't belong in your body. It is non-self. It is foreign.*

Your immune system is a wonderful work of God and nature. It distinguishes self, things that are meant to be inside you from anything else, that is foreign, non-self. If you inject a person with a genetic sequence that instructs your body to become a factory for some protein that doesn't belong in you, your immune system will detect that and it will attack every cell that has done that instruction and kill it.

Now, these materials, when injected in your arm, didn't stay in your arm, they travelled around your heart, your lungs, your kidneys, your brain, your ovaries. And in every place it landed, if it was taken up and expressed, your body registered that as foreign invasion and it attacks and kills every cell doing it. There is no other possible consequence from doing that. So that is step one and no one can argue that is not what they did. That is the design of them. It also picks a particular protein. I'm not really sure where spike protein came from, if it's really real, but proteins like the one they claim was encoded in these gene-based materials are known to be toxic.

There are loads of experiments, lots of published experiments, showing that proteins like that one cause blood coagulation, damaged nerves, damaged heart tissue. So they injected you with something that would make your body make a protein that doesn't belong there, knowing axiomatically, automatically, unavoidably, your immune system would attack that. It would be like rejecting an organ transplant. [my italics]

Your body would say, that's foreign, got to go, uses your immune system to kill it. And then they also inject you with something that is inherently toxic. So if it got out into your body or wherever it was made [to go], it would harm you.

And I've got a third one that cannot be argued with. The mRNA products from Pfizer and Moderna were encapsulated in something called lipid nano-particles. It's really a blob of fat, a complicated, technical blob of fat, that is what it is after all. And what that material did was to allow your injection to glide all around your body across all biological barriers, and get everywhere in your body. So of course, it is not what you would want, is it? For something they told you was inhaled into your nose and lungs. But no, it went all around your body, into your brain, your blood vessels.

But in particular, I need to tell you, there were publications that are now more than 10 years old in peer-reviewed journal articles. There were peer-reviewed journal articles showing that lipid nanoparticles were recognised over a decade ago of having a particular property, which you are not going to like to hear, which shocked me when I learned it. They tend to deposit their payload into the ovaries.

That is exactly what happened with these injected materials. There was at least one study performed with the Pfizer agents, with the Japanese regulatory authorities. Lo and behold, the material accumulated in the ovaries of the test animals.

I remember the day I read that paper I really couldn't sleep. *The person who chose to use lipid nanoparticles to formulate the Moderna and Pfizer products knew perfectly well that what they would do is allow them to drift all through your body, through membranes as if they weren't there, and disproportionately deposit them in your ovaries.* That is what has happened, Ladies and Gentlemen, to every woman and girl injected with these materials.

Remember what I said about designing molecules to do things deliberately with objectives in mind? They picked lipid nanoparticles, knowing they accumulate the payload in the ovaries. It is not an accident. Mistakes were not made. *So I tell you, as a professional who spent his whole honest scientific career in an industry I did not realise was corrupt, trying to make experimental medicines for respiratory and allergy diseases, that my experience tells me that there are multiple independent, unnecessary and obvious mechanisms of toxicity built into these so-called vaccines.* [my italics]

And then by sheer luck, all four companies, Moderna, Johnson & Johnson, AstraZeneca and Pfizer, all chose basically the same formula for their so-called vaccines. That would never happen in reality. For a start, I would call my opposite numbers and say, we should do different things because if something goes wrong, if we are wrong in an assumption, all of the so-called vaccines will fail for the same reason. We should do different things. It's called diversification. But no, they all did the same things because they are just lying. They were making intentionally dangerous material, passing them off as vaccines to having you and your children injected. And that is what they did. Of course, I didn't get injected and neither did my children and most of my relatives. So the big picture, what happens, I think from the research I've done, and of course, I am an expert in research and development, not in politics, but I believe that very wealthy people, the kind of people who run foundations with names, have planned, as have their antecedents for a couple of generations, to take over the world, to remove the freedoms of ordinary people like us that they regard as "useless eaters." [the words originally used by Henry Kissinger and recently by Yuval Harari] They don't want us around anymore.

And their intention is to strip us of our freedoms by persuading us that there are very frightening events occurring in the world, and we need them to lead us to safety. There are documents you can find from a group called The Club of Rome, who in the late 1960's, was commissioned by some of these people who run the nameless global foundations that have hundreds of billions of pounds of worth. They were asked to come up with scenarios that would produce challenges for countries that couldn't be solved by countries on their own, so they would have to look outwards and upwards to supranational solutions; organisations like the United Nations, the World Health

Organisation, the Bank for International Settlements, the World Economic Forum, which are populated by the people who have orchestrated this attack on humanity and they are going to do it again. There are [gain-of-function] factories all around the world busy manufacturing these so-called "vaccines" and formulating them in the way I just described, and they are going to come up with contrived reasons why you need to roll your sleeve up. And I am telling you, for the love of God, please don't do it!

Now guess what? The two things they came up with, pandemics of infectious diseases, which I know as an immunologist are not possible and have never happened. The other thing they said to account for or plan for were climate change crises. I've done enough research now, Ladies and Gentlemen, I've spoken to people who have spent as long in climate atmospheric research as I have in pharmaceutical R&D, and they have explained to me, and I understand very well, that there's all of this nonsense about carbon dioxide, global boiling, net zero.

It is all a complete scam from the same people who bought you the Covid scam and the dangerous injections. It is the same people. They want one world government, they want to deprive you of your liberty, and then I'm afraid I think they will kill us using these injections because they're going to do it again. All over the world, factories to make mRNA-based materials are being thrown up, billions of doses are being made, and if we let them, they will stick them in our arms and people will sicken and die. So those of you who have been injured or bereaved, in my mind, no blame whatsoever attaches to you. How could you know that people you trusted and thought you could trust were lying to you? Well, you didn't know, but if you let them inject you again, you have no sympathy from me because they have lied to you, you've been injured or killed, and I've explained to you that they are liars and they have attacked us.

So if you go along with it, you cannot be saved. All we need to do is enough of us continue to speak out about this and say we are not having it anymore, get lost, don't listen to liars anymore. People who have lied to you forfeit your trust forever, in my view, and so anyone who is in the political process, for example in Northern Ireland, looking at this so-called public health bill, which if you pass it would allow these supra-national criminals to take you from your house, to inject you by force if necessary, they are aiding and abetting a global crime.

I saw someone online say recently that if you pass that legislation, I don't think it would be unreasonable to interpret that as an act of war. It is as serious as that. So, politicians, you may well be under pressure from shadowy figures, but if you go along with it and hope for an easier time of it, you will have unlocked the doors of hell and pushed everybody in it and you along with them as well. So this is your time to do what I am doing, which is to speak out, no matter what the consequences. I say to you if you are frightened about what happens if you speak out, you should be absolutely terrified about what is going to happen if you don't. So really that is all I've got to say.

I do think these criminals are going to do it again; they are continuing to threaten us with pandemics like bird flu, monkey pox and so on. It is all nonsense. Stop listening to liars right now. Put things right between you, the people you love, and between you and God if you haven't already. And for goodness' sake, be one of the people who speaks out no matter what the consequences, because if you don't, we will lose our freedom and then our lives. Thank you.

The Colossus
Francisco de Goya (1746–1828), Museo del Prado

Chapter Thirteen: Part Two

The Abuse of Power: Transhumanism

God's powers have passed into our hands. The powers themselves are not evil,
but in the hands of man they are an appalling danger — in evil hands.
— C.G. Jung

The death of human empathy is one of the earliest and most telling signs
of a culture about to fall into barbarism.
— Hannah Arendt

It is the hallmark of the technological imperative to run the world on AI.
The assertion that intelligence can be artificial is yet another insane
permutation of the Archontic Lie.
— John Lamb Lash, *Not in His Image*

Man's conquest of Nature, if the dreams of some scientific planners are
realized, means the rule of a few hundreds of men over billions
and billions of men.
— C.S. Lewis, *The Abolition of Man*

When we observe a human being, we merely perceive an object which makes a
certain variety of motions and noises. The same is true, however, when we
observe a dog or a Ford car.
— Technology Study Course 1934

We are at a time of greater change than at any time in our history.
— Yuval Noah Harari

Scientists say that the hand on the Doomsday Clock has reached eighty-nine seconds to mid-night (29/1/25). But the scientists who are calculating this risk are only thinking in terms of nuclear attack. I believe there is a threat to our survival as great or greater than the nuclear threat. That threat is Transhumanism. It is not AI that is the problem, but what technocrats and transhumanists could do with it. Once they have gathered the data on all life forms on the planet in a central place of digital control, they can use it to manipulate this data in any way they choose. We humans will be part of the data, part of what is being manipulated. We will no longer have free will. We will be subject to the insane will of those who wish to control the planet and all life on it. The first phase of the Plan — the development of the virus and the bio-weapons — was detailed in part One of this Chapter and the Interlude. This Chapter will look at the next phase of the Plan. I feel incredulity writing this chapter. I find it hard to believe what I am communicating because it is so evil and so utterly destructive of the values that we, as a species, have fought for centuries to articulate and defend — values that are enshrined in our political institutions, however fragile these may be. It is, above all, utterly inimical to the concept and vision of the Divine Feminine.

Is this the change that Yuval Harari has in mind when he said that we are at a time of greater change than at any time in our history? As explained by Dr David Martin in Part 1 of this Chapter, a Plan has been prepared over the last sixty or so years — a Plan to reduce the population of the planet sufficiently to allow a handful of powerful technocrats to take complete control of it. The deliberate creation of the 'virus,' the forcible imposition of the Lockdowns and the mRNA bio-weapons saw the implementation of the first phase of the Plan. In his second address to the European Parliament in September 2023, Dr David Martin said, "We did not have a pandemic; we had a genocide."He described what has happened since 2020 as "the greatest crime against humanity in our history."

We are faced with two utterly different perspectives: one advanced by Klaus Schwab, founder of the World Economic Forum, and his spokesman, Yuval Noah Harari, the other by David Martin. Professor Harari sees our species as "hackable animals." [1] Dr David Martin sees us as soul-endowed beings. We will need to choose between them, taking care not to demonize the supporters of the path we may reject while we still have the freedom to do so.

Were it not for the fading of Christianity and its moral constraints and guidance over the last two hundred years, none of this could have been envisaged, let alone implemented. But with the vacuum left by Christianity's weakening influence and its inability to challenge the beliefs of Scientific Materialism, this ideology has been able to establish itself in our schools and universities with hardly any challenge and, together with our accelerating technological skills, has been able to create a belief system of power over Nature, with no ethical or moral constraints to inhibit its forward momentum.

Transhumanism as a New Version of Naziism

Eugenics tends to repeat itself at intervals. Lawrence Rees, in a recent book, *The Nazi Mind: Twelve Warnings from History*, says that we should never forget the techniques that would-be tyrants are likely to use to subdue our freedoms. [2] Two of the foremost techniques are Fear and Propaganda and the division of people into two categories: "us" and "them." Once this polarized situation is established, archaic instincts are activated which are very difficult to contain. We have seen this in the recent pandemic with the attacks and even the forced physical restraint (in Australia) of people who chose not to be vaccinated, and in the constant attacks on "conspiracy" theories or theorists. The phrase "useless eaters," used by Henry Kissinger originally and more recently by Yuval Harari, is a dangerous one to use. Who is to decide who are the useless eaters and who not? After the Holocaust, we said "Never Again." Yet, here we are, potential victims of another Plan of mass extermination.

In 1943, C.S. Lewis published *The Abolition of Man*. Presciently, he wrote:

> Man's conquest of Nature, if the dreams of some scientific planners are realized, means the rule of a few hundreds of men over billions upon billions of men... Each new power won by man is a power over man as well. The final stage is come when Man by eugenics, by pre-natal conditioning, and by an education and propaganda based on a perfect applied psychology, has obtained full control over himself. Human nature will be the last part of Nature to surrender to man. The battle will then be won.... We shall be henceforth free to make our species whatever we wish it to be.... The power of Man to make himself what he pleases means, as we have seen, the power of some men to make other men what they please. [3]

We are now, eighty years on, at the final stage that C.S. Lewis was writing about, the stage where the Transhumanist Plan to design an improved version of humanity may be put in place. Ray Kurzweil has predicted that this "up-grade" will occur in 2045. He calls it "The Singularity." [4] Our species, as we know it, could be abolished by Transhumanism — an ideology conceived by men who have exchanged their souls for power — whose intention is to control the planet, with them as the elite in charge of its "management," overriding the laws, political institutions and hard-won human rights of different nations and controlling the lives of billions from a central digitally-controlled authority. Transhumanism appears to be an extension of Chinese Communism, but imposed on the whole world, where there is one central authority in control of billions of people, with that control exercised by digital means. Hannah Arendt warned us about how totalitarianism advances and spreads, but vast numbers of us are unable to see what is happening under our noses because its tentacles are already so deeply embedded in our lives and our technological culture that they are almost invisible to those who are not aware of what is happening. Fortunately, there are a growing number of people who are aware of what is happening, among them Dr David Martin and the authors David Hughes, Patrick M. Wood and Gregg Braden, whose words I am quoting in this chapter and to whom I would like to express my heartfelt gratitude.

What is psychologically interesting about this Plan, is that it takes the discoveries of quantum physics — that we are all One life, connected to each other at the quantum level — and transposes this to One System of Control to be imposed on the entire planet. It converts astounding scientific discoveries into a totalitarian System of Control, whereby everything that people have fought for in Western Civilization, above all freedom and human rights — as superbly defined in the Constitution of the United States — is to be sacrificed to this ideology. It is enabled to do this because it has repudiated the idea that there is a transcendent reality beyond the material reality of this planet, taking the beliefs of Scientific Materialism or Physicalism (not Science itself) to their furthest limit. It has arrogated to itself rulership of the planet because it recognizes no higher authority to which it is accountable. It has usurped the Creator role of God and stepped into His shoes.

The *hubris* involved in this Plan, bordering on psychosis, is almost beyond comprehension, but the dawning light of insight and information given to us by those who have seen the danger of this Plan, is revealing the truth for those who want to see it and are courageous enough to speak out about what has happened and will continue to happen unless we come together to prevent it achieving its aims. Soon, we may expect an announcement by the WHO of another pandemic, most probably bird-flu, then another series of "vaccines" to control it and another Lockdown. The fact that President Trump has already withdrawn the US from the WHO the day after his inauguration may be a hopeful sign of light dawning.

Transhumanism

On page 1 of his minutely referenced book, *Covid 19: Psychological Operations and the War for Technocracy*, the historian David Hughes elaborates on this Plan or Omniwar as he calls it, that has been decades in preparation. This exceptionally detailed book is essential reading for anyone who wants to understand what is happening beneath the surface. It is available as a free download if you sign up to David Hughes on substack.

> With the World Health Organization's declaration of the "Covid-19 pandemic" on March 11, 2020, an undeclared global class war was initiated, aimed at the controlled demolition of liberal democracy and the institution of global technocracy, a novel, biodigital form of totalitarianism. The largest psychological warfare operation in history was waged transnationally against unwitting

populations to cripple their resistance to the intended transition to technocracy… If successfully implemented, technocracy will be worse than anything imaginable by Hitler or Stalin, because it amounts to the biodigital enslavement of humanity through biometric technologies, the "Internet of Bodies," constant surveillance and monitoring, central bank digital currencies, and a Chinese-style social credit system. Moreover, if allowed to happen, such a control system could prove irreversible."[5]

> It is quite within the bounds of possibility for a man to recognize the relative evil of his nature, but it is a rare and shattering experience for him to gaze into the face of absolute evil.   Carl Jung

The Great Red Dragon and the Woman Clothed with the Sun
William Blake (1757–1827)

Another author, Patrick M. Wood, in his book, *The Evil Twins of Technocracy and Transhumanism,* published in 2022, explains how this Plan was incubated many decades ago, tracing the beginning of Transhumanism to the 1930's and to The Trilateral Commission, founded in 1973 by David Rockefeller and Zbigniew Brzezinski, whose stated goal was to develop "A New International Economic Order." [6] Drawn from North America, Europe and Japan, its members consisted of influential or high-ranking lawyers, politicians, journalists, scientists, international bankers and academics, a membership that appears to be comparable to that of the World Economic Forum today.

In 1970 Brzezinski published a book, *Between Two Ages: America's role in the Technetronic Era,* which attracted the attention of David Rockefeller and led to the founding of the Trilateral Commission, whose aims bear a strong resemblance to The Great Reset agenda of the WEF (World Economic Forum) that I will come to shortly. The conceived end for both was and is the total re-structuring of civilization. In his book, Brzezinski wrote,

> Such a society would be dominated by an elite whose claim to political power would rest on allegedly superior scientific know-how. It would not hesitate to achieve its political ends by using the latest modern techniques for influencing public behavior and keeping society under close surveillance and control. Under such circumstances, the scientific and technological momentum of the country would not be reversed but would actually feed on the situation it exploits.[7]

Wood quotes another author — Max More — who, he says, defined Transhumanism when he wrote:

> The dawn of the new millennium will see the ability to use engineered viruses to alter the genetic structure of any cell, even adult, differentiated cells. This will give us pervasive control over our physiology and morphology. Molecular nanotechnology, an emerging and increasingly funded technology, should eventually give us practically complete control over the structure of matter, allowing us to build anything, perfectly, atom-by-atom. We will be able to program the construction of physical objects (including our bodies) just as we now do with software. The abolition of ageing and most involuntary death will be one result. We have achieved two of the three alchemist dreams: we have transmuted the elements and learn to fly. Immortality is next.[8]

Wood comments:

> When this was written nearly 20 years ago, its resemblance to science fiction novels and films caused most observers to laugh at early transmuted humanists like Max More. Few are laughing now. In the intervening years the transhumanist philosophy and the applied science of NBIC (Nanotechnology, Biotechnology,

Information technology and Cognitive Science) have been spreading like wildfire through the world's top academic institutions and emerging biotech companies. [9]

Wood describes how and when the Plan to establish Transhumanism was launched:

By early 2020 enough progress had been made to spring the transhuman trap on all of humanity. The trap took the form of the SARS-COV-2 virus, which big Pharma and the biotech industry used as an opportunity to launch a revolutionary new vaccine technology based on messenger ribonucleic acid or mRNA... To quell growing public fear that mRNA injections might somehow affect our DNA, the mRNA injection manufacturers, scientists, the CDC, the FDA, and other health authorities all united in a vehement denial that any such thing could ever happen. *However, the denials were proven unfounded when, on February 22, 2022, a study was released by Lund University in Sweden, describing a process of reverse transcription, whereby foreign mRNA can indeed find its way back into one's DNA.* [10] [my italics]

The biological attack of SARS-COV-two (Covid-19) is the most egregious attack on humanity in history. Not that the virus itself was so damaging, but the response to it was a crushing blow. Billions of citizens in almost every country were forced to submit to mandates that were not only useless, but destructive to health, wealth, and well-being. Facemasks did nothing to stop contagion; if anything, they caused illness and emotional pain. Quarantine and isolation, also unnecessary for the most part, were comparable to martial law. In America, the Bill of Rights was virtually suspended — make that eviscerated. Churches were ordered closed. Public gatherings were forbidden. Government ceased to respond to the pleas of citizens, issuing tyrannical dictates.

Then came the experimental mRNA injections that were rushed through without the rigorous and lengthy testing on humans that is traditionally required (actually, mandated) by the Food and Drug Administration [FDA]. Of the billions who have been "vaccinated" worldwide, many millions have suffered adverse effects, some so severe as to cause death. Even those who have been given one or more injections but have so far suffered no side effects still face possible long-term health issues.

Legitimate doctors, scientists, and medical scholars have pleaded with government officials to halt these experimental drugs. But instead of being heeded, they are ignored, shunned, decertified, fired, and branded as conspiracy theorists, or "vaccine" deniers. The manufacturers of mRNA injections are resolute in their quest to continue blanketing the global population with additional mRNA-based "therapies."

The effect of the pandemic crisis that started in early 2020 has been to demoralize, disrupt, and degrade the general mental, spiritual, and bodily health of individuals throughout the world. Furthermore, it has caused major damage to the global economy, to the global supply chain, and to the global financial system. In sum, the crisis precipitated by the pandemic planners has been nothing short of an all-out war against mankind. [11]

The world has never before experienced such sustained, intensive, deceptive propaganda. The problem, of course, is that many people believe the lies and become willing participants in their own capture by the forces of technocracy and transhumanism. [12]

Wood adds that much of this takeover of humanity was achieved by propaganda:

The propaganda machine is meant to deceive, manipulate, and condition its subjects into adopting positions and actions that they would otherwise never adopt. The response to the pandemic narrative was proof that propaganda is one of the most frightening tools of control imaginable. [13]

Propaganda was the primary tool that Hitler used to condition the population of Germany to accept his agenda of eliminating the Jews. Developed by a man called Edward Bernays, a nephew of Sigmund Freud, who published a book of that title in 1928, the propaganda tool later became rapidly and widely used by governments to influence their citizens. Bernays wrote, "Those who manipulate the unseen mechanism of society constitute an invisible government which is the true ruling power of our country." [14] Propaganda is the same invisible and immensely powerful tool used to control and deceive us during the Covid years. The population, particularly the young adults and the middle-aged, is still suffering from the severe trauma that was disgracefully inflicted on them by their governments. David Hughes, referring to the techniques of psychological warfare described in Naomi Klein's book, *The Shock Doctrine*, writes on page 61 of his book, "Consistent with the "shock doctrine," the "Covid-19" operation hit the public with the gamut of psychological warfare techniques — all at once. The scale, intensity, and coordination of the operation are testament to the transnational deep state behind it." But who was organizing the propaganda and the psychological warfare and who oversaw the censoring all the news outlets during these years?

The Covid Dossier and the Control by the Military

To answer these questions, one of the most extraordinary recent disclosures about the Covid Plan has been the fact that, from 2020, the whole operation was taken over and controlled by the military. According to the Dossier (published February 3rd, 2025) compiled by Debbie Lerman, a research investigator and Sasha Latypova, a former big pharma executive, all COVID counter-measures, including the biological warfare agents marketed as 'Covid-19 vaccines' were created, produced, and distributed in a covert military program, where the pharma manufacturers only worked as sub-contractors. This confirms what Robert Kennedy said in November 2024 about the vaccines being created in a military laboratory and distributed under the name of Pfizer and Moderna, and the Dutch Minister for Health, Fleur Agema, confirming in the same month that the Dutch Ministry for Health was under the control of NATO.

In their Dossier, they write: "It is crucially important to understand that COVID was a globally coordinated response based on legal frameworks intended for biodefense/ biowarfare situations. The attack that initiated the global COVID response could have been real, perceived, or invented — regardless of the trigger, the lockdown-until-vaccine paradigm originated in the military/ intelligence biodefense playbook, not in any scientifically based or epidemiologically established public health plan."

"This means that nothing about the response — masking, distancing, lockdowns, vaccines — was part of a public health plan to respond to a disease outbreak. Rather, every aspect of the response was intended to induce public panic in order to gain compliance with biodefense operations, culminating with the injection of unregulated mRNA products, which were legally treated as biodefense military countermeasures (MCMs), into billions of human beings."

"The COVID Dossier is a compilation of the evidence we have amassed over the last three years supporting the following claim:

> **COVID was not a public health event, although it was presented as such to the world's population. It was a global operation, coordinated through public-private intelligence and military alliances and invoking laws designed for CBRN (chemical, biological, radiological, nuclear) weapons attacks."**

The Dossier contains information regarding the military/intelligence coordination of the COVID biodefense response in the US, UK, Australia, Canada, the Netherlands, Germany, and Italy. For some countries, we have extensively documented information. For others, we have some documentation of military/ intelligence involvement but not all the details. For as many countries as possible, we list the military/intelligence agencies in charge of their country's COVID response; dates on which emergency declarations were made in each country; military/intelligence-related agencies and bodies in charge of censorship/ propaganda; and top people with military/intelligence jobs who were known or reported to hold leadership positions in the response. We also list connections to global governing bodies, including the EU and UN/ WHO, through which the response was coordinated. In the final section, we provide a list of military/ intelligence/ biodefense alliances and agreements that provide multinational frameworks for responding to a bioterror/ bioweapons attack.

By providing all of this information in one place, we hope to dispel the notion that COVID was a public health event, managed independently by each country's public health agencies, with some limited, logistically focused military involvement. We also hope to drive home the shocking realization that not only were military and intelligence agencies in charge of COVID in all of these countries, but the response to what was represented as a public health crisis was coordinated through military alliances, including NATO.

They ask: "Who ordered and directed these operations? Who benefited from them? Who was and still is covering them up? We have been investigating these questions for the last several years, and we hope many who read this will join us moving forward." (https://substack.com/@sashalatypova).

As Debbie and Sasha say, this should be the subject of front-page news everywhere, yet, apart from their interview with Neil Oliver, they have been unable to get this dossier published in main-line news outlets, proving that censorship is still controlling the news outlets. [15]

Do We Still Have a Choice?

We face a choice while there is still time. Do we want to be changed into an "up-graded" species through implants, nano-particles, and more mRNA vaccinations? Do we want to lose the inherent human genius that has given us Pythagoras, Parmenides, Plato, the Gnostics, and the Essenes, Marsilio Ficino, Raphael, Shakespeare, Kepler, Galileo, Rembrandt, Mozart, Beethoven, Dostoevsky, Goethe, Einstein, Solzhenitsyn, Jung, and other supremely creative individuals, not forgetting the great luminaries of the Indian, Persian and Chinese civilizations? Included in this list are all the architects, engineers, builders, sculptors of genius who have raised the great buildings we admire today — buildings like the Parthenon, the Romanesque and Gothic Cathedrals, the exquisite mosques of Islam, the temples of India and China. It is as if our species has been reduced by scientific materialism to physical bodies stripped of their souls. The phenomenal creative genius of our species as well as the subtlety and range of our emotions, passes transhumanists by.

How has it happened that we have been reduced to the situation where, like sheep, we can be corralled into a technocratic sheepfold by a handful of men who deny the existence of God and the soul and any transcendent meaning and purpose to our lives?

Sheep penned in a fold — North of England

How has human intelligence become so degraded that it can betray the greatest minds of the past in its desire permanently to alter something as magnificently creative and extraordinary as the human being? Our species is a part of Nature and now we are faced with the possibility that a few members of our species are trying to change us into something that Nature never intended us to become. Our DNA is part of Nature, existing for some 200,000 years. Transhumanists want to change our DNA and transform us into a transhuman or post-human 'improved' species. One may agree with them that our species needs improvement, but I cannot agree that this is the best way to achieve it. Who will write poems like this in a transhuman future?

Expectancy by William Moore

I do not care for sleep, I'll wait awhile
For Love to come out of the darkness, wait
For laughter, gifted with the frequent fate
Of dusk-lit hope, to touch me with the smile
Of moon and star and joy of that last mile
Before I reach the sea. The ships are late
And mayhap laden with the precious freight
Dawn brings from Life's eternal summer isle.

> And should I find the sweeter fruits of dream —
> The oranges of love and mating song —
> I'll laugh so true the morn will gayly seem
> Endless and ships full laden with a throng
> Of beauty, dreams and loves will come to me
> Out of the surge of yonder silver sea. [16]

Transhumanism, Klaus Schwab and The Great Reset

In 1932 Aldous Huxley published a book called *Brave New World*. In 1957 his younger brother Julian wrote this in his book, *New Bottles for New Wine*:

> The human species can, if it wishes, transcend itself — not just sporadically, an individual here one way, and individual there in another way, but in its entirety, as humanity. We need a name for this new belief. Perhaps transhumanism will serve: man remaining man, but transcending himself, by realizing new possibilities of and for his human nature.

Klaus Schwab, one of the principal promoters of transhumanism, was born in Ravensburg, Germany in 1938. In 1971, he founded the European Management Forum (renamed the WEF or World Economic Forum in 1987), on the suggestion of Henry Kissinger, at about the same time as the Trilateral Commission was established. Highly qualified, Schwab holds doctorates in economics and engineering and a Masters degree in Public Administration from Harvard where he studied under Kissinger. Based in Geneva, where he was Professor of Business Studies in the University from 1972 to 2003, he has worked assiduously over the last fifty years to build the WEF into an organization of great power, wealth, and influence. It holds its annual meeting in Davos every January and February, inviting top industrialists, political leaders, business men and scientists to participate in its discussions and listen to its plans. Klaus Schwab's son Olivier married a Chinese woman and has managed the World Economic Forum office in Beijing since 2011. Chinese officials have attended the WEF since 2009, including Xi Jinping in 2017.

The intention of Klaus Schwab and the basic Plan for what he calls the Great Reset and the New World Order is to move the world from the financial system we currently have, which is called Free Market Capitalism, to Stakeholder Capitalism.

Richard Jeffs created a film on Stakeholder Capitalism. This shows that Klaus Schwab is the master-mind planning to take the whole planet into a digitalised totalitarian system of government by 2030, a system where, we are told, "we will own nothing but be happy."

Klaus Schwab is the author of a book called *The Fourth Industrial Revolution*, published in 2013. Here is his description of it:

> Previous industrial revolutions liberated humankind from animal power, made mass production possible and brought digital capabilities to billions of people. This Fourth Industrial Revolution is, however, fundamentally different. It is characterised by a range of new technologies that are fusing the physical, digital and biological worlds, impacting all disciplines, economies and industries, and even challenging ideas about what it means to be human. [17]

An article on the WEF website in 2018, written by Schwab, reveals his views on Transhumanism:

> The central premise of transhumanism is that biological evolution will be overtaken by advances in genetic, wearable and implantable technologies that artificially expedite the evolutionary process.
>
> To date, areas to improve on include natural aging (including for the die-hards, the cessation of "involuntary death") as well as physical, intellectual and psychological capacities. Some distinguished scientists, such as Hans Moravec and Raymond Kurzweil, even advocate a post-human condition: the end of humanity's reliance on our congenital bodies by transforming "our frail version 1.0 human bodies into their more durable and capable version 2.0 counterparts."[18]

Elsewhere, he wrote:

> The ability to edit biology can be applied to practically any cell type, enabling the creation of genetically modified plants or animals, as well as modifying the cells of adult organisms including humans. [19]

The Alliance of the United Nations and the World Economic Forum

In 2019, the WEF and the UN signed The Strategic Partnership Framework, which aimed to "jointly accelerate the implementation of the 2030 Agenda for Sustainable Development." The Seventeen Sustainable Goals (SSG) of the UN's Climate Change Agenda, which were defined at a Climate Conference in Rio in 1992, and were due to be achieved by 2030, henceforth became part of the WEF's Great Reset programme.

Patrick Wood comments:

> If sustainable development can be represented by a bird, the two wings that allow the bird to fly are the United Nations and the World Economic Forum. Both

organizations are tightly aligned at all levels. The UN provides countries with a common legal framework treaties, agreements, and memorandums of understanding. The WEF, meanwhile, steers the global economic community towards fake solutions to imaginary problems – solutions that choke off capitalism and provide massive financing of climate reduction goals. [20]

The sustainable development dogma was based on a two-pronged lie — namely, that there was a need to overhaul the entire economic system and that this need was precipitated by global warming (now called climate change). In fact, there was no such need and no such causal connection between the two.

In both cases — the 2015 pretence that global warming was a threat and the 2020 pretence that the pandemic was a threat — the objective was to destroy capitalism and replace it with sustainable development, aka Technocracy. The UN's self-declared crisis, followed five years later by the WEF's self-declared crisis, pushed a confused and fearful worldwide populace into going along with the globalist preconceived agenda. There was never any other agenda or "fix" offered…The world had been conned by two false fears and one false solution. [21]

Not everyone approved of the terms of the SSG's. Wood mentions the late Rosa Quire and what she wrote in the preface of her acclaimed book, *Behind the Green Mask: UN Agenda 21*:

Under the mask of green our civil liberties are being restricted, constricted, and suffocated in every village and hamlet. The plan is imposed locally." In her talks and video presentations, she defined the UN Sustainable Development Plan as follows: "It is the Inventory and Control Plan: Inventory and control of all land, all water, all minerals, all clerks, or animals, or construction, or means of production, all food, or energy, or information, and all human beings in the world. [22]

The Launching of the WEF's Great Reset

The WEF launched the Great Reset Initiative in June 2020 in response to the COVID-19 pandemic which, Schwab said, "represents a rare but narrow window of opportunity to reflect, reimagine, and reset our world." The inaugural announcement was delivered by Prince Charles, now King Charles. In a short but dramatic video, he declared that "the natural world was in a state of crisis and that there is a desperate need to reimagine, rethink, reinvent, re-design our response to it."

The introductory statement on the WEF's Great Reset Initiative page proclaims:

There is an urgent need for global stakeholders to cooperate in simultaneously managing the direct consequences of the Covid-19 crisis. To improve the state

of the world, the World Economic Forum is starting the Great Reset Initiative…
The Covid-19 crisis, and the political, economic and social disruptions it has
caused is fundamentally changing the traditional context for decision-making.
The inconsistencies, inadequacies and contradictions of multiple systems —
from health and financial to energy and education — are more exposed than ever
amidst a global context of concern for lives, livelihoods and the planet. Leaders
find themselves at a historic crossroads, managing short-term pressures against
medium — and long-term uncertainties. [23]

The first step in the Plan was to reduce the population of the planet. This was
achieved through the deliberate creation of the virus, the so-called "pandemic"
and the bio-weapon vaccines which have been responsible for the deaths
of some 15 to 17 million people up to 2022 (see Part 1 of this Chapter). [24]
Their long-term effects are unknown. Another important step, described by
Wood, was to persuade businesses to join the ESG initiative. ESG stands for
Environmental, Social and Governance, collectively called sustainability. In
a business context, sustainability is about the company's business model, i.e.
how its products and services contribute to sustainable development. Whereas
this appears to be a positive initiative, by July 2021, Wood writes, the ESG
data-driven assets hit $35 trillion, or more than one third of the world's largest
asset markets.[25] The Great Reset is well underway, as evidenced by the ESG
investing what is already some trillions of dollars in available capital into
sustainable development projects.

Another step will be the use of AI technology to take over people's jobs,
leaving them with no income and dependent on the State for support. A further
step will be the introduction of CBDC's or digital IDs for *everyone* which will
make the world population dependent on those who are "managing" them.
If this insane project succeeds, we will find ourselves enmeshed in the most
extreme totalitarian system that has ever existed, driven like sheep into a
prison devised by the WEF with the complicity of the UN and the WHO. All this
is covered in David Hughes' magisterial book, where, on page 34, he writes:
"Totalitarianism comes for everyone in the end, which is why the global technocratic coup must be put down before it is too late," and on page 12:

If CBDC is implemented, central banks will be able to freeze individuals' bank
accounts, or take money out of them, or impose conditions on the way that "money" (just a voucher system by this point) is spent, and no financial transaction
anymore will be private (Davis, 2023). Put bluntly, it is a system of financial
enslavement, more "direct" than "debt slavery." Dissidents will be financially
outcast, as already indicated by the abortive move to freeze Canadian truckers'
bank accounts and those of their supporters in January 2022.

Brave New World?

Wood explains that with the new sciences of Nanotechnology, Biotechnology, Information Technology and Cognitive Science — collectively called NBIC — transhumanists believe that, as Yuval Harari has announced, man himself can now take on the role of "intelligent designer" and can create the future in accordance with his own desires and technical power. The dark side of NBIC "applied science," however, is that its practitioners' goal is to programme evolution and take control of future life on earth. Nearly all of them do not recognize that there already exists an intelligent design to life nor do they recognize the existence of an "Intelligent Designer." They are all apparently devotees of the ideology of Scientific Materialism. [26] This paragraph from Mattias Desmet's book sums up the danger of the proposed Plan:

> Man may not realize it, but his humanity does not really matter, it is nothing essential. His whole existence, his longing and his lust, his romantic lamentations and his most superficial needs, his joy and his sorrow, his doubt and his choices, his anger and unreasonableness, his pleasure and his suffering, his deepest aversions, and his most lofty aesthetic appreciations, in short, the entire drama of his existence, can ultimately be reduced to elementary particles that interact according to the laws of mechanics. [27]

Transhumanists anticipate that they will ultimately be able to eliminate death when they have discovered how to upload the content of the human brain into the 'Cloud.' What happens if there is a cyber attack and their brain cannot be downloaded? The irony of this is that there is no necessity to try to achieve this goal since they will discover, when they transition, that their consciousness survives the death of the physical body.

Wood says that several conclusions can be drawn from this exploration of transhumanism. "Once transhumanists regard DNA as something to be exploited and manipulated, disregarding individual sovereignty and nature's design, they experiment with ways to use DNA more efficiently than it is used in its present state." They will therefore adulterate the DNA codes that have been passed down the generations for tens of thousands of years. Here is his summary of NBIC technology (Nanotechnology, Biotechnology, Information Technology and Cognitive Science) in seven points:

1. Transhumanists regard DNA as something to be exploited and manipulated. Disregarding individual sovereignty and nature's design, they experiment with ways to use DNA more efficiently than it is used in its original state.

2. When transhumanists refer to "biodiversity," they really mean "genetic resources."

3. "Genetic resources" in turn, refers to genetic material that is to be owned, exploited, and controlled through genetic engineering performed by the biotech industry.

4. UNCED (UN Conference on Economic Development) and Agenda 21 were largely smokescreens to obscure the reality of conclusions one through three.

5. The Third World is being set up to be plundered yet again — this time in the name of sustainable development and biodiversity. The plunderers' prize is genetic engineering and ownership of the resulting genetically engineered products.

6. Biodiversity is not about preserving species but is rather; using species as a source of raw materials for the biotech industry, whose mission is to sequence the DNA of all living entities on earth.

7. After being digitally sequenced, these living things are placed in a globally accessible database, are recognised as a global common asset, and are made available for "licensing" by biotech firms. [28]

The Great Reset must be seen as a two-part achievement. The first part is the economic restructuring of the world. The second part is the restructuring of the humans who live in that economically reconstructed future world. Economic restructuring refers to sustainable development — that is, the rebirth of 1930s technocracy. The end result of technocracy/sustainable development is scientific dictatorship. Dictatorship of any sort is hardly the Utopia its fanatical adherents insanely envision and glowingly describe.[29]

If the Archons that I wrote about in Part 2 of Chapter Seven on the Gnostics, exist, this is exactly the field where they would be directing their malevolent efforts, driving humanity towards perpetual war and preparations for war on the one hand and Transhumanism on the other. I think these dark spiritual energies or entities do indeed exist and their entry point into influencing the direction of events on this planet and taking control of it is through the twin portals of Power and Greed. A book called *The Controligarchs* by Seamus Bruner, published in 2023, reveals how five immensely wealthy and powerful men: Bill Gates, George Soros, Mark Zuckerberg, Jeff Bezos and Klaus Schwab [and Elon Musk], already control virtually every aspect of our lives and how the top twenty-five members of the World Economic Forum (WEF), who together are worth more than $10 trillion, have already amassed more economic power than the United States government.[30] Do we want to have bi-annual mRNA vaccines, as Klaus Schwab has recently suggested (30/1/25), when we now know that these bio-weapons are designed to alter our DNA and destroy our immune systems?

Transhumanists remind me of the myth of Prometheus, who stole the fire from the gods and gave it to humans. These transhumanists are the new Prometheans. In his Commentary on *The Secret of the Golden Flower*, Jung said of modern consciousness that is unable to listen to the Spirit of the Depths: "Consciousness thus torn from its roots possesses a Promethean freedom, but it also partakes of the nature of a godless *hybris*." The transhumanists' envisioned "upgrade" of humanity will make it impossible for us to go back to the human beings we are now. Anything more terrifying than this can hardly be imagined, yet technocracy and scientific materialism make it possible. Whether you look at the greed of the pharmaceutical companies, the government departments and medical institutions that accept large sums of money from them, or the colossal wealth of the so-called benefactors like Bill Gates and the other Controligarchs, the driving motive of all of them is the immense power that immense wealth brings, power that may not necessarily be exercised in the best interests of humanity.

The most infamous idea of the technocrats who seek to take over the planet and control us through digital technology, is to alter the biology of our bodies by "improving" it through digital technocracy, through sub-cutaneous implants and nano-technology and even through giving us pills and vaccinations via nose-sprays. Their Plan, presenting technology as our "saviour" and "the next step in our evolution," is to alter and upgrade our DNA. This Agenda to "improve" us is evil. It is evil because it arrogates to itself the right to interfere with and alter human biology which, some of us believe, was given to us by divine intent.

Drawing on the fallacious idea that we are a flawed species in need of "upgrading," it aims to create a "super-human" species that will be an improvement on the current one. The prospect of using technology radically to enhance human performance has been the subject of intense debate over the last two decades. The military will undoubtedly try to create soldiers with an 'improved' ability to kill. To unite against this Agenda, we need to understand the pathology of its formulators, how inflated, omnipotent, and even insane they have become, wanting to control everything and everyone through the technology that is giving them the God-like power to create the "New Human." We are being ensnared in a Dystopian totalitarian future from which, if we allow it to trap us, we will be unable to escape. What is coming ever closer is the technocratic enslavement of humanity.

The Warning of Gregg Braden [31]

In his recently published book, *Pure Human*, Gregg Braden says that transhumanism has its roots in the belief that we are a flawed species that needs improving or up-grading, thereby repeating the belief diffused by the Myth of the Fall. Technology is being presented as our saviour and as the next step in our evolution, replacing us with a new form of humanity that will be an 'advance' over the present one. The means of achieving this will be a convergence of technology and human biology, technology that will drastically alter our DNA and our immune system. Once established, there will be no possibility of going back to our present form. He says, and I agree with him, that we are engaged in a battle between good and evil. "Evil is at the core of the transhumanist movement that wants to replace the natural biology of our bodies with machines." [32] He asks whether we have the intelligence and the willpower to destroy this 'Plan.' Our focussed attention on what is going on beneath the radar is vital if our current species is to survive the transhumanist threat.

Because I think this book is exceptionally interesting, clearly expressed, and timely, I am quoting extracts from the Introduction to his book:

> For the first time in our history, we have the power not only to change the world around us but the world within us.... We now have at our fingertips the technology to alter ourselves — to re-write the code of our DNA and the neural networks that define us — in ways that, once implemented, can never be reversed, and will forever change what it means to be human. What we stand to lose in this transformation of ourselves, is our imagination, intuition, innovation, and creativity.
>
> We stand at the precipice of giving away our humanness — the biological bridge to our divinity.... We owe it to ourselves to recognize the deep truth of what it means to be human before we give ourselves away to the technology now being proposed by the transhumanist movement.... We are on a destructive path that will degrade and possibly end the human species as we know it. [33]

The next steps that we take regarding artificial intelligence (AI) and the merging of our natural bodies with technology by implanting computer chips in the brain and injecting gene therapies into our blood will set the course that determines how much of ourselves we preserve and how much of our humanness we forever give away to technology. The choice is ours and we are already making it. [34]

For the first time in human history, we're implementing technology that irreversibly changes our bodies on a biological level. If we continue on the current technological path, guided by the current trends in thinking, by the year 2030 we will have made the ultimate choice: We'll be well on our way to one of two kinds of societies.

We will either be locked into a "futuristic" society of human-machine hybrids where we have traded our cherished qualities of intuition, empathy, and creativity and the soul-stirring bonds of love, intimacy, and sexual conception for the convenience of AI that creates our music, poetry, and art, and virtual realities that replace genuine relationships and human contact. [35]

Or we will awaken to the deep truth of our extraordinary largely untapped natural human potential and, for the first time as a species, discover what it means to be fully human. We stand to lose the source of our imagination, innovation, and creativity. What is at stake is our divinity — the part of us that allows us to rise above our circumstances and become more than any limitations and expectations that we've accepted for ourselves in the past. [36]

Ultimately, he says, "We stand at the precipice of giving away our humanness — the biological bridge to our divinity. [37] The steep price that we would pay for such achievements is the creation of individuals, who have lost the ability to feel; who are driven by efficiency, logic, and algorithms, who no longer experience what transhumanists view as the human "flaws" of uncomfortable emotions, such as grief, suffering, broken love, and loss." [38]

He agrees with Patrick Wood that the 2019 partnership between The United Nations and the WEF is a nefarious alliance because it furthers the aims of the WEF. He says that the problem is not with the 17 Sustainable Goals as such but with the methods the UN has agreed to achieve them, fusing the aims of the WEF Great Reset with its 17 Sustainable Goals. [39] These Goals, to be achieved in such a brief time — by 2030, "have triggered much of the economic and social turmoil we see in the world today." [40] They have had a particularly harmful effect on agriculture and on small farms which are being forcibly transformed into large corporate farms that require pesticides and GMO technologies as well as conforming to climate change goals. [41]

He defines the Great Reset vision as one that "aims to merge us and all the present-day systems of finance, business, manufacturing, transportation, and food production that we use, as well as our consumption, travel, lifestyle choices, and spending habits, into one vast network that is managed and regulated through the oversight of an advanced AI." [42]

> The public proceedings from the WEF reveal that the vision for this vast data sphere is for the entire system to be governed automatically by sophisticated algorithms, deep surveillance, and an advanced system of AI. Schwab and other members of the WEF view the convergence of our physical, digital, and biological lives as the inevitable next stage of progress in the evolution of civilization and humankind. [43]

Braden views the proposed integration of the human body and consciousness into the digital landscape envisioned by the WEF as irresponsible and dangerous because it poses an irreversible threat to our lives and our humanness. [44]

Replacing our Biology with Technocracy

One of the technological feats envisaged by transhumanists is the creation of life in an artificial womb. After 200,000 years of child-bearing, woman's role in the creation of new life would become redundant. The sexual union of a man and a woman (even artificial insemination) would no longer be necessary for the continuation of the human species.

> In the light of these technologies, it is not so far-fetched to envisage a world of baby-producing factories consisting of large warehouse-like structures where rows of artificial wombs contain living human foetuses. During their development the foetuses might be "optimized" for specific functions such as athletic performance or increased IQ — or to become super-soldiers — with gene-editing technology, and monitored by computers and AI until the moment of their... birth? It wouldn't be accurate to say that these babies are "born," as there would be no actual delivery as typically occurs with their emergence through the birth canal. [45]

Who would receive and handle these babies — a robot? What would happen to love, empathy, the essential bonding between mother and child? Would their growing up be supervised by robots or hybrids instead of parents? Would there be any need for homes, families, grandparents, relationships? The aim of this inhuman technology seems to be to eliminate our emotional intelligence: our capacity to feel, to imagine, to create, to dream, to love as well as to hate and to fear; to banish or degrade the relationship between child and parent, man and woman and between human beings in general. Who would decide what characteristics and qualities would be mechanically "given" to the foetus? What gender would be assigned to it? If the population of a country is declining, who would decide whether males or females should be gestated in these artificial wombs and how many of each? All this sounds like a re-creation of Aldous Huxley's *Brave New World*, published in 1932. Here, I will reluctantly leave Gregg Braden and turn to Climate Change.

Climate Change

Climate anxiety was launched when Al Gore held up his famous chart with a line going vertical after having been horizontal for centuries. He confidently predicted in 2009 that the Arctic ice would be melted by 2014. Since then, we have been indoctrinated with anxiety and guilt for having been responsible for bringing about that vertical line through the extraction and use of fossil fuels since the time of the Industrial Revolution. The achievement of the UN's Seventeen Sustainable Goals by 2030, and reaching Net Zero by 2050, are the goals imposed on countries that, we are told, must be achieved if we are to save ourselves from Global Warming going out of control and destroying all life on Earth.

The method of bringing about this new system is to use fear and guilt as the two agents to induce conformity. As with the virus, the first step was to instil fear in the population by means of propaganda. Create fear and guilt, and you can then impose an agenda for controlling or reversing the supposed threat of Climate Change.

The first Climate Change Conference took place in 1979 in Geneva and the first UN Climate Change Conference in 1995, in Berlin. Ever since, Climate Change has gradually taken on the character of a religious cult with its devotees, promoters, activists, and martyrs. Since the Paris Climate Change Conference of 2015 and the creation of the UN's 17 Sustainable Goals, we have been programmed to accept changes which are drastically affecting our lives, government financial and environmental planning, and the future of the technologies that provide us with light and heat. Climate Change is what we have long been programmed to believe in, and what the media continually draws our attention to with every unusual storm, hurricane, typhoon or fire — even the recent terrible inferno in California (January 2025).

We have been indoctrinated for decades with the belief that Climate Change is a threat caused by our extraction and use of fossil fuels, that CO_2 is a danger to the planet and that we must not cross the 1.5°C warming threshold — a critical limit that certain climate scientists have warned against exceeding; that we must live in 15-minute cities, that cows' burps and farts release methane into the atmosphere and must be reduced or even cows themselves eliminated; that we must stop eating food grown naturally in the Earth on small farms and eat synthetic food manufactured artificially in factories, or food that has been geo-engineered in huge farms; that we must cover the landscape with wind-turbines and solar panels in order to supply millions of people with electricity; that we must get rid of petrol and diesel cars and move to electric ones instead. No-one mentions that China is continuing to burn coal, and is developing energy with thorium (rather than uranium) reactors that do not leave lethal plutonium residues. Nor that China and Saudi-Arabia's Net Zero's target date is 2060 or India's 2070.

Many international meetings have been held to discuss the problem of how to accelerate Net Zero and replace fossil fuels with other sources of energy. We are not told that a change in the climate may be part of the Earth's own cycles of change from a warmer climate to a cooler one or vice versa. All this is blatant propaganda and disinformation, cleverly disseminated over many decades and designed to programme us to believe what we are told and to obey. Mike Yeadon said in his address to the Irish Parliament that the warnings about climate change started with the Club of Rome in the 1960's and have continued ever since. He told us not to be taken in by them.

Gregg Braden, who has studied this situation for decades, and who has the required qualifications to comment, concludes in his book:

> Contrary to the public narrative promoted in mainstream media and classrooms, the geologic data from diverse sources reveal that Earth's climate is not static. It's a dynamic and complex system that is constantly changing. The changes we are seeing today in global climate and localized weather patterns are (1) part of Earth's rhythms and cycles seen in the past, and (2) that the bulk of the increased CO_2 in the atmosphere comes from the outgassing of oceans rather than from the burning of fossil fuels. Without a doubt, CO_2 levels are definitely higher today than they have been for recent decades. And without a doubt, today's CO_2 levels actually pale in comparison to levels they've achieved in ages past.
>
> It is no coincidence that the periods of geologic history that saw high levels of CO_2 also correlate with the time that Earth experienced lush forests and a healthy diversity of life. These demonstrable facts are in direct contradiction to the frightening predictions coming from "experts," mis-informed activists, and many of our political leaders today.
>
> Clearly, he continues, it is to our benefit as a species to develop clean, green, and sustainable forms of energy that are available to everyone that wants access to this energy. If our leaders were serious about doing so, however, the technologies discovered over the last seventy years would have been developed and made available to replace the fossil fuels that we rely on today. [46]
>
> These include the use of the element thorium, for example, to power base-load electric power plants as validated during the Manhattan Project in the mid-20th century; allowing the carburettors developed in the 1970's that achieve 90

miles per gallon of gasoline to be used in the automobile industry; and access to the resonant technology that draws energy from the Planck vacuum of "empty" space to be made available for commercial use. [47]

Essential to the formula of mass indoctrination is to tell us that there is no way out. We are doomed if we don't acquiesce in the agenda laid out for us — whether in relation to the vaccinations forced on us, digital technology or climate change.

> The most seductive part of this kind of manipulation is how it uses a mix of factual, real-world events to promote guilt and then to justify extreme forms of social engineering as a means to an end. The means detracts from our lives by destroying entire industries and traditional ways of life and living, while the end we are headed towards will enrich a select few who know how to build and invest in technology and financial instruments that align with mandated changes.… The magnitude of social engineering that is being attempted based upon the false narratives of climate change is making the availability of objective information even more valuable than ever. The better informed we are, the better equipped we are to make informed and responsible choices. [48]

(see Gregg's videos on this subject on his website: Gregg Braden.com) Near the end of his book, he sums up our situation:

> Two hundred thousand years ago, something miraculous happened here on Earth, something so extraordinary that it left us with godlike abilities that have never before and have never since been given to any other form of life — at least not to any life form that we're currently aware of. It was at that time that we were imbued with the power to self-regulate our consciousness and self-heal physically as well as the ability to do so consciously and on demand. We're the only form of life on Earth that can access via brain states and advanced realms of deep intuition intentionally, when we choose to do so. We're the only form of life that can create a super immune response and super resilience to our rapidly changing world, awaken longevity enzymes, and create elevated states of super learning, super memorization, super cognition, and more — all at the time and place of our personal choosing.
>
> The DNA evidence shows us that our anatomically modern human ancestors were given these extraordinary abilities, and many more, on the day they myste-riously appeared on the Earth. These abilities have been with us every day since that time, and they remain with us today. Although we're seldom informed or reminded of our exceptional abilities that give us deeper meaning to our lives they are part of us, nonetheless. It's the undeniable fact of these extraordinary powers that points us to our inevitable destiny: we're a species meant to express our powers and live the truth of our human divinity. And we're wired to awaken the innate abilities that we thought of in the past as supernatural powers. And we're wired to embrace these abilities as a natural part of our everyday lives. [49]

As we stand in the fullness of our power, it is impossible for us to be deceived by the dark forces that are sweeping through our societies and across the nations of the Earth today. In the fullness of our power, we can no longer be reduced to the status of powerless victims in the battle between good and evil.

As we learn to trust our divinity, we will also awaken our natural desire for the freedom that leads us to become the best versions of ourselves and create the best world possible. The key to living up to our pure human destiny is that we must choose to embrace it. [50]

I suggest that anyone reading this who is deeply concerned about climate change should watch **Climate: The Movie (The Cold Hard Truth)** written and directed by Martin Durkin and released (20/3/24). The movie shows that the alarm we have been conditioned to accept is not supported by facts, only by computer models. CO_2 is a red herring — a tiny 0.04% — and irrelevant in a living system.

Reviewing *Climate: The Movie*, Peter Murphy writes that it features a series of interviews of prominent and credentialed scientists, including Steven Koonin, NYU professor and former Assistant Secretary of Energy in the Obama administration; Richard Lindzen, retired atmospheric physicist from Harvard University and the Massachusetts Institute of Technology; Roy Spencer, meteorologist at the University of Huntsville in Alabama and an award-winning veteran of NASA; Willie Soon, an astrophysicist and aerospace engineer at Harvard and the Smithsonian; and others, some of whom were blackballed for daring to challenge the prevailing climate change group-think narrative.

In an article published in *The Week That Was*: January 18, 2025, a publication of The Science and Environmental Policy Project (www.SEPP.org), Steven Koonin, one of the climate scientists in *The Movie*, presents physical evidence (data) showing that nothing unusual is taking place. He begins by describing *hubris*.

Hubris is a Greek word that means dangerously overconfident. Based on my research, hubris fairly describes our current response to the issue of climate change. Here's what many people believe:

One: The planet is warming catastrophically because of certain human behaviors.

Two: Thanks to powerful computers we can project what the climate will be like 20, 40, or even 100 years from now.

Three: That if we eliminate just one behavior, the burning of fossil fuels, we can prevent the climate from changing for as long as we like. Each of these presumptions — together the basis of our hubris regarding the changing climate — is either untrue or so far off the mark as to be useless.

Yes, it's true that the globe is warming, and that humans are exerting a warming influence upon it. But beyond that, I do not think the "Science" says what you think it says.

The globe has warmed and cooled many times in the past as it is doing now. From the early 1600s to the early 1800s, the surface of the River Thames froze over 24 times. Sometimes it stayed frozen for several weeks and people enjoyed skating on it.

Koonin continues:

> Why aren't these reassuring facts better known? Because the public gets its climate information almost exclusively from the media. And from a media perspective, fear sells. 'Things aren't that bad' doesn't sell. Very few people, and that includes journalists who report on climate news, read the actual science. I have. And what the data — the hard science — from the US government and UN Climate reports say is that… 'things aren't that bad.'
>
> Nor does the public understand the questionable basis of all catastrophic climate change projections: computer modelling. Projecting future climate is excruciatingly difficult. Yes, there are human influences, but the climate is complex. Anyone who says that climate models are 'just physics' either doesn't understand them or is being deliberately misleading. I should know. I wrote one of the first textbooks on computer modelling. While modellers base their assumptions upon both fundamental physical laws and observations of the climate, there is still considerable judgment involved. And since different modelers will make different assumptions, results vary widely among different models.

Koonin then shows that 73 models *overestimate* the warming of the globe. These models are the ones cited by the **UN Intergovernmental Panel on Climate Change and its collaborators**, as proof of human caused global warming. I would add that these models are another aspect of the lies we have been told. One problem that Koonin discusses is the failure of these models correctly to forecast clouds. As Koonin states:

> Natural fluctuations in the height and coverage of clouds have at least as much of an impact on the flows of sunlight and heat as do human influences. But how can we possibly know global cloud coverage say 10, let alone 50 years from now? Obviously, we can't. But to create a climate model, we have to make assumptions. That's a pretty shaky foundation on which to transform the world's economy.
> **Moreover, creating more accurate models isn't getting any easier. In fact, the more we learn about the climate system, the more we realize how complex**

it is. Rather than admit this complexity, the media, the politicians, and a good portion of the climate science community attribute every terrible storm, every flood, every major fire to 'climate change.' Yes, we've always had these weather events in the past, the narrative goes, but somehow 'climate change' is making everything 'worse.' Even if that were true, isn't the relevant question, how much worse? Not to mention that 'worse' is not exactly a scientific term. And how could we make it better? For the alarmists, that's easy: we get rid of fossil fuels. Not only is this impractical—we get over 80% of the world's energy from fossil fuels—it's not scientifically possible. That's because CO_2 doesn't disappear from the atmosphere in a few days like, say, smog. It hangs around for a really long time. About 60 percent of any CO_2 that we emit today will remain in the atmosphere 20 years from now, between 30 and 55 percent will still be there after a century, and between 15 and 30 percent will remain after one thousand years."

To this interesting and clarifying contribution from Koonin, *That Was The Week That Was* added: "The enormous growth in human CO_2 emissions is coming from China and south Asia. The hubris of western politicians is amazing. Without even a hint of expertise in climate science, they pretend to "know" that CO_2 is ruining the climate, fail to put "blame" on the biggest CO_2 emitters, fail to acknowledge the benefits of increasing CO_2, and enact laws to control their own citizenry under the guise of saving the planet."

The Attack on Agriculture

Patrick Wood describes how, in the original 1934 Technocracy Study Course, the transhumanist agenda was described as follows:

> All present farms and land divisions would be eliminated. Agriculture would be only one division of a vast chemical industry which would convert the raw materials of the land into use products and in turn supply to the land its requirements in fertilisers and plant food. Tracts probably tens of miles square would be worked at a unit. [51]

"The obsessive need to control Nature and consolidate industries explains the technocrats' war on family farms over the last eighty years as well as the massive accumulation of farmland by multinational corporations in the US and elsewhere." [52] Bill Gates and others have apparently bought up enormous tracts of land in the US. Farmers in the UK are infuriated by the 20% inheritance tax imposed by the Labour Government Budget (30/10/2024) that will lead to their being taxed out of existence and cause food shortages, as the supermarkets have predicted. This new tax has aroused their furious anger as well as their despair — leading a few to commit suicide, unable to face the loss of everything they have built up and hoped to leave to their children. The new tax will prevent many from being able to do so because of the high cost of replacing farm machinery.

The absurd lengths governments are going to conform to this agenda, include Bill Gates' synthetic foods and controlling the climate by extensive geo-engineering. The centuries' old relationship of farmers to their land is being attacked and undermined, most recently in the Netherlands and Ireland but in many other places as well. All this causes great distress and anxiety to people whose whole life is centred on the care of the land and who feel a deep sense of responsibility towards it. This agenda is a repudiation of Nature, of the deep roots of agriculture, of how we have grown food for thousands of years. It is the most devastating blow governments could inflict on the world-wide farming community that produces our food — food that is essential for our survival. This too, is an insidious aspect of the Plan.

In this Chapter, the disclosure by concerned individuals of this dark vision of our future has come in time to wake us up from our too great a trust in governments, the medical profession and the scientific community, although Science per se, as a methodology, is not included in this warning. Behind the terrifying transhuman vision of our future are the beliefs of scientific materialism which have been taught to generations of our children, indoctrinating them with the fallacious idea that we are the only conscious beings in a universe that is without life, consciousness, intelligence, purpose or meaning, narrowing their horizon to this planet and ignoring the vast Intelligence of the Cosmos and its multiple dimensions, as well as the presence of its other inhabitants.

Where is the voice of the Divine Feminine in this distorted view of reality and its desire for power and control over Nature? One of the main reasons we are in a time of crisis is the belief that we human beings are separate from the natural world in which we live, and that we can therefore interfere with its physical, chemical, and biological systems without these alterations having any effect on us. We need now to come together to create a new kind of civilization, based on beliefs and behaviour that respect Nature's wisdom, the miraculous immune system of our bodies and our evolutionary destiny on this planet. Our young people are suffering from depression and the belief that life has no meaning beyond what they hear and see on social media. They need hope and trust that this challenging passage we are in can be navigated and that they will come through it as co-creators of a new kind of civilization that honours and trusts our humanness and our innate, extraordinary creativity.

They need to re-imagine the education they will give to their children —

to help them to appreciate and value the marvel of their life and the marvel of the world they are born into; to help them cultivate the qualities and skills that contribute to the richness and beauty of their humanity: empathy, creativity, trust in their divinity, intelligence and intuition, their curiosity, enthusiasm, joy, and their capacity to love and care for other forms of life.

I will end this Chapter with a poem by David Lorimer

It is Always Time

The silent mountains
Speak eternal truth
Within our souls
From their depth of time.

It is always time to be still
To remember who we are
To be present in the centre of our being
To flow towards the One,
And towards each other.

It is always time for compassion,
To be rooted and grounded in love,
To comfort the afflicted
To care and share with each other.

It is always time
To be true and loyal,
To be noble and civil,
To be courteous and kind
Towards each other.

It is always time
For honour and integrity,
Time for courage,
It is always time for truth,
Time for wisdom,
It is always time for goodness,
Time for beauty.

This meeting of eternity and time
Is always here and now,
Is always present,
Is always to be embodied,
To be enacted by each and all
Together.

Notes:

1. According to Professor Harari:
    "Many tyrants and governments wanted to hack millions of people in the past, but nobody knew biology well enough. Nobody had enough computing power and data to hack millions of people. Neither the Gestapo nor the KGB could do it. But soon, at least some corporations and governments will be able to systematically hack all the people. We humans should get used to the idea that we are no longer mysterious souls. We are now hackable animals. Data may allow human elites to do something even more radical than just build physical dictatorships. By hacking organisms, elites may gain the power to re-engineer the future of life itself. Because once you can hack something, you can usually also engineer it. And if indeed, we succeed in hacking and engineering life, this will be not only the greatest revolution in the history of humanity. This will be the greatest revolution in biology since the very beginning of life four billion years ago. For four billion years, nothing fundamental changed in the basic rules in the game of life. All of life for four billion years — dinosaurs, amoeba, tomatoes, humans — all of life was subject to the laws of natural selection and to the laws of biochemistry.

    But this is now about to change. Science is replacing evolution by natural selection with evolution by intelligent design. Not some intelligent design of some God above the clouds but our intelligent design — the IBN Cloud, the Microsoft Cloud. These are the new driving forces of evolution. And science may enable life, after being confined for 4 billion years to the limited realm of organic compounds, science may enable life to break out into the inorganic realm. So, after 4 billion years of life shaped by natural selection, we are entering the era or inorganic life, shaped by Intelligent Design. So does the data about my DNA, my brain, my body, my life, belong to me? Does it belong to me, or to some corporation, or perhaps to the government or perhaps to the human collective?" End of transcript from his 2020 Davos talk.
    https://www.youtube.com/watch?v=gG6WnMb9Fho
2. Rees, Laurence (2025) *The Nazi Mind: Twelve Warnings from History*, Viking
3. Lewis, C. S. (1947) *The Abolition of Man*, Macmillan, New York, p. 58. Quoted in Patrick M. Wood, 2022, *The Evil Twins of Technocracy and Transhumanism*, Coherent Publishing, Meza, AZ, pp. 22-23

4. Kurzweil, Ray (2024) *The Singularity is Nearer*, Bodley Head, London also his earlier book (2005) *The Singularity is Near: When Humans Transcend Biology*, Penguin, London.

5. Hughes, David (2025), *Covid 19: Psychological Operations and the War for Technocracy.* Free download of his book if you sign up to substack
    see https://dhughes.substack.com/p/interview-with-alex-jones-february 2025

6. Wood, Patrick M. (2022), *The Evil Twins of Technocracy and Transhumanism*, Coherent Publishing LLC, Mesa AZ

7. Brzezinski, Zbigniew (1970) *Between Two Ages: America's role in the Technetronic Era*, p. 253, quoted in Wood, p. 35

8. More, Max (1994) *On Becoming Posthuman,* quoted in Wood p. 59

9. Wood, p. 59

10. ibid, p. 60

11. ibid, pp. 203-204. It has recently emerged 21/2/25 that the FDA banned the use of Ivermectin to cure the symptoms of Covid and instead promoted the mRNA vaccines. In so doing, it was and is responsible for the death and injury of thousands.

12. ibid, p. 205

13. ibid, p. 101

14. Bernays, Edward L. (1928) *Propaganda: The Public Mind in the Making*, Horace Liveright, New York, Chapter 1

15. See Neil Oliver interview
    https://www.youtube.com watch?v=999QK1NTE_E&t=73s

16. "Expectancy" by William Moore is featured in Negro Poets and Their Poems (The Associated Publishers, Inc., 1923

17. Wood, p. 9

18. ibid, p. 86

19. Quoted by Wood, p. 86

20. ibid, p. 76

21. ibid, p. 76

22. ibid, p. 89

23. ibid, pp. 74-75

24. "The overall risk of death induced by injection with the COVID-19 vaccines in actual populations, inferred from excess all-cause mortality and its synchronicity with rollouts, is globally pervasive and much larger than reported in clinical trials, adverse effect monitoring, and cause-of-death statistics from death certificates, by 3 orders of magnitude (1,000-fold greater)."
    Conclusion from a study by Denis Rancourt, Marine Baudin, Joseph Hickey and Jérémie Mercier of COVID-19 vaccine-associated mortality in the Southern Hemisphere. September 2023.

25. Wood, p. 88

26. ibid, p. 18

27. Desmet, Mattias, op. cit., p. 17

28. Wood, op. cit. pp. 70-71

29. ibid, p. 86

30. Bruner, Seamus (2023), *Controligarchs*, Sentinel, Penguin Random House, London

& New York

31. Braden, Gregg (2025) *Pure Human: The Hidden Truth of Our Divinity, Power, and Destiny*, Hay House LLC, Carlsbad, California, New York City, London, Sydney, New Delhi.
   Gregg Braden is the author of many books. He has a background in geology, earth-sciences, and computer systems. Throughout his life he has travelled and explored the world widely. He has given innumerable fascinating webinars, some of them with Nassim Haramein for Humanity's Team in the US.
32. Braden, op. cit. p. xvii
33. ibid, pp. xii-xiii
34. ibid, p. xii
35. ibid, pp. xii-xiii
36. ibid, p. xiii
37. ibid, p. xiv
38. ibid, p. xv
39. ibid, p. 165
40. ibid, p. 160
41. ibid, p. 166
42. ibid, p. 161
43. ibid, p. 161
44. ibid, p. 161
45. ibid, p. 175
46. ibid, p. 222
47. ibid, p. 223
48. ibid, pp. 223-224
49. ibid, p. 233
50. ibid, p. 234
51. Wood, op. cit. p. 52
52. ibid, p. 53

https://unpackthelies.com/film/ — video about the power of propaganda and corruption in government and its health departments.

https://live.childrenshealthdefense.org/chd-tv/events/the-big-picture-life-inside-the-control-grid/the-big-picture-life-inside-the-control-grid-premiere/?utm_source=lumi-nate&utm_medium=email&utm_campaign=marketing&utm_id=20250225
— video about the Plan to trap us all into digital control.

Chapter Fourteen

THE SACRED MARRIAGE: AN EVOLUTIONARY IMPERATIVE

The world will be saved by beauty.
— Fyodor Dostoevsky, *The Idiot*

We are experiencing a moment of significance far beyond what any of us can imagine… The historical mission of our times is to reinvent the human.
— Thomas Berry, *The Great Work*

Spiritual Awakening is the most essential thing in human life; it is the only purpose of our existence.
— Khalil Gibran

Learn how to see. Realize that everything connects to everything else.
— Leonardo da Vinci

Love is the Water of Life
— Rumi

Humanity is too clever to survive without Wisdom
— E.F. Schumacher

The Sacred Marriage is about reconnecting the Great Above and the Great Below, orienting our lives to the Light and Love of the Divine Ground. It is roughly ten thousand years since we had slowly and painfully to recover from the great cataclysm and the Younger Dryas period that wiped out ancient civilizations. Other great civilizations have come and gone, bequeathing us the quintessence of their genius. At the beginning of a new phase in our evolutionary journey and a new astrological Age when humanity and the planet are said to be ascending from the third to the fifth dimension, we are beginning to awaken to what I have called the *Dream of the Cosmos* — the Dream of an enlightened humanity engaging in a new role on this planet: a role that is in harmony with the evolutionary intention of the Cosmos; that is no longer driven by the quest for power, conquest and control and the appropriation of the Earth's resources for the benefit of the few. As we begin to align ourselves with this luminous ground of reality, our minds will serve the deepest longing of our heart, the deepest wisdom of our soul. We will know who we are and why we are here.

The greatest spiritual teachers of the world have spoken about our innate Divinity: The writers of the *Upanishads* about the atman or divine core of our being, The Buddha about our underlying Buddha nature, Jesus about the kingdom of heaven within us and around us, the Sufi mystics about the realization that everything is saturated with Divinity. Abraham Abulafia, a Jewish mystic living in Spain in the thirteenth century, said that through meditation, "we are no longer separated from our source, and behold we *are* the source and the source is us. We are so intimately united with It, we cannot by any means be separated from It, for we are It." All have said that our ego, broadly associated with our left-hemispheric mind and our survival instincts, may prevent us from experiencing the truth of who and what we are, inhibiting us from experiencing union with our Source and expressing that awareness of union as love, compassion, and service of Life.

Rejecting the Divine Feminine millennia ago, we cut the umbilical cord that connected us to nature and ancient shamanic sources of wisdom. We were left with only the masculine archetype carried in the patriarchal image of God. In the Christian Church, nature and the body were split off from spirit, viewed as contaminated by the sin of the Fall. Today, we can view the death-throes of Patriarchy in the events described in the previous two chapters.

In the Introduction to this book, I said that cultures that have no image of the Mother in the god-head are vulnerable to powerful unconscious feelings of fear and anxiety, particularly when the emphasis of their religious teaching is on sin and guilt. The compensation for fear is an insatiable need for power and control. Those who for centuries have been the transmitters of the patriarchal traditions may not appreciate how deep this need and this longing are; as acutely felt by men as by women. Just as the presence of the mother comforts and reassures the child, so the image of the Divine Mother awakens the feeling of trust in us because it reflects our personal experience of our containment in the womb and our earliest human relationship.

No-one has portrayed this relationship of trust between Mother and Child better than the artists of the Renaissance as in this beautiful painting by Botticelli. At Christmas 2024, I was sent an article written by Claire Lehmann after a visit to the Louvre with her child. She writes: "We can see Botticelli depicting a level of emotional depth not previously seen in Western art… Botticelli shows us Baby Jesus standing up on his mother's lap, gazing up at her with the natural curiosity of an infant exploring his mother's face. Mary meets his gaze, her soft cheek and comforting hands creating a cradle for her child's movement. The sacred is no longer expressed through golden halos and formal arrangements, but through an intimate interaction between mother and child… What Raphael and Botticelli did was different. Through [their art] they made the vulnerability of infanthood sacred; the gentleness of femininity divine… We can still see the simple truth that they captured — in witnessing the care of a mother for her child we can look through a window into the sublime."

Virgin and Child — Botticelli

Mother and Child — Raphael

Scientific Materialism and its Denial of the Soul

In stark contrast with the new, dawning concept of reality described above, Scientific Materialism has cut us off from our soul because it does not recognize its existence. It has banished the heart, love, and the whole feeling aspect of life. It has banished wisdom, and philosophy as the love of wisdom. It has closed off the visionary right-hemisphere of our brain. As a result of its pervasive influence, we are living in an increasingly unbalanced, even insane society. Technocracy has become an obsession with men, who are being drawn towards dangerous discoveries and to actions that do not serve humanity or the planet.

Where today are the creations of the visionary imagination that has gifted our species with so many incomparable riches — riches expressed in art, architecture, poetry, music, literature, philosophy, and revelatory experience?

The whole foundation of our lives is missing because this materialist science has disconnected us from the priceless legacy of ancient civilizations, including our own: disconnected us from the shaman, the artist, the poet, the mystic, the stonemason and sculptor, the philosopher and the inventor — all those who have given expression to their celebration of Life.

We have become a one-eyed culture which has lost the visionary eye, the eye of the imagination. Our culture is incomplete and impoverished because this vital aspect of the total range of our human experience has been shut down. The visionary imagination is a supremely important faculty of our nature, just as our capacity to feel and our rational intellect are vital faculties of our nature.

Richard Tarnas, Professor of Philosophy at the California Institute for Integral Studies, asks the looming question of our time:

> What is the ultimate impact of cosmological disenchantment on a civilization? What does it do to the human self, year after year, century after century, to experience existence as a conscious purposeful being in an unconscious purposeless universe? What is the price of a collective belief in absolute cosmic indifference? What are the consequences of this unprecedented cosmological context for the human experiment, indeed, for the entire planet? [1]

The consequences are a planetary-wide increase in mental illness, addictions of every kind and regression to the most primitive, brutal, and unconscious kinds of behaviour — all of which we can see on our television screens, mobiles, and cell phones. We live in a decadent culture that promotes deception, lying and corruption that have infiltrated government, academia, and social media. We are, in the words of psychiatrist, philosopher and author Dr Iain McGilchrist, engaged in a spiritual battle of unprecedented importance. Our mind is the battlefield in which this battle is taking place. [2] As he explains in his books, we have become conditioned over recent centuries to experience life mainly through the lens of the left hemisphere of the brain. The right hemisphere, to which we are connected through the heart, has become atrophied through lack of use, closed off by our too limited view of reality, our too great reliance on the "rational" mind. The right hemisphere, seat of the creative imagination, gives us a different view of reality, where we experience ourselves as part of the Oneness of all Life and feel empathically related to the life around us and to everyone and everything on the planet. [3]

The different ways of relating to life through the two hemispheres of the brain, have been brilliantly described by Jill Bolte Taylor in her book, *My Stroke of Insight.* After she had a stroke which disabled the left hemisphere of her brain, she had the revelation of how differently life was experienced through her right hemisphere. As she gradually regained the use of her left hemisphere, she realized what a confined space she had lived in until her stroke and was able to modify the tendency of the left hemisphere to want to be in control. "My stroke of insight is that at the core of the right hemisphere is a character that is directly connected to my feeling of deep inner peace. It is completely committed to the expression of peace, love, joy, and compassion in the world." [4]

Andrew Harvey, in an interview with Father Bede Griffiths before he transitioned, wrote down his words: "I know for certain only two things about the time we are about to enter: The first is that we will see on every level, a ruthless battle between those forces that want to keep humanity enslaved to the past — and these include religious fundamentalism, nationalism, materialism, and corporate greed — and those forces that will awaken in response to a hunger for a new way of living and doing everything. The second thing I know — and I know this from my own inmost experience — is that God will shower help, grace and protection on all those who sincerely want to change and are brave enough to risk the great adventure of transformation." [5]

Birthing a New Story or a new paradigm of Reality is an evolutionary imperative at this time of unprecedented crisis and unprecedented opportunity. Without this awakening, we have no future as a species.

The Return of the Divine Feminine

The Sleeping Beauty
Edward Burne-Jones

Against the very dark background of what is happening in the world, in this final book I have endeavoured to give the history of the Divine Feminine: what it was originally, what it became; how, why, and when it was lost and what the effects of this loss have been on civilization.

Like the Sleeping Beauty, the soul of humanity is stirring to life from a four-thousand-year-long coma. The Feminine Archetype is coming back into our consciousness as a new and very ancient image of the Sacred, bringing with it a new revelation, a New Story. In the language of The Great Work of Alchemy, we are moving from the darkness of the *Nigredo* into the dawning clarity of the *Albedo*. As this great evolutionary impulse gains momentum, our rational left-hemispheric mind is beginning to open again to the right hemisphere, and to reconnect us with our heart and our long-silenced soul. What, in its deepest archetypal sense, does the word 'Feminine' mean in today's world? It stands for the arduous creation of a new kind of civilization, and a new kind of human — one who is in a conscious relationship with the Cosmos and has a profound respect for the divine laws which order it.

Awakening to the Feminine requires a receptivity not only to the events occurring in the world around us but to the long-ignored voice of the spirit that speaks to us through dreams and visions, through intuitions, and through its longing for relationship with us. The spirit communicates through the soul, through the heart, through our deepest feelings, many of which are denied recognition and expression in our culture.

The traditional values of the Feminine Principle are Wisdom, Compassion, Love, Justice, Truth, Harmony, and Beauty. All these have their origin in our human instinct to love and to create, to heal, nurture, protect and cherish. Our technological culture, enslaved by the materialist mind, and addicted to weapons and war and control of the environment, has forgotten these values but they are returning through the inspired work of many thousands, even millions, of individuals. The call goes out to the people of the world to speak with one voice on behalf of these values, on behalf of Life, on behalf of Love — for the precious life of the planet on which all our lives depend. Love and Wisdom need to become the keystone of a new civilization based on the unity of spirit and nature. This could be called the Sacred Marriage.

An Annunciation

Something of immense significance is happening: we are recovering the image of the Sacred, not as something to worship but as something we are part of, that we have always been part of. A new cosmology is being born; a new vision of our profound relationship with a conscious, intelligent, living universe. The two-and-a-half millennia-old severance of nature from spirit is being healed. Instead of seeing ourselves as fallen, sinful creatures in need of redemption by the sacrificial death of the Son of God, or as the random manifestations of a dead universe, we are beginning to realize that, as Parmenides observed long ago, we are divine beings having a human experience. We can answer the question asked by Plotinus, "But we, who are we?" We can say, with the initiates of the Orphic Mysteries, "I am a child of earth and starry heaven but my race is of heaven alone." We are travelling on a journey into the Light, realizing that we are that Light, have always been part of it. We belong to the life of the Cosmos as well as to the life of the Earth.

The Annunciation — Fra Angelico, Cortona

All this to me is like an Annunciation. We are living through a profound alchemical transformation that is transmuting the lead of our partially developed consciousness into the gold of a fully awakened one. The revelation that we are all manifestations of and participants in Cosmic Mind, part of the Earth's life as well as the life of the Cosmos, gives me hope that we may rescue ourselves from our predatory and exploitive habits in time to avoid the danger of destroying not only millions more species, but our own as well. It invites us to recognize that we have a future role in the service of the planet and ultimately the Cosmos, to know ourselves in our innermost nature as Cosmic Beings, incarnated here for a purpose, fully aware of our divinity and immortality.

Birthing a New Story

Birthing a New Story is an evolutionary imperative at this time of unprecedented crisis: a New Story that can free us from the materialist beliefs and limited left-hemispheric perspective that have increasingly imprisoned and controlled us.

If there is a single idea that has facilitated the subjugation of nature and the devastation of the planet, it is the belief that the Earth has no consciousness and that we are separate from its life. Now, we are beginning to define a new cosmology and a new relationship with the Earth. Many of us are feeling a profound love and respect for the Earth — our Mother and our home in the Cosmos. This new experience of love and empathy has the power to raise our consciousness to a higher level, bringing us into closer relationship with our soul and the higher reaches of the Cosmos, helping us to relinquish old beliefs, old struggles for power that were rooted in fear and ignorance and are still being acted out in the absurd struggle for supremacy between America, Russia, and China and in the attempts to control the climate.

The New Cosmology coming into being is that the whole universe is a Unified Field. In the words of cosmologist and physicist Nassim Haramein "A new cosmology is being born — a new vision of our profound relationship with a conscious, intelligent and interconnected universe." This new cosmology invites what the philosopher Owen Barfield called 'Final Participation,' and the alchemists 'Stellar Consciousness,' when the Great Above and the Great Below are reconnected to each other, when we are reunited with our Source. There is an emerging consensus among certain physicists, astro-physicists, and cosmologists that consciousness, not matter is the primary ground of reality; that the material world exists within consciousness. Physicist Amit Goswami, in his book *The Self-Aware Universe*, states unequivocally that

"Consciousness is the ground of all being, and our self-consciousness is That consciousness." [6] Physicist and cosmologist Jude Currivan says that "We do not *have* consciousness. We *are* consciousness."

These scientists see the universe as a living organism, not a mindless mechanism, with the seen and unseen aspects of it functioning as a unified whole. Our consciousness is part of an underlying Ground, Field, or Plenum, inseparable from it and certainly not created by the neurons of our physical brain. Each of us carries the holographic imprint of the entire universe within us. We are all equally part of the living, breathing, connecting Web of Life which connects all life forms in the universe and on our planet. Following Plato, I call this Web of Life the Soul of the Cosmos.

The realization that we participate in a Cosmic Consciousness that is the source and ground of our own consciousness shatters the belief that material reality is all there is; that we exist in a randomly created universe and that there is no life beyond death. The discoveries now being made challenge what materialist science has indoctrinated us to believe — that we, as humans, are separate from all other species and from the life of the planet as well as the life of the entire universe.

Nor are we alone in the universe. As I said in the Preface, this vital fact has been kept secret by the American government which has, during the last eighty years, concealed the information that our planet has been visited by extra-terrestrials. But the Disclosure Act of December 21st, 2023, signed by President Biden, has broken the spell of this secrecy, and has set a limit for the disclosure of the facts and events to Congress that have previously been a closely guarded secret of certain government departments. To admit publicly that this planet has been visited by extra-terrestrials opens a totally new chapter in our history and invites relationship with our cosmic brothers and sisters. The danger we need to be aware of is that we may be told that these extra-terrestrials are enemies who must be defeated by us. There is indeed a dark aspect to the universe but we are protected from becoming subject to it.

I see this emerging revelation as the fulfilment of what I call the Dream of the Cosmos. We are rediscovering at a new turn of the spiral of evolution what was known to shamans millennia ago in the Lunar Culture of the Great Mother and described in minute detail in the cosmology of Kabbalah.

We are not separate from the divinity we have been worshipping for thousands of years; we are an intrinsic part of its life, its mind, and its soul. Nor is this divinity a bearded Father-God in the sky. The greatest spiritual teachers, including the writers of the *Upanishads*, the Gnostics, the Essenes, the Sufis, the mystics, East and West, have told us that we carry divinity within our nature; that divinity is the ground of all that we call Life. At the heart of the cosmos is a love of unimaginable dimensions; a Love and a Light that sustain the entire universe and are the source of our own capacity to love and to create. As he was burnt at the stake in Rome in 1600, Giordano Bruno, philosopher, poet, alchemist, astrologer, and cosmologist said, "A single force — Love — links and gives life to infinite worlds." [7]

The Great Awakening

Over the past fifty years a gradual restoration of a sense of the sacred has been taking place beneath the surface of our culture, called forth by the multi-faceted crisis of our times. Now, through the awakening power of the environmental movement as well as new scientific discoveries, we are entering a new era, where nature — the life of the earth — and all the miraculous processes and invisible patterns of life can once again be recognized as sacred, as they once were in ancient shamanic cultures. This new movement is beginning to heal the separation between spirit and nature and the wound in the image of God which has so tragically flawed the three patriarchal religions.

Thousands, if not millions of individuals today are searching not only for the unified field in science but for a unified vision of life — a unified vision of spirit, nature and humanity that could be in time to mitigate the catastrophic effects of our fragmented view of life. The birthing of this vision asks us to relinquish many cherished beliefs and requires a fundamental transformation of our values. Our knowledge about the world and the universe is accelerating geometrically. We are overwhelmed with information about every aspect of what we observe, yet we understand so little about the mystery of why we are here and what the evolutionary role of our species on this planet might be.

The Old Image of God is undergoing an alchemical transformation

In the Preface of this book, I wrote about the need for a new image of God. Originally created millennia ago in Jerusalem, and adopted by Christianity and later, Islam, the image of the God of the patriarchal religions — a distant male Creator in a place called heaven — is undergoing an alchemical transformation. God or Spirit may be redefined as the invisible Ground of the entire manifest universe and the Ground of our own consciousness. Divine Mind is not something separate or distant from us. We are within it, part of it, co-existing and co-creating with it. This to me is one of the great revelations of our time. If God or Spirit is the intelligence and creative energy of the life process itself, pulsing forth at every instant in every region of this vast universe, then how we treat so-called inanimate matter, planetary life and each other becomes a matter of how we are treating God. We cannot separate any aspect of life from this new image or concept of God. *In splitting the atom and creating weapons of mass destruction, and in killing others who are our soul-brothers and sisters, we are mutilating and desecrating the body of God.*

This new emerging image suggests that the world is not a random assembly of parts but resonates with a unifying and coherent intelligence. The physical universe is a divine hologram that reflects in its tiniest parts the presence of the higher unifying intelligence that created it. To injure the Earth or to inflict pain and suffering on other human beings is to injure the Universal Consciousness and, since we participate in that Consciousness, to injure ourselves. Everything we do affects the whole. This is such a different concept of God and of ourselves that it takes some time to assimilate its implications. The insight that divinity is present in every single atom of life is precisely what has been missing in our concept of God and it is this which has led to the separation between spirit and nature and, ultimately, to that between religion and science as well as to our growing capacity to inflict destruction on each other and on the life of the planet.

This realization calls for a fundamental change in our values. The Genesis Myth about the creation of the earth by a Father-God needs to be superseded by a new image of 'God' as the intelligence and energy of the life process itself, flaring forth at every instant in every region of this vast universe as well as in ourselves. It transforms obedience to God's commands into love and respect for God's creation, including ourselves, our neighbour and, most importantly, our enemy.

We are moving from the story of a dead insentient cosmos to a new story of a Cosmos that is vibrantly alive and the primary ground of our own consciousness. But more than this, we are moving towards a new concept of God and of our relationship with God which is a revelation as great as any we have ever had. We are moving from an image of God as a creator separate from creation to an image of spirit as the sublime Intelligence *within* the process of cosmic and planetary evolution. An Eternal Consciousness participates in the life of this universe and we are a manifestation of that Consciousness just coming to the awareness that we participate in its life, that we are co-creators with it; that we are, essentially, divine beings.

New Wine in New Bottles: The New Spirituality

On the one hand the image of deity that has presided over Christian civilization for two thousand years is dying and this process of the decay or waning of an archetype is affecting the whole world. On the other hand, beneath the surface concerns of our culture, we can see that a spiritual awakening on a planetary scale is taking place in response to the challenges we face and the general political insanity of our times. This awakening is beginning to heal the great split in the patriarchal psyche between spirit and nature and the dissociation between thinking and feeling that lies at the core of scientific materialism.

Mother and Child — Painting by Robin Baring

The old idea that we are separate from God is breaking, cracking, beginning to move. The extraordinary discoveries about the size, complexity and incredible beauty of the universe are opening the door to a new cosmology, a new way of living and relating to each other and the planet. This dawning meta-narrative is bringing about a breakdown of old beliefs, old images of God and nature and our own human nature. It is challenging our political and economic structures, our enslavement to obsolete beliefs and atavistic habits of behaviour. It is awakening our heart, our soul, often through means which may seem threatening.

The deep malaise and depression in society may help us to grow beyond the current secular mind-set and beyond the patriarchal religions of the past which carry so much dead wood, towards a new spirituality which unifies the two great archetypes of life in a sacred marriage of spirit and nature.

This new spirituality, which incorporates the best aspect of the great spiritual traditions of the past, including the Indigenous traditions, could open the door to a new understanding of our role in a mind-blowing cosmic drama. Many people are discovering that their experience of spirit is utterly different from what they had accepted as 'truth' in the past. In these discoveries there is no division of God. There is nothing outside God. What we have called 'God' is all cosmic life.

As we assimilate this incredible story, the realization is dawning that we are participating in a Cosmic Consciousness or Intelligence which is co-inherent with every particle of our being and every particle of 'matter.' If we connect these ideas to God, then God or Spirit or Divine Mind is not something transcendent to and separate from ourselves. We are co-inherent with It, at the very heart of It. To co-inhere means to be together, to abide together.

Cosmic Consciousness

The great teachers who have come to this planet from the higher reaches of the Cosmos have spoken of our divine, immortal nature and the path to the experience of it. Mystics like Hildegarde of Bingen and Meister Eckhart and poets like Dante, Rumi and Kabir have had the revelatory experience of our nature. A hundred years ago Richard Maurice Bucke wrote a book called *Cosmic Consciousness* in which he predicted that this experience would become accessible to many in the future. [8]

Over the last fifty years, a door has been opening onto this new consciousness, bringing together many individuals and initiatives that are creating new bottles to hold the new wine. In the West, Pierre Teilhard de Chardin and Father Bede Griffiths were forerunners of this new consciousness. Incredible new insight into the life of the planet and the effect we have had on its species and its wellbeing has been brought to us by the biologist, Sir David Attenborough. We have access to ancient Wisdom Traditions, like the *Vedas* and the *Upanishads* and the teachings of the Buddhist and Daoist sages.

Truths that were known thousands of years ago are being rediscovered. Indigenous Prophecies and beliefs are being listened to. Astrological insights, Peruvian Shamanic Trainings and hundreds of teachers bringing healing to body and soul through their outstanding Courses have been offered by organizations in America like the Shift Network and Humanity's Team, working to awaken human consciousness. The HeartMath Institute in California has discovered the extraordinary importance of the heart as a vital centre of consciousness that connects us to the quantum field, and has been teaching people how to connect with their heart and to engage with life through it. None of this may reach the mass of humanity but it may be enough that it reaches a few, who are like the leaven in bread that can raise the whole loaf.

His Holiness, the Dalai Lama, has been one of the greatest teachers of this era, calling repeatedly for an end to weapons and war. Sri Ramana and Paramhansa Yogananda were two enlightened teachers who had a great influence in the last century. I was fortunate to visit Sri Ramana's Ashram in 1956 and pondered his great question, "Who am I?" for decades until I was able to answer it. Teachers from the East like Thich Nhat Hanh have come to the West, establishing Buddhist communities and practices of meditation. Many people from the West have travelled to India to be taught there by great teachers and have come back to transmit what they have learned from them to others. Transcendental Meditation, introduced by the Maharshi Mahesh Yogi, has millions of followers worldwide. All this might be called "The Activation of the Sacred."

Sri Aurobindo, one of the greatest Indian sages, wrote these words in his book, *The Life Divine*. "If it be true, that Spirit is involved in Matter and apparent Nature is secret God, then the manifestation of the divine in himself and the realization of God within and without are the highest and most legitimate aim possible to man upon earth." [9] These words have been my guide ever since I discovered them in his prophetic book which clearly lays out the evolutionary path of humanity.

Annunciation — detail from the painting by Simone Martini (c. 1284 – July 1344)

The Deuteronomists banished the angels, the Hosts of Heaven in 623 BCE. However, they return in Christianity and in the experience of the great Christian Mystics, Dionysius the Areopagite, Hildegarde of Bingen and St. Thomas Aquinas and are found in the Bible, particularly in the marvellous encounter of Esdras with the Archangel Uriel and the story of Tobias and the Archangel Raphael in the *Apocrypha*. The theologian Matthew Fox and biologist Rupert Sheldrake have just published a book called *The Physics of Angels*, which explores the theme of angelic presences. Angels and Archangels need to come back into our awareness.

The Near-Death Experience

Another of the doors opening to a new consciousness is the Near-Death Experience and the realization that the death of the physical body is not the end of consciousness. Courses exist on how to communicate with loved ones who have left this world, and how to connect with the help and guidance that is available to us from higher dimensions.[10] There is now undeniable evidence of the afterlife that has been revealed through many Near-Death Experiences. These experiences offer proof that our relationships with our loved ones, including our pets, continue beyond the death of the physical body in an adjacent dimension of reality, inaccessible to us while living in this dimension because of the different vibrational rate between them. No-one who we were close to in past lives or in this life is gone forever. Angels, guides, ancient teachers can be contacted. People are receiving messages and guidance from distant stars like Sirius and Arcturus, and the constellations of the Pleiades and Andromeda. Help is coming to us from Cosmic Beings who are standing with the Children of Light against the powers of Darkness that, for millennia have tried to gain control of this planet.[11] As I have shown in this book, channeled messages from the Atlanteans and the Essenes have been received through carefully trained mediums.[12]

This new wine began to appear in the last century when the psychiatrist Elisabeth Kübler-Ross gathered thousands of these experiences through her work with the dying and published ground-breaking books showing that there is no death for the soul.[13] In this century Anita Moorjani has told of her cure from terminal cancer in her book *Dying to be Me*. The eminent neurosurgeon Dr Eben Alexander has recounted his extraordinary near-death-experience in three remarkable books.[14] As a result of this experience, he has written: "Consciousness is fundamental in the universe, not derivative from physical matter. *All* of the apparent physical world exists *within* consciousness." [15]

Witnesses to the all-embracing Light they see and the Unconditional Love they experience comes from the descriptions of the thousands of people who have had a Near-Death experience but also an Out-of-the-Body one. One such account moved me deeply. It is the visionary experience of a man called Mellen–Thomas Benedict, who described what happened to him during the hours after he had clinically died of cancer. He describes the journey he took into the Light and how the Light answered his questions and took him on a cosmic journey deeper and deeper into Itself. I have, with his permission, included his journey as an appendix to my book, *The Dream of the Cosmos*, in the hope that it will inspire and reassure others. His experience offers a message of hope for humanity, delivered with a joy and clarity that is astonishing and authentic.

Four Questions

There are Four Questions that neither Religion nor Science have answered: Who are we? Where do we come from? Where do we go when we die? Why are we here? These questions were answered two millennia ago by the Gnostics and the Essenes and are beginning to be answered again now, not least because of the Near-Death Experience and because many Gnostics and Essenes have reincarnated now.

There is one extraordinary book, written by an emeritus professor who taught Philosophy and Religious Studies at an American University for many years, that helps to answer some of these questions. He embarked on a 20-year journey into the Mind of the Cosmos, taking carefully controlled and recorded psychedelic drugs to accomplish this, assisted by his wife who sat beside him through every session. His name is Christopher Bache and his book is called *LSD and the Mind of the Universe*. Taken in stages through the enormous suffering humanity has endured on its long and heroic journey on this planet, and experiencing this suffering multiple times himself, he was given many revelations and visions by the Consciousness or Intelligence of the Cosmos who initiated him into these experiences and whom he calls 'The Beloved.' With his permission, I am including some passages from his book in this final chapter because I think they are of great interest and value. However, I would add a note of caution because this opening to the transcendent is not without dangers. It must never be embarked on casually, without someone in attendance, preferably someone with medical experience. [16]

> Everyone must choose a name for the Absolute, a title that approximates its truth, power, and beauty. Though I will use many terms to describe it in this book, in my heart of hearts I call it my Beloved. Once held in her embrace, once dissolved into her radiant splendor, I was hers forever. I will be hers until my last breath

and after still. If my description tilts towards the feminine, it is because of two things — the specific story of creation that emerged on this journey and the love that reuniting with this reality awakened in me. [17]

In *The Dream of the Cosmos*, I included this passage, among others, from a book he published in 2000, called, *Dark Night, Early Dawn,*

> Just when Western culture had convinced itself that the entire universe was a machine, that it moves with a machine's precision and a machine's blindness, the ability to experience the inner life of the universe is being given back to us... The entire human endeavor has been emptied of existential purpose and significance because it has been judged to be a product of blind chance. When one gains access to the inner experience of the universe, one learns that, far from being an accident, our conscious presence here is the result of a supreme and heroic effort. Far from living our lives unnoticed in a distant corner of an insentient universe, we are everywhere surrounded by orders of intelligence beyond reckoning. [18]

Returning to his recent book, *LSD and the Mind of the Universe*, he writes:

> The core vision of our future that has emerged in the sessions is that humanity is coming into a time of Great Awakening, a profound shift in the fundamental condition of the human psyche. But for there to be a Great Awakening, there must first be a Great Death. We must be emptied of the old before the new can emerge. I have come to believe that the twenty-first century will be such a time. It will begin the dark night of our collective soul, a time of emptying, of intense anguish, of loss of control and breakdown. A global purification unto death that will last generations. But through this hard labor, we will give birth to something extraordinary. More than just a new civilization, what is emerging is nothing less than a new order of human being. I believe that through the global systems crisis, our planet is giving birth to the Future Human. [19]

Taken on a revelatory and deeply moving journey of discovery, he describes how he was...

> ...brought to an encounter with a unified energy field underlying all physical existence. I was confronting an enormous field of blindingly bright, incredibly powerful energy. This energy was the single energy that composed all existence. All things that existed were but varied aspects of its comprehensive existence. Experiencing it was extremely intense and carried with it a sense of ultimate encounter. [20]

> What stood out for me in the early stages was the interconnectedness of everything to form a seamless whole. The entire universe was an undivided, totally unified, organic whole... The unified field underlying physical existence completely

dissolved all boundaries. As I moved deeper into it, all borders fell away, all appearances of division were ultimately illusory. No boundaries between incarnations, between human beings, between species, even between matter and spirit. The world of individuated existence was not collapsing into an amorphous mass, as it might sound, but rather was revealing itself to be an exquisitely diversified manifestation of a single entity. [21]

Though these experiences were extraordinary in their own right, the most poignant aspect was not the discovered dimensions of the universe themselves but what my seeing and understanding them meant to the Creative Consciousness I was with. It seemed so pleased to have someone to show Its work to. I sensed that it had been waiting for billions of years for embodied consciousness to evolve to the point where we could at last begin to see, to understand, and to appreciate what had been accomplished in our self-evolving universe, I felt the loneliness of this Intelligence, having created such a masterpiece and having no one to appreciate Its work, and I wept. I wept for its self-isolation and in awe of the profound love which had accepted this isolation as part of a larger plan. Behind creation lies a Love of extraordinary proportions, and all of existence is an expression of this Love. The Intelligence of the universe's design is matched by the depth of Love that inspired it. [22]

I was taken back to the beginning of creation and there experienced human evolution in the context of a larger cosmic agenda. Suddenly, I was overwhelmed by the most extraordinary LOVE. It was as if a dam had burst and that Love was coming at me from every direction, so much Love that I could barely take it in, even in my expanded state.…

I experienced all the suffering that humanity had endured throughout history as taking place inside this Love. I realized that all the suffering inherent in evolution was noble beyond words. It was all part of a cosmic plan that had been entered in freely by all the participants, however unconscious of the fact we have become along the way. The nobility of great suffering voluntarily shouldered in the name of divine Love, suffering that would stretch across millions of years, suffering that would become so inscrutable that it would be used as evidence that the universe was devoid of compassion, this was the nobility of humanity's gift to the Creator. [23]

Towards the end of his journey, he writes about our collective awakening:

Out of the seething desires of history, out of the violent conflicts and the awakening of individuals and nations, there is now driving forward a new awareness in human consciousness, Its birth in us is no less difficult or violent than the birth of a new continent. It drives upwards from the floor of our being, requiring a transposition of everything that has gone before to make room for its new organization patterns.

The great difficulty I have is describing the enormity of what is being birthed. The true focus of this creative process is not individuals but all humanity. It is actually trying to awaken our entire species. What is emerging is a consciousness of unprecedented proportions, the entire human family integrated in a unified field of awareness. The species reconnected with its Fundamental Nature. Our thoughts tuned to Source Consciousness. This unified field did not suffocate our individuality but liberated it into new orders of self-expression. [24]

I saw humanity climbing out of a steep valley and just ahead, on the other side of the mountain was a brilliant, sun-drenched world that was about to break over us. The time frame was enormous. After millions of years of struggle and ascent, we were poised on the brink of a sunrise that would forever change the conditions of life on this planet. All current structures would quickly become irrelevant. All truths would quickly be rendered passé. Truly a new epoch was dawning. The lives of everyone living on the edge of this pivotal time in history had been helping to bring this global shift about.... In being given glimpses of our future, in touching the edges of the Creator's intent, I saw that evolution was indeed no accident but a creative act of supreme brilliance and that humanity is being taken across a threshold that would change it forever." [25]

In one of the most insightful passages in this book he says,

The physical universe is not a punishment or trap into which we have fallen and from which we must be saved. It is not a spiritual wasteland we should escape from as quickly as possible. The purpose of rebirth is not to spiritually awaken and then leave the universe. The purpose is to awaken and become a conscious player in its continuing growth and transformation. [26]

Reaching the end of his book, he says he had to learn to balance the two poles of his existence — transcendence and immanence. Adjusting again to life in the world was difficult and took some time and much effort. Summing up what he has learned from his journey into the heart of the universe he says he has learnt:

…that the universe is the manifest body of a Divine Being of unimaginable intelligence, compassion, clarity and power; that we are all aspects of this Being, never separated from It for a moment, that we are growing ever more aware of this connection, that physical reality emerges out of Light and returns to Light continuously, that Light is our essential nature and our destiny, that all life moves as One, that reincarnation is true, that there is a deep logic and significance to the circumstances of our lives, that everything we do contributes to the evolution of the whole, that our awareness continues in an ocean of time and a sea of bliss when we die, that we are loved beyond measure and that humanity is driving towards an evolutionary breakthrough that will change us and life on this planet at the deepest level. [27]

The New Visionaries

I think we can look to certain physicists and cosmologists as the new visionaries. With the astounding view of the universe offered by Hubble and the new James Webb telescope, the incredible beauty and complexity of what we are being shown seems miraculous, numinous. Even more extraordinary are the discoveries of Quantum Physics which reveal that we are deeply and indissolubly connected to the life of the planet and the entire life of the universe.

Dr Jude Currivan is a physicist and cosmologist, one of the new visionaries, whose field of exploration is the unfolding life of the Cosmos. In her book *The Story of Gaia*, published in 2023, she explores the evolutionary journey of our conscious planet and our own gradual emergence as self-aware members of our planetary home. She describes the universe as a unified and innately sentient entity. She explains how mind and consciousness are not what we possess but what we and the whole world are. She reveals our Universe to be "a great thought of cosmic mind," manifesting as a cosmic hologram of infolded information that exists to evolve. She says that the universe did not emerge suddenly as a Big Bang but gently, as a Big Breath, and explains how evolution is not driven by random occurrences and mutations but by profoundly resonant and harmonic interplays of forces and influences, each intelligently informed and guided. [28]

The New Cosmology is also coming from Nassim Haramein who says, as I wrote earlier, "A new cosmology is being born; a new vision of our profound relationship with a conscious, intelligent and interconnected universe." He has now moved from California to France, to Cluses, near Geneva and set up his new Institute there, called International Space Federation. In 2023, he presented to the scientific community a 200-page paper holding thousands of equations, the fruit of decades of research, showing how quantum theory and relativity theory can be reconciled. He has recently discovered the missing equation that completes his theory. He compares the astounding recent scientific discoveries to the unfolding of the petals of a rose. The revelation of our profound connection to the deepest ground of life and to each other could have a powerful effect on how we live our lives, how we relate to the planet and how we interact with each other, recognizing that our every act and even every thought affects the underlying Intelligent Field.

Unified Physics tells us that *the whole universe is a Unified Field*, a Cosmic Web of Life which connects all life forms in our universe and on our planet. Every atom of life interacts with every other atom, no matter how great the distance between them. None of us is truly separate from others or from other species of life on this planet or from the life of the three trillion galaxies of the universe. These discoveries reflect and confirm the revelatory insights Christopher Bache received on his journey into the Mind of the Universe.

Unified Field Cosmology shows us that the material world exists *within* a stupendous Field of Consciousness that is the ground-state of the universe. Our human consciousness is part of the Consciousness which sustains not only our world, but the entire universe. Each one of us carries the holographic imprint of the universe within us. No matter what our race, nation, gender, or caste, each of us is part of the living, breathing, connecting Web of Life which underlies and connects all life forms in the universe and on our planet.

Quantum physics tells us that our world of matter is like a visible foam resting on a very deep ocean of Light that permeates every cell of our physical being. We are not only connected with each other through the astonishing reach of the Internet but through the infinitesimal particles of sub-atomic matter that are non-locally connected with each other throughout the entire universe. In our essence, we are beings of Light, Cosmic Beings, incarnated many times on this planet for an evolutionary purpose. All life at the deepest level is essentially One. Each of us is an expression of that One, inseparable from it.

These discoveries challenge the assumption that we humans are the only conscious beings in a universe that is without life, intelligence, purpose or meaning. In the nick of time, we are leaving behind us the story of a dead, insentient universe and entering a new phase in our understanding of a universe that is vibrantly alive and the ground of all that we call Life.

The Discoveries of Nassim Haramein

Now I want briefly to focus on the quintessence of Nassim Haramein's discoveries, not in mathematical equations but in words you can understand. This summary is taken from a Course I did with him in 2013 and from a lecture on the Unified Field [approved by him] that I gave in 2015 in the Great Hall at Dartington, Schumacher College, and which is on my Playlist. For Nassim, the whole Field of his exploration is Sacred. He says that beneath the visible universe is an underlying electro-magnetic Field or Matrix, like a fabric woven of energy, or a Lattice or a Web. There is no such thing as empty space. Space is full and it is seething with energy.

> We cannot separate consciousness from this Field because the Field itself *is* consciousness: imprinting, exchanging, and transmitting information every nano second. Consciousness orders and organizes the field and its complex intercon-

nected systems at all levels and the evolution of the universe itself. We are part of this stupendous organization of energy, part of that consciousness. Nor can we separate so-called inanimate matter, animate self-organizing systems like plants and animals, and self-aware organisms like ourselves. All may come to be seen as integrated components of a continuous evolutionary path of information or consciousness growing and unfolding through what we call time.

The entirety of spacetime is full of fields. From the electromagnetic field of a single atom, to that of each cell in our body, to the heart's electromagnetic field, to the fields of the earth, the sun, and the two trillion galaxies—the whole of what we call space is full of electro-magnetic fields of different magnitudes interacting with each other. Even the atom is a field and the proton and electron within it are also fields.

There are 100 trillion cells in our body and 100 trillion atoms in every one of these 100 trillion cells. Each one of these atoms contains a proton. Each proton holds trillions of the infinitesimal units of matter called Planck units. Everything in the entire universe is connected through the network of these Planck units. The size of a single Planck unit is like a grain of sand compared to the size of the whole universe. Untold numbers of these electro-magnetic oscillators constitute the ground of the material universe. *All so-called 'matter' is vibrantly alive, made out of protons and these infinitesimal Planck units.* [my italics]

These basic particles in the Field are oscillating and vibrating so rapidly that there is no *apparent* space between them. This electro-magnetic oscillation is the ground-state of the universe. This continuous oscillation is so rapid that it makes matter appear to us as a steady state.

All these Planck units, protons, atoms and cells are connected to each other and to every observer in the universe, forming a stupendous field of energy in a continuous state of oscillation. They produce a holographic structure and a dynamic wormhole-like network which connects all points across scales, generating a connected living universe.

Conclusion

The conclusion I draw at the end of this book on the Feminine Face of God is that Divine Spirit is the core of our being. The soul is the intermediary between spirit and body. The body is the sacred temple of the soul and the means of our being able to incarnate on this planet. At the same time, it can offer us access to the many dimensions of the inner universe and relationship with the Divine Spirit that ensouls it. The more we develop love and reverence for life, the more we will be in touch with this Holy Spirit within and around us. This new kind of consciousness is what I call the Sacred Marriage of body, soul, and spirit, when we see the world of nature around us as transparent to divinity, with ourselves as part of that divinity.

The New Story is about relinquishing the fear of death; knowing that we survive the death of the body, that we are in our essence, immortal beings whose life continues after the death of the physical body.

The New Story tells us that Cosmic Light and Love are the Source of all manifestations of Life and are the foundation of our being: our consciousness, our creativity, and our capacity for love.

Imagine this revelation being born in our heart, unfolding within it, like the petals of a rose. If the whole universe is one integrated, living organism, one symphony of cosmic sound, then we are part of that whole. We participate as co-creators in the unfolding of our life in this miraculous evolutionary process. The last chapter of *The Dream of the Cosmos*, is called 'Light and Love as the Pulse of the Cosmos.' The Gnostics and the Essenes identified the Creative Ground or Source with the image of Light. They did not give it a name like 'God.' At the heart of the Cosmos is a Love of unimaginable dimensions, a Love that sustains the entire universe and is the origin of our own capacity to love and to create. To feel embraced by this Love could enable us to heal the pathology and terrible traumas of the past, to replace fear and doubt and the need for power and dominance with trust and joy. To know this is the secret longing of the life that lives us.

The *Vedas*, the *Upanishads*, the *Bhagavad Gita*, the Jewish mystical tradition of Kabbalah, the Christian and Sufi mystics, the Buddhist, and Daoist sages, all suggest that spirit is omnipresent, at once transcendent to and immanent within the forms of life, present within the core of our being. We are bathed in, permeated by spirit every moment of our existence, in every breath we take. In the light of this different understanding, spirituality invites us to focus more on the experience of illumination than on faith and belief.

For at least five thousand years, possibly far longer, the great sages of India have taught the underlying unity of all creation and never separated the visible and invisible dimensions of reality. In their view, the entire organism of the world we know as well as the organism of our human selves is the expression, manifestation, and dwelling place of Brahman or spirit. Professor Ravi Ravindra tells us in his book Science and the Sacred,

> The one central insight into Truth to which all Indian wisdom points is *the one-ness of all that exists*. Although the truth is easily stated as "All is one," the sages have also said that the realization of this truth in the core of one's being can take many lifetimes. And the realization of this truth is held to be the purpose of human existence. All art, philosophy and science, if they are true, reflect this vision and further its realization. [29]

The artist, the late Cecil Collins in his book, *The Vision of the Fool*, echoes the words of Joachim of Flora, given in the Introduction to this book:

> We are entering the period of the free-flowing, universal, creative spirit of life, the unlocalised God, accessible to all men in all places… I believe the age of the Father is over. The age of the Son is over. This is the age of the Holy Spirit. This is the age of the universal principle — the open, flexible field of consciousness, the understanding of the unity of life in the multiplicity of human experience. [30]

In a booklet called *Angels*, he wrote:

> In our education we need to rediscover our relationship with nature, with organic life, our friendship with all created things. We need to rediscover our relationship with the divine world.

The Sacred Marriage

Men and women come together in harmony to create a new civilization.

The visible and invisible dimensions of life are experienced as unified aspects of a living universe.

We no longer feel separate from the universe but connected to the heart of its being. Our body, mind, soul and spirit are seen as components of a single cosmic organism.

We are aware that we carry divinity in every atom of our being, because we are not separate from the Divinity we have been worshipping for thousands of years, but are an intrinsic part of its life, its mind and its soul.

This divine element within our nature is expressed in our lives as the longing to create, invent, discover, and transform, to nurture and protect, to love and be loved.

Divine Spirit is no longer imagined as remote and transcendent to ourselves but experienced as the very process of Life pouring into manifestation — expressing Itself as our life as well as all aspects of planetary life and the life of the entire Cosmos.

Nature is no longer treated as our servant but recognized and respected as the manifestation of spirit in this dimension of reality.

We can communicate consciously with other beings in our universe, asking for their guidance and receiving their help.

Death is no longer feared because it is seen as a rite of passage into another dimension of reality.

The Alchemical Wedding
Painting by Emily Balivet

Net of Indra

Notes:

1. Tarnas, Richard (2006) *Cosmos and Psyche: Intimations of a New Word View*, Viking Penguin, New York, p. 33
2. McGilchrist, Dr Iain, from a talk given at a Conference on *The Future of Humanity*, October 26th, 2024.
3. McGilchrist, Dr Iain (2021), *The Matter with Things: Our Brains, Our Delusions and the Unmaking of the World*, Volumes 1-2, Perspectiva Press, London
4. Bolte Taylor, Jill Ph.D. (2008), *My Stroke of Insight*, Hodder & Stoughton Ltd., London
5. Harvey, Andrew, *Servant of a Transformed Future: A Meeting with Bede Griffiths*, Alternatives Magazine, no. 33 (quoted in Bache, *LSD and the Mind of the Universe*, p. 235)
6. Goswami, Amit, (1993) with Richard E. Reed and Maggie Goswami, *The Self-Aware Universe*, Jeremy P. Tarcher, p. 270
7. Faggin, Federico (2021) Silicon, *Waterside Production*, Cardiff, CA, p. 282
8. Bucke, Richard Maurice (1901), *Cosmic Consciousness*, E. P. Dutton & Co. New publication 2018
9. Aurobindo, Sri (1990) *The Life Divine*, Lotus Light Publications, Wilmot, WI, p. 4
10. Humanity's Team – Wayne Dyer Communications
11. Salmon, Saira (2024) *Understanding Ascension: The Sacred Science of Ascension Mechanics*

12. Wilson, Stuart & Prentis, Joanna, (2005) *The Essenes, Children of the Light*. (2009) *The Power of the Magdalene*. (2011) *Atlantis and the New Consciousness*, Ozark Mountain Publishers, Huntsville AR

13. Kübler-Ross, Elisabeth (1975) *On Death and Dying*, Spectrum, US, (1991) *On Life After Death*, Celestial Arts, Berkeley, CA

14. Alexander 111, Dr Eben (2012), *Proof of Heaven, A Neurosurgeon's Journey into the Afterlife*, Simon & Schuster, US. (2014) *The Map of Heaven*. (2017) with Karen Newell, *Living in a Mindful Universe: A Neurosurgeon's Journey into the heart of Consciousness*

15. (2017) *Living in a Mindful Universe*

16. Psychedelic drugs have been used in a medical situation to treat severe depression and to help patients suffering from cancer to experience hope and deeper understanding. In a small study of adults with major depression, Johns Hopkins Medicine researchers report that two doses of the psychedelic substance psilocybin, given with supportive psychotherapy, produced rapid and large reductions in depressive symptoms, with most participants showing improvement.

17. Bache, Christopher Ph.D. (2019) *LSD and the Mind of the Universe*, Park Street Press, Rochester, Vermont, p. 22

18. Bache, Christopher Ph.D. (2000), *Dark Night, Early Dawn*, University of New York Press, p. 332

19. *LSD and the Mind of the Universe*, p. 209

20. ibid, p. 112

21. ibid, p. 123

22. ibid, p. 115

23. ibid, p. 213

24. ibid, p. 131

25. ibid, p. 214-15

26. ibid, p. 203

27. ibid, p. 310

28. Dr Jude Currivan is a cosmologist, planetary healer, futurist, author of seven books and co-founder of WholeWorld-View. website: www.WholeWorld-View.org

29. Ravindra, Ravi Prof. (2002) *Science and the Sacred*, Quest Books, Wheaton, Ill. p. 27

30. Keeble, Brian (2002), Cecil Collins, *The Vision of the Fool and Other Writings*, Golgonooza Press, 3 Cambridge Drive, Ipswich, p. 122

Christ in Majesty
from the Basilica of Saint Mary Magdalene at Vézelay

Messages from a Transcendent Dimension

To end this book, I would like to share with you some of the prophetic channeled Messages received by my mother and a friend from 1943 to 1965. In 2023 I published them in a book called *Messages from a Transcendent Dimension*. These Messages show that we are not alone in the universe: a higher assembly of Beings who have our welfare at heart are watching over this planet, observing what is happening here, strengthening the Children of Light against the Forces of Darkness.

They began in February 1943 in an apartment in New York, where my mother and a small group of women close to her were gathered to talk about the life-and-death struggle that was tearing Europe apart. Suddenly, although the windows of the apartment were closed because of the cold, they heard a roar like thunder and the glass door onto the terrace was blown inwards by a powerful blast of air. Lightning flickered all around them although there was no storm. They cried out in terror, and went to shut the door, but suddenly felt a tremendous presence in the room and, falling on their knees, were overcome with awe.

Then they heard a voice which told them to write down what they heard. The voice said: "Be sure of thy spirit as I am of being the wine and the bread of the One who is above the Fire and the Light and Foremost." The voice warned of a future catastrophe for the earth if human beings did not change course and stop killing each other. The women asked what they should do. They were told to follow the guidance of their heart. For the next twenty years, my mother and a close friend wrote down the Messages that came to them from Jesus and St. Francis. I think they are more relevant now than they were then.

* * * * * * *

Man is on the threshold of his greatest trial since the day of My coming. This is the time when My teaching has to be fully understood. Humanity has lived for two thousand years in a state of adolescence. Now it must become adult or sink into general criminality that will bring chaos, confusion, and final destruction. If humanity chooses adulthood and responsibility to life, it will have the millennium of peace and happiness and Earth will join the circle of planets which have already completed their evolution and have reached the state of Paradise — the state where human beings through their own decision, will have regained the angelic state.

Everywhere on this planet the call has gone out. From far distant realms in the universe come Great Beings to your poor benighted planet to stand with the children of the Light in their effort to overthrow the tyranny of evil once and for all so that never again shall it overpower the world. If enough people stand in the Light when the darkness would engulf it, then with this help from the Cosmos, you will succeed in overcoming the darkness. But there is a danger that many will be intimidated into weak compromise or indifference. You need to become as wise as serpents and as gentle as doves.

All the great prophets have been heralding this moment which is truly the moment of judgement of which I spoke to My disciples at the beginning of this cycle. You are all meant to work for unity and understanding. You can, by concentration, meditation, and the humility of prayer, learn to use the force of blessing in your words, your gestures, your writings, your approach to other human beings and to all other species.

Peace is Harmony. War and destruction are discordance. Only when men learn not to shed their brother's blood can the House of God be built on its true foundations. Until this moment comes, shall Caesar unjustly usurp the power that is God's, because those who ought to have chosen God, chose Caesar, and you see the results today. Caesar's spirit came into the first Church and sat enthroned in Rome, and the Church fought with the arms of man instead of with the arms of God, which are prayer, meditation, and service of the Divine Plan.

We may witness another catastrophe unless we call on the Divine Mother to help us receive the influx of power coming with the New Age. There will be crisis after crisis that will completely upset the human mind and split the frame of civilization. The core of the evil lies in the East, near the sands of Palestine. The wanton thirst to kill will be roused more and more. For no logical reason blood is being shed and more will follow, so pray that your mind will be lifted above the vibration of the suffering earth, for only those who have that ability will be given the strength to resist the madness that will be the fourth horseman of these times.

There will be greater and more terrible discoveries than the splitting of the atom. More devastating weapons are being worked upon in secret; forces powerful enough to reverse the laws of Nature. Already you see the results around you of man's presumptuous endeavour to use the elements of matter, not for beneficial purposes but to destroy life. Destructive energy emanates from places where scientists are working to develop new weapons. This energy affects human bodies and human minds, creating split psyches which are the equivalent on the human plane of what the splitting of energy is on the cosmic plane. There is a danger of collective insanity.

If you mix the waters of knowledge with the thought of destruction,

destruction will come. The control of Nature, now nearly acquired, can be used for love and blessing or for malediction and hate.

It is only through humanity that man can solve the problem of his inhumanity… only by lifting his consciousness to a higher level of unity and awareness of Oneness can man acquire the wisdom rightly to use the power over Nature that his intelligence has given him. This power is only beneficial through the application of wisdom, otherwise it risks becoming all-destroying.

The breaking up of the established churches is but a question of time and will be accomplished partly by their inability to satisfy the spiritual needs of man and partly by the atheists [materialists] who will play a greater and greater part in world events. Harmony must be found at every level as Man can no longer survive the disintegration of his psyche caused by his own destructive civilization. Only those who have reached an inner harmony between their knowledge and their intuition, their thoughts, and their actions; those who are able to listen to and accept the guidance of their heart, will be given the strength and the knowledge to help their fellow men. It is through the intuition of the weak that the Light will be found again, not through the will of the strong.

Man has progressed in his intelligence and his mastery of scientific discoveries, but his wisdom and love have not progressed to the same extent. He is as the labourer who knew how to sow but who has forgotten to put in the living seed so that when harvest comes his fields are barren and he suffers the pangs of hunger. Today man is truly hungry for what he lost since the words of My apostles died in the rituals of indifference and the greed of those who used My Church to serve Caesar instead of God. The result is the destruction and suffering you are witnessing today. Where there is blood, greed, and hate, My Kingdom has been denied.

It was our beloved Father's wish that man should learn slowly the working of His laws and discover the secrets of the house he was called to live in. It was not the plan that he should consider himself the architect and start building on his own. When man attempts to substitute himself for God, if he is not attuned to the Cosmic Law as it is reflected in Nature, he may create discord, disharmony, which finally expresses itself as illness — illness of the body, sickness of the mind, national and international diseases — and what are wars but outbreaks of international diseases?

Do not offend Nature. Do not offend God by tampering with the laws of Nature, trying to bend them to your destructive purposes. Every act of a human being must be judged according to the rule: Does it offend Nature? Does it offend God? Does it injure Life?

Listen to the despairing voice of your Mother, the Earth. Only by raising your consciousness to the realization of the Oneness of life can you escape destruction and acquire the wisdom rightly to use the power that your intelligence has given you over Nature. Scientific knowledge must be raised to the level of this realization. Blessed are those who see behind and beyond the veils of separateness to the Divine Unity of all life.

The Divine Mother is the Holy Spirit who presides over the New Age. Only water and its healing strength can extinguish the over-riding fires of Mars. Inspired by her, women, through their love and understanding, have been given the task of awakening in men the compassion and devotion to life taught by Me at the beginning of the Piscean Age. Man through woman, will realize in himself the sense of his mission on earth and see clearly as in a mirror, the Law of the Universe. When that time comes, the secrets of Nature will be understood.

The Divine Mother will be the Redeemer of the New Age. Like the alchemist of the Middle Ages, she will transform and fuse the harder elements in the surging waters of compassionate Love. Only she can re-establish an Equilibrium between the destructive forces and the ever-building principle of Life and Love.

If man uses his control of Nature for love and for blessing, this Aquarian Age will be the fulfilment of My coming. The universe is changing and the cosmic rays which strike your planet are now potent with the power to create or destroy. The choice is man's: will he choose to be the Son or the Rebel? It would be better for those of this generation never to have been born, than having been born, not to become fully awakened to the moral responsibility of this dangerous yet promise-fulfilling age.

The time has come when the Children of Light need to assemble to create the great invisible church which will be built on many planes of life, and will be the only protection against the destructive powers which are starting to gnaw again at the roots of this unhappy planet.

Think often of the Source. Feel the presence of it. Think of its messengers and the amplifiers of the message. Learn to express in your own time and space what is eternal, indivisible, and holy. You should no more lead an ill-fitted life than wear an ill-fitting garment. Learn to divide your time between the duties of your daily life and those of your inner self and give them your undivided attention.

A human soul is like an instrument. It is tuned or it rings flat. When your soul is harmonious it can vibrate with all the vibrations of the spirit and take part in the wonderful concert of the universe. Then God's harmony can be heard on the lowest level of the mineral world. You do not know how precious in the eyes of the Son are the souls He can use to orchestrate the symphony of the universe.

Create gardens to protect the purity of Nature from all destructive rays. Protect the birds. Tell other people about angels. Make the stars weep for joy. Your channels can be blocked through grief and doubt. Throw doubt away in the name of Christ. Do not try to sort out the threads of your many lives. You will waste your time. Concentrate on the thread you are spinning now. We do the tapestry. Give us good thread.

Do not despair over your lack of achievement. It only needs a few years, days or hours of complete realization and service in one incarnation to make worthwhile the eternal spiral and your arduous way back to the heavenly spheres.

Keep knocking and gently, very gently the door will open so that you will have time to prepare and bear the radiance of the vision that will fill your mind with the realization of the immortal truth. Each day, each minute is a preparation. Only through awareness and longing from you to Me can I bring you the blessing of the millennium. When the Light comes, it is all the more luminous because of the darkness that has gone before.

Verily, verily, I say unto you, receive My blessings, receive My Dove, because now unity has to become the law of the earth and those who respect it and make it their own will enter with Me the Kingdom of Heaven.

Peace be with you. It is from Peace that I want to speak to you for verily, verily, I say unto you, My future name will be the Peacemaker and it is as the Master of Peace that I am appearing to those who are gathered in My Name throughout the world. Peace is the Castle of shining Truth where the hidden can be revealed and the soul can don its Robe of Glory.

Love be with you
Love be with the World
Love be the only eternal blessing

Credits

p. xv   *The Eternal Bride* — painting by Cecil Collins (1908-1989)

p. xvi   *Completion of the Great Work* — engraved by Matthäus Merian ca. 1630

p. xix   *The Creation of the World* — from the painting by Giovanni di Paolo ?-1482 CE

p. xx   *The Fall and Expulsion (Adam and Eve) from the Garden of Eden* — From the fresco in the Sistine Chapel ceiling by Michelangelo 1475-1564 CE

p. xx   *The Trinity with Christ Crucified* — Austrian c.1410, National Gallery, London

p. xxi   *Portrait of René Descartes* (1596-1650) by Frans Hals c.1583–1666

p. xxii The Sublimation of the King from the *Philosophia Reformata* 1622 by Johann Daniel Mylius

p. xxix *The Cyclops* Odilon Redon 1840-1916

p. 2   *The Younger Dryas Boundary Field.* (Europe)"The red boundary line defines the current known limits of the YDB field of cosmic-impact proxies, spanning 50 million square kilometers" — Image credit: *Richard B. Firestone*

p. 3   *The Younger Dryas Boundary Field.* (World)

p. 4   Graham Hancock for his book *Magicians of the Gods* and Netflix Series

p. 6   *The Lost City of Atlantis* — easyscienceforkids.com

p. 8   *Artemis of Ephesus* — Naples. Photo attribution: Barnaby Rogerson

p. 10   Ozark Mountain Publishing for permission to quote from *Atlantis, The Essenes* and *The Power of the Magdalene* by Stuart Wilson and the late Joanna Prentis

p. 17   Susanne Schaup for her book *Sophia: Aspects of the Divine Feminine, Past and Present*

p. 17   Professor Richard Tarnas to quote from *The Passion of the Western Mind*

p. 19   *Goddess of Laussel,* rock carving, Dordogne. c.25,000 BCE Archaelogical Museum, Bordeaux. *Goddess of Lespugue* c. 25,000 BCE, mammoth ivory statue, Musée de l'Homme, Paris.

p. 21   *Neolithic Great Mother,* Romania c. 5,500-5,000 BCE
          Neolithic Great Mother, Danube Valley 5,000 BCE

p. 22   Steve Taylor, to quote from *The Fall* (2005 & 2018)

p. 24   John Lamb Lash for his book *Not in His Image: Gnostic Vision, Sacred Ecology, and the Future of Belief*

p. 31   *Surrealist Landscape 1945* — painting by Cecil Collins

p. 35   Diagram of the Separation of Spirit and Nature — author's own work

p. 38   Dr Margaret Barker for permission to quote from her books, particular her latest one, *The Great Lady*

p. 46   *The Essene Gospel of Peace* for two quotations from Book Four

p. 62   *The Holy Trinity,* Urschalling, Bavaria, 9th Century fresco on the church ceiling. Licensed under the Creative Commons International license.

p. 65   *Wisdom* — Sculpted relief from the Cathedral of Notre Dame, Paris.

p. 71   *Catholic cathedral dedicated to Sophia* — Island of Murano, Venice, Italy

p. 72   *Orthodox cathedral dedicated to the Holy Wisdom* — Kyiv, Ukraine

p. 79   Neil Douglas-Klotz for permission to quote from his book *Prayers of the Cosmos*

p. 82   *Wisdom* Ms. 64 (97.MG.21), fol. 11, probably 1170s, unknown artist/maker
p. 85   *Map of Alexandria* Based on: Shepherd, William (1911) Historical Atlas New York: Henry Holt & Co. p. 34-35. Courtesy of the University of Texas Libraries, Texas at Austin. Perry-Castañeda Library Map Collection
p. 89   *The Nag Hammadi Library*, E. J. Brill, Leiden
p. 93   *The Eight-Petallled Rosette,* at the Temple of Eleusis — photograph attribution: Rebecca Battles ALSO Princeton University Press for illustrations from *The Lost World of Old Europe*
p. 107 Timothy Freke and Peter Candy for their book *Jesus and the Goddess*
p. 119 Dan Morse for his book, *The Divine Spark Within*
p. 123 The Theosophical Society, Quest Fall 2011 for Raul Branco's article *Pistis Sophia*
p. 131 *Christ before the Judge,* Cecil Collins — on loan to Winchester Cathedral
p. 144 *Map of the Holy Land,* at the time of the Essenes
p. 168 Jehanne de Quillan for permission to use the Map of the Holy Land in *The Gospel of the Beloved Companion* and permission to quote from *The Gospel of the Beloved Companion* in the Chapter on Mary Magdalene pp. 185-188
p. 173 Dr Annine van der Meer for her book *Mary Magdalene Unveiled*
p. 183 *Jesus and Mary Magdalene at The Last Supper*, Sculpture in the Church of St.Volusien, Foix, Ariège, France — courtesy of Dr Annine van der Meer
p. 184 *The Last Supper* — Leonardo De Vinci
p. 195 *The Journey to France* — Giotto di Bondone c1266-1337 Lower Church Assisi
p. 200 *The Black Virgin,* from Beaulieu-sur-Dordogne, and *Notre-Dame de St-Gervasy* — both in Public Domain
p. 203 *The Knights and the Vision of the Grail* — Knights of the Round Table
p. 204 Dr Betty J. Kovàcs for permission to quote from *Merchants of Light: The Consciousness that is Changing the World*
p. 207 *La Belle Verrière* — Chartres Cathedral, France
p. 210 *Labyrinth* — Chartres Cathedral, France
p. 211 *Women and men as troubadours* — from a Renaissance painting
p. 214 *Splendor Solis* — Harley Manuscript, British Museum. Permission applied for from M. Moleiro Editor, Barcelona
p. 220 Castle of Foix, Ariège
p. 221 *Courtly Love* from a Renaisance illustration
p. 230 Fortress of Monségur
p. 248 *Fresco of the three aspects of the Goddess,* the throne room, Palace of Knossos, Crete
p. 248 *The Phaestos Disc*, Palace of Phaestos, Crete
p. 249 *Funeral wreath of Philip of Macedon*, tomb of Philip of Macedon, Vergina, Greece
p. 251 *The Labyrinth*, Chartres Cathedral
p. 258 *Madonna de la Misericordia* Piero della Francesca, Museo Civico di Sansepolcro
p. 259 *Le Livre du Cueur d'Amour Épris*, written and illustrated by the Roi René, Count of Provence 1434 to 1480
p. 263 *Adam and Eve, the Serpent, and the Tree of Knowledge*, William Blake 1757-1827
p. 272 *Tobias and the Angel Raphael* — Andrea del Verrochio 1435-1488
p. 285 *The Fight with the Dragon* — Lambsprinck, c.1625
p. 301 Dr Mike Yeadon for his address to the Irish Parliament.

p. 304 *Cosmos* — Robin Baring

p. 312 *The Colossus* — Francisco de Goya (1746–1828), Museo del Prado

p. 316 Patrick M. Wood for his book *The Evil Twins of Technocracy and Transhumanism*

p. 316 David Hughes for his book *Covid 19: Psychological Operations and the War for Technocracy.*

p. 317 *The Great Red Dragon and Woman Clothed with the Sun,* William Blake (1757–1827)

p. 322 *Penned Sheep*, Northern England — This file is licensed under the Creative Commons Attribution-Share Alike 4.0 International license

p. 328 *Brave New World* ?

p. 331 Gregg Braden for his book *Pure Human*

p. 341 David Lorimer for his poem "It is always time"

p. 347 *Virgin and Child*, Botticelli (1445-1510) — *Mother and Child*, Raphael (1483-1520)

p. 349 *The Sleeping Beauty* — Edward Burne-Jones

p. 351 *The Annunciation* — Fra Angelico (1395-1455)

p. 352 Nassim Haramein for his brilliant Course on Unified Physics.

p. 356 *Mother and Child* — Painting by Robin Baring

p. 358 *Annuciation* — Painting by Simone Martini (c. 1284 – July 1344) licensed under the Creative Commons International license. Photo attribution: Diego Delso

p. 360 Emeritus Professor Christopher Bache for permission to quote passages from his book *LSD and the Mind of the Cosmos*

p. 360 *The Alchemical Wedding* — artist Emily Balivet, for licence to use her painting,

p. 370 Net of Indra

p. 372 *Christ in Majesty* from the Basilica of Saint Mary Magdalene at Vézelay

p. 378 *Messages from a Transcendent Dimension* — cover image, Archive Publishing.

Bibliography

Alexander 111, Dr Eben (2012), *Proof of Heaven, A Neurosurgeon's Journey into the-After life*, Simon & Schuster, US.

Alexander, Dr Eben (2014) *The Map of Heaven*, Piatkus

Alexander, Dr Eben (2017) with Karen Newell, *Living in a Mindful Universe: A Neuro-surgeon's Journey into the heart of Consciousness*, Piatkus

Allan, D.S. & Delair, J.B., (1995) *When the Earth Nearly Died*, Gateway Books, Bath

Anthony, Mark (2021) *The Afterlife Frequency*, New World Library, Novato, CA

Apuleius, Lucius (1950) *The Golden Ass*, trans. Robert Graves, Penguin Books Ltd., Harmondsworth

Ardis, Dr Bryan Ardis, (2024) *Moving Beyond the COVID-19 Lies*, Harvest Creek Publishing. His book is now available from Amazon UK

Aurobindo, Sri (1990) *The Life Divine*, Lotus Light Publications, Wilmot, WI

Bache, Christopher Ph.D. (2000), *Dark Night, Early Dawn*, University of New York Press,

Bache, Christopher Ph.D. (2019) *LSD and the Mind of the Universe*, Park Street Press, Rochester, Vermont

Baigent, Michael & Leigh, Richard (1991) *The Dead Sea Scrolls Deception*, Jonathan Cape, London

Barfield, Owen (1988) *Saving the Appearances: A Study in Idolatry*, Wesleyan University Press, Connecticut

Baring (Anne Gage), (1961) *The One Work, A Journey Towards the Self*

Baring, Anne & Cashford, Jules (1992) *The Myth of the Goddess: Evolution of an Image*, Penguin, London

Baring, Anne (2013 & 2020), *The Dream of the Cosmos: A Quest for the Soul*, Archive Publishing, Shaftesbury, Dorset

Baring, Anne (2023) *Messages from a Transcendent Dimension*, Archive Publishing, Shaftesbury, Dorset

Barker, Dr Margaret (2003) *The Great High Priest*, T & T Clark International

Barker, Dr Margaret (2004) *Temple Theology*, SPCK, London

Barker, Dr Margaret (2004), *The Hidden Tradition of the Kingdom of God*, SPCK, London.

Barker, Dr Margaret (2023) *The Great Lady: Restoring Her Story*, Sheffield Phoenix Press, UK

Bayley, Harold (1909) *A New Light on the Renaissance*, J.M. Dent & Co., London

Bayley, Harold (1912) *The Lost Language of Symbolism*, Williams and Norgate, London

Benton, Michael (2015) *When Life Nearly Died: The Greatest Mass Extinction of All Time*, Thames & Hudson, London

Bernays, Edward L. (1928) *Propaganda: The Public Mind in the Making*, Horace Liveright

Bolte Taylor, Jill Ph.D. (2008), *My Stroke of Insight*, Hodder & Stoughton Ltd., London

Bougeault, Cynthia (2010) *The Meaning of Mary Magdalene*, Shambhala Publications Inc.

Bowden, Rev. John (1989), *Jesus: The Unanswered Questions*

Braden, Gregg (2025) *Pure Human: The Hidden Truth of Our Divinity, Power, and Destiny*, Hay House LLC, Carlsbad, California, New York City, London, Sydney, New Delhi

Brzezinski, Zbigniew (1970) *Between Two Ages: America's role in the Technetronic Era*, Viking Press, New York

Bruner, Seamus (2023), *Controligarchs*, Sentinel, Penguin Random House, London & New York

Bucke, Richard Maurice (1901), *Cosmic Consciousness*, E. P. Dutton & Co. New publication Waking Lion Press 2018

Campbell, Joseph (1986) *The Inner Reaches of Outer Space*, St James Press Ltd., Toronto

Churchward, James (1939), *The Lost Continent of Mu*, Neville Spearman, London. (Reprinted 2020)

Churton, Tobias (1987) *The Gnostics*, George Weidenfeld & Nicolson Ltd., London

Clarke, Lindsay (2001) *Parzival and The Stone from Heaven*, HarperCollins, London

Collins, Cecil (2004) *Angels, Fool's Press*, London. see also *The Vision of the Fool and Other Writings*, Edited and with an Introduction by Brian Keeble, Golgonooza Press, Ipswich

Currivan, Dr Jude, (2022) *The Story of Gaia*, Inner Traditions, Bear & Co, Rochester, Vermont

Dalrymple, William (2024), *The Golden Road: How Ancient India Transformed the World*, Bloomsbury Publishing, London

Deakin, Michael, (2007) *Hypatia of Alexandria*, Prometheus Books, Amherst, NY

de Quillan, Jehanne trans. (2010) *The Gospel of the Beloved Companion*, Éditions Athara, Foix, Ariège, France

Dennis, Kingsley L. (2023), *The Inversion: How We Have Been Tricked into Perceiving a False Reality*, Aeon Books,

Desmet, Mattias (2022), *The Psychology of Totalitarianism*, Chelsea Green Publishing, London

Douglas-Klotz, Neil (1990), *Prayers of the Cosmos: Meditations on the Aramaic Words of Jesus*, HarperSanFrancisco

Edinger, Edward (1984) *The Creation of Consciousness, Jung's Myth for Modern Man*, Inner City Books, Toronto

Freke, Timothy and Candy, Peter (2001) *Jesus and the Goddess*, Thorsons, London

Gardner, Laurence (2005) *The Magdalene Legacy*, Element, London, 2005

Gardner, Laurence, (2008) *The Grail Enigma 2008* HarperElement, London.

Gimbutas, Marija (1991) *The Civilization of the Goddess: The World of Old Europe*, HarperSanFrancisco

Faggin, Federico (2021) *Silicon*, Waterside Production, Cardiff, CA

Fox, Matthew (1983), *Original Blessing*, Bear & Co. Inc.

Freeman, Charles (2003) *The Closing of the Western Mind, The Rise of Faith and the Fall of Reason*, Pimlico, London

Freeman, Charles, (2008) *AD 381: Heretics, Pagans and the Christian State and The Closing of the Western Mind*, Pimlico, London

Freke, Timothy and Candy, Stephen (2001) *Jesus and the Goddess*, Thorsons

Goswami, Amit, (1993) with Richard E. Reed and Maggie Goswami, *The Self-Aware Universe*, Jeremy P. Tarcher

Grant, Robert, (1961) *Gnosticism, An Anthology*, Collins, London

Griffiths, Father Bede (1976) *Return to the Centre*, Collins, London

Hancock, Graham (2015), *Magicians of the Gods*, Coronet

Harvey, Andrew, *Servant of a Transformed Future: A Meeting with Bede Griffiths*, Alternatives Magazine, no. 33

Hays, Gregory, *Marcus Aurelius*, Meditations

Hoeller, Stephan (1982) *The Gnostic Jung and The Seven Sermons to the Dead*, Quest Books, Wheaton, Illinois

Hoeller, Stephan (1989) *Jung and the Lost Gospels*, Quest Books, Wheaton, Illinois

Hoeller, Stephan (2002) *Gnosticism*, Quest Books, Wheaton, Illinois

Hughes, David (2025), *Covid 19: Psychological Operations and the War for Technocracy* Palgrave Macmillan. Free download of his book from substack

Inayat Khan, Hazrat, *from Immortality: A Traveller's Guide*

James, E.O. (1959) *The Cult of the Mother Goddess*, Thames and Hudson, London

Jonas, Hans (1958) *The Gnostic Religion*, Beacon Press, US

Jung, C. G. (1931) *The Secret of the Golden Flower*, Routledge & Kegan Paul, London

Jung, C. G. (1954) *Answer to Job*, trans. R. F.C. Hull, Routledge & Kegan Paul Ltd., London

Jung, C. G. (1958) *The Undiscovered Self*, Routledge & Kegan Paul Ltd., London

Jung, C. G. (1964) *Man and His Symbols*, Aldus Books, London

Jung, C. G. (1967) *Memories, Dreams, Reflections*, The Fontana Library of Theology and Philosophy

Jung, C. G. (1983) *Memories, Dreams, Reflections*, Collins and Routledge & Kegan Paul

Jung, C.G. *Collected Works*, Vol. 11 Psychology and Religion: West and East

Jung, C. G. (2009) *The Red Book*, W.W. Norton & Co, New York and London

Keeble, Brian (2002), *Cecil Collins, The Vision of the Fool and Other Writings*, Golgonooza Press, 3 Cambridge Drive, Ipswich, p. 122

Keepin, William Ph.D. (2016) *Belonging to God, Spirituality, Science & a Universal Path of Divine Love*, Skylight Paths Publishing, Woodstock, Vermont

Kennedy, Robert F, Jr, (2023) *The Wuhan Cover-Up and the Terrifying Bioweapons Arms Race*, Skyhorse Publishing, New York

Kingsley, Peter (1999) *In the Dark Places of Wisdom*, London: Element Books; (2010)

Kingsley, Peter (2018) *A Story Waiting to Pierce You: Mongolia, Tibet and the Destiny of the Western World*, The Golden Sufi Center, California

Kovács, Dr Betty J. (2019) *Merchants of Light: The Consciousness that is changing the World*, The Kamlak Center, CA

Kübler-Ross, Elisabeth (1975) *On Death and Dying*, Spectrum, US, (1991) *On Life After Death*, Celestial Arts, Berkeley, CA

Kurzweil, Ray (2024) *The Singularity is Nearer*, Bodley Head, London.

Lamb, Christina (2020) *Our Bodies, Their Battlefield: What War Does to Women*, William Collins, London

Lash, John Lamb (2006 & 2021) *Not in His Image*, Chelsea Green Publishing, Vermont USA & London UK

Lee, Desmond (1971) trans. *Plato: Timaeus and Critias*, Penguin Books Ltd., Harmondsworth, London

Leloup, Jean-Yves (2002) *The Gospel of Mary Magdalene*, Inner Traditions, Rochester, Vermont, USA

Lewis, C. S. (1947) *The Abolition of Man*, Macmillan, New York

Malachi, Tau (2006) *St. Mary Magdalene, The Gnostic Tradition of the Holy Bride*, Llewelyn Publications, Woodbury, Minnesota

Matt, Daniel (1995) *The Essential Kabbalah: The Heart of Jewish Mysticism*, HarperSanFrancisco

McGilchrist, Dr Iain (2021), *The Matter with Things, Our Brains, Our Delusions and the Unmaking of the World*, Volumes 1-2, Perspectiva Press, London

McKinnon, Tricia (2015) *Return of the Divine Sophia: Healing the Earth through the Lost Wisdom Teachings of Jesus*, Isis and Mary Magdalene, Bear & Co. Rochester, Vermont

Mead, G. R. S. (1908) *The Wedding Song of Wisdom*, Theosophical Publishing House

Mead, G. R. S. (1931, *Fragments of a Faith Forgotten*, John M. Watkins, London

Mead G. R. S. (1947) *Pistis Sophia*, John M. Watkins, London

Merkur, Dan (1983) *Gnosis: An Esoteric Tradition of Mystical Visions and Unions*, State University of New York Press, Albany

Morse, Dan (2022) *The Divine Spark Within*, Sophonia Press

Muhl, Lars (2017) *The Magdalene*, Watkins, London

Nixey, Catherine (2017), *The Darkening Age: The Christian Destruction of the Classical World*, Macmillan, London

Ophuls, William, (2018), *Apologies to the Grandchildren*.

Page, Barry (2015) *The Historical Jesus Found*, MPM Publication

Patai, Raphael (1990) *The Hebrew Goddess*, Wayne State University Press

Pagels, Elaine (1980) *The Gnostic Gospels*, Weidenfeld and Nicolson Ltd., London

Phillips, John A. (1984) *Eve, The History of an Idea*. Harper & Row, San Francisco

Querido, René (1987) *The Golden Age of Chartres: The Teachings of the Mystery School and the Eternal Feminine*, Floris Books, Edinburgh

Quispel, Gilles, (1973) *Eranos Lectures 3: Jewish and Gnostic Man*

Ravenscroft, Trevor (1981) *The Cup of Destiny: The Quest for the Grail*, Rider & Co., London

Ravindra, Ravi Prof. (2002) *Science and the Sacred, Quest Books*, Wheaton, Illinois

Reeves, Minou, (2013) *Europe's Debt to Persia from Ancient to Modern Times*, Ithaca Press, Reading, UK

Rees, Laurence (2025) *The Nazi Mind: Twelve Warnings from History*, Viking

Rigoglioso, Marguerite Ph.D. (2009) *The Cult of Divine Birth in Ancient Greece*, Palgrave Macmillan

Rigoglioso, Marguerite Ph.D. (2010) *Virgin Mother Goddesses of Antiquity*, Palgrave Macmillan

Rigoglioso, Marguerite Ph.D. (2021) *The Mystery Tradition of Miraculous Conception: Mary and the Lineage of Virgin Births*, Bear & Co., Vermont

Rigoglioso, Marguerite Ph.D. (2024) *The Secret Life of Mother Mary: Divine Feminine Power for Personal Healing and Planetary Awakening*. Bear & Co., Vermont

Roalfe Cox, Marian (1983) *Cinderella*, The Folk-Lore Society

Roi René, *Le Livre du Cueur d'Amours Épris* (1975) The National Library, Vienna. Thames and Hudson, London

Sabini, Meredith (2016) *C. G. Jung on Nature, Technology and Modern Life*, North Atlantic Books, Berkeley, CA

Sagar, Keith (2005) *Literature and the Crime Against Nature*, Chaucer Press, London

Salmon, Saira (2024) *Understanding Ascension: The Sacred Science of Ascension*

Mechanics

Schaup, Susanne (1997), *Sophia: Aspects of the Divine Feminine*, Nicolas-Hays, Inc., York Beach, Maine

Scholem, Gershom, (1974) *Kabbalah*, Keter publishing House Jerusalem Ltd.

Scholem, Gershom G. (1941) *Major Trends in Jewish Mysticism*, Schocken Publishing House, Jerusalem

Shengold, Leonard (1989) *Soul Murder: The Effects of Childhood Abuse and Deprivation*, Yale University

Shlain, Leonard (1998) *The Alphabet versus the Goddess: The Conflict Between Word and Image*, Viking, New York

Starbird, Margaret (1993) *The Woman with the Alabaster Jar*, Bear & Co, Rochester, Vermont

Stern, P (1969), *Prehistoric Europe from Stone Age Man to the Early Greeks*

Strachan, Gordon, (2003) *Sacred Geometry, Sacred Space*, Floris Books, Edinburgh,

Szekely, Edmond B. (1981) *The Essene Gospel of Peace, Book Four, Teachings of the Elect* Brussels: International Biogenic Society

Tarnas, Richard (1991), *The Passion of the Western Mind*, Ballantine Books, Random House

Tarnas, Richard (2006) *Cosmos and Psyche: Intimations of a New Word View*, Viking Penguin, New York

Taylor, Steve (2005) *The Fall*, O Books, Ropley, Hampshire and Iff Books, 2018

The Nag Hammadi Library (NHL) in English (1977) editor James R. Robinson, E. J. Brill, Leiden

van der Meer, Dr Annine Ph.D. (2019), *The Black Madonna from Primal to Final Times*, Pan Sophia Press, English edition transl. Catriona O'Daly

van der Meer, Dr Annine Ph.D. (2024), *Mary Magdalene Unveiled*

van der Meer, Dr Annine Ph.D. (2025), *Magdalene's Ascension: Mary's Journey to Becoming Light*, Bear & Co.Vermont

Vermes, Geza (2011) *The Dead Sea Scrolls*, Penguin Classics

von Franz, Marie-Louise (1966) *Aurora Consurgens*, Routledge and Kegan Paul, London, Bollingen Foundation, New York

von Franz, Marie-Louise, (1975), *C.G. Jung, His Myth in Our Time*, C.G. Jung Foundation for Analytical Psychology

Wilson, Stuart & Prentis, Joanna (2005), *The Essenes, Children of the Light*,

Wilson, Stuart and Prentis, Joanna (2008), *The Power of the Magdalene*,

Wilson, Stuart & Prentis, Joanna (2011) *Atlantis and the New Consciousness*

Wilson, Stuart and Prentis, Joanna (2012) *Beyond Limitations* All published at: Ozark Mountain Publishing, Huntsville, AR 72740

Wolf, Naomi (2022) *The Bodies of Others: The New Authoritarians, Covid-19 and the War Against the Human*, All Seasons Press, Port Lauderdale, Florida

Wolf, Naomi (2023) *Facing the Beast, Courage, Faith and Resistance in a New Dark Age.* Chelsea Green Publishing New York and London

Wolf, Naomi (2024) *The Pfizer Papers*, Simon & Schuster, New York & London

Wolkstein, Diane & Kramer, Samuel Noah (1984) *Inanna*, Rider & Co

Wood, Patrick M. (2022) *The Evil Twins: Technology and Transhumanism*, Coherent Publishing, LLC, Messa, AZ 85208

Index

A

K

X

Y

Z